LIBRARY OF NEW TESTAMENT STUDIES

566

Formerly Journal of the Study of the New Testament Supplement Series

T&T CLARK • LIBRARY OF BIBLICAL STUDIES •

THE EARLIEST PERCEPTIONS OF JESUS IN CONTEXT

Essays in Honour of John Nolland on His 70th Birthday

Edited by

Aaron W. White, Craig A. Evans and David Wenham

t&tclark

LONDON • NEW YORK • OXFORD • NEW DELHI • SYDNEY

T&T CLARK
Bloomsbury Publishing Plc
50 Bedford Square, London, WC1B 3DP, UK
1385 Broadway, New York, NY 10018, USA

BLOOMSBURY, T&T CLARK and the T&T Clark logo are
trademarks of Bloomsbury Publishing Plc

First published 2018
Paperback edition first published 2019

A catalogue record for this book is available from the British Library.
A catalog record for this book is available from the Library of Congress.

ISBN: HB: 978-0-5676-7177-6
PB: 978-0-5676-9006-7
ePDF: 978-0-5676-7178-3

Series: Library of New Testament Studies, volume 566

Typeset by Forthcoming Publications (www.forthpub.com)

To find out more about our authors and books visit
www.bloomsbury.com and sign up for our newsletters.

CONTENTS

ABBREVIATIONS

A	Atrahasis Epic
AB	Anchor Bible (Commentary)
ABD	D. N. Freedman (ed.), *The Anchor Bible Dictionary*, 6 vols (New York: Doubleday, 1992)
AJP	*American Journal of Philology*
AJT	*American Journal of Theology*
ANRW	W. Haase and E. Temporini (eds.), *Aufstieg und Niedergang der römischen Welt* (Berlin: de Gruyter, 1979–)
ASOR	American Schools of Oriental Research
ATANT	Abhandlungen zur Theologie des Alten und Neuen Testaments
AV	Authorized Version
BAIAS	*Bulletin of the Anglo Israel Archaeology Society*
BAR	*Biblical Archaeology Review*
BAZ	Biblische Archäologie und Zeitgeschichte
BBB	Bonner biblische Beiträge
BBR	*Bulletin for Biblical Research*
BDAG	Walter Baur, Frederick W. Danker, William F. Arndt, F. Wilbur Gingrich, *Greek-English Lexicon of the New Testament and Other Early Christian Literature*, 3rd edn (University of Chicago Press, 2000)
BECNT	Baker Exegetical Commentary on the New Testament
BETL	Bibliotheca ephemeridum theologicarum lovaniensium
Bib	*Biblica*
BibInt	*Biblical Interpretation*
BJS	Brown Judaic Studies
BNTC	Black's New Testament Commentary
BSW	*Biblical Studies on the Web*
BTB	*Biblical Theology Bulletin*
BWANT	Beiträge zur Wissenschaft vom Alten und Neuen Testament
BZNW	Beihefte zur *Zeitschrift für die neutestamentliche Wissenschaft*
CBQ	*Catholic Biblical Quarterly*
CCSL	Corpus Christianorum: Series Latina
CEV	Contemporary English Version
CGTC	Cambridge Greek Testament Commentaries
CIIP	*Corpus Inscriptionum Iudaeae/Palaestinae*
CIJ	J. B. Frey (ed.), *Corpus Inscriptionum Judaicarum* (1936–52)
CIL	*Corpus Inscriptionum Latinarum*

CJO	L. Y. Rahmani, *A Catalogue of Jewish Ossuaries* (1994)
CSEL	Corpus Scriptorum Ecclesiasticorum Latinorum
DBSup	*Dictionnaire de la Bible, Supplément*
DJG	J. B. Green, S. McKnight, I. H. Marshall (eds.), *Dictionary of Jesus and the Gospels* (1992; rev. edn, 2013)
EDNT	H. R. Balz and G. Schneider (eds.), *Exegetical Dictionary of the New Testament* (Grand Rapids: Eerdmans, 1990–93)
EE	*Enuma Elish*
EKK	Evangelisch-katholischer Kommentar
ESI	*Excavations and Surveys in Israel*
EstBíb	*Estudios bíblicos*
ESV	English Standard Version
ETL	*Ephemerides theologicae lovanienses*
EvQ	*Evangelical Quarterly*
EWNT	H. Balz and G. Schneider (eds.), *Exegetisches Wörterbuch zum Neuen Testament*
ExpTim	*Expository Times*
FC	The Fathers of the Church
FRLANT	Forschungen zur Religion und Literatur des Alten und Neuen Testaments
GNB	Good News Bible
HA-ESI	*Hadashot Arkheologiyot — Excavations and Surveys in Israel*
HBT	*Horizons in Biblical Theology*
HCSB	Holman Christian Standard Bible
HNT	Handbuch zum Neuen Testament
HS	*Hebrew Studies*
HTKNT	Herders theologischer Kommentar zum Neuen Testament
HTR	*Harvard Theological Review*
HvTSt	*Hervormde teologiese studies*
IAA	Israel Antiquities Authority
IBS	*Irish Biblical Studies*
ICC	International Critical Commentary
IEJ	*Israel Exploration Journal*
IG	*Inscriptiones Graecae* (Berlin: G. Reimer, 1873–)
Int	*Interpretation*
JAAR	*Journal of the American Academy of Religion*
JB	A. Jones (ed.), *Jerusalem Bible*
JBL	*Journal of Biblical Literature*
JBT	*Jahrbuch für biblische Theologie*
JGRChJ	*Journal of Greco-Roman Christianity and Judaism*
JJS	*Journal of Jewish Studies*
JPOS	*Journal of the Palestine Oriental Society*
JPTSup	Journal of Pentecostal Theology Supplement Series
JSHJ	*Journal for the Study of the Historical Jesus*
JSJ	*Journal for the Study of Judaism in the Persian, Hellenistic and Roman Period*

JSJSup	*Journal for the Study of Judaism in the Persian, Hellenistic and Roman Period*, Supplements
JSNT	*Journal for the Study of the New Testament*
JSNTSup	*Journal for the Study of the New Testament*, Supplement Series
JSOTSup	*Journal for the Study of the Old Testament*, Supplement Series
JTI	*Journal of Theological Interpretation*
JTS	*Journal of Theological Studies*
KEK	Kritisch-exegetischer Kommentar über das Neue Testament
KJV	King James Version
LCL	Loeb Classical Library
LEC	Library of Early Christianity
LNTS	Library of New Testament Studies
MAMA	*Monumenta Asiae Minoris Antiqua*
Moffat	James Moffat Translation of the Bible
NASB	New American Standard Bible
NCB	New Century Bible
NCBC	New Cambridge Bible Commentary
NCV	New Century Version
NEB	New English Bible
Neot	*Neotestamentica*
NETS	New English Translation of the Septuagint
NET	New English Translation
NF	Neue Folge
NICNT	New International Commentary on the New Testament
NICOT	New International Commentary on the Old Testament
NIDB	K. D. Sakenfeld (ed.), *The New Interpreter's Dictionary of the Bible* (2009)
NIDOTTE	M. Silva (ed.), *New International Dictionary of Old Testament Theology and Exegesis*, 5 vols (Grand Rapids: Zondervan, 2014)
NIGTC	New International Greek Testament Commentary
NIV	New International Version
NLT	New Living Translation
NovT	*Novum Testamentum*
NovTSup	Novum Testamentum, Supplements
NRSV	B. M. Metzger and R. E. Murphy (eds.), *New Revised Standard Version*
NTAbh	Neutestamentliche Abhandlungen
NTD	Das Neue Testament Deutsch
NTL	New Testament Library
NTS	*New Testament Studies*
PEQ	*Palestine Exploration Quarterly*
PNTC	Pillar New Testament Commentary
QDAP	*Quarterly of the Department of Antiquities in Palestine*
RB	*Revue biblique*
RevQ	*Revue de Qumran*

RGG	K. Galling (ed.), *Religion in Geschichte und Gegenwart: Handwörterbuch für Theologie und Religionswissenschaft*, 3rd edn (Tübingen: Mohr [Siebeck], 1957)
RH	*Revue historique*
RSV	Revised Standard Version
SBL	Society of Biblical Literature
SC	Sources chrétiennes
SEG	*Supplementum Epigraphicum Graecum*
SJLA	Studies in Judaism in Late Antiquity
SJOT	*Scandinavian Journal of the Old Testament*
SNTSMS	Society for New Testament Studies Monograph Series
SNTU	*Studien zum Neuen Testament und seiner Umwelt* (journal)
SP	Sacra Pagina
SPB	Studia postbiblica
SSEJC	Studies in Scripture in Early Judaism and Christianity
ST	*Studia theologica*
SUNT	Studien zum Umwelt des Neuen Testaments
SVTP	Studia in veteris testamenti pseudepigrapha
TANZ	Texte und Arbeiten zum neutestamentlichen Zeitalter
TAPA	*Transactions of the American Philological Association*
TBei	*Theologische Beiträge*
TDNT	G. Kittel and G. Friedrich (eds.), *Theological Dictionary of the New Testament* (1964–74)
THKNT	Theologischer Handkommentar zum Neuen Testament
TNIV	Today's New International Version
TNTC	Tyndale New Testament Commentaries
TOTC	Tyndale Old Testament Commentaries
TPINTC	Trinity Press International New Testament Commentaries
TSAJ	Texte und Studien zum antiken Judentum
TWNT	G. Kittel and G. Friedrich (eds.), *Theologisches Wörterbuch zum Neuen Testament*
TynBul	*Tyndale Bulletin*
TZ	*Theologische Zeitschrift*
UTB	Urban–Taschenbücher
VC	*Vigiliae christianae*
VT	*Vetus Testamentum*
WBC	Word Biblical Commentary
WMANT	Wissenschaftliche Monographien zum Alten und Neuen Testament
WTJ	*Westminster Theological Journal*
WUNT	Wissenschaftliche Untersuchungen zum Neuen Testament
ZAW	*Zeitschrift für die alttestamentliche Wissenschaft*
ZECNT	Zondervan Exegetical Commentary on the New Testament
ZKWL	*Zeitschrift für kirchliche Wissenschaft und kirchliches Leben*
ZNW	*Zeitschrift für die neutestamentliche Wissenschaft*
ZTK	*Zeitschrift für Theologie und Kirche*

Profile and Appreciation of John Nolland

John Nolland is known to many people because of his prodigious publications. It is my pleasure in this brief profile to provide a broader picture of this Christian gentleman, concerned churchman and paradigmatic scholar whom I have had the privilege of knowing in each capacity.

John was born in Australia where he grew up with his parents and one sister. As a young man he came to faith in Christ through the Anglican Church of Australia. His first degree was in Mathematics from the

University of New England in Armidale, Australia. But he increasingly felt drawn to Christian ministry, to the chagrin of his father, and in due course went to study at Moore Theological College in Sydney, receiving his BD from London University. In 1971, he was ordained by the Archbishop of Sydney for parish ministry in a deprived neighbourhood. His growing passion for the Gospels led him on to pursue his doctoral studies at the University of Cambridge; he completed his PhD thesis on 'Luke's Readers in Luke/Acts' in 1978. During this he was also caring for Gail, his wife who was terminally ill, and his young son, David.

John secured his first teaching post at Regent College in Vancouver in 1978 as Assistant Professor of New Testament. He quickly gained a reputation as an excellent teacher, who could draw out the best in students and one who could identify with and integrate pain and suffering with joy. It was during his early years here that his wife died. Some years later he married Lisa Severine, sharing her interest and very active involvement in Christian social ethics, most recently in questions of sexuality. In 1986 they left for Bristol, England where he began his work his work at Trinity College as Tutor in New Testament. His grasp of the biblical text, his love of New Testament studies and his passion to communicate this material resulted in delighted students, who wanted to study under him. But John was and is not content with only head knowledge. His goal is discipleship, which he defines as 'Christians living transformed lives that make them visibly different from their neighbours and church life that is a corporate version of the same. [Discipleship] is a multi-dimensional matter, but one of the important matters here is knowledge of and confidence in biblical and Kingdom values.' His two-prong approach to teaching was infectious and students longed to drink from the deep well from which he drew.

His deep commitment to the truth and discipleship also made him a highly sought-after supervisor. Scores of men and women have written their dissertations under his careful eye and have gone on to have their work published and to find teaching positions around the world. Being one of these people, I can say unequivocally that his input into my life during this period of time formed me indelibly as a person, teacher, writer and scholar. Many others would echo that, some of whom are contributing to this Festschrift.

John also had the rare combination of being an excellent teacher as well as an excellent administrator. While many academics go to great lengths to avoid any administrative responsibility, seeing it as an encumbrance to teaching and research, he embraced it as a means of improving the quality of students' education and therefore a service to the Church and the furtherance of God's kingdom. He was for some years Vice-Principal of Trinity. He was also a sought-after counsellor by many generations of students and colleagues, and brought to the college a rich mix of teaching, administrative and pastoral skills, as well as his scholarship.

In spite of a heavy teaching and administrative load, John was a dedicated, conscientious and productive scholar. He published his first article in the year he graduated from Cambridge. John continued to produce important, significant articles for journals though he dedicated a large amount of his time to two seminal works: his three-volume commentary on Luke in the Word Biblical Commentary Series and his single-volume commentary on Matthew in the New International Greek Testament Commentary Series.

Two things stand out about his scholarship. First, he has an uncanny ability to listen to one argument and present it judiciously and then press pause and listen to another argument and present its merits with equal fairness. Upon representing the different biblical and theological arguments he would then, with Solomon-like wisdom and discernment, present his own position.

Second, he could engage in critical debate with other scholars while avoiding the temptation to belittle or denigrate them. I remember a student describing Dr Nolland as 'a kind man but a stern scholar'. He was and remains ruthless in his pursuit of the true meaning of the text but in a way that respects other scholars and their opinions.

Third, he is well read, writing recently on the Old Testament as well as the New Testament. John has always been adamant about reading the primary literature and equally concerned about reading the secondary material. I have chuckled to myself sometimes when I consider that the length of the bibliography in his commentaries is about the same length as many books on the subject. He rarely leaves a stone unturned.

He not only contributed to the academic life of the colleges and universities where he taught, but he was a willing and able participant in academic societies, such as the British New Testament Conference and the Tyndale Fellowship for Biblical and Theological Research. His notable contributions were recognized in 2009 when the University of Bristol appointed him to an honorary professorship.

John has never thought of academics and the church as mutually exclusive, rather that they inform one other. For this reason he has always had one foot securely rooted in the church, being involved in and committed to the ministry of the local church, but also deeply concerned for the wider church and for its witness in society.

John has many loves apart from biblical studies and teaching. He is devoted to his family; Lisa, his son David, and his daughter Elisabeth, his mother Jean and sister Barbara. He loves history, classical music, and walking in the British countryside. He is a deeply conscientious, unassuming and kind man, who has inspired love and loyalty. It is to this man, whom we have appreciated and had the privilege to know, that this Festschrift is dedicated.

Craig A. Smith

John Nolland Selected Bibliography

Dissertation

'Luke's Readers – A Study of Luke 4.22-8; Acts 13.46; 18.6; 28.28 and Luke 21.5-36' (PhD diss., University of Cambridge, 1977).

Commentaries

Luke 1–9:20, WBC 35A (Dallas: Word, 1989).
Luke 9:21–18:34, WBC 35B (Dallas: Word, 1993).
Luke 18:35–20:53, WBC 35C (Dallas: Word, 1993).
The Gospel of Matthew: A Commentary on the Greek Text, NIGNT (Bletchley: Paternoster/ Grand Rapids: Eerdmans, 2005).

Edited Volumes

(With Daniel M. Gurtner) *Built upon the Rock: Studies in the Gospel of Matthew* (Grand Rapids/Cambridge: Eerdmans, 2008).

Articles and Essays

'A Misleading Statement of the Essene Attitude to the Temple', *RevQ* 9, no. 4 (1978): 555–62.
'Classical and Rabbinic Parallels to "Physician, heal yourself": (Lk 4:23)', *NovT* 21, no. 3 (1979): 193–209.
'Do Romans Observe Jewish Customs (Tertullian, Ad Nat. 1.13; Apol. 16)?', *VC* 33, no 1 (1979): 1–11.
'Impressed Unbelievers as Witnesses to Christ (Luke 4:22a)', *JBL* 98, no. 2 (1979): 219–29.
'Proselytism or Politics in Horace Satires I, 4, 138–143?', *VC* 33, no. 4 (1979): 347–55.
'*Sib Or* III:265-94: An Early Maccabean Messianic Oracle', *JTS* NS 30, no. 1 (1979): 158–66.
'A Fresh Look at Acts 15:10', *NTS* 27, no. 1 (1980): 105–15.
'Uncircumcised Proselytes', *JSJ* 12, no. 2 (1981): 173–94.
'Women in the Public Life of the Church', *Crux* 19, no. 3 (1983): 17–23.
'Words of Grace (Luke 4:22)', *Bib* 65, no. 1 (1984): 44–60.
'Grace as Power', *NovT* 28, no. 1 (1986): 26–31.

'Luke's Use of ΧΑΡΙΣ', *NTS* 32, no. 4 (1986): 614–20.

'Acts 15: Discerning the Will of God in Changing Circumstances', *Crux* 27, no 1 (1991): 30–34.

'Reading and Being Read: New Insights into the Parables of Jesus', *Crux* 29, no. 3 (1993): 11–17.

'The Gospel Prohibition of Divorce: Tradition History and Meaning', *JSNT* 58 (1995): 19–35.

'Genealogical Annotation in Genesis as Background for the Matthean Genealogy of Jesus', *TynBul* 47, no. 1 (1996): 115–22.

'No Son-of-God Christology in Matthew 1.18-25', *JSNT* 62 (1996): 3–12.

'What Kind of Genesis Do We Have in Matt 1.1?', *NTS* 42, no. 3 (1996): 463–71.

'The Four (Five) Women and Other Annotations in Matthew's Genealogy', *NTS* 43, no. 4 (1997): 527–39.

'Jechoniah and his Brothers (Matthew 1:11)', *BBR* 7 (1997): 169–77.

'Salvation-history and Eschatology', in Darrell L. Bock, ed., *A Theology of Luke and Acts: God's Promised Program, Realized for All Nations* (Grand Rapids: Eerdmans, 1998), 63–81.

'The Sources for Matthew 2:12', *CBQ* 60, no. 2 (1998): 283–300.

'"In such a manner it is fitting for us to fulfil all righteousness": Reflections on the Place of Baptism in the Gospel of Matthew', in Stanley E. Porter and Anthony R. Cross, eds, *Baptism in the New Testament and the Church: Historical and Contemporary Studies in Honour of R. E. O. White*, JSNTSup 171 (Sheffield: Sheffield Academic Press, 1999), 63–80.

'Romans 1:26-27 and the Homosexuality Debate', *HBT* 22, no. 1 (June 2000): 32–57.

'The Mandate: Love our Enemies Matt. 5:43-48', *Anvil* 21, no. 1 (2004): 23–33.

'The Role of Money and Possessions in the Parable of the Prodigal Son (Luke 15:11-32): a Test Case', in Craig G. Bartholomew, Joel B. Green, and Anthony C. Thistelton, eds, *Reading Luke: Interpretation, Reflection, Formation* (Bletchley: Paternoster; Grand Rapids: Zondervan, 2005), 178–205.

'The Purpose and Value of Commentaries', *JSNT* 29, no. 3 (2007): 305–11.

'The Gospel of Matthew and Anti-Semitism', Daniel M. Gurtner and John Nolland, eds, *Built upon the Rock: Studies in the Gospel of Matthew* (Grand Rapids/Cambridge: Eerdmans, 2008), 154–69.

'The King as Shepherd: The Role of Deutero-Zechariah in Matthew', in Thomas R. Hatina, ed., *Biblical Interpretation in Early Christian Gospels*. Vol. 2, *The Gospel of Matthew* (London: T&T Clark International, 2008), 133–46.

(With R. T. France) 'Reflections on the Writing of a Commentary on the Gospel of Matthew', in Daniel M. Gurtner and John Nolland, eds, *Built upon the Rock: Studies in the Gospel of Matthew* (Grand Rapids/Cambridge: Eerdmans, 2008), 270–89.

'Sexual Ethics and the Jesus of the Gospels', *Anvil* 26, no. 1 (2009): 21–30.

'The Times of the Nations and a Prophetic Pattern in Luke 21', in Thomas R. Hatina, ed., *Biblical Interpretation in Early Christian Gospels*. Vol. 3, *The Gospel of Luke* (London: T&T Clark International, 2010), 133–47.

'Luke and Acts', in T. Holmén and S. E. Porter, eds, *The Handbook of the Study of the Historical Jesus* (Leiden: Brill, 2011), 3:1901–31.

'Blessing and Woe' and 'Sabbath', in J. B. Green, J. K. Brown, N. Perrin, eds, *Dictionary of Jesus and the Gospels*, 2nd edn (Nottingham/Downers Grove: IVP, 2013), 88–90, 820–23.

'Preaching the Ethics of Jesus', in Ian Paul and David Wenham, eds, *'We Proclaim the Word of Life': Preaching the New Testament Today* (Leicester/Downers Grove: IVP, 2013).
'In Search of Undocumented Uses of Greek Connective: The Case of a Causal καὶ', *EstBib* 72, no. 2 (2014): 237–56.
'Does the Cultic אשׁם Make Reparation to God?', *ETL* 91, no. 1 (2015): 87–110.
'Sin, Purity and the חטאת Offering', *VT* 65, no. 4 (2015): 606–20.

List of Contributors

Armin D. Baum, Professor of New Testament, Freie Theologische Hochschule Giessen, Germany, and Evangelische Theologische Faculteit, Leuven, Belgium.

Darrell Bock, Executive Director for Cultural Engagement, Howard G. Hendricks Center for Christian Leadership and Cultural Engagement, and Senior Research Professor of New Testament Studies, Dallas Theological Seminary, USA.

Robert L. Brawley, Albert G. McGraw Professor of New Testament Emeritus, McCormick Theological Seminary, Durham, North Carolina, USA.

Peter H. Davids, Visiting Professor of Bible and Applied Theology, Houston Graduate School of Theology, Texas, USA.

Roland Deines, Professor of Biblical Theology and Ancient Judaism, Internationale Hochschule Liebenzell, and Emeritus Professor University of Nottingham

Craig A. Evans, John Bisagno Distinguished Professor of Christian Origins, Houston Baptist University, Texas, USA.

Daniel M. Gurtner, Ernest and Mildred Hogan Professor of New Testament Interpretation, The Southern Baptist Theological Seminary, Louisville, Kentucky, USA.

Thomas R. Hatina, Professor of Religious Studies, Trinity Western University, Vancouver, Canada, and Visiting Professor, Charles University, Prague, Czech Republic.

Eeva John, Director of Pastoral Studies at Ridley Hall, Cambridge, UK.

Yongbom Lee, Lecturer in Theology, Universitas Pelita Harapan, Jakarta, Indonesia.

Douglas Sean O'Donnell, Senior Lecturer in Biblical Studies and Practical Theology, Queensland Theological College, Brisbane, Australia.

Rainer Riesner, Professor Emeritus of New Testament, Instititut für Evangelische Theologie, University of Dortmund, Germany.

Eckhard J. Schnabel, Mary F. Rockefeller Distinguished Professor of New Testament, Gordon Conwell University, South Hamilton, Massachusetts, USA.

Craig A. Smith, Professor of Biblical Studies, Co-Director of the DMin Program, Carey Theological College, University of British Columbia, Vancouver, Canada.

Christoph Stenschke, Dozent, Biblisch-Theologische Akademie, Forum Wiedenest, Bergneustadt, Germany; Professor Extraordinary, Department of Biblical and Ancient Studies, College of Humanities, University of South Africa, Pretoria, South Africa.

Steve Walton, Professor in New Testament, St Mary's University, Twickenham, UK

David Wenham, Associate Tutor, Trinity College Bristol, UK, and Wycliffe Hall, Oxford, UK.

Aaron W. White, PhD (The University of Bristol); Associate Pastor, Faith Presbyterian Church, Quincy, Illinois, USA.

N. T. Wright, Research Professor of New Testament and Early Christianity, University of St Andrew's, UK.

Introduction

These essays have been written by a number of friends, colleagues and students, to mark John Nolland's 70th birthday and to express, on our own behalf and on behalf of many others, our appreciation of John and of his work. They were presented to John at a meeting of the Tyndale Fellowship for Biblical and Theological Research in Cambridge in July 2017.

The essays range widely over John's own range of interests. Some of them are very much related to the context of Jesus and of the Gospels: Rainer Riesner's discussion of the latest archaeological and historical evidence surrounding Nazareth falls very clearly into this category. Craig Evans describes the importance of Julia Livia, the second wife of the emperor Augustus, not least in the estimation of Philip the tetrarch. He suggests that Philip's plan to build a temple to Julia in Bethsaida in 50 CE as well as his renaming of the town after her may have been the context of Jesus' famous promise to Peter, 'On this rock I will build my church'.

The Gospels themselves are obviously among the earliest perceptions of Jesus to which we have access, and Armin Baum considers the much-debated question of the genre of the Gospels, concluding that they are closest generically to Old Testament and Jewish narratology, though with slight influence from Graeco-Roman biography. Thomas Hatina writes of the importance of social memory perspectives for an appreciation of the Gospels, considering particularly Jesus' quotations of Scripture and relating these to the culture and context of the evangelists.

Most of our essays are studies of the perception of Jesus within the New Testament. Tom Wright argues that Psalm 8 is a key christological text in the Gospels, and in a wide-ranging essay explores the text in relation to a range of themes, from Adam to Davidic Messianism to the Son of Man, to priesthood and temple, concluding with reflection on the coming of Yahweh and the divine identity of Jesus.

Others focus on particular Gospels, notably on Luke–Acts and on Matthew, as is appropriate in a volume dedicated to John Nolland. Darrell Bock explores one particular part of the central section of Luke, namely 11.24–13.9, pointing out the themes of authority and accountability running through those verses. Robert Brawley looks at the characterization of the Pharisees in Luke–Acts, finding the Lukan portrayal of their relations with Jesus to be more positive and less confrontational than has often been recognized. Yongbom Lee looks at Jesus as Son of Adam and Son of God in Luke–Acts, identifying places where Adamic Christology is important to Luke. Steve Walton focuses on the Ascension theme in Acts, showing its importance with significant implications for the divine identity of Jesus. Christoph Stenschke looks at the missionary speeches of Acts, and notices how Luke, for all his interest in the Gentile world, brings out the Jewish context of Jesus.

Daniel Gurtner takes in both Luke and Matthew, examining the theme of the temple in both Gospels, finding a rather positive view. Douglas O'Donnell looks just at Matthew, examining the vocative *kurie* as it is used in addressing Jesus, and concludes that it has divine resonances and it is not just respectful address. Roland Deines offers a rather comprehensive and insightful discussion of the generally neglected subject of the Holy Spirit in Matthew. David Wenham supports those who see the Matthaean Beatitudes as having a very coherent, almost poetic shape, related to its Matthaean context.

Of course, the rest of the New Testament apart from the Gospels and Acts gives us insight into the earliest perceptions of Jesus. Craig Smith explores the theme of rest, *sabbatismos*, in Hebrews and relates it to Mt. 11.28–12.14. Peter Davids looks at James and 1 Peter, noting many echoes of the traditions of Jesus in both letters, but explaining how their use of the traditions reflects their particular contexts.

John Nolland's interests range much more widely than just the Gospels, and indeed than the New Testament. He has been involved for many years in ministerial training, and it is good to have an essay by former colleague Eeva John on that subject, relating it to Luke's portrayal of Jesus as teacher. It is also appropriate to have Eckhard Schnabel's essay on Rom. 12.1, the point in Romans where Paul moves from doctrine into ethics; the study explores the meaning of worship that is *logikē*. Schnabel recognizes the strength of the traditional translations 'reasonable' or 'spiritual', but prefers to look towards the 'word' sense of *logos*, suggesting that Paul is exhorting the Romans to offer their bodies as a living sacrifice that speaks and communicates with the world. This is an appropriate conclusion to our volume of essays both because John Nolland has done so much to help students to engage with detailed and responsible study of the Greek text (especially in his class on 'Advanced Greek' on 2 Corinthians), and because his interests have included both a concern for mission – for communication – but also for Christian life and ethics.

In bringing these essays together we honour John as someone who has 'investigated things accurately', so that we may 'know the reliability of the things we have been taught' (Lk. 1.3-4), and as a teacher, 'discipled for the kingdom of heaven, who is like a man bringing out of his treasure things old and new' (Mt. 13.52). He is also a humble and self-effacing Christian scholar who would want to say 'we do not proclaim ourselves, but Christ Jesus as Lord, and ourselves as your servants for Jesus' sake' (2 Cor. 4.5). We are grateful for all his service to us and to many others.

As editors we are grateful to Bloomsbury T&T Clark for their willingness to publish these essays and for all their help in doing so.

Aaron W. White, Craig A. Evans, David Wenham

1

The Nazareth of Jesus*

Rainer Riesner

I. *Did Nazareth Exist in the Time of Jesus?*

In the 19th century several scholars asserted that Nazareth did not exist in the time of Jesus and some of them made out that Jesus did not exist either. In his famous history of pre-20th-century Jesus research, Albert Schweitzer had to dedicate two whole chapters to these questions.[1] Today, these kinds of opinions are dominant in some atheistic circles in the United States.[2] But serious archaeological work proves the opposite, as a summary of the most important finds and insights will show.

Modern archaeological activity started in the 1950s and 1960s with the work of the Franciscan scholar Bellarmino Bagatti before the construction of the mighty Basilica of the Annunciation.[3] He excavated a

* My gratitude goes to Anna-Lena Beck and to Dr David Wenham for improving my English, and to Christoph Kraft for his help in procuring literature.

1. Albert Schweitzer, *The Quest of the Historical Jesus*, ed. John Bowden (1906; Minneapolis: Fortress Press, 2001), 355–436.

2. René Salm, *The Myth of Nazareth: The Invented Town of Jesus* (Cranford: American Atheist Press, 2008); Salm, 'Christianity at the Crossroads – Nazareth in the Crosshairs', *American Atheist* 4 (2010): 8–12. See the devastating critiques of Stephen Pfann and Yehudah Rapuano, 'On the Nazareth Village Farm Report: A Reply to Salm', *BAIAS* 26 (2008): 105–8; Ken Dark, Review of René Salm, *The Myth of Nazareth*, *BAIAS* 26 (2008): 140–6.

3. Bellarmino Bagatti, *Excavations in Nazareth*. Vol. 1, *From the Beginning till the Twelfth Century*, trans. Eugene Hoade, Studii Biblici Franciscani, Collectio Maior 17 (Jerusalem: Franciscan Printing Press, 1969). Summarized in Bagatti, 'Nazareth', *DBSup* VI, ed. Henri Cazelles (Paris: Letouzey et Ané, 1960), 318–33; Bagatti,

system of natural and man-made caves, cisterns and underground silos hewn in the soft limestone, including olive- and wine-presses, but he did not find actual walls. For some scholars, the results suggested the picture of a settlement mainly of cave-dwellers.[4] But the evidence is better explained by the fact that in the Byzantine period and afterwards, earlier houses were dismantled for the purpose of building churches and monasteries in the area venerated by Christians. Some linear rock-hewn depressions can be interpreted as the basements of walls. Pottery finds stemming from the Iron Age and from the Late Hellenistic-Roman period point to a settlement gap for the time in between. This evidence fits the general picture of the settlement history of Galilee. The Assyrian conquest of 732 BCE (2 Kgs 17.5-6) resulted in a catastrophic depopulation, especially of Lower Galilee, and this territory remained only sparsely inhabited in the Babylonian and Persian times.[5] During the Hellenistic period the population increased to some extent, but a lasting change was only brought about by the Hasmonaean conquest of Galilee in 104–103 BCE by Aristobulus I (cf. Josephus, *War* 1.76; *Ant.* 13.318-19).[6] Destroyed places were rebuilt and many new settlements were founded mainly by Jews coming from Judaea.[7] Based on a false understanding of Mt. 4.15, quoting 'the Galilee of the Gentiles (Γαλιλαία τῶν ἐθνῶν)' from Isa. 9.1 LXX, the idea of a largely or at least partly pagan Galilee was popular in the first half of the 20th century.[8] The

'Nazareth: Excavations', in *The New Encyclopedia of Archaeological Excavations in the Holy Land* 3, ed. Ephraim Stern (Jerusalem: Israel Exploration Society & Carta; New York: Simon & Schuster, 1993), 1103–5.

4. Willibald Bösen, *Galiläa – Lebensraum und Wirkungsfeld Jesu* (Freiburg: Herder, 1985), 105–10. Strangely, Gerd Theissen and Annette Merz restate this false assumption in *The Historical Jesus: A Comprehensive Guide* (Minneapolis: Fortress Press, 1998), 165.

5. Zvi Gal, *Lower Galilee during the Iron Age*, trans. Marcia Reines Josephy, ASOR Dissertation Series 8 (Winona Lake: Eisenbrauns, 1992).

6. Morten Hørning Jensen, 'The Political History in Galilee from the First Century BCE to the End of the Second Century CE', in *Galilee in the Late Second Temple and Mishnaic Periods*. Vol. 1, *Life, Culture, and Society*, ed. David A. Fiensy and James Riley Strange (Minneapolis: Fortress Press, 2014), 51–77 (52–7).

7. Uzi Leibner, *Settlement and History in Hellenistic, Roman, and Byzantine Galilee: An Archaeological Survey of the Eastern Galilee*, TSAJ 127 (Tübingen: Mohr Siebeck, 2009), 315–44.

8. Michael Schröder, 'Das Galiläa der Heiden – ein heidnisches Land oder ein hoffnungsvolles Zeichen für die Völker? Untersuchungen zu einer Galiläakonzeption im Matthäusevangelium' (PhD diss., University of Dortmund, 2016), 95–140.

archaeological work of the last decades has exposed this conception as a scholarly myth.[9]

In 1997/98 the Israeli archaeologist Yardenna Alexandre did some limited excavations at Mary's Well, a spring located about 500m north-east of the Late Hellenistic-Roman village. She did not find ruins but only ceramics from this time.[10] The most important was the find of 165 coins, including eighteen from the Late Hellenistic–Early Roman period: two Hellenistic coins, ten Hasmonaean coins from Alexander Jannaeus (103–76 BCE), two coins from Herod the Great (37–4 BCE), one from Archaelaos (4 BCE–6 CE), one from Antonius Felix (dated to 54 CE) and two coins from the first half of the 2nd century CE.[11] The accumulation of coins from Alexander Jannaeus coincides with the Jewish re-settlement of Lower Galilee and points to a founding of Nazareth in the 1st century BCE. In 2003 a trial excavation by Yoram Tepper in the Rashidiya school produced some sherds from the Late Hellenistic and Early Roman times.[12] In 2008/2009 Yardenna Alexandre did a salvage excavation before the erection of the International Marian Center just opposite the Franciscan Church of Saint Joseph. The archaeologist unearthed a building consisting of two rooms and a courtyard.[13] Fragments of pottery vessels suggest the establishment of the house in the 1st century CE. Walls of another house underneath the Convent of the Sisters of Nazareth had been known since 1884,[14] but were only recently re-examined in 2006–2010 by the English archaeologist Ken Dark from the University of Reading and can be dated to the 1st century CE or somewhat earlier by modern

9. Mark Chancey, *The Myth of a Gentile Galilee*, SNTSMS 118 (Cambridge: CUP, 2002); Mordechai Aviam, 'Distribution Maps of Archaeological Data from the Galilee: An Attempt to Establish Zones Indicative of Ethnicity and Religious Affiliation', in *Religion, Ethnicity and Identity in Ancient Galilee: A Region in Transition*, ed. Jürgen Zangenberg, Harold W. Attridge and Dale B. Martin, WUNT 210 (Tübingen: Mohr Siebeck, 2007), 115–32.

10. Yardenna Alexandre, *Mary's Well, Nazareth: The Late Hellenistic to the Ottoman Periods*, IAA Reports 49 (Jerusalem: Israel Antiquities Authority, 2012), 57–61, 153–4.

11. Ariel Berman, 'The Numismatic Evidence', in Alexandre, *Mary's Well*, 107–20.

12. Yotam Tepper, 'Nazareth', *HA-ESI* 121 (2009): A-3953.

13. For a brief report see 'Nazareth', *Welt und Umwelt der Bibel* 14, no. 2 (2010): 67.

14. Bellarmino Bagatti, 'Gli scavi presso le Dame di Nazaret', *Studii Franciscani* 34 (1937): 253–65; Marie de Nazareth, 'La Maison de Saint Joseph à Nazareth', *Cahiers de Joséphologie* 4 (1956): 243–71.

archaeological methods.[15] In an unbuilt-on area 0.5 km south-west of the Hellenistic-Roman village, Stephen Pfann, Ross Voss and Yehudah Rapuano discovered agricultural installations such as artificial terraces, three watch-towers and a wine-press.[16] The earliest pottery finds stemming from the Late Hellenistic and Early Roman periods testify to a beginning of agricultural activities in this time coinciding with the foundation of the village. The boundaries of the village are marked by several tombs, including kokhim-tombs, which had been in use from the 1st century BCE to the 1st and 2nd centuries CE, as the finds of Hellenistic and 'Herodian' oil lamps demonstrate.[17] These tombs reveal that Nazareth was a typical Jewish village from the period comprising an area of about 60 acres and hosting 200 to 500 inhabitants.[18] It is the small size and not the supposed non-existence of the village, as Robert H. Eisenman assumed,[19] which explains why Josephus never mentions Nazareth. According to the Jewish historian, Galilee had 204 villages (κῶμαι) and cities (πόλεις) (*Life* 235). Even if these numbers are exaggerated, we can only know some of these settlements and their names. Josephus was interested in the places that were involved in the First Jewish War (*Life* 188). Thus he mentions the great town of Japhia, 3 km south-west of Nazareth, because it was fortified by him (*War* 2.573) and later the place of a fierce battle (*War* 3.289-306).

II. *How Pious Were the Inhabitants of Nazareth?*

The archaeological discoveries can contribute to an answer to this question. Underneath the present Basilica of the Annunciation and the adjoining Church of Saint Joseph, two stepped pools have been excavated

15. Ken Dark, 'Early Roman-Period Nazareth and the Sisters of Nazareth Convent', *Antiquaries Journal* 92 (2012): 37–64.

16. Stephen Pfann, Ross Voss and Yehudah Rapuano, 'Surveys and Excavations at the Nazareth Village Farm (1997–2002): Final Report', *BAIAS* 25 (2007): 19–79.

17. E. T. Richmond, 'A Rock-Cut Tomb at Nazareth', *QDAP* 1 (1931): 53–4; Clemens Kopp, 'Beiträge zur Geschichte Nazareths', *JPOS* 18 (1938): 187–228 (191–207); Bagatti, *Excavations in Nazareth*, 1:237–49; Arfan and Nissim Najar, 'Nazareth', *HA-ESI* 16 (1995): 49–50; Zvi Yavor, 'Nazareth', *ESI* 18 (1998): 48* (English summary 32).

18. James F. Strange, 'Nazareth', *ABD* 5:1050–1 (less than 500); John Dominic Crossan and Jonathan L. Reed, *Excavating Jesus: Beneath the Stones, Behind the Texts* (San Francisco: Harper, 2001), 34 (between 200 and 400). There is no evidence for about 2,000 (Andreas J. Köstenberger, *John*, BECNT (Grand Rapids: Baker, 2004), 81).

19. Robert H. Eisenman, *James the Brother of Jesus* (New York: Penguin Books, 1997), 952.

that can be interpreted as *miqvaot*, Jewish ritual baths.[20] There was sensationalist media-hype about the ruins of a bath-house near Mary's Well,[21] but it only goes back to the Crusader period.[22] In the excavations in the area of the Basilica of the Annunciation[23] and the International Marian Center,[24] a number of stone vessels have been found. These unpractical but ritually clean utensils (cf. Jn 2.6) were used by rather strictly Torah-observant Jews. Whereas stone vessels of this kind are known in Judaea, the Golan and Galilee, they are missing in Samaria. There was stone-vessel manufacturing only 3 km north of Nazareth.[25] In the years 2007/08, Ken Dark conducted a survey of the rural areas between Nazareth and Sepphoris, which had been Herod Antipas' capital of Galilee until 19/20 CE. For the Early Roman period, this survey led to a very interesting result:

> In the south part of the area people may have used Jewish purity laws as a form of passive resistance against the Roman state and/or associated cultural change. These communities used only Jewish-made products, even if they had to source these more distantly than available Roman imports available at Sepphoris. The settlements closer to Sepphoris show more imported material, and so perhaps had a less strict interpretation of Jewish purity laws than those around Nazareth. A cultural frontier is, therefore, visible running through the valley between communities that, while both Jewish, accepted some part of Roman provincial culture and those that asserted a more strongly Jewish and more overtly religious identity.

Dark proposes a further explanation of this evidence in that it is 'perhaps suggesting opportunistic settlement of good-quality agricultural land by recently arrived Judaean farmers rather than their placement by urban

20. Bagatti, *Excavations in Nazareth*, 1:119–23, 228–33.

21. Jonathan Cook, 'Is This Where Jesus Bathed?', *The Guardian*, October 22, 2003.

22. Tzvi Shacham, 'Bathhouse from the Crusader Period in Nazareth', in *Spa – sanitas per aquam. Tagungsband des Internationalen Frontinus-Symposiums zur Technik und Kulturgeschichte der antiken Thermen*, ed. R. Kreiner and W. Letzner, Babesch Supplements 21 (Leuven: Peeters, 2012), 319–26.

23. Bagatti, *Excavations in Nazareth*, 1:318; Roland Deines, *Jüdische Steingefäße und pharisäische Frömmigkeit: Ein archäologisch–historischer Beitrag zum Verständnis von Joh 2,6 und der jüdischen Reinheitshalacha zur Zeit Jesu*, WUNT 2/52 (Tübingen: Mohr Siebeck, 1993), 145.

24. See n. 13.

25. Zvi Gal, 'A Stone-Vessel Manufacturing Site in the Lower Galilee', *'Atiqot* (Hebrew Series) 20 (1991): 25*–6* (179–80 English summary).

authorities'.[26] For that reason, it is probably no coincidence that the excavations in Nazareth lack imported *terra sigillata*.[27] In the 1st century CE, there was an increasing trend among pious Jews to avoid Roman coins.[28] The near absence of Roman coins in the excavation at Mary's Well is at the very least noteworthy.

Around 570 an anonymous pilgrim from the north Italian city of Piacenza visited a synagogue in Nazareth (*Itinerarium* 5 [*CSEL* 39, p. 161]). Several locations for this building have been suggested from which the so-called 'Synagogue Church' within the enclosure of the 19th-century Melkite church can now be excluded.[29] North-east of the Church of Saint Joseph, Bellarmino Bagatti discovered simple capitals, column drums and bases resembling architectural fragments from Galilean synagogues of the 3rd and 4th century CE.[30] Bagatti thought that the synagogue of the 1st century had stood at the same place. In view of the small size of the village, such a building was probably only a modest house-synagogue, perhaps without identifying architectural features. According to the Synoptic Gospels, Nazareth had a synagogue, and this cannot be explained as a purely redactional feature. Nazareth's synagogue is attested not only by the Markan tradition (Mk 6.2, cf. Mt. 13.54) going back to the memories of Peter (Papias, in Eusebius, *Hist. Eccl.* 3.39.15).[31] As Joachim Jeremias[32] and John Nolland[33] have convincingly demonstrated: 'there can be little doubt that Luke had access to an

26. Ken Dark, 'Roman-Period and Byzantine Landscapes between Sepphoris and Nazareth', *PEQ* 140 (2008): 87–102 (98).

27. James F. Strange, 'Nazareth', in *Galilee in the Late Second Temple and Mishnaic Periods*. Vol. 2, *The Archaeological Records from Cities, Towns, and Villages*, ed. David A. Fiensy and James Riley Strange (Minneapolis: Fortress Press, 2015), 167–80 (176).

28. Niclas Förster, *Jesus und die Steuerfrage: Die Zinsgroschenperikope auf dem religiösen und politischen Hintergrund der Zeit mit einer Edition von* Pseudo-Hieronymus De haeresibus Judaeorum, WUNT 294 (Tübingen: Mohr Siebeck, 2012), 83–143.

29. Ken Dark and Eliya Ribak, 'A Report on the Unpublished Excavation by Roland de Vaux at the "Synagogue Church" in Nazareth, Israel', *Reading Medieval Studies* 35 (2009): 93–100.

30. Bagatti, *Excavations in Nazareth*, 1:23–5, 233–4 and Plate XI.

31. Richard Bauckham, *Jesus and the Eyewitnesses: The Gospels as Eyewitness Testimony*, 2nd edn (Grand Rapids/Cambridge: Eerdmans, 2017), 202–39.

32. Joachim Jeremias, *Die Sprache des Lukasevangeliums: Redaktion und Tradition im Nicht-Markus-Stoff des dritten Evangeliums*, KEK Sonderband (Göttingen: Vandenhoeck & Ruprecht, 1980), 119–28.

33. John Nolland, *Luke 1–9:20*, WBC 35A (Dallas: Word Books, 1989), 192–5.

additional account of Jesus' ministry in Nazareth'.[34] It was part of the Lukan special tradition going back to conservative Jewish Christians in Judaea and Jerusalem, gathering around James the Brother of the Lord and other relatives of Jesus.[35] Luke 4.16-20 is independent testimony to a synagogue in this village and our earliest literary source describing a synagogue service. As Israeli specialist Lee I. Levine comments: 'The importance of Luke's pericope cannot be overestimated for our understanding of the first-century Judaean synagogue'.[36] We now know of archaeological remains from a synagogue in Magdala and probably also from Khirbet Qana, the Cana of the New Testament (Jn 2.1, 11; 4.46; 21.2), and from Capernaum (Mk 1.21-23 // Lk. 4.31-33).[37] With the presence of ritual baths, stone vessels and a synagogue, three of the most important indicators of a pious Jewish population are attested for Nazareth.

III. *Which Languages Were Being Spoken in Nazareth?*

There is an increasing consensus that in the 1st century CE, Eretz Israel / Palestine was characterized by a trilingual situation. In the words of John C. Poirier: 'A judicious arrangement of the thousands of pieces to the puzzle...supports a sort of trilingualism of Aramaic, Hebrew, and Greek, but one very noticeably tilted toward Aramaic'.[38] To some extent, this trilingual situation is illustrated by the epigraphical evidence from

34. Nolland, *Luke 1–9:20*, 192.

35. Rainer Riesner, 'Die Emmaus-Erzählung (Lukas 24,13-35). Lukanische Theolo gie, judenchristliche Tradition und palästinische Topographie', in *Emmaus in Judäa: Geschichte – Exegese – Archäologie*, ed. Karl Heinz Fleckenstein, Mikko Louhivuori and Rainer Riesner, BAZ 11 (Giessen: Brunnen, 2003), 150–207; Riesner, 'From the Messianic Teacher to the Gospels of Jesus Christ', in *Handbook for the Study of the Historical Jesus*. Vol. 1, *How to Study the Historical Jesus*, ed. Tom Holmén and Stanley E. Porter (Leiden: Brill, 2011), 405–46 (431–41).

36. Lee I. Levine, *The Ancient Synagogue: The First Thousand Years*, 2nd edn (New Haven: Yale University Press, 2005), 46.

37. Lee I. Levine, 'The Synagogues of Galilee', in Fiensy and Strange, eds, *Galilee in the Late Second Temple and Mishnaic Periods*, 1:129–50; Anders Runesson, 'The Historical Jesus, the Gospels, and First-Century Jewish Society: The Importance of the Synagogue for Understanding the New Testament', in *A City Set on a Hill: Essays in Honor of James F. Strange*, ed. Daniel A. Warner and Donald D. Binder (Mountain Home: BorderStone Press, 2014), 265–97.

38. John C. Poirier, 'The Linguistic Situation in Jewish Palestine in Late Antiquity', *JGRChJ* 4 (2007): 55–134 (133–4).

the central Jewish necropolis (2nd to 4th century CE) of Sepphoris. Of fourteen tomb inscriptions one is in Greek, seven in Aramaic, three in Hebrew, one in Hebrew and Greek, one in Greek and Aramaic, and one in Hebrew and Aramaic.[39] The very limited evidence from Nazareth is not incompatible with this picture. A marble fragment excavated under the Basilica of the Annunciation and, on palaeographical grounds, dated to the end of the 1st or the beginning of the 2nd century CE, has the Aramaic words וביר גווי 'and a well within' on one side and the Hebrew word נעצוץ 'thorn bush' (Isa. 55.13) on the other side.[40] Another Hebrew fragment of a sepulchral inscription, only stemming from the 4th century CE at the earliest, reads 'So'em the son of Menachem, may his soul find peace'.[41] In the 19th century, an imperial edict against tomb-robbery was sent from Nazareth to the Sorbonne in Paris (*SEG* VIII no. 13).[42] Probably this inscription was written in the 1st century CE,[43] but it cannot be taken as evidence for the knowledge of Greek in Nazareth, because it is uncertain whether the fragment was excavated in this city or only sold at its flourishing antiquities market. Nevertheless, some knowledge of Greek by merchants and artisans is likely given the proximity to the ancient capital of Sepphoris.[44] Two factors speak for a current use of Middle or Proto-Mishnaic Hebrew: like other Galilean settlements, Nazareth was founded by Jews from Judea where in post-exilic times Hebrew used to be a spoken language.[45] In addition, the piety of the people of Nazareth would probably have included the cultivation of the holy language. It seems to be quite sure that in the synagogue of Nazareth, the Law and the Prophets were being read publicly in Hebrew.

39. Mordechai Aviam and Aharoni Amitai, 'The Necropolis of Sepphoris: The Results of Field Survey', in Warner and Binder, eds, *A City Set on a Hill*, 4–16 (15).

40. Bagatti, *Excavations in Nazareth*, 1:170–1.

41. Ibid., 1:248.

42. François Cumont, 'Un rescript impérial sur la violation de sépulture', *RH* 163 (1930): 241–66.

43. Rainer Riesner, *Paul's Early Period: Chronology, Mission Strategy, Theology* (Grand Rapids: Eerdmans, 1998), 103–4; Craig A. Evans, *Jesus and the Ossuaries: What Jewish Burial Practices Reveal about the Beginning of Christianity* (Waco: Baylor University Press, 2003), 35–7.

44. Craig A. Evans, 'In the Shadow of Sepphoris: Growing Up in Nazareth', in *Jesus and His World: The Archaeological Evidence* (Louisville: Westminster John Knox Press, 2012), 13–37 (21–2).

45. Guido Baltes, *Hebräisches Evangelium und synoptische Überlieferung*, WUNT 2/312 (Tübingen: Mohr Siebeck, 2011), 70–150.

IV. *Why Was Nazareth Called Nazareth?*

In 1962 two fragments of a 3/4th-century inscription were discovered at Caesarea Maritima, containing a list of priestly courses and their settlements, either from the time after the destruction of Jerusalem in 70 CE or after the Bar-Kokhba war (132–135 CE).[46] Another fragment had been found earlier at Ashkelon and later other fragments from Kissufim and Tel Rehov,[47] and possibly even from Nazareth,[48] became known. The fragments form into a complete list of the twenty-four priestly courses, included in two 9th-century lamentations on the destruction of the temple for the 9th of Ab by Eleazar ha-Qalir,[49] which proves the faithful preservation of these lists. In one of the fragments from Caesarea the spelling נצרת for Nazareth is attested (*IEJ* 12 [1962]: 138). Jerome in his *liber interpretationis hebraicorum nominum* knew this spelling (*CCSL* 62, pp. 24–27). Although צ is usually transliterated by σ and not by ζ, numerous exceptions to this rule exist in the Septuagint and in Josephus.[50] The etymological derivation of the place name Nazareth is disputed,[51] but Hans Peter Rüger did a very thorough and convincing philological analysis of the name.[52] The normal Hebrew form was *năṣrat* (נֲצְרַת). In the New Testament Ναζαρέθ, or sometimes Ναζαρέτ, goes back to the Hebrew secondary form *nāṣæræt* (נָצֶרֶת). The form Ναζαρά, attested by the better text in Mt. 4.13 // Lk. 4.16,[53] was derived from the normal Hebrew form

46. Michael Avi-Yonah, 'A List of Priestly Courses from Caesarea', *IEJ* 12 (1962): 137–9 and plate 13.

47. Stuart S. Miller, 'Priests, Purities, and the Jews of Galilee', in Zangenberg, Attridge and Martin, eds, *Religion, Ethnicity and Identity in Ancient Galilee*, 375–402 (374 n. 3).

48. Hanan Eshel, 'Fragments of an Inscription of the Twenty-Four Priestly Courses from Nazareth?' [Hebrew], *Tarbiz* 61 (1992): 159–61 (English summary vii).

49. Samuel Klein, *Beiträge zur Geographie und Geschichte Galiläas* (Leipzig: R. Haupt, 1909), 97–102.

50. George F. Moore, 'Appendix B: Nazarene and Nazareth', in *The Beginnings of Christianity Part I: The Acts of the Apostles.* Vol. 1, *Prolegomena I: The Jewish, Gentile and Christian Backgrounds*, ed. F. J. Foakes Jackson and Kirsopp Lake (1920; Grand Rapids: Baker Books, 1979), 426–32 (427).

51. Horst Kuhli, 'Ναζαρέτ, Ναζαρηνός, Ναζωραῖος', *EWNT* 2, 3rd edn (Stuttgart: W. Kohlhammer, 2011), 1113–21.

52. Hans Peter Rüger, 'ΝΑΖΑΡΕΘ / ΝΑΖΑΡΑ ΝΑΖΑΡΗΝΟΣ / ΝΑΖΩΡΑΙΟΣ', *ZNW* 72 (1981): 257–63.

53. According to Shawn Carruth and James M. Robinson, *Q 4:1–13.16: The Temptation of Jesus, Nazara. Documenta Q: Reconstruction of Q through Two Centuries of Gospel Research Excerpted, Sorted and Evaluated*, Vol. 1, ed. Christoph Heil

by changing the feminine ending *–at* into the other feminine ending *–a*, as was the case with other place-names. According to Yoel Elitzur, the ending *–t* points to the name's origin in post-exilic times[54] and this would fit the archaeological and historical evidence for a founding of Nazareth in the 1st century BCE. Obviously, the founders of Nazareth knew Hebrew. The most probable meaning to be linked with the place-name Nazareth is *nezær* (נֵצֶר) 'branch' or 'bud'.

The meaning 'branch' or 'bud' for Nazareth is strengthened by a passage in the Gospel of Matthew. It is a fulfillment citation that is untypically formulated and hence likely to stem from pre-Matthaean tradition;[55] Joseph 'made his home in a town (πόλις)[56] called Nazareth, so that what was spoken through the prophets might be fulfilled, that he will be called a Nazorean (Ναζωραῖος)' (Mt. 2.23).[57] Connections to various Old Testament passages had been suggested by several scholars and critically reviewed by Robert H. Gundry.[58] In his Commentary on Matthew (*c.* 398 CE [SC 242, p. 88]) and in one of his letters (*Epistolae* 57.7 [*CSEL* 54, p. 515]), Jerome combined Mt. 2.23 with the prophecy in Isa. 11.1: 'A shoot shall come out

(Leuven: Peeters, 1996), 391–442, Ναζαρά was part of Q. In this case, it would have stood for the transition between the temptation of Jesus in the wilderness and his Galilean ministry. Narrative elements of this sort give rise to doubts about Q being a pure sayings source. See Stephen Hultgren, *Narrative Elements in the Double Tradition: A Study of Their Place within the Framework of the Gospel Narrative*, BZNW 13 (Berlin: W. de Gruyter, 2002).

54. Yoel Elitzur, *Ancient Place Names in the Holy Land: Preservation and History* (Jerusalem: Hebrew University, Magnes Press; Winona Lake: Eisenbrauns, 2004), 11, 227–8, 334.

55. Ulrich Luz, *Matthew 1–7: A Commentary*, trans. W. Linss (Minneapolis: Augsburg, 1989), 150.

56. When Nazareth is called a πόλις (Mt. 2.23; Lk. 1.26; 2.4, 39; 4.29), this might be explained by the rendering of the ambiguous term עיר/עירה, as in the Septuagint. According to Arieh Ben-David, *Talmudische Ökonomie: Die Wirtschaft des jüdischen Palästina zur Zeit der Mischna und des Talmud* (Hildesheim: Georg Olms, 1974), 49, עירה is used in Mishnaic Hebrew for a country town of 600 to 7,500 inhabitants. Josephus, too, has not always been consistent in his use of κώμη and πόλις. Sometimes he would use both expressions for one and the same place. See Ze'ev Safrai, 'Urbanization and Industry in Mishnaic Galilee', in Fiensy and Strange, eds, *Galilee in the Late Second Temple and Mishnaic Periods*, 1:272–96 (273 n. 3).

57. For this translation see W. Barnes Tatum, 'Matthew 2.23 – Wordplay and Misleading Translations', *Bible Translator* 27 (1976): 135–8.

58. Robert H. Gundry, *The Use of the Old Testament in St. Matthew's Gospel with Special Reference to the Messianic Hope*, NovTSup 18 (Leiden: Brill, 1967), 97–104.

from the stump of Jesse, and a branch (נֵצֶר) shall grow out of his roots' (NRSV). But later, in his Commentary on Isaiah, he changed his mind and opted for a connection with the Nazirite, but not without mentioning: '*Quoniam Nazaraeus vocabitur* [Mt. 2.23]: *eruditi Hebraeorum de hoc loco* [Isa. 11.1] *assumptum putant*' (*CCSL* 73, p. 147). The 'learned from the Hebrews' were probably Jewish Christians, who combined Mt. 2.23 with this messianic promise.[59] In the uncensored version of a Baraitha in the Babylonian Talmud, Jesus is called יֵשׁוּ הַנּוֹצְרִי (*Sanh.* 43a *bar.*)[60] and in a later commentary on this tradition the condemnation of a disciple named נֵצֶר is connected to Isa. 11.1 (see below). This passage was interpreted messianically in the Targum and the 'branch' is directly identified with the Messiah: 'And a *king* shall come forth from the *sons* of Jesse, and *the Messiah* shall be exalted from *the sons of his sons*'.[61] Even in the Isaiah *pesher* from Qumran, Isa. 11.1-5 is related to the Davidic Messiah (*4Q161* frags. 8-10 3:11–25).[62] Since Mt. 2.23 refers to the prophets in the plural, other passages like Isa. 42.6 and 49.6, connected by the root נצר as a catch-word, may have been in the background.[63] Still, the main reference is the clearly Davidic promise Isa. 11.1, fitting the strong Davidic colouring of Matthew 1–2, as seems to be the majority view of modern commentators.[64] Against all proposals of connecting Mt. 2.23 and the term

59. Ray A. Pritz, *Nazarene Jewish Christianity from the End of the New Testament Period until its Disappearance in the Fourth Century*, SPB 37 (Jerusalem: Magnes Press; Leiden: Brill, 1988), 12–13 n. 9.

60. David Instone-Brewer, 'Jesus of Nazareth's Trial in the Uncensored Talmud', *TynBul* 62 (2011): 262–94 (274–6).

61. Bruce D. Chilton, *The Isaiah Targum*, Aramaic Bible 11 (Wilmington: Michael Glazier, 1987).

62. The partially reconstructed text in Florentino García Martínez and Eibert J. C. Tigchelaar, *The Dead Sea Scrolls Study Edition*. Vol. 1, *1Q1–4Q273* (Leiden: Brill, 1997), 316–17. See also Johannes Zimmermann, *Messianische Texte aus Qumran: Königliche, priesterliche und prophetische Messiasvorstellungen in den Schriftfunden von Qumran*, WUNT 2/104 (Tübingen: Mohr Siebeck, 1998), 59–71.

63. Rainer Riesner, 'Nazarener / Nazareth', in *Neues Bibel-Lexikon* 2, ed. Manfred Görg and Bernhard Lang (Solothurn: Benziger Verlag, 1995), 908–12 (909); John Nolland, *The Gospel of Matthew*, NIGTC (Grand Rapids: Eerdmans; Bletchley: Paternoster Press, 2005), 128–31.

64. Robert H. Gundry, *Matthew: A Commentary on His Literary and Theological Art* (Grand Rapids: Eerdmans, 1982), 39–40; Alexander Sand, *Das Evangelium nach Matthäus* (Regensburg: Friedrich Pustet, 1986), 57–8; Donald A. Hagner, *Matthew 1–13*, WBC 33A (Dallas: Word Books, 1993), 39–42; Wolfgang Wiefel,

Ναζωραῖος with the Old Testament Nazirite (נָזִיר, Ναζιραῖος)[65], as indeed advocated by Tertullian (*Adv. Marc.* 4.8) and Eusebius (*Dem. Evan.* 7.2), the Hebrew spelling of Nazareth (נצרת) speaks against this view, as well as the fact that Jesus is distinguished from John the Baptist by not being depicted as an ascetic (Mt. 11.18-19 // Lk. 7.33-34). When Nathanael objects to Philip: 'Can anything good come out of Nazareth?' (Jn 1.46; cf. 7.52), the evangelist could presuppose that most of his readers knew that the opposite was true.[66] It is possible that the Matthaean infancy narrative, which, in contrast to the Lukan account, is told from the perspective of Joseph, took shape among the circle of Jesus' relatives in Galilee and the neighbouring areas like Gaulanitis and Batanaea.[67]

Possibly, the Christian polyhistor Julius Africanus (*c.* 160–240 CE), a friend of Origen, met personally some of the remaining relatives of Jesus.[68] In any case he preserved among their traditions the following report: There 'were those, of whom we have already spoken called desposynoi (δεσπόσυνοι), for their relationship with the Lord. From the Jewish villages of Nazareth and of Cokhaba (ἀπό τε Ναζάρων καὶ Κωχαβα κωμῶν Ἰουδαϊκῶν) they were scattered in various regions and they gathered with the greatest possible diligence the above-mentioned genealogy from the Book of Days' (Eusebius, *Hist. Eccl.* 1.7.14 [Schwartz, p. 23]). Not only can the name of Nazareth be derived from a messianic prophecy (Isa. 11.1) but also that of Cokhaba, namely from Bileam's oracle: 'A star (כּוֹכָב) shall come out of Jacob, and a sceptre shall rise out of Israel; it shall crush the borderlands of Moab, and the territory of all the Shetites. Edom will become a possession… ' (Num. 24.17-18 NRSV). This cannot be accidental but is best explained by people naming two new settlements

Das Evangelium nach Matthäus, THKNT 1 (Leipzig: Evangelische Verlagsanstalt, 1998), 49; Craig S. Keener, *A Commentary on the Gospel of Matthew* (Grand Rapids: Eerdmans, 1999), 114.

65. Eduard Schweizer, 'Er wird Nazoräer heißen zu Mc. 1,24; Mt 2,23', in *Neotestamentica* (Zurich: TVZ Verlag, 1963), 51–5; Ernst Zuckschwerdt, 'Nazōraios in Matth. 2,23', *TZ* 31 (1975): 65–77; Klaus Berger, 'Jesus als Nasoräer/Nasiräer', *NovT* 38 (1996): 323–35.

66. George R. Beasley-Murray, *John*, WBC 36 (Waco: Word Books, 1987), 118.

67. Rainer Riesner, 'Bethlehem, the Birth Stories and Archaeology', in *The Gospels: History and Christology: The Search of Joseph Ratzinger – Benedict XVI*, vol. 1, ed. Bernardo Estrada, Ermenegildo Manicardi and Armand Puig i Tàrrech (Vatican City: Libreria Editrice Vaticana, 2013), 473–507 (480–2).

68. Christoph Markschies, 'Stadt und Land des Christentums in Palästina', in *Römische Reichsreligion und Provinzialreligion*, ed. Hubert Cancik and Joachim Rüpke (Tübingen: Mohr Siebeck, 1997), 265–97 (280).

of Davidic families in a way that alludes to great messianic prophecies, and so testifies to their still fervent eschatological hopes.[69] In the Jewish-Christian *Apocalypse of John* which has connections to the Lukan special tradition[70] the two prophecies of Isa. 11.1 and Num. 24.17 are combined: 'I (Jesus) am the root and the descendant of David, the bright morning star' (Rev. 22.16 NRSV). If Joseph, who was of Davidic descent and had originally dwelt in Bethlehem (Mt. 2.1, 10),[71] later resettled into Nazareth (Mt. 2.19-23), then that can be explained by his connection to another Davidic clan.[72] When Nazareth is called the πατρίς of Jesus (Mk 6.1, 4 // Mt. 13.53, 57 // Lk. 4.24), this does not necessarily mean the place of birth, but only the place of dwelling.[73]

V. *Was Nazareth the Home Town of Jesus?*

The adjectival designation Ναζαρηνός in Mark (1.24; 10.47; 14.67; 16.6) and Luke (4.34; 24.19) is in apposition to the name of Jesus. According to a widespread ancient usage, this term designates provenance from the so-named place. The surname is identical with the expression Jesus ὁ ἀπὸ Ναζαρέθ (Mt. 21.11; Jn 1.45; Acts 10.38). In Matthew (2.23; 26.71) and John (18.5, 7; 19.19) exclusively, and in Luke–Acts (Lk. 18.37; Acts 2.22; 3.6; 4.10; 6.14; 22.8; 26.9) preponderantly, Jesus is called Ναζωραῖος. It is also philologically possible to derive this designation from the place-name, probably from another secondary Hebrew form *naṣōr* (נָצוֹר),[74] expressing the provenance of Jesus from Nazareth. In Luke–Acts

69. Étienne Nodet and Justin Taylor, *The Origins of Christianity: An Exploration* (Collegeville: Liturgical Press, 1998), 154–5; Bargil Pixner, *Paths of the Messiah and Sites of the Early Church from Galilee to Jerusalem: Jesus and Jewish Christianity in Light of Archaeological Discoveries*, ed. Rainer Riesner (San Francisco: Ignatius Press, 2010), 3–4.

70. Rainer Riesner, 'Genesis 3,15 in der vorlukanischen und johanneischen Tradition', *SNTU* 29 (2004): 119–78 (141–4).

71. Markus Bockmuehl, *This Jesus: Martyr, Lord, Messiah* (Edinburgh: T. & T. Clark, 1994), 24–9.

72. Rainer Riesner, '"Gedeutete, konzentrierte Geschichte": Benedikt XVI. und die Geburt Jesu in Bethlehem', in *Zu Bethlehem geboren? Das Jesus-Buch Benedikts XVI. und die Wissenschaft*, ed. Thomas Söding (Freiburg: Herder, 2013), 104–27 (110–16).

73. Charles E. B. Cranfield, *The Gospel according to St Mark*, CGTC (Cambridge: CUP, 1972), 192–3; Robert A. Guelich, *Mark 1–8:26*, WBC 34A (Dallas: Word Books, 1989), 308.

74. Rüger, "NAZAPEΘ', 262.

the more strongly semitizing form Ναζωραῖος likely shows the influence of his special tradition,[75] rather than being part of Luke's redactional activity. In the hymns from Qumran נֵצֶר 'branch' is used collectively as a designation for the eschatological community of the sectarians (1QH 6.15; 7.19; 8.6, 8, 10). In Acts 24.5 messianic believers around James the brother of the Lord are called Ναζωραῖοι. Behind the name of this group the messianic connotation was probably stronger than the memory of the place-name Nazareth. An Amoraic tradition in the Babylonian Talmud (*b. Sanh.* 43a [*Str-B* I, p. 95]) may suggest that the Jewish Christians called themselves נוֹצְרִים after Isa. 11.1 (see above). Usually, in Patristic literature, Nazarenes or Nazoraeans are designations of christologically orthodox Jewish Christians in contrast to the Ebionites.

Even in the 20th and 21st centuries, some attempts had been made to separate Jesus from Nazareth. One line of argumentation tries to derive Ναζωραῖος from a pre-Christian religious movement and so to separate the name from the village of Nazareth. According to J. Spencer Kennard, the evangelist Mark invented the connection between Jesus and Nazareth to distance him from this movement.[76] Kennard goes on to say that the real home of Jesus was Capernaum. In 1969 Hartmut Stegemann, the respected Qumran scholar, proposed a similar hypothesis in a public lecture, which gained great attention in the media but was never published.[77] D. B. Taylor shows how desperate the attempt of separating Jesus from Nazareth can be in reasoning that Jesus 'described his ministry in terms borrowed from Isa 49:6 [the Servant of the Lord restoring the preserved (נְצוּרֵי) of Israel]; and that half of his audience completely misunderstood his meaning'.[78] The most ambitious recent attempt to separate Jesus from Nazareth was proposed by Volker Wagner, building his case on four very debatable arguments.[79] First, the references to Nazareth concentrate on

75. For Lk. 18.35–42 as influenced by his Semitizing special tradition see Eduard Schweizer, 'Eine hebraisierende Sonderquelle des Lukas?', *TZ* 6 (1950): 161–85 (175–6); James R. Edwards, *The Hebrew Gospel and the Development of the Synoptic Tradition* (Grand Rapids: Eerdmans, 2009), 131, 134–5, 138.

76. J. Spencer Kennard, 'Was Capernaum the Home of Jesus?', *JBL* 65 (1946): 131–41; Kennard, 'Nazorean and Nazareth', *JBL* 66 (1947): 79–81. He was severely criticized by William F. Albright, 'The Names "Nazareth" and "Nazoraean"', *JBL* 65 (1946): 397–401.

77. See the detailed report and critique by Josef Blinzler, 'Die Heimat Jesu. Zu einer neuen Hypothese', *Bibel und Kirche* 25 (1970): 14–20.

78. D. B. Taylor, 'Jesus – of Nazareth?', *ExpTim* 92 (1981): 336–7 (337).

79. Volker Wagner, 'Mit der Herkunft Jesu aus Nazaret gegen die Geltung des Gesetzes?', *ZNW* 92 (2001): 273–82.

the childhood stories and the passion narrative of the Gospels and are rare during his public career, but this is not astonishing if Jesus was rejected in Nazareth (Mk 6.1-6 // Mt. 13.53-58; Lk. 4.16-30) and for some time chose Capernaum as his Galilean headquarters (Mt. 4.12-13; Jn 2.12). Second, 1st-century Nazareth was not a permanently, but only occasionally, inhabited place. In respect to the archaeological situation, Wagner referred only to sparse and largely irrelevant secondary literature. Third, although he conceded that the philological analysis of Hans Peter Rüger is possible, Wagner revived in a slightly modified form an old hypothesis of Mark Lidzbarski,[80] which had been refuted by Hans Heinrich Schaeder[81] long ago and more recently by Robert H. Gundry.[82] According to Wagner, Jesus belonged to a Jewish group called 'keepers' (from the root נצר 'to keep, preserve') of the Law. Fourth, this etymological derivation was obscured, if not falsified, when the Christians tried to distance Jesus from the Torah. But it is the Jewish Christian Gospel of Matthew that establishes the closest link between Jesus' designation as Ναζωραῖος and his provenance from Nazareth (Mt. 2.23). Just out of curiosity, it is worth mentioning that even Sepphoris was recently proposed as Jesus' home town. This is supposedly 'proven' because Jesus told dramatic parables and Sepphoris had a theatre...[83] Against such one-man-theories, James H. Charlesworth stated that 'Jesus grew up in Nazareth' is the 'remarkable consensus... among leading scholars'.[84] If Jesus was a member of a Davidic clan there, he had been raised and had lived in the traditions of the Old Testament and of his family.[85]

80. Mark Lidzbarski, *Mandäische Liturgien*, Abhandlungen der Gesellschaft der Wissenschaften zu Göttingen (Philologish-historische Klasse) NF 17/1 (Berlin: Weidmann, 1920), xvii–xix.

81. Hans Heinrich Schaeder, 'Ναζαρηνός, Ναζωραῖος', *TWNT* 4:879–84 (880–3).

82. Gundry, *The Use of the Old Testament in St. Matthew's Gospel*, 100–102.

83. Eberhard Martin Pausch, 'Jesus aus Sepphoris: Eine Abduktion zum historischen Jesus', *Deutsches Pfarrer-Blatt* 116 (2016): 151–3.

The existence of a theatre in the 1st century AD is contested. See Ze'ev Weiss, 'Sepphoris: From Galilean Town to Roman City, 100 BCE – 200 CE', in Fiensy and Strange, eds, *Galilee in the Late Second Temple and Mishnaic Periods*, 2:53–75 (67–8).

84. James H. Charlesworth, 'Should Specialists in Jesus Research Include Psychobiography?', in *Jesus Research: New Methodologies and Perceptions: The Second Princeton-Prague Symposium on Jesus Research*, ed. James H. Charlesworth with Brian Rhea and Petr Pokorný (Grand Rapids: Eerdmans, 2014), 436–66 (439).

85. Rainer Riesner, *Jesus als Lehrer: Eine Untersuchung zum Ursprung der Evangelien-Überlieferung*, 3rd edn, WUNT 2/7 (Tübingen: J. C. B. Mohr (Paul

VI. *What Can We Learn from Nazareth in the Time after Jesus?*

The archaeological evidence speaks against the assumption that in 67 CE 'the Nazareth of the Gospels was utterly wiped out'.[86] After the destruction of Jerusalem in 70 CE or after the catastrophe of the Bar-Kokhba war (132–135 CE), Nazareth became the home of the priestly class ha-Pizzez (1 Chron. 24.15).[87] This proves the Jewish character of Nazareth, but does it also prompt to the conclusion that there were no more Jewish Christians in town? Bellarmino Bagatti's assumption that the remains of a pre-Byzantine building underneath the Basilica of the Annunciation, including many graffiti, point to the presence of such messianic believers in the 3rd century CE[88] is disputed.[89] We have some evidence about Galilean Jewish Christians from the 2nd to the 4th century in Kefar Sekhanyah (*t. Hul.* 2.24; *b. 'Abod. Zar.* 16b–17a)[90] and Sepphoris (*Gen. Rab.* 14.7;

Siebeck), 1988), 210–36; Roland Deines, 'Der Messiasanspruch Jesu im Kontext frühjüdischer Messiaserwartungen', in *Der jüdische Messias und sein jüdischer Apostel Paulus*, ed. Armin D. Baum, Detlef Häußer and Emmanuel L. Rehfeld, WUNT 2/425 (Tübingen: Mohr Siebeck, 2016), 49–106 (95–100).

86. Clemens Kopp, *The Holy Places of the Gospels* (Freiburg: Herder; Edinburgh: Nelson, 1963), 53.

87. See nn. 46–9. By denying the literary sources and ignoring the archaeological facts, the foundation of Nazareth is ascribed to these priests by Ernst Axel Knauf, 'Writing and Speaking in Galilee', in *Zeichen aus Text und Stein: Studien auf dem Weg zu einer Archäologie des Neuen Testaments*, ed. Stefan Alkier and Jürgen Zangenberg, TANZ 42 (Tübingen: Francke, 2003), 336–50 (349).

88. Bagatti, *Excavations in Nazareth*, 1:114–73; Bellarmino Bagatti, *The Church from the Circumcision: History and Archaeology of the Judaeo-Christians*, Studii Biblici Franciscani, Collectio Minor 2 (Jerusalem: Franciscan Printing Press, 1971), 19–21, 122–9.

89. Critical are Joan E. Taylor, *Christians and the Holy Places: The Myth of Jewish Christian Origins* (Oxford: OUP, 1993), 221–67; Eric M. Meyers and Mark A. Chancey, *Alexander to Constantine*, Archaeology of the Land of the Bible 3 (New Haven: Yale University Press, 2012), 187–90; somewhat more sympathetic are Sean Freyne, 'Christianity in Sepphoris and in Galilee', in *Galilee and Gospel: Collected Essays*, WUNT 125 (Tübingen: Mohr Siebeck, 2000), 299–307 (304–5); James F. Strange, 'Archaeological Evidence for Jewish Christianity', in *Jewish Believers in Jesus: The Earliest Centuries*, ed. Oskar Skarsaune and Reidar Hvalvik (Peabody: Hendrickson, 2007), 710–41 (723–7).

90. Freyne, 'Christianity in Sepphoris and in Galilee', 301–2; Roland Deines, 'Religious Practices and Religious Movements in Galilee: 100 BCE–200 CE', in Fiensy and Strange, eds, *Galilee in the Late Second Temple and Mishnaic Periods*, 1:78–111 (100–101).

b. Sanh. 38b),[91] from Rabbinic sources. Philip S. Alexander even comes to the conclusion: 'Jewish Christianity was a more significant movement in the Jewish communities of Palestine than it might at first sight appear. Jewish Christians were one of a range of ideological opponents of the rabbis, who struggled with them for dominance in the Judaism of the post-70 era… Jewish Christians were scattered through the Jewish towns and villages of Galilee.'[92] It is rather improbable that all the members of the extended family of Jesus, living in Nazareth in the time of his public career (Mk 6.3 // Mt. 13.55-56), after Easter resettled into Jerusalem like his mother and some of his brothers (Acts 1.14). Indeed, during the persecution of Decius (249–251 CE), we hear from a martyr named Konon who affirmed: 'I am of the city of Nazareth in Galilee, I am of the family of Christ to whom I offer cult from the time of my ancestors' (*Analecta Bollandiana* XVIII, 180).[93] Apparently, Julius Africanus could have met some relatives of Jesus in Nazareth. A remark of the Pilgrim of Piacenza (*Itinerarium* 5 [*CSEL* 39, p. 161]) may presuppose the presence of some Jewish Christians, even in the 6th century CE.[94]

If there was a personal continuity of relatives of Jesus and other Jewish Christians in Nazareth from New Testament times until the 4th century, then the oldest local traditions merit attention. Ken Dark was able to re-discover the second Byzantine church of Nazareth underneath the Convent of the Sisters of Nazareth.[95] According to the Pilgrim Arculf (*c.* 670 CE) it stood at the place of the house where Jesus was educated as a child '*domus, in qua noster nutritius est salvator*' (*De locis sanctis* 2.26 [*CSEL* 39, p. 274]). Indeed, underneath the Byzantine church, the walls of a house from the 1st century CE have been found and Dark thinks it might be possible that this was the house of Joseph.[96] If so, the family

91. Frédéric Manns, 'Un centre judéo-chrétien important: Sepphoris', in Manns, *Essais sur le Judéo-Christianisme*, Studii Biblici Franciscani, Analecta 12 (Jerusalem: Franciscan Printing Press, 1977), 165–90.

92. Philip S. Alexander, 'Jewish Believers in Early Rabbinic Literature (2nd to 5th Centuries)', in Skarsaune and Hvalvik, eds, *Jewish Believers in Jesus*, 659–709 (686).

93. Richard Bauckham, *Jude and the Relatives of Jesus in the Early Church* (Edinburgh: T. & T. Clark, 1990), 121–5.

94. Simon C. Mimouni, *Le Judéo-christianisme ancien: Essais historiques*, Patrimoines (Paris: Éditions du Cerf, 1998), 63–6.

95. Ken Dark, 'The Byzantine Church of the Nutrition in Nazareth Rediscovered', *PEQ* 144 (2012): 164–84.

96. Ken Dark, 'Has Jesus' Nazareth House Been Found?', *BAR* 41, no. 2 (2015): 54–63, 72.

of Jesus inhabited a decent dwelling. The house had well-built walls and a chalk floor and perhaps even a second storey.[97] Stone vessels point to Jewish inhabitants and some glassware shows a modest prosperity. There is a growing consensus that Galilee, before the Jewish War, was not an impoverished region, but rather economically stable.[98] Bradley W. Root summarizes the present majority view: 'The preponderance of evidence concerning Galilee's socio-economic conditions is more consistent with the picture of harmony. Although, by today's standards, economic hardship and oppression were common in all ancient societies, these problems were generally less pronounced in 1st-century Galilee than they were in most parts of the Mediterranean.'[99] Martin Hengel and Anna Maria Schwemer characterize the family of Jesus as members not of the proletarian class of day-labourers without landed property, but as artisans (Mk 6.3) belonging to the modest middle-class.[100]

VII. *Some Conclusions*

First, Jesus grew up and lived for about thirty years in Nazareth in a pious Jewish environment. Identifying him with the line of Cynic preachers was not a critical advance. Second, in view of the general socio-economic situation of Galilee, possible archaeological evidence from Nazareth and the background of his family, Jesus did not belong to the impoverished underclass. Third, because Nazareth was a settlement of pious Jews from Judaea, Hebrew was used in the synagogue, yet probably not only liturgically, but colloquially, too. Owing to the Semitic background of the words of Jesus, one should not confine oneself to an Aramaic origin, but also ask for a possible Hebrew substratum. Fourth, in the synagogue of Nazareth, Jesus could hear the Law and the Prophets through public

97. A possible reconstruction of houses in Nazareth in Robert K. McIver, 'First-century Nazareth', in *Glaube und Zukunftsgestaltung*, ed. Bernhard Oestreich (Frankfurt: Peter Lang, 1999), 139–59.

98. David A. Fiensy, 'Assessing the Economy of Galilee in the Late Second Temple Period: Five Considerations', in *The Galilean Economy in the Time of Jesus*, ed. David A. Fiensy and Ralph K. Hawkins (Atlanta: SBL, 2013), 165–86; Morten Hørning Jensen, 'Rural Galilee and Rapid Changes: An Investigation of the Socio-Economic Dynamics and Developments in Roman Galilee', *Bib* 93 (2012): 43–67.

99. Bradley W. Root, *First Century Galilee: A Fresh Examination of the Sources*, WUNT 2/378 (Tübingen: Mohr Siebeck, 2014), 184.

100. Martin Hengel and Anna Maria Schwemer, *Jesus und das Judentum*, Geschichte des frühen Christentums 1 (Tübingen: Mohr Siebeck, 2007), 294.

readings in the Shabbat services, but he also had the possibility to study the holy Scriptures during the week there. Citations and allusions to the Old Testament in his words should not automatically be ascribed to the post-Easter Christian community. Jesus was not an uneducated peasant uttering some short popular wisdom proverbs, but acted as a messianic teacher living in the holy scriptures of his people. Fifth, the settlement history of Nazareth strengthens the tradition of a Davidic descent of Jesus (Rom. 1.3). In his Davidic clan, both the hope for a universal peace-king (Isa. 11.1) and for a messianic warrior (Num. 24.17) were alive. Faced with these differing expectations, Jesus had to find out what the will of his heavenly Father was for his messianic role

2

'On This Rock I Will Build My Church' (Matthew 16.18): Was the Promise to Peter a Response to Tetrarch Philip's Proclamation?

Craig A. Evans

In a piece of satire, attributed to Seneca (*c.* 4 BCE–65 CE), one Diespiter, a fictitious politician and vendor of Roman citizenship, says of the recently deceased Emperor Claudius (ruled 41–54 CE):

> Inasmuch as the blessed Claudius [*divus Claudius*] is akin to the blessed Augustus [*divum Augustum*], and also to the blessed Augusta [*divam Augustam*], his grandmother, whom he ordered to be made a goddess [*deam*], and whereas he far surpasses all mortal men in wisdom… I propose that from this day forth blessed Claudius [*divus Claudius*] be a god [*deus*], to enjoy that honour with all its appurtenances in as full a degree as any other before him…[1]

Apocolocyntosis Divi Claudi, or 'Pumpkinification of Divine Claudius',[2] is a wickedly funny satire, in which the passing of the emperor on 13 October 54 is welcomed with relief. The authorship of the tract is not

1. Trans. based on William Henry Denham Rouse, 'Seneca: Apocolocyntosis', in Michael Heseltine, *Petronius*, rev. Eric Herbert Warmington, LCL 15 (Cambridge, MA: Harvard University Press; London: Heinemann, 1969), 463.

2. The word *apocolocyntosis*, which is coined of course, is based on the Greek κολοκύνθη ('pumpkin') and is intended as a parody of *apotheosis* ('transformed into deity'), which in pre-Christian imperial Rome was sometimes applied to the emperor or someone in his family. The point of Seneca's spoof is that Claudius has not been transformed into a *god*; he has been transformed into a *pumpkin*.

certain, of course, but no modern scholar has raised a fatal objection against the tradition that it was penned by Seneca.[3] For all its satire, it nevertheless truthfully conveys popular 1st-century Roman beliefs regarding the *apotheosis* of the emperor. Of particular interest here is the reference to blessed or divine (*diva*) Augusta, better known as Livia, the long-time wife of Emperor Augustus, who ruled Rome absolutely for almost forty-five years.

The Deification of Livia and the Refounding of Bethsaida

Livia Drusilla was born in 58 BCE and died in 29 CE, at the age of 87. No other imperial spouse had more influence or gained more notoriety, both positive and negative. In her time the only woman who rivalled Livia was Cleopatra, the queen of Egypt. But in the end, it was Livia, wife of Rome's first emperor and mother of Rome's second emperor, who left an enduring stamp on the Roman imperial cult.[4]

At fifteen Livia married Tiberius Claudius Nero, to whom she bore Tiberius the future emperor and Drusus Julius Caesar. In 39 BCE she divorced in order to marry Octavian, the future Augustus, to whom she bore no children. Octavian himself had divorced Scribonia, who bore him Julia, his only child, in order to marry Livia. The marriage was stable and effective, enduring until the death of Augustus in 14 CE.

Contemporary opinion of Livia varied. All agreed that she was intelligent, resourceful and beautiful. In many ways she was a traditional role model, even 'old school' as one historian puts it (Tacitus, *Ann.* 5.1). Livia exemplified the Roman matron at her finest. But not all were so generous to Livia. Critics rumored that she was involved in a number of intrigues and murders and manipulated Augustus near the end of his life. Most of our historical data comes from Tacitus (*c.* 56–*c.* 120 CE), who seems more than willing to believe the worst about Livia. He apparently accepts the rumors that Livia was behind the murders of various

3. See the brief comments in Rouse, 'Seneca: Apocolocyntosis', 432–5.

4. Scholarly interest in Livia has revived in recent years. See Claudia-Martina Perkounig, *Livia Drusilla – Iulia Augusta: Das politische Porträt der ersten Kaiserin Roms* (Vienna: Böhlau, 1995); Eric D. Huntsman, 'The Family and Property of Livia Drusilla' (PhD diss., University of Pennsylvania, 1997); Antony A. Barrett, *Livia: First Lady of Imperial Rome* (New Haven: Yale University Press, 2002); Eric D. Huntsman, 'Livia Before Octavian', *Ancient Society* 39 (2009): 121–69; Chapter 1, 'La vie de Livie, femme d'Auguste', in Gérard Minaud, *Les vies de 12 femmes d'empereur romain: Devoirs, intrigues & voluptés* (Paris: L'HarMattan, 2012), 13–38.

family members, motivated in part to clear the way for her son Tiberius (Tacitus, *Ann.* 1.3, 6; Suetonius, *Tib.* 22). In this connection, Tacitus reminds his readers of the dark maxim: 'Livia – as a mother, a curse to the realm; as a stepmother, a curse to the house of the Caesars' (Tacitus, *Ann.* 1.10).

Augustus bequeathed a fortune to Livia. But his greatest bequest was adopting her into the Julian family and granting her the name *Julia Augusta* (Tacitus, *Ann.* 1.8; 5.1; Suetonius, *Aug.* 101.1; *Claud.* 11.2). Senators heaped praise on her, suggesting she receive titles like 'Parent of her Country' or 'Mother of her Country'. A few senators, much to the annoyance of Tiberius, suggested that the new emperor be called Caesar Augustus 'son of Julia' (Tacitus, *Ann.* 1.14; Suetonius, *Tib.* 50.3). Tiberius was further annoyed when his mother had an inscription made for the Theatre of Marcellus, in which the name of the emperor appeared *after* her name (Tacitus, *Ann.* 3.64).[5]

Her long relationship to Augustus and the benefits her late husband bestowed upon her through his will solidified her place of power and influence, well beyond that of other imperial widows. Livia's power guaranteed the emperorship for her son Tiberius. Her adoption into the Julian family transformed her son into a Julian and assured his succession (Dio 57.2-3).[6] Her influence advanced a number of persons, including future emperors Galba and Otho (Suetonius, *Galb.* 5.2; *Otho* 1.1; Plutarch, *Galb.* 3.2). As it turned out, however, Tiberius had little affection for his mother. It was believed that he moved to the island of Capreae (now Capri) in 26 CE to avoid her and to keep his paedophilia and perversities out of the public eye (Suetonius, *Tib.* 40–45; 50.2; 51.1-2). When Livia became ill, Tiberius did not visit her (Suetonius, *Tib.* 51.2). When she died, Tiberius delayed then greatly simplified her funeral (at which he was not present), would not execute her will and forbade her deification (Tacitus, *Ann.* 5.1-2; Suetonius, *Tib.* 51.2; *Cal.* 16.3; *Galb.* 5.2). Her will was not executed until the reign of Caligula and her postponed deification did not take place until the reign of Claudius (Suetonius, *Claud.* 11.2: *divinos honores*).[7]

5. The inscription reads (*CIL* I no. 316): *Signum divo Augusto patri ad theatrum Marcelli Iulia Augusta et Ti. Augustus dedicarunt* ('Julia Augusta and Tiberius Augustus dedicated the image to the divine Augustus their father on the Theatre of Marcellus'). More will be said about this inscription below.

6. David C. A. Shotter, 'Julians, Claudians and the Accession of Tiberius', *Latomus* 30 (1971): 1117–23.

7. Hans-Werner Ritter, 'Livias Erhebung zur Augusta', *Chiron* 2 (1972): 313–38.

Notwithstanding the emperor's lack of affection for his mother, a number of influential persons clamoured for her deification. Among those who admired her and supported the movement calling for her deificiation was Philip the tetrarch of Gaulanitis, the territory to the north and east of Galilee. The evidence, which will be reviewed below in greater detail, is primarily seen in Philip's upgrading Bethsaida from village (κώμη) to city (πόλις) and renaming it Julias, referring to the name given to Livia on the death of Augustus. It is also seen in an issue of coins in the year 30 CE, to coincide with the dedication of Bethsaida-Julias.[8]

After relating the death of Augustus, who had appointed Antipas and Philip as tetrarchs, and the subsequent enthronement of Tiberius, Rome's new emperor, Josephus says: 'Philip built Caesarea near the sources of the Jordan, in the district of Paneas, and Julias in lower Gaulanitis; Herod (Antipas) built Tiberias in Galilee and a city which also took the name of Julia, in Peraea' (Josephus, *War* 2.168). Further details are provided in the parallel passage in *Antiquities*, written about twenty years later:

> (Antipas) also threw a wall about another city, Betharamphtha, which he called Julias after the name of the emperor's wife. Philip too made improvements at Paneas, the city near the sources of the Jordan, and called it Caesarea. He also raised the village of Bethsaida on Lake Gennesaret to the status of city by adding residents and strengthening the fortifications. He named it after Julia, the emperor's daughter (*Ant.* 18.27-29).

All of these cities have been founded or refounded and named after members of the Roman imperial family. Antipas, tetrarch of Galilee, founded Tiberias, on the western shore of the Sea of Galilee, and named it after Emperor Tiberius. He then upgraded biblical Beth-haram (Num. 32.36; Josh. 13.27) and renamed it Julias, after Livia, the wife of Emperor Augustus, who had been given the name Julia Augusta. Philip does likewise: he upgraded Paneas, renaming it Caesarea, or, more fully, Caesarea Philippi. He also upgraded Bethsaida, the fishing village on the north shore of the Sea of Galilee, giving it the name Julias 'after Julia, the emperor's daughter'.

In their translations of *Jewish War* and *Antiquities* Henry Thackeray and Louis Feldman understand 'Julia, the emperor's daughter' in reference to Octavian's daughter by his wife Scribonia, who was disgraced and sent into exile in 2 BCE (Tacitus, *Ann.* 1.53; 3.24; 4.44; 6.51; Suetonius, *Aug.* 65.1; Dio 55.10.4). Because it is most unlikely that Bethsaida or any other

8. Nikos Kokkinos, 'The Foundation of Bethsaida-Julias by Philip the Tetrarch', *JJS* 59 (2008): 236–51.

city would have been named after such a well-known person so publicly disgraced, Thackeray and Feldman suggest the upgrade of Bethsaida must have taken place in 4 BCE, immediately after the young Philip became tetrarch of Gaulanitis and before Julia's disgrace.[9] But this seems unlikely. In the context of the relevant passages in *Jewish War* and *Antiquities*, Josephus is speaking of what Antipas and Philip did during the reign of Tiberius, not at the beginning of their respective administrations, during the rule of Augustus.[10] And in any case, it seems unlikely that a city named in honor of Julia in 4 BCE would have retained this new name in the aftermath of her disgrace just two years later.

One way to resolve the problem is to conclude that Josephus is simply mistaken.[11] He should have said, 'Julia, the emperor's wife'. Support for this is seen in the older passage in *War* 2.168 where Josephus is speaking of the accession of Tiberius, son of Julia and then speaks of the founding and refounding of cities named in honor of the new emperor and his mother. In the parallel passage in *Ant.* 18.28, written years later, Josephus adds a few details but mistakenly refers to Julia as the emperor's *daughter* rather than his *wife*.

In a recent study Fred Strickert calls our attention to important evidence that suggests that Josephus may be quite correct but that we moderns have not understood him.[12] In the will of Augustus, who died in 14 CE, both

9. Henry St. John Thackeray, *Josephus II: The Jewish War Books I–III*, LCL 203 (London: Heinemann; Cambridge, MA: Harvard University Press, 1927), 388–9 n. d; Louis H. Feldman, *Josephus IX: Jewish Antiquities Books XVIII–XX*, LCL 433 (London: Heinemann; Cambridge, MA: Harvard University Press, 1965), 25 n. g. Both Thackeray and Feldman appeal to Emil Schürer, *The History of the Jewish People in the Age of Jesus Christ*, 3 vols, rev. Geza Vermes, Fergus Millar and Matthew Black (Edinburgh: T. & T. Clark, 1973–87), 2:171–2. Schürer remarks that it is 'inconceivable that Philip would subsequently have named a town after her', that is, after her disgrace and exile.

10. For this reason Mary Smallwood believes Josephus is guilty of an anachronism. She too understands 'Julia, the emperor's daughter' in *Ant.* 18.28 in reference to Julia, disgraced and exiled in 2 BCE. See E. Mary Smallwood, *The Jews under Roman Rule: From Pompey to Diocletian: A Study in Political Relations*, SJLA 20 (Leiden: Brill, 1976), 118 n. 50.

11. Or intentionally vague, as suggested by John T. Greene, 'The Honorific Naming of Bethsaida-Julias', in *Bethsaida: A City by the North Shore of the Sea of Galilee*, ed. Rami Arav and Richard A. Freund, 4 vols (Kirksville: Truman State University Press, 1999), 2:307–31 (317–27).

12. Fred Strickert, 'The Renaming of Bethsaida in Honor of Livia, a.k.a. Julia, the Daughter of Caesar, in Josephus, *Jewish Antiquities* 18.27-28', in Arav and Freund, eds, *Bethsaida: A City by the North Shore of the Sea of Galilee*, 3:93–113.

Tiberius and Livia were adopted. With the deification of Augustus Livia became Julia Augusta, *daughter* of the late emperor. Strickert cites a statement made by Velleius Paterculus in the year 30 CE, one year after Livia's death:

> Take for example Livia. She, the daughter of the brave and noble Drusus Claudianus, most eminent of Roman women in birth, in sincerity, and in beauty, she, whom we later saw as wife of Augustus, and after his deification as his priestess and daughter [*sacerdotem ac filiam*][13] (*Hist. Rom.* 2.75.3).

Strickert then draws our attention to the Velleia Livia statute, in which Livia is seated, wearing the apparel of a priestess. The accompanying inscription reads: 'To Julia Augusta, daughter of Divus Augustus, mother of Tiberius Caesar the son of Divus Augustus and of Nero Claudius Drusus'.[14] Another inscription reads: 'To Julia Augusta [Σεβαστήν], daughter of Augustus [Σεβαστοῦ Θυγατέρα], the new Hera'.[15] And, of course, in the inscription already mentioned above (*CIL* I no. 316), Divine Augustus is said to be the *father* (*divo Augusto patri*) of Julia Augusta and Tiberius Augustus.

The partially reconstructed inscription, base and statues at Apollonia, which at one time included the *Res Gestae* of Augustus, included Livia/ Julia alongside Augustus and other deified members of the Julian family. The Greek inscription reads: 'The people of the Apollonian, Lycian, and Thracian colonists (honor) the public and private Augustan gods and their children. To Germanicus. To Tiberius Caesar. To god Augustus. To Julia Augusta. To Dusus.'[16]

This monument and inscription, erected after the death of Augustus in 14 CE but probably no later than 20 CE (given the presence of Germanicus), includes the emperor's wife among the 'Augustan gods' (θεοὺς Σεβαστούς).[17] The inscription at Apollonia clearly reflects the emperor's wishes for Livia, as expressed in his will, even if the Roman Senate had not yet formally deified her at the time of the construction of

13. Translation based on Strickert, 'The Renaming of Bethsaida', 98.

14. Translation based on ibid., 100. In the inscription 'daughter' (*filia*) is abbreviated '*f*'.

15. Ibid., 100–101.

16. *MAMA* IV no. 143. For text, translation and discussion I follow Alison E. Cooley, *Res Gestae Divi Augusti: Text, Translation, and Commentary* (Cambridge: CUP, 2009), 16–18. See also M. B. Flory, 'Livia and the History of Public Honorific Statues for Women in Rome', *TAPA* 123 (1993): 287–308.

17. For a facsimile of the monument and its inscription, see Cooley, *Res Gestae Divi Augusti*, 17 + fig. 7.

the monument. Alison Cooley speculates that the people of Apollonia set up such a grand and expensive monument, in order to display publicly the *Res Gestae* of Augustus, at the prompting of the 'emperor-loving elite', perhaps in rivalry with the more prestigious Antioch. Both Apollonia and Antioch were on the Augustan Road (*via Sebaste*).[18] The presence of a monument of this nature would have enhanced the reputation and status of Apollonia, perhaps propelling it toward the status enjoyed by Antioch, which was a full Roman colony.

One can only wonder if that was part of Philip's intention. He did not elevate the status of Bethsaida and rename it Julias simply to honor the late empress; he probably hoped to gain for the city and for himself enhanced status in the Roman Empire. Indeed, given the presence of the Roman legion Fretensis X, some of whose members lay buried on the eastern side of the Sea of Galilee,[19] it is possible that a few Roman colonists either already lived or would live in the enhanced and refounded city of Bethsaida-Julias. The discovery of non-kosher faunal remains in Bethsaida-Julias in the period in question points to the presence of at least some Gentiles in the refounded city.[20]

Coins also provide evidence of the effort to deify Livia. In some cases she is depicted as Demeter/Ceres, the goddess of grain. Philip issued coins in honor of Livia in the year 30 CE, some stamped with the inscription καρποφόρος 'fruit-bearer', a clear allusion to Demeter/Ceres.[21] Philip's coins leave no doubt as to his commitment to the Roman imperial

18. Ibid., 18.

19. Which may be presupposed in the eerie encounter with the demonized man who lived among tombs on the eastern side of the Sea of Galilee and called himself 'Legion; for we are many' (Mk 5.9). For archaeological evidence of the presence of Legio Fretensis X in Israel, see *CIIP* nos. 1235, 1353 and 1354.

20. Toni Fisher, 'Faunal Analysis: Zooarchaeology in Syro-Palestinian/Israeli Archaeology', in *Bethsaida in Archaeology, History and Ancient Culture: A Festschrift in Honour of John T. Greene*, ed. J. Harold Ellens (Newcastle upon Tyne: Cambridge Scholars Press, 2014), 84–121. The evidence of the faunal remains suggests that in the time of Philip the tetrarch the population of Bethsaida-Julias remained overwhelmingly Jewish. Nevertheless, the presence of pork bones and catfish bones – as much as 3% of the faunal remains – is clear indication that some of the inhabitants of Bethsaida were Gentiles.

21. Gertrude Grether, 'Livia and the Roman Imperial Cult', *AJP* 67 (1946): 222–52; Fred Strickert, 'The Coins of Philip', in Arav and Freund, eds, *Bethsaida*, 1:165–89 (171–3, 179–84); idem, 'The First Woman to be Portrayed on a Jewish Coin: Julia Sebaste', *JSJ* 33 (2002): 65–91; idem, 'The Dying Grain Which Bears Much Fruit: John 12:24, the Livia Cult, and Bethsaida', in Arav and Freund, eds, *Bethsaida*, 3:149–82 (here 155–70).

cult and his specific loyalty to Livia herself. The linkage between the honoring of Livia and the refounding of Bethsaida is seen in coins issued in 30 CE that read 'by Philip the tetrarch, founder' and 'Julia Sebaste'. 'Founder' (κτίστης) refers to the refounding of Bethsaida.[22]

The heights of Bethsaida rest on a rocky ridge of volcanic basalt. The earliest phase of the city reaches back to the Bronze Age. The site was chosen because it is the highest ground along the north shore of the Sea of Galilee, the ridge provides plenty of rock for building and defensive purposes, there is ready access to fresh water (such as the Jordan and Meshosim Rivers, as well as the Sea of Galilee) and there is also abundant arable land surrounding the ridge.[23] Indeed, the original name of Bethsaida may have been Zer ('rocks').[24] It was on this 'rock' that Philip the tetrarch refounded Bethsaida and began building the new city of Julias in honor of a Roman matriarch, now divinized in death (by order of the will of Augustus).

The renaming and refounding of Bethsaida required a temple dedicated to Livia, now Julia Augusta. The proper location of the temple would of course be on the city's acropolis, which at Bethsaida is a rocky rise made of volcanic basalt. A temple situated there would have a commanding view of the Sea of Galilee to the south. And, of course, those below the precipice and on the sea itself would see the impressive temple. But did Philip build a temple for Livia? Archaeological work thus far has not uncovered such a structure that can with confidence be dated to the late 20s or early 30s. The non-discovery of a temple dedicated to Livia may be due to the fact that Philip died in 34 and so may not have been able to fulfill his plans.[25]

22. Ya'acov Meshorer, *Ancient Jewish Coinage*. Vol. 2, *Herod the Great through Bar Cochba* (Dix Hills: Amphora Books, 1982), 148; Arie Kindler, 'The Coins of the Tetrarch Philip and Bethsaida', in Arav and Freund, eds, *Bethsaida*, 2:245–9.

23. J. F. Shroder Jr and M. Inbar, 'Geological and Geographic Background to the Bethsaida Excavations', in Arav and Freund, eds, *Bethsaida*, 1:65–98, esp. p. 76, in reference to the rocky ridge providing advantages of defence. See also ibid., figs. 3 and 4.

24. As seen in the old geographical list in Josh. 19.35, which lists 'the fortified cities…Ziddim, Zer [צֵר], Hammath, Rakkath, Kinneret', cities that encircle the Sea of Galilee.

25. Even so, it is likely that some new construction and enhancement took place in Bethsaida-Julias prior to Philip's death. Pliny the Elder (*c.* 23–79 CE) says the Sea of Galilee is 'skirted by the pleasant towns [*amoenis circumsaeptum oppidis*] of Bethsaida and Hippo on the east' (*Hist. Nat.* 5.15.71). It is improbable that the fishing village in which Simon and Andrew grew up would have warranted a description of this nature from a member of the Roman elite.

Rami Arav, who directs the excavation at Bethsaida, believes the temple has been found.[26] The foundation of a building has been uncovered in 'squares G–K 51–53 in Stratum 2'.[27] Not all agree.[28] The problem is that the foundation of this structure dates to an earlier period. The evidence suggests that the foundation of this structure dates to the Ptolemaic/Seleucid period and that the building was put to new uses in later periods. The discovery of an incense shovel and a figurine that bears a striking resemblance to Livia[29] leaves open the possibility that the building had been remodeled to serve as a temple in honor of Livia and that perhaps Philip had plans to build a new temple.

Whatever we may think of the temple, there is little doubt that Philip, almost certainly in the year 30, one year after the death of Livia, refounded Bethsaida, naming it Julias, and did so out of his loyalty to the Augustan family and as part of the movement to deify the late emperor's widow. There should also be little doubt that the renaming of this ancient Jewish village would have angered not only its Jewish inhabitants, but Jews throughout Gaulanitis and Galilee. That Bethsaida was to be renamed after Livia, whom Roman elites wished to deify – and eventually did so – would have been especially abhorrent to Torah-observant Jews. We should expect some reaction to this move on the part of the tetrarch. I think the words of Jesus to Peter were a reaction to it.

26. Rami Arav, 'Bethsaida Preliminary Report, 1994–1996', in Arav and Freund, eds, *Bethsaida*, 2:3–113, here 18–24; idem, 'Bethsaida', in *Jesus and Archaeology*, ed. James H. Charlesworth (Grand Rapids: Eerdmans, 2006), 145–66 (162–5 + fig. 39, which provides a depiction of the temple in honor of Livia).

27. Carl E. Savage, *Biblical Bethsaida: An Archaeological Study of the First Century* (Lanham: Lexington Books, 2011), 145–58, with quotation from 145. For a facsimile of the footprint of the temple, see 155. I thank Professors Arav and Savage for discussing the 'temple' with me on site and pointing out a number of features of interest.

28. The principal objections are that the temple-like structure that has been unearthed does not fit the pattern of Roman temples and that the structure may be too early. On the latter problem, see H.-W. Kuhn, 'Jesu Hinwendung zu den Heiden im Markusevangelium im Verhältnis zu Jesu historischen Wirken in Betsaida, mit einem Zwischenbericht zur Ausgrabung eines vermuteten heidnischen Tempels auf et-Tell (Betsaida)', in *Die Weite des Mysteriums: Christliche Identität im Dialog; für Horst Buerkle*, ed. K. Kraemer and A. Paus (Freiburg: Herder, 2000), 222–9. Mark Chancey finds the evidence thus far presented unconvincing: see M. A. Chancey, *The Myth of a Gentile Galilee*, SNTSMS 118 (Cambridge: CUP, 2002), 106–8; idem, *Greco-Roman Culture and the Galilee of Jesus*, SNTSMS 134 (Cambridge: CUP, 2005), 91–4.

29. Strickert, 'The Renaming of Bethsaida', 107–9 + figs. 2 and 3.

That Jesus and his following reacted to aspects of the Roman Empire should not occasion surprise, at least it should no longer. Detecting the presence of reaction against or engagement with Roman power and culture should no longer surprise us, especially in light of the ever-growing number of studies that clarify in what ways Roman power and culture impacted Israel and the emerging Christian church. Until recently, New Testament interpreters by and large have underestimated the extent of this influence.[30] Put bluntly, we should not think that Jesus and his disciples were unaware of or had no interest in the power and influence of Rome.[31] Philip the tetrarch's announcement that the hometown of Peter and other members of the inner circle was to be renamed and dedicated in honor of Livia, the recently deceased widow of the Roman emperor Augustus, worshipped as a god, would have been very offensive to Jewish sensitivities. Moreover, the clash with the very message of Jesus – namely, the kingdom of God has come and the kingdom of Satan is collapsing – would have almost certainly required a response. Philip may have gotten away with the refounding of Paneas as Caesarea Philippi, complete with its grand temple atop the ridge overlooking the natural springs below, but the refounding of Bethsaida, a mere stone's throw from Galilee, whose Jewish population was strongly dedicated to Israel's ancient faith, would have been inflammatory. We should expect a response. Jesus' promise to Peter in Mt. 16.17-19 may very well have been such a response.

The Refounding of Bethsaida and the Promise to Peter

One of the best-known scenes in the ministry of Jesus is the confession of Peter and the promise Peter receives from Jesus in return. Some commentators think that the longer, fuller version of the story in Matthew

30. See now the timely Adam Winn, ed., *An Introduction to Empire in the New Testament*, Resources for Biblical Study 84 (Atlanta: SBL, 2016). For an example of a detailed study that takes into account New Testament engagement with Roman power and society, see Gabriella Gelardini, *Christus Militans: Studien zur politisch-militärischen Semantik im Markusevangelium vor dem Hintergrund des ersten jüdisch-römischen Krieges*, NovTSup 165 (Leiden: Brill, 2016). Gelardini probes the political and military backdrop to a number of passages in Mark. As does Winn, in his essay that appears in the collection he edited, Gelardini focuses especially on the triumph of Vespasian, who had successfully prosecuted the war against the Jewish people.

31. Richard A. Horsley, 'Jesus-in-Movement and the Roman Imperial (Dis)order', in Winn, ed., *An Introduction to Empire in the New Testament*, 47–69. Horsley builds a strong case for seeing important aspects of Jesus' teaching and activities as responses to Roman imperialism.

(in contrast to the shorter version in Mark) is either more original or from an older, distinct form of tradition.[32] It is not my intention here to enter this debate, but I think if my proposal below is persuasive then the authenticity of the longer version receives additional support. Matthew's version reads:

> 13. Now when Jesus came into the district of Caesarea Philippi, he asked his disciples, 'Who do men say that the Son of man is?' 14. And they said, 'Some say John the Baptist, others say Elijah, and others Jeremiah or one of the prophets'. 15. He said to them, 'But who do you say that I am?' 16. Simon Peter replied, 'You are the Christ, the Son of the living God'. 17. And Jesus answered him, 'Blessed are you, Simon Bar-jona! For flesh and blood has not revealed this to you, but my Father who is in heaven. 18. And I tell you, you are Peter, and on this rock I will build my church, and the gates of Hades[33] shall not prevail against it. 19. I will give you the keys of the kingdom of heaven, and whatever you bind on earth shall be bound in heaven, and whatever you loose on earth shall be loosed in heaven' (Mt. 16.13-19, RSV).

This passage raises a number of questions. One of the most critical focuses on the name Peter, 'Rock' (Πέτρος), given to Simon, and on the promise that Jesus will build his church 'on this rock' (ἐπὶ ταύτῃ τῇ πέτρᾳ). In what sense is Simon *rock* and what does it mean to build the church on the (bed)rock?[34]

That Jesus gave Simon a new name is not remarkable. He gave some of his disciples nicknames. One thinks of the sons of Zebedee, called 'sons of Thunder' (Mk 3.17), or Simon called the 'zealot' (Lk. 6.15; Acts 1.13). Judging by Jewish literature, inscriptions and epitaphs the practice was not uncommon. Sometimes the epithets are not so much nicknames as

32. John Nolland, *The Gospel of Matthew*, NIGTC (Grand Rapids: Eerdmans; Bletchley: Paternoster Press, 2005), 658: 'None of the verses is likely to be simply Matthean redaction'. See further discussion in Ben F. Meyer, *The Aims of Jesus* (London: SCM Press, 1979), 185–97, 215–17, 302–5; R. T. France, *The Gospel of Matthew*, NICNT (Grand Rapids: Eerdmans, 2007), 613–14 and n. 9. For arguments that Matthew has conflated Mark's shorter account (in 8.27-29) with a longer independent account, see Dale C. Allison Jr and W. D. Davies, *A Critical and Exegetical Commentary on the Gospel according to Saint Matthew.* Vol. 2, *Commentary on Matthew VIII–XVIII*, ICC (Edinburgh: T. & T. Clark, 1991), 602–15.

33. The RSV translates 'powers of death'. That may be correct, but I think it is best to translate πύλαι ᾄδου literally, for these words may be better understood another way.

34. On the different nuances of πέτρος and πέτρα, see Nolland, *Matthew*, 669.

references to former occupations. We find the 'wool-dresser' (Masada no. 420), the 'baker' (Mas no. 429), the 'chief' (*m. Sheq.* 8.5), the 'messenger' (*CIJ* no. 1285), the 'butcher' (Mas no. 440; *m. Ket.* 2.9), the 'painter' (*CIJ* no. 1285), the 'hunter' (Mas no. 440), the 'captive physician' (*CJO* no. 80), 'Simo [*sic*] the builder' (Mas no. 561), 'Nehunia the trench digger' (*m. Sheq.* 5.1; *t. Sheq.* 2.14), one 'Jonathan called the digger' (1 Macc. 2.5), 'Yehudah the scribe' (*CIJ* no. 1308), 'Joseph, son of Hananya the scribe' (*CJO* no. 893), 'Eleazar son of the scribe' (Mas. no. 667), 'Judah, son of the druggist' (Mas. no. 471).[35] Most of these date to the pre-70 CE period.

Of great interest are two names and epithets found on ossuaries from the first half of the 1st century CE. The first reads 'Simon, builder of the Temple' (*CJO* no. 200) and the second 'Nicanor of Alexandria, who built the doors' (*CIJ* no. 1256).[36] The former contributed to the building of the temple (either literally, or perhaps financially). The latter was remembered for financing the construction of Nicanor Gate.

There is a striking point of comparison between Simon Peter and the individual mentioned in the ossuary that reads 'Simon, builder of the temple'. We immediately think of Mt. 16.18, where Jesus tells Simon, 'I will build my church'. I am not suggesting that either Jesus or the Matthaean evangelist alluded to the person mentioned on this ossuary. Rather, it may well be that the occupational description 'builder of the temple' was as much metaphorical as it was literal. This Simon and many others were builders of the temple of Jerusalem, a building project that commenced before Jesus was born and that finally concluded some thirty years after Jesus' death. Building the temple, therefore, was a constant throughout the lifetime of the Simon mentioned on the ossuary. While literally building the temple, this Simon was also building Israel's faith. Perhaps mimicking this way of speaking, as reflected in the Simon ossuary inscription, Jesus declares that his Simon Peter will become the builder of Jesus' church, something parallel to and perhaps over against the temple.

35. I review these and other nicknames in Craig A. Evans, *Jesus and the Ossuaries* (Waco: Baylor University Press, 2003), 56–7, 67–8. See also Rachel Hachlili, 'Hebrew Names, Personal Names, Family Names and Nicknames of Jews in the Second Temple Period', in *Families and Family Relations as Represented in Early Judaisms and Early Christianities: Texts and Fictions*, ed. Jan Willem van Henten and Athalya Brenner, Studies in Theology and Religion 2 (Leiden: Deo, 2000), 83–115.

36. For text, comments and bibliography, see Evans, *Jesus and the Ossuaries*, 91–4.

But I wonder if Philip's recent announcement to rename Simon's home town and to build a temple in honor of Livia atop its rocky precipice was the actual incident that prompted Jesus to call Simon *rock* and promise to build his church on solid bedrock? Philip the tetrarch, the faithless son of Herod the Great, has betrayed the God of Israel and his people by embracing and promoting the rank paganism of the Romans, who worship humans and regard them as gods (see, for example, the sentiment of Paul the former Pharisee in Rom. 1.22-23, 25). Philip has announced that he will rename Bethsaida, the home town of Peter and other disciples, to honor Livia, the widow of Augustus, whose divine name became Julia Augusta. In her honor and probably to support the cult of Livia and the drive to deify her Philip the tetrarch intends to build a temple on the rocky prominence of Bethsaida. In reaction to this plan Jesus promises to build his church, a community of confessing followers like Simon Peter, against which the very gates of Hades will not prevail. That is, the *political and demonical powers* (and not simply 'powers of death', as in the RSV's translation) that back Philip will not overcome the community that Jesus foresees growing up around the confession of Peter, namely, that Jesus is the Anointed One, the Son of God.

The announced refounding of Bethsaida flew in the face of the very essence of Jesus' proclamation that the rule of God had come and that the rule of Satan was coming to an end (Mk 1.15; 3.26-27; Lk. 11.20).[37] If the promise to Simon Peter is seen as a reaction to Philip's plans, then we should infer that the promised church stands over against the planned temple, and the Lord of the church stands over against the exalted priestess of the planned temple, which further suggests that Jesus, the true Son of God, stands over against the false diva Augusta, daughter of divus Augustus.

Whatever christological and ecclesiological implications may arise from Mt. 16.13-19 and whatever traditional elements may clarify them, we should ask if something provocative and local has occurred, perhaps reflective of the Roman world in which Jesus and his disciples lived, that may have occasioned Jesus' remarkable promise. Philip's announcement regarding Bethsaida deserves consideration.

37. There can be no détente between the kingdoms of God and of Satan. See Craig A. Evans, 'Inaugurating the Kingdom of God and Defeating the Kingdom of Satan', *BBR* 15 (2005): 49–75.

3

Biographies of Jesus in Old Testament and Rabbinic Style: The Genre of the New Testament Gospels

Armin D. Baum

Many studies have investigated the genre of the New Testament Gospels.[1] It is contested whether the Gospels should be classified as ancient *bioi* or biographies (I). It is also controversial whether they belong to cultivated Graeco-Roman literature (II), to popular Graeco-Roman literature (III), to Jewish literature in Old Testament style (IV) or to Jewish literature in rabbinic style (V).

I. *The Gospels as Texts* sui generis

In the middle of the 19th century David Friedrich Strauss began his second Jesus book with the thesis that it is impossible to write a biography of the Christ of faith. The doctrine of the church about his person (the incarnate Son of God) and about his life (particularly his death and resurrection for the redemption of mankind) cannot be the subject of a (historical) biography. The reason is, according to Strauss, that the Christ of faith stands above the laws of nature and, therefore, outside of historical reality: 'The Christ of the church is no subject for biographical narrative, and the idea of making it one is not only modern but self-contradictory'.[2] Strauss did not, however, apply these notions to the genre of the Gospels. He did not deal with the question as to whether the Gospels with their mix of historical and mythical content were ancient biographies.

1. An earlier, German version of my reflections on this topic was published in *Bib* 94 (2013): 534–64.

2. D. F. Strauss, *A New Life of Jesus* (London: Williams & Norgate, 1865), 1:3.

I.a. *The Gospels as Expanded Cult Legends*

This is the question which Rudolf Bultmann answered negatively in the first half of the 20th century. In the final chapter of his *History of the Synoptic Tradition* and in a related *RGG* article about the Gospels of the New Testament, Bultmann wrote: The Gospels 'should not be considered part of the genre of biography'.[3] Rather, they are 'an original Christian creation', a work *sui generis*.[4]

In support of his view Bultmann pointed out that in the Gospels, historical Jesus tradition merged with the myth of the incarnate Son of God. Therefore, the Gospels were out of touch with reality: 'There is no historical-biographical interest in the Gospels, and that is why they have nothing to say about Jesus' human personality, his appearance and character, his origin, education and development'. Rather, the Gospels were developed as a supplement to and as an illustration of the Christian kerygma (Rom. 1.3-4; 1 Cor. 15.3-7; Acts 10.37-38, etc.). The kerygmatic and mythical stories were not only read in the Christian cult but they emerged from it. Thus, the Gospels are not biographies but expanded 'cult legends' that focus entirely on the Christ of faith, the death and resurrection of the Son of God, not on the historical Jesus.[5]

Regarding the genre of the Gospels, Bultmann also drew on several formal features. He identified various analogies to smaller forms embedded in the Synoptic Gospels (logia, apophthegms, miracle stories, etc.) in extra-biblical literature. Because of their anonymity he associated the Gospels with popular rather than with cultivated ancient literature. He referred to a lack of more elaborate techniques of composition that were typical of cultivated literature. And he pointed out that the absence of chronological and topical cohesion and of psychological characterization and motivation in the Gospels was typical of popular literature.[6] But Bultmann did not regard ancient popular biographies as a real analogy because they did not presuppose a myth and a cult, while the Gospels had a mythical and a cultic origin. In Bultmann's assessment of the Gospels' genre, their mythical content was more important than their literary form.

The thesis that the Gospels are books *sui generis* has been widely accepted in New Testament scholarship. Werner Georg Kümmel adopted it in his *Introduction to the New Testament*: the Gospels are 'a new

3. R. Bultmann, 'Evangelien (gattungsgeschichtlich)', *RGG* 2 (2nd edn, 1928): 418–22 (418).

4. R. Bultmann, *The History of the Synoptic Tradition* (Oxford: Blackwell, 1968), 372.

5. Ibid., 371.

6. Bultmann, 'Evangelien', 418–20.

and distinctive literary genus'.[7] Philipp Vielhauer concluded that the Gospels are 'a unique literary phenomenon without precedent'.[8] Udo Schnelle concedes that the form of the Gospels is most similar to that of Hellenistic biography. Still, primarily because of its contents, 'the gospel is in fact *sui generis*, and cannot be incorporated as a subgenre into any higher category'.[9] These statements help to explain an observation which Albrecht Dihle made in 1983: 'every theological student is warned in his first semester against reading the four canonical Gospels as biographies of Jesus'.[10]

More recent studies on the Gospel genre question this consensus from different angles (see sections II-V below). And yet, some scholars continue to support the *sui generis* hypothesis. In her discussion with scholars such as Burridge and Dormeyer, Eve-Marie Becker emphasizes that the Gospel of Mark should not be classified as ancient biography:[11] while it displays 'biographical features',[12] Mark has 'no biographical interest per se'.[13] In particular, in contrast to ancient biography, Mark did not evaluate the character of his main protagonist.[14] For these reasons Becker regards the Gospel of Mark as a composition *sui generis*.

I.b. *The Biographical Character of the Gospels*

In this paper I do not want to address Bultmann's premise (which he shared with Strauss) that God only acts in line with the laws of nature. Rather, I would like to call into question both his understanding of the concept of reality in ancient biographies and the adequacy of the formal criteria which he and others employed.

Both of Bultmann's arguments regarding the New Testament Gospels' relation to reality have been called into question. A first objection has to do with the fact that other ancient biographies also contained myths (stories about gods) or mythical elements. Charles Talbert identified

7. W. G. Kümmel, *Introduction to the New Testament*, trans. H. C. Kee (London: SCM Press, 1975), 37.

8. Ph. Vielhauer, *Geschichte der urchristlichen Literatur* (Berlin: W. de Gruyter, 1975), 282.

9. U. Schnelle, *The History and Theology of the New Testament Writings*, trans. M. E. Boring (Minneapolis: Fortress Press, 1998), 161; cf. 155.

10. A. Dihle, 'The Gospels and Greek Biography', in *The Gospel and the Gospels*, ed. P. Stuhlmacher (Grand Rapids: Eerdmans, 1991), 361–86 (361).

11. E.-M. Becker, *Das Markus-Evangelium im Rahmen antiker Historiographie*, WUNT 194 (Tübingen: Mohr, 2006), 64–5.

12. Ibid., 52.

13. Ibid., 408.

14. Ibid., 65, 300, 411.

mythical elements in Pseudo-Callisthenes' biography of Alexander the Great. This biography tells of a miraculous prediction of Alexander's death[15] and of a kind of ascension of Alexander.[16] Similar mythological elements can be found, for instance, in Suetonius' *Life of Augustus*,[17] in Diogenes Laertius' biography of Empedocles[18] and in Philostratus' *Life of Apollonius of Tyana*.[19] In this regard, the Gospels are far from unique.[20]

Further, the (partially) mythical or unhistorical contents of a narrative text do not speak against its classification as a biography. In Literary Studies, not only the Gospels but also subsequent early Christian texts which described 'the life of saints and martyrs in their legendary form, uncritical and obsessed with miracles and more interested in the example of divine grace than in real life'[21] are regarded as biographies. Therefore, the question if the Gospels should be considered biographies cannot be answered on the basis of our convictions regarding the reality of their biographical contents.

The argument that the Gospels are unique and not biographies because they arose out of the early Christian cult has also been criticized as unconvincing. One objection is that some Graeco-Roman biographies were just as cult-related as the Gospels. Charles Talbert called the *Life of Alexander the Great* an enlarged form of a cult legend.[22] He also believed that biographies such as Philo's *Life of Moses* were developed and used by religious communities with the purpose of presenting their spiritual values.[23] It has to be admitted, however, that this last observation may not be entirely relevant to Bultmann's thesis that the Gospels emerged in the context of the Christian cult.

Further, Bultmann's thesis is also historically questionable.[24] It is certainly correct that not only the Gospels but also the oral Jesus tradition were cited in Christian worship services (Col. 3.16, etc.) and in

15. *Vita Alexandri Magni* 3.30.1-7.

16. *Vita Alexandri Magni* 3.33.5

17. Suetonius, *Aug*. 94.4.

18. Diogenes Laertius 8.68-70.

19. Philostratus, *Vit. Apoll.* 1.4; 8.30-31.

20. C. H. Talbert, *What Is a Gospel? The Genre of the Canonical Gospels* (Philadelphia: Fortress Press, 1977), 31–5.

21. G. von Wilpert, *Sachwörterbuch der Literatur*, 7th edn (Stuttgart: Kröner, 1989), 104–5.

22. Talbert, *Gospel*, 101–2.

23. Ibid., 104–5.

24. K. Berger, 'Hellenistische Gattungen im Neuen Testament', *ANRW* 2.25.2 (1984): 1031–432 (1243–44).

missionary sermons (Acts 2.22-24, etc.). According to Luke's prologue (Lk. 1.1-4) and the oldest early Christian witnesses,[25] however, the main source of the Gospels was not the early Christian worship service or cult but the traditions of Jesus' eyewitnesses.[26] There is no historical evidence which supports the thesis that the Christian cult was the source of the Gospels. The Gospel authors gathered the material for their Jesus books from oral and written eyewitness testimonies, just as other ancient biographers did.

A more general objection concerns the formal criteria which Bultmann and others have used to distinguish the Gospels from ancient biographies. Bultmann referred to the lack of information about Jesus' education, appearance, etc. Others have pointed to the structure of the Gospels (their vague chronology, etc.). But such arguments have no historical basis, neither in ancient literary theory nor in ancient biographical practice.

Ancient writers mentioned specific features of particular genres such as speeches, letters and other kinds of texts. But in antiquity there was 'no clear definition of biography. Literature that describes individual persons…was no particular genre with its own stylistic and methodological norms.'[27] There are no ancient statements which prescribed that a biography had to contain a certain degree of chronological precision or had to present its main character in a certain way or must not be mythical or cult-related.

Likewise, ancient biographical practice does not reveal that ancient biographers had to follow specific (unwritten) genre rules. According to the classicist Albrecht Dihle, 'the major proportion of extant Greek "lives" are marked by the absence of formal structure'. They consisted 'of the material the biographer communicates, without regard to any formal rules'.[28]

Accordingly, some biographies outside the New Testament, such as those by Plutarch, contain a minimum of chronological information.[29] It would, therefore, be mistaken to regard a detailed chronology as a necessary feature of ancient biographies.

25. Papias in Eusebius, *Hist. Eccl.* 3.39.15, etc.

26. R. Bauckham, *Jesus and the Eyewitnesses: The Gospels as Eyewitness Testimony* (Grand Rapids: Eerdmans, 2006), *passim*.

27. H. Sonnabend, *Geschichte der antiken Biographie: Von Isokrates bis zur Historia Augusta* (Darmstadt: Wissenschaftliche Buchgesellschaft, 2003), 222.

28. Dihle, 'Gospels', 374.

29. W. Steidle, *Sueton und die antike Biographie* (Munich: Beck, 1951), 10–11; D. Frickenschmidt, *Evangelium als Biographie: Die vier Evangelien im Rahmen antiker Erzählkunst* (Tübingen: Francke, 1997), 278–81.

Also the presentation of the development of Jesus' character, which some New Testament scholars miss in the Gospels, was no feature of ancient biographies. In his book about Joseph, Philo of Alexandria did not even think of describing the development of his hero. But that was not a deficiency because generally 'ancient biographers hardly gave this a moment's thought'.[30]

It is true that some ancient biographies share a number of features: a three-part structure, a genealogy of the main character, the presentation of his personality through the description of his deeds, the comparison with other people (*synkrisis*), the citation of final words, etc.[31] Still, these features were not consistently present and therefore cannot be regarded as genre criteria.

All modern efforts to define specific genre criteria of ancient biographies are confronted by this theoretical and practical plurality of ancient biography. The simple definition by the historian Arnaldo Momigliano makes the best sense of the ancient sources: 'An account of the life of a man from birth to death is what I call biography'. This definition 'has the advantage of excluding any discussion of how biography should be written. It is not for a historian of biography to decide what biography should be.'[32]

Only two of the four New Testament Gospels, that of Matthew and that of Luke, correspond exactly to the definition by Momigliano since they narrate the birth of Jesus, while those of Mark and of John begin only with Jesus' public ministry. In order to avoid an artificial distinction between biographical and non-biographical Gospels in the New Testament, a slightly adjusted definition is preferable: a biography is an account of the life of a person until his death. According to this definition, all four New Testament Gospels are ancient biographies.[33]

The next question has to be what kind of ancient biographies the New Testament Gospels resemble most closely or which type influenced them the most. There are four subgenres to be considered (see Figure 1): biographies of cultivated Graeco-Roman literature (II), biographies of popular Graeco-Roman literature (III), biographies in the style of Old Testament historiography (IV) and biographies in the style of rabbinic literature (V).

30. U. von Wilamowitz-Moellendorff, *Die griechische Literatur des Altertums*, 3rd edn (1912; repr. Stuttgart: Teubner, 1995), 182.

31. Frickenschmidt, *Evangelium*, 505–6.

32. A. Momigliano, *The Development of Greek Biography*, exp. edn (Cambridge, MA: Harvard University Press, 1993), 11.

33. D. E. Aune, *The New Testament and Its Literary Environment*, LEC (Philadelphia: Westminster Press, 1987), 17–76.

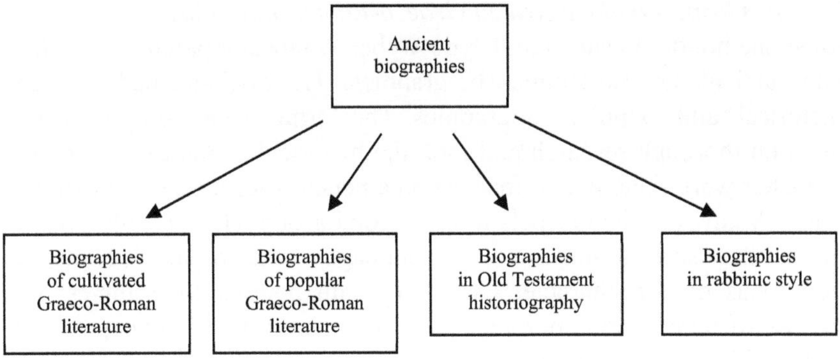

Figure 1

II. *The Gospels and the Biographies of Cultivated Graeco-Roman Literature*

Plutarch (*c*. 45–125 CE) and Suetonius (*c*. 70–125 CE) are among the best-known Greek and Roman biographers of the Hellenistic period and many of their biographies have survived. Klaus Berger has assembled a very useful 'Summary of Graeco-Roman biographical literature in chronological order' from the 5th century BCE to the 4th century CE.[34] Some of the more important biographies are:

Isocrates, *Evagoras* (4th cent. BCE)
Xenophon, *Agesilaus* (4th cent. BCE)
Xenophon, *Cyropaedia* (4th cent. BCE)
Xenophon, *Memorabilia* (4th cent. BCE)
Cornelius Nepos, *De Viris Illustribus* (1st cent. BCE)
Philo of Alexandria, *De Vita Mosis* (1st cent. CE)
Plutarch, *Vitae Parallelae* (1st–2nd cent. CE)
Tacitus, *Agricola* (1st–2nd cent. CE)
Suetonius, *De Vita Caesarum* (1st–2nd cent. CE)
Lucian, *Demonax* (2nd cent. CE)
Philostratus, *Vita Apollonii* (2nd cent. CE)
Diogenes Laertius, *Vitae Philosophorum* (3rd cent. CE)
Iamblichus, *Vita Pythagorae* (3rd–4th cent. CE)

34. Berger, 'Hellenistische Gattungen', 1232–6; Frickenschmidt, *Evangelium*, 79–80.

II.a. *The Gospels and Cultivated Graeco-Roman Literature*

Some one hundred years ago, Clyde Weber Votaw compared the Gospels with ancient Graeco-Roman biographies. He distinguished between 'historical' and 'popular' biographies. The former were comprehensive, relied on thorough research and took the historical context into account. The latter were sketchy and focused on a person's teachings and exhortations.[35] Votaw put the Gospels in the second group. He correctly pointed out that they shared their use of the language of the common people and their focus on the character's teaching with popular biographies. But because of their serious purpose Votaw compared the Gospels predominantly with cultivated works such as Plato's and Xenophon's biographies of Socrates and Philostratus's *Life of Apollonius*.[36]

More recently, Richard Burridge rejected Bultmann's assessment of the Gospels as works *sui generis* and, after a brief review of ancient Jewish literature, looked for analogies to the Gospel genre exclusively in Graeco-Roman literature. Burridge compared the Gospels with the biographies of Isocrates, Xenophon, Satyrus, Cornelius Nepos, Philo, Tacitus, Plutarch, Suetonius, Lucian and Philostratus, all of which belonged to cultivated Graeco-Roman literature.

Burridge enumerated nearly twenty generic features of Graeco-Roman biographies which he divided into four groups:[37]

> *1. Opening Features*:
> Title: often just the name of the subject, sometimes accompanied by the word *bios*
> Opening Formulae: often including the name of the subject, sometimes in a formal prologue
>
> *2. Subject*:
> Verb Subjects: the person described is the subject of most of the verbs
> Allocation of Space: not necessarily an even coverage of the subject's life
>
> *3. External Features*:
> Mode of Representation: prose narrative
> Size: medium length (between 3,000 and 82,000 words)
> Structure: chronological framework with room for topical material

35. C. W. Votaw, 'The Gospels and Contemporary Biographies', *AJT* 19 (1915): 45–73, 217–49 (49).

36. Ibid., 53–5.

37. R. A. Burridge, *What Are the Gospels? A Comparison with Graeco-Roman Biography*, 2nd edn (Grand Rapids: Eerdmans, 2004), 124–84.

Scale: limited to the subject's life
Literary Units: anecdotes, sayings, stories, discourses, speeches, etc.
Use of Sources: a wide range of oral and written sources
Methods of Characterization: indirectly through words and deeds

4. Internal Features:
Setting: all over the ancient world
Topics: ancestry, birth, boyhood, deeds, virtues, death, etc.
Style: often formal and highbrow and sometimes popular
Atmosphere: respectful and serious or popular and light-hearted
Quality of Characterization: stereotypic element
Social Setting and Occasion: within the educated and ruling class
Authorial Intention and Purpose: economastic, exemplary, informative, entertaining, etc.

On the basis of these criteria, Burridge described the canonical Gospels as Graeco-Roman biographies: they begin with a prologue or a sentence that mentions the name of the main character. Jesus is the subject of most verbs. The external and internal features also fit with those of the comparative material.[38] But Burridge highlighted one peculiarity: 'the style and social setting are probably further down the social scale than our *bioi*, but it is likely that other *bioi* were available at these levels which have not survived'.[39] Burridge did not, however, include popular biographies into his analysis.

Christopher Bryan mainly followed Burridge's methods and results.[40] He also noticed that the stylistic level of the Gospel of Mark is below that of biographies by authors such as Xenophon or Plutarch.[41]

According to Dirk Wördemann, the Gospels are not *bioi* in Plutarch's sense. They do not describe how a person develops a virtuous or heinous character. Nevertheless, Wördemann regarded Plutarch's biographies as 'the closest analogy to the genre of the Gospels'.[42]

38. Ibid., 185–232.

39. Ibid., 212.

40. Ch. Bryan, *A Preface to Mark: Notes on the Gospel in Its Literary and Cultural Setting* (Oxford: OUP, 1993), 9–64.

41. Ibid., 53–6.

42. D. Wördemann, *Der bios nach Plutarch und das Evangelium nach Markus: Eine Untersuchung zur literarischen Analogie des Charakterbildes des Helden und des Christusbildes im Evangelium Jesu Christi*, Studien zur Geschichte und Kultur des Altertums I/19 (Paderborn: Schöningh, 2002), 286–90.

II.b. *The Gospels' Resemblances to Cultivated Graeco-Roman Literature*

The criteria developed by Burridge are relatively unspecific: the fact that the main character is the subject of most verbs applies most probably not just to Graeco-Roman biographies but to all biographies from different time periods and cultures. And the characterization of a person by his or her deeds and words is also not limited to Hellenistic *bioi*. Therefore, Burridge's analysis supports the classification of the Gospels as biographies, but his observations (and similar ones by other scholars) cannot prove the Gospels' particular affinity to biographies of cultivated Graeco-Roman literature.

It is important to note (as Burridge and Bryan did) that the stylistic level of the Gospels is significantly below that of the biographies by Plutarch, Philo, Lucian and so on. In contrast to many Hellenistic biographers who wrote their texts in a literary Koine or even in the language of Atticism, the Gospel authors made use of a simple Hellenistic prose that resembled the contemporary spoken language.[43]

The fact that Graeco-Roman biographies as a rule mention the name of the main character in the title does not distinguish them from the Gospels. The first and the second Gospel open with sentences that mention the name of the main character: 'Book of the history of Jesus Christ, the son of David, the son of Abraham' (Mt. 1.1).[44] And: 'The beginning of the good news about Jesus Christ (happened) as is written in the prophet Isaiah…' (Mk 1.1).[45] The fourth Gospel mentions the main character's name in the original epilogue (Jn 20.30) as well as in the secondary epilogue (Jn 21.25). And the prologue of the book of Acts says retrospectively with regard to Luke's Gospel that this first volume presented the words and deeds of Jesus (Acts 1.1).

There are, however, some obvious differences between the Gospels and cultivated Graeco-Roman biographies: In contrast to Graeco-Roman biographies the Gospel authors wrote their books anonymously.[46] Further,

43. M. Reiser, *Sprache und literarische Formen des Neuen Testaments. Eine Einführung*, UTB 2197 (Paderborn: Schöningh, 2001), 29–33.

44. Cf. W. D. Davies and D. C. Allison, *The Gospel according to Matthew*, ICC (Edinburgh: T. & T. Clark, 1988), 1:151–2.

45. Cf. R. Pesch, *Das Markusevangelium*, HTKNT 2/1 (Freiburg: Herder, 1976), 1:74–7.

46. M. Wolter, 'Die anonymen Schriften des Neuen Testaments. Annäherungsversuch an ein literarisches Phänomen', *ZNW* 79 (1988): 1–16; A. D. Baum, 'The Anonymity of the New Testament History Books: A Stylistic Device in the Context of Graeco-Roman and Ancient Near Eastern Literature', *NovT* 50 (2008): 120–42.

in contrast to Plutarch,[47] the Gospels speak neither about their sources nor about alternative reports in their source texts. Moreover, about half of the Gospels' content consists of speech material, in contrast to Graeco-Roman biographies. And the Gospel authors presented their speech material nearly exclusively in *oratio recta*,[48] and they loved dialogue.[49] These are differences to Plutarch's and other cultivated Greek biographies.

The studies by Burridge and others confirm that we should not hesitate to consider the Gospels as biographies. But a more detailed comparison calls into question the view that the New Testament Gospels have their closest analogy in cultivated Graeco-Roman literature. Rather it confirms Dihle's judgement that 'specific similarities between Greek biography and the canonical as well as the extracanonical gospels...definitely seem to be absent'.[50] That explains why the Gospels have also been compared to popular biographies of Graeco-Roman literature.

III. *The Gospels and the Biographies of Graeco-Roman Popular Literature*

Besides the ancient biographies that belong to cultivated Greek literature there were also those which classicists count among popular literature. The main difference is 'the primacy of content over form' in popular literature and 'the primacy of form over content' in cultivated literature. Accordingly, cultivated literature is intellectually demanding and inviting to ponder while popular literature is easy to read and quickly engaging.[51]

Common features of popular literature are a low stylistic level, anonymity and an episodic style.[52] Furthermore, popular biographies differ from cultivated biographies by their preference for direct speech and especially dialogue. Moreover, many popular stories exclusively served the purpose of entertainment.[53]

47. Plutarch, *Alex.* 15.1-2.

48. R. I. Pervo, 'Direct Speech in Acts and the Question of Genre', *JSNT* 28 (2006): 285–307; A. D. Baum, 'Paulinismen in den Missionsreden des lukanischen Paulus: Zur inhaltlichen Authentizität der *oratio recta* in der Apostelgeschichte', *ETL* 82 (2006): 405–36.

49. M. Reiser, 'Die Stellung der Evangelien in der antiken Literaturgeschichte', *ZNW* 90 (1999): 1–27 (12–15); idem, *Sprache*, 98–105.

50. Dihle, 'Gospels', 379.

51. W. Hansen, *Anthology of Ancient Greek Popular Literature* (Bloomington: Indiana University Press, 1998), xi–xvii.

52. Ibid., xx–xxi.

53. Ibid., xiv–xv, 3, 77.

The most important biographies of ancient popular literature from the 1st to the 4th century CE that have survived are:[54]

Vita Aesopi (*c*. 2nd cent. CE)
Vita Homeri (*c*. 2nd cent. CE)
Vita Alexandri Magni (*c*. 3rd cent. CE)
Vita Secundi Philosophus (2nd–3rd cent. CE)

III.a. *The Gospels as Popular Graeco-Roman Literature*

Karl Ludwig Schmidt refused to label the Gospels as (fully developed) biographies, even though he admitted that this is a quarrel about words. According to Schmidt, everyone who wants to designate the Gospels as biographies may use the term 'folk biography, that is, popular biography'[55] because 'a Gospel is by nature not high literature, but low literature'.[56] Schmidt not only counted ancient writings such as the *Life of Homer* among popular literature but also German texts such as *Till Eulenspiegel* and *Doctor Faustus* as well as (with H. Gunkel) the biblical book of Genesis. According to Schmidt, the Gospels are at most popular biographies that correspond to the preliminary stages of fully developed biographies.[57] Schmidt listed some features of popular literature: It is anonymous and uses an episodic style without a tight connection between the single episodes. Its material is largely timeless and not connected to specific locations. It lacks a description of 'the life of a person, including both inward and outward development'.[58] But rather than settling for a definition of popular biography as 'easy to understand', or 'simple', Schmidt called it 'aboriginal' or 'native' (like a folk song).[59] With these labels he probably meant to say that this literature is not produced and transmitted by individuals, but that 'it was the people who originally created and bore along the tradition'.[60]

According to Klaus Berger, the Gospels show a special resemblance to ancient biographies of philosophers. 'More specifically the Gospels demonstrate a particularly close affinity to those lives of philosophers

54. Compare with H.-G. Beck, *Geschichte der Byzantinischen Volksliteratur*, Byzantinisches Handbuch 2/3 (Munich: Beck, 1971), 28–35.

55. K. L. Schmidt, *The Place of the Gospels in the General History of Literature*, trans. B. R. McCain (Columbia: University of South Carolina Press, 2002), 33.

56. Ibid., 27.

57. Ibid., 36.

58. Ibid., 32 and *passim*.

59. Ibid., 80.

60. Ibid., 52; cf. 76.

which incorporate a great diversity of material related to individual scenes, words and deeds'.[61] According to Berger, not only the biographies of Pythagoras but also the *Life of Aesop* is very similar to the Gospels. The popular *Life of Aesop* tells the story of a clever Phrygian slave and his coarse jests and is comparable to the stories about Till Eulenspiegel. The original version of the biography of Aesop was composed sometime between 30 BCE and 100 CE in Egypt.[62] The author and the redactors wrote anonymously. The language of the *Vita Aesopi* is very simple. The book largely consists of a collection of single episodes which probably existed originally as independent stories. Recent studies have shown, however, that these episodes are not stitched together carelessly but were carefully assembled into a biography with five parts.[63] The *Life of Aesop* is fond of direct speech and natural dialogues. The most thorough comparison between the Gospels and the *Life of Aesop* has been undertaken by Lawrence Wills.[64]

Marius Reiser compared the Gospels with the *Life of Alexander the Great*. Its Greek version was probably composed in the 3rd century CE, six centuries after Alexander. It drew from two main sources, a novel about Alexander and a number of pseudo-historical letters. That material was supplemented with imaginary additions.[65] Originally the novel about Alexander was probably composed anonymously. (Only later was it ascribed to Callisthenes, Alexander's court historian.) The full narrative consists of many individual episodes. Instead of long speeches that were so typical of classical ancient historiography, the Alexander novel made use of natural dialogues which were absent from the works of Thucydides or Polybius. The style level corresponds to that of the New Testament. In contrast to Josephus, Pseudo-Callisthenes did not try to follow the stylistic rules of Atticism. He did not desire to satisfy expectations of the educated elite but sought to address a broad audience which wanted to be entertained. According to Reiser, in terms of 'compositional and narrative

61. Berger, 'Hellenistische Gattungen', 1245.

62. B. E. Perry, *Aesopica*. Vol. 1, *Greek and Latin Texts* (Urbana: University of Illinois Press, 1952), 22.

63. N. Holzberg, 'Der Äsop-Roman', in *Der Äsop-Roman: Motivgeschichte und Erzählstruktur*, ed. N. Holzberg, Classica Monacensia 6 (Tübingen: Narr, 1992), 31–75.

64. L. M. Wills, *The Quest of the Historical Gospel: Mark, John, and the Origin of the Gospel Genre* (London: Routledge, 1997), 23–50.

65. R. Merkelbach, *Die Quellen des griechischen Alexander-Romans*, 2nd edn (Munich: Beck, 1977), 20–92.

technique, language, and style' the Alexander Romance offers 'perhaps the closest analogy to the Gospels'.[66]

III.b. *The Gospels' Resemblances to Popular Graeco-Roman Literature*

The New Testament Gospels shared their anonymity with Graeco-Roman popular literature. However, the reason the Gospels were published anonymously was not to present them as the composition of a large group of nameless Christians. Schmidt's thesis that popular texts are created collectively by the poetic spirit of the folk has been rejected in more recent research. 'The people as a collective entity have never...demonstrated its creativity, the masses have never been able to compose a verse, to develop a concept, or to envision or create a particular work of art. Every piece of literature, from the most insignificant to the most important, is the work of one author'. Even if this author

> had no concept of his own individuality and did not demand recognition of himself as an individual, preferring to disappear behind the folkloric contents of his work...he was still always present as its personal creator. The part played by the folk – a plurality of individuals – in the creation of folklore is therefore restricted merely to its oral transmission.[67]

The striking fact that the New Testament Gospels do not mention their authors' names has its literary counterpart in the anonymity of the Old Testament history books and has to be explained against this background (see below, section IV.b).

Further, popular Graeco-Roman biographies display various formal similarities to the Gospels: simple language, episodes that are loosely connected and their preference for direct speech, in particular the (natural) dialogue. At the same time, the New Testament Gospels distinguish themselves from Graeco-Roman biographies by their use of the *parallelismus membrorum*, both on sentence level and on pericope level, their use of chiasms and concentric structures,[68] the style of their parables which

66. M. Reiser, 'Der Alexanderroman und das Markusevangelium', in *Markus-Philologie: Historische, literargeschichtliche und stilistische Untersuchungen zum zweiten Evangelium*, ed. H. Cancik, WUNT 33 (Tübingen: Mohr, 1984), 131–63 (131).

67. Von Wilpert, *Sachwörterbuch Literatur*, 1010–11.

68. E. Norden, *Agnostos Theos*, 5th edn (Stuttgart: Teubner, 1971), 360–4; F. Rehkopf, 'Der "Parallelismus" im NT. Versuch einer Sprachregelung', *ZNW* 71 (1980): 46–57; J. W. Welch, ed., *Chiasmus in Antiquity: Structures, Analyses, Exegesis* (Hildesheim: Gerstenberg, 1981); A. Berlin, *The Dynamics of Biblical Parallelism* (Bloomington: Indiana University Press, 1985).

make up about a third of their speech material,[69] as well as the many lexical and syntactical Semitisms[70] which permeate their prose.

Moreover, popular Graeco-Roman biographies wanted to entertain their readers, which was not the purpose of the New Testament Gospels. The popular biographies did not have a serious didactic purpose. In this regard the Gospels resemble more the biographies of the cultivated Graeco-Roman literature, which aimed primarily at teaching the audience.

The suggestion that the Gospels derive from popular Graeco-Roman literature is also confronted with a chronological problem. All the above-mentioned biographies of Aesop, of Alexander, of Homer and of Secundus are younger than the New Testament Gospels.[71]

To conclude: The Gospels bear more similarities to the popular Graeco-Roman biographies than to the cultivated Graeco-Roman biographies. And yet, they also differ in several respects from popular literature and can for chronological reasons not be derived from this group of ancient texts.

IV. *The Gospels and Old Testament Biographies*

The Old Testament contains biographical narratives about the patriarchs and their sons, Moses and his successors, the judges and the kings of Israel and the prophets. These biographies are, however, not independent texts but form part of larger history books:[72]

Abraham (Gen. 12–25)	call to death
Isaac (Gen. 17–35)	birth to death
Jacob (Gen. 25–50)	birth to death
Joseph (Gen. 37–50)	youth to death
Moses (Exod. 2–Deut. 34)	birth to death
Samuel (1 Sam. 1–25)	birth to death

69. A. D. Baum, 'Bildhaftigkeit als Gedächtnishilfe in der synoptischen Tradition', *TBei* 35 (2004): 4–16 (10–13).

70. K. Beyer, *Semitische Syntax im Neuen Testamen*. Vol. 1, *Satzlehre*, part 1, 2nd edn (Göttingen: Vandenhoeck & Ruprecht, 1968); E. C. Maloney, *Semitic Interference in Marcan Syntax*, SBL Dissertation Series 51 (Chico: Scholars Press, 1981); H. P. Rüger, 'Die lexikalischen Aramaismen im Markusevangelium', in Cancik, ed., *Markus-Philologie*, 73–84; R. A. Martin, *Syntax Criticism of the Synoptic Gospels*, Studies in Bible and Early Christianity 10 (Lewiston: Edwin Mellen Press, 1987); A. D. Baum, 'Mark's Paratactic *kai* as a Secondary Syntactic Semitism', *NovT* 58 (2016): 1–26.

71. Reiser, 'Stellung', 5.

72. See also K. Baltzer, *Die Biographie der Propheten* (Neukirchen-Vluyn: Neukirchener Verlag, 1975), 22–3.

Saul (1 Sam. 9–31)	youth to death
David (1 Sam. 16–1 Kgs 2)	call to death
Solomon (1 Kgs 1–11)	public ministry to death
Rehoboam (1 Kgs 12–14)	public ministry to death
Elijah (1 Kgs 17–2 Kgs 2)	public ministry to ascension
Elisha (1 Kgs 19–2 Kgs 13)	call to death

Some Old Testament books focused on the life of one individual, but only rarely did they narrate a life until death. With the exception of the book of Tobit, the following independent narratives do not fit the definition of a biography offered above:

Ruth (book of Ruth)	marriage to birth of a son
Esther (book of Esther)	election as queen to Purim
Jonah (book of Jonah)	commission to correction
Tobit (book of Tobit)	youth to death

IV.a. *The Gospels as Biographies in Old Testament Style*

According to Johann Gottfried Herder, the Gospels bear the most similarity to Hebrew historiography: 'Are their Gospels history and biography according to the norms of the Greeks and the Romans? No... Every historian belongs to his nation, time, and language... Working to identify Attic or Roman historians behind the Gospels is futile labour...because of their conceptual and compositional genius.'[73] The genealogies, parables and miracle stories which are presented in the 'style of most simply told stories' belong to the 'historical prose of the Hebrews'.[74]

More than a century ago, Theodor Zahn also ascribed the Gospels not to Graeco-Roman but to Old Testament and Jewish literature: 'The author of our first Gospel was clearly not familiar with the art and technique of Greek historiography. It reads like an Old Testament history book.'[75]

Martin Hengel rendered a similar judgement: 'The model for the collection and the literary presentation of the "biographical" Jesus tradition is... to be sought...in the accounts of history to be found in the Old Testament and Judaism, which to a large degree are composed of "biographical" sections'.[76]

73. J. G. Herder, *Vom Erlöser der Menschen: Nach unsern drei ersten Evangelien*, Sämtliche Werke 19 (Hildesheim: Olms, 1967), 135–252 (194–5).

74. Ibid., 195–6, 216–24.

75. Th. Zahn, 'Der Geschichtschreiber und sein Stoff im Neuen Testament', *ZKWL* 9 (1888), 581–96 (588).

76. M. Hengel, *Acts and the History of Earliest Christianity* (Eugene: Wipf & Stock, 2003), 30–1.

More recently, Marius Reiser emphasized that the narrative style of the Gospels is more like that of Jewish rather than Graeco-Roman literature. Old Testament narratives were the Gospel authors' model for their simple language, the episodic style, the avoidance of the first person singular of the author and the preference for direct speech and the dialogue: Regarding the 'style of the language as well as in formal respects', the Gospels show 'the most similarities with the biographical narratives of the Old Testament and the Septuagint'. According to Reiser, the biographical stories of Jeremiah (Jer. 36–46 = LXX 43–51) show the closest parallels.[77]

IV.b. *The Gospels' Resemblances to Old Testament Historiography*

The literary proximity of the New Testament Gospels to the Old Testament and to the biographical narratives of the Septuagint can be summarized as follows:

1. The four New Testament Gospels were composed anonymously, just as the historical books of the Old Testament.[78] The authorial intent of the Gospels' anonymity can be deduced from its Old Testament background. Unlike the Greek or Roman historians who, among other things, wanted to earn praise and glory for their literary achievements from both their contemporaries and posterity, the Gospel authors sought to disappear as much as possible behind the material they presented and to become its invisible mouthpieces. By means of the anonymity of their books they implied that their subject matter deserved the full attention of the readers.[79]
2. In addition, the narrators of both the New Testament and the Old Testament commented only rarely on the origins or qualities of their books.
3. The technical prologue so typical of Graeco-Roman literature is absent from three of the four Gospels just as from all historical books of the Old Testament. At the same time, the opening sentences of the Gospels are very similar to those of Old Testament books:

77. Reiser, 'Stellung', 20–4.

78. J. Weinberg, 'Authorship and Author in the Ancient Near East and the Hebrew Bible', *HS* 44 (2003): 157–69; A. Millard, 'Authors, Books and Readers in the Ancient World', in *The Oxford Handbook of Biblical Studies*, ed J. W. Rogerson and J. M. Lieu (Oxford: OUP, 2006), 544–64.

79. Baum, 'The Anonymity of the New Testament History Books'.

'The book of the history of Jesu Christ, the son of David, the son of Abraham…' (Mt. 1.1).	'The book of the acts of Tobit (the son) of Tobiel, (son of) Ananiel…' (Tob. 1.1 LXX)
'The beginning of the good news of Jesus Christ, the Son of God…' (Mk 1.1).	'The beginning of the word of the Lord to Hosea…' (Hos. 1.2).
'There was in the days of Herod, the king of Judea, a certain priest…' (Lk. 1.5).	'And it came to pass in the days of Jehoiakim, son of Josias king of Juda…' (Jer. 1.3).
'In the beginning was the Word, and the Word was with God…' (Jn 1.1).	'In the beginning God created the heavens and the earth…' (Gen. 1.1).

4. The episodic style that is so common in many sections of the Gospels is also prevalent in the historical books of the Old Testament.[80] We not only encounter it in the synoptic presentation of Jesus' Galilean ministry (Mt. 4–18; Mk 10; Lk. 4–9) and of his last journey to Jerusalem (Mt. 19–20; Mk 10; Lk. 9–19). It is also used in the narratives of Elijah and Elisha. The single events follow a loose chronological or geographical order or are linked paratactically (2 Kgs 2.9–8.15).
5. The speech material in the Gospels (*c.* 40–65%) resembles that of the Old Testament history books in scope as well as with regard to the preference for direct speech and dialogue.[81]
6. The level of style in the Gospels corresponds to that of Hellenistic prose in the Septuagint.[82]
7. With regard to smaller forms contained in the Gospels, they closely resemble the Old Testament miracle stories and call narratives. In the Elijah- and Elisha-cycle of the Old Testament there are a number of episodes that are similar to certain Gospel pericopes. Among these is the narrative of Elisha's call through Elijah in 1 Kgs 19.19-21. The parallel episodes in Lk. 9.59-60 and 9.61-62 mention similar

80. Reiser, *Sprache*, 98–105.

81. Ibid.; S. Bar-Efrat, *Narrative Art in the Bible*, JSOTSup 70, Bible and Literature Series 17 (Sheffield: Almond Press, 1989), 147, and A. D. Baum, 'Zu Funktion und Authentizität der *oratio recta*: Hebräische und griechische Geschichtsschreibung im Vergleich', *ZAW* 115 (2003): 586–607.

82. L. Rydbeck, *Fachprosa, vermeintliche Volkssprache und Neues Testament: Zur Beurteilung der sprachlichen Niveauunterschiede im nachklassischen Griechisch*, Acta Universitatis Upsaliensis: Studia Graeca Upsaliensis 5 (Uppsala: Almqvist & Wiksell, 1967); Reiser, *Sprache*, 29–33.

requirements for potential disciples. The narrative about the multiplication of oil by Elisha in 2 Kgs 4.1-7 also has synoptic parallels in the pericopes about the multiplication of bread, particularly in the story about the feeding of the 4,000 (Mt. 15.32-38).

In two respects, however, the New Testament biographies differ from those found in the Old Testament:

1. The historical books of the Old Testament contain no parallels to the paratexts of the Gospels, namely Luke's technical prologue (Lk. 1.1-4) and John's technical epilogues (Jn 20.30-31; 21.24-25). Luke's prologues were derived from Graeco-Roman historiography.[83]
2. In contrast to the New Testament, the Old Testament contains, no independent biographical narratives that do not form part of larger historical books (with the exception of the rather late book of Tobit).

Finally, the Gospels display features that have analogies in later ancient Jewish literature.

V. *The Gospels and the Biographical Narratives of the Rabbis*

There are no full biographies of Jewish scribes in rabbinic literature. All we have are collections of individual statements made by various rabbis. Tractate *Avot of Rabbi Natan* contains many episodes with words and deeds of different rabbis. But it does not offer a full biography of one rabbi.[84]

Although there was sufficient biographical material available for rabbis such as Rabbi Eliezer ben Hyrcanus, on the beginning of his Torah studies, on his words and deeds and on his death, no one ever compiled them into one biographical account. That only happened in modern Judaic Studies. The *Encyclopedia Judaica* (1971), for example, contains biographical articles on many Tannaim and Amoraim which draw from the biographical material of ancient rabbinic tradition. 'The reason Tannaitic and Amoraic authors did not compose biographies is simply

83. D. Earl, 'Prologue-form in Ancient Historiography', *ANRW* 1.2 (1972): 842–56; A. D. Baum, 'Lk 1,1-4 zwischen antiker Historiografie und Fachprosa: Zum literaturgeschichtlichen Kontext des lukanischen Prologs', *ZNW* 101 (2010): 33–54.

84. J. Neusner, *Why No Gospels in Talmudic Judaism?*, BJS 135 (Atlanta: Scholars Press, 1988), 49–72.

that they didn't consider the individual Rabbi so outstanding that they regarded it as indispensable to write his biography'.[85]

V.a. *The Gospels as Biographies in Rabbinic Style*

Nevertheless, some scholars have suggested classifying the Gospels as rabbinic biographies or biographies in rabbinic style. Many formal features of Old Testament and early Jewish literature are also prevalent in rabbinic literature.

This was already emphasized by Adolf Schlatter. He identified early rabbinic culture as the closest background of the Gospels, particularly the biographical parts of rabbinic literature. In his study about the Jewish scribe Yohanan ben Zakkai (1st century CE), Schlatter wrote that to the New Testament Gospels there are 'stylistically no closer parallels than the reminiscences of the words and deeds of the teachers of the 1st century, which are found in the casuistic literature'.[86]

Philip Alexander thinks that an early Jewish life of Eliezer 'could have looked something like Lucian's *Life of Demonax* or the Gospel of Mark'. There is, according to Alexander, one main reason why such biographies of the rabbis were never written: 'The centre of Rabbinic Judaism was Torah; the centre of Christianity was the person of Jesus'.[87] In rabbinic Judaism, biographical stories about the rabbis served merely as illustrations for the interpretation of Torah. In early Christianity, the biographical stories about Jesus were used as the building blocks for a complete biography of Jesus.

V.b. *The Gospels' Resemblances to Rabbinic Traditional Literature*

A number of stylistic features are shared by biographical episodes in the rabbinic traditions and in the Gospels of the New Testament:

1. Rabbinic literature was anonymous,[88] just as the New Testament Gospels were.
2. Rabbinic narrative technique was highly episodic. Most of the episodes were self-contained units and probably existed separately

85. P. Fiebig, *Der Erzählungsstil der Evangelien im Lichte des rabbinischen Erzählungsstils untersucht* (Leipzig: Hinrichs, 1925), 88.

86. A. Schlatter, *Jochanan Ben Zakkai, der Zeitgenosse der Apostel* (Gütersloh: Bertelsmann, 1899), 8.

87. P. S. Alexander, 'Rabbinic Biography and the Biography of Jesus: A Survey of the Evidence', in *Synoptic Studies*, ed. C.M. Tuckett (Sheffield: JSOT Press, 1984), 19–50 (40–1).

88. Neusner, *Why No Gospels*, 70–2.

before they were integrated into rabbinic literature.[89] The same is true of many of the synoptic episodes.

3. Many of the biographical episodes in rabbinic literature were comprised of speech material which appeared nearly exclusively in *oratio recta*. 'In contrast to Latin and Greek…in Hebrew/Aramaic there is hardly any indirect speech'.[90] This was also true for the speech material in the Gospels.
4. The biographical anecdotes in rabbinic literature contained a high percentage of dialogues,[91] just like many pericopes in the Gospels.
5. Many statements of the rabbis followed the rules of the Semitic *parallelismus membrorum*.[92] This is also true of the words of Jesus in the Synoptic Gospels. The following example can serve as an illustration:

Mt. 5.23-24	*m. Pes.* 3.7
'So when you are offering your gift at the altar, if you remember that your brother or sister has something against you, leave your gift there before the altar and go; first be reconciled to your brother or sister, and then come and offer your gift'.	'If a man was on the way to slaughter his Passover-offering… and he remembered that he had left *hametz* in his house… let him go back and remove it…'.

Further, the biographical material in rabbinic literature also offers many parallels to the smaller forms in the Gospels. Over a hundred years ago Paul Fiebig already demonstrated that the Tannaitic literature contained many examples of proverbs, parables, prayers and events that closely resemble those in the Gospels.

The rabbinic parables show more similarities to the synoptic parables regarding structure, use of images, and contents than any other ancient texts.[93] A parable ascribed to Johanan ben Zakkai (*c.* 90 CE) tells of a king who only permits guests to a feast that are properly dressed whereas improperly dressed guests are sent away. Jesus told a very similar parable:

89. Fiebig, *Erzählungsstil*, 108–9.

90. Ibid., 72–3.

91. Ibid., 73, 89, 91, etc.; Alexander, 'Rabbinic Biography', 34–7.

92. Fiebig, *Erzählungsstil*, 31, 89.

93. P. Fiebig, *Die Gleichnisreden Jesu im Lichte der rabbinischen Gleichnisse des neutestamentlichen Zeitalters* (Tübingen: Mohr, 1912); R. M. Johnston and H. K. McArthur, *They Also Taught in Parables: Rabbinic Parables from the First Centuries of the Christian Era* (Grand Rapids: Academic Books, 1990).

Mt. 22.1-14	*b. Shab.* 153a
'Once more Jesus spoke to them in parables, saying:	'R. Jochanan b. Zakkai said:
The kingdom of heaven may be compared to a king who gave a wedding banquet for his son …	This may be compared to a king who summoned his servants to a banquet without appointing a time…
But when the king came in to see the guests, he noticed a man there who was not wearing a wedding robe,	Suddenly the king desired (the presence of) his servants: the wise entered adorned, while the fools entered soiled.
and he said to him, "Friend, how did you get in here without a wedding robe?" And he was speechless. Then the king said to the attendants, "Bind him hand and foot, and throw him into the outer darkness, where there will be weeping and gnashing of teeth". For many are called, but few are chosen.'	The king rejoiced at the wise but was angry with the fools. "Those who adorned themselves for the banquet", ordered he, "let them sit, eat and drink. But those who did not adorn themselves for the banquet, let them stand and watch."'

In addition, the separation between wise and foolish servants and virgins in *b. Shab.* 153a has a close parallel in Jesus' parable of the ten virgins (Mt. 25.1-13).

At least some of the rabbinic miracle stories about Honi the Circle Maker (died 65 BCE) and Hanina ben Dosa (1st century CE) are very similar to those of the Synoptic Gospels.[94] A rabbinic miracle story about Hanina ben Dosa, for instance, shows close parallels to the story about the healing of the official's son in Jn 4.46-53:

Jn 4.46-53	*b. Ber.* 34b
'Now there was a royal official whose son lay ill in Capernaum.	'Once the son of R. Gamaliel fell ill.
When he heard that Jesus had come from Judea to Galilee, he went and begged him to come down and heal his son, for he was at the point of death…	He sent two scholars to R. Hanina b. Dosa to ask him to pray for him…
Jesus said to him, "Go; your son will live"…	When he came down he said to them: "Go, the fever has left him…"

94. Vgl. P. Fiebig, *Jüdische Wundergeschichten des neutestamentlichen Zeitalters unter besonderer Berücksichtigung ihres Verhältnisses zum Neuen Testament bearbeitet* (Tübingen: Mohr, 1911); M. Becker, *Wunder und Wundertäter im frührabbinischen Judentum*, WUNT 2/144 (Tübingen: Mohr, 2002), 291–378.

So he asked them the hour when he began to recover, and they said to him, "Yesterday at one in the afternoon the fever left him". The father realized that this was the hour when Jesus had said to him, "Your son will live". So he himself believed, along with his whole household.'	They sat down and made a note of the exact moment. When they came to R. Gamaliel, he said to them: "By the temple service! You have not been a moment too soon or too late, but so it happened: at that very moment the fever left him and he asked for water to drink."'

With regard to their form and content, these rabbinic parallels to individual episodes of the Synoptic Gospels are sometimes even closer than those between the Gospels and Old Testament and certainly closer than those with Graeco-Roman literature.[95] While early rabbinic tradition could not serve the Gospels as a model for a full biography of Jesus, it provides the closest analogies to many Gospel pericopes.

VI. *The Place of the Gospels in the Ancient History of Literature*

Strict generic rules for biographical writings were unknown in antiquity. Authors of ancient biographies were free to follow personal preferences and to combine elements from both cultivated and popular literature as well as from Jewish and Graeco-Roman literary style. It is, therefore, quite legitimate to categorize the Gospels as mixed biographical forms (or biographical hybrids). Klaus Berger, for example, identified an affinity of the Gospels with both the cultivated biographies of Plutarch and the popular *Life of Aesop* and with Old Testament texts.[96] Hubert Cancik also interpreted the Gospels as texts 'between two worlds…as the sequel to the Old Testament, but with a stronger awareness that their audiences were Hellenists'. According to Cancik, ancient pagan readers of Mark 'would have read his Gospel as a biography of Jesus, though a rather exotic one'. Cancik believed that this exotic nature was due to the influence of the prophetic traditions of the Old Testament and in particular of the book of Kings.[97]

If the Gospels are biographical hybrids that reveal different influences, the question is which influence dominated. Detlef Dormeyer described the Gospels as a 'special form of Old Testament prophetic biography

95. Alexander, 'Rabbinic Biography', 41–2.

96. Berger, 'Hellenistische Gattungen', 1244, etc.

97. H. Cancik, 'Die Gattung Evangelium: Das Evangelium des Markus im Rahmen der antiken Historiographie', in Cancik, ed., *Markus-Philologie*, 85–115 (94–9).

and Hellenistic ideal biography' with an emphasis on the Graeco-Roman tradition.[98] Marius Reiser, on the other hand, compared the Gospels first to Graeco-Roman popular literature[99] and later to Old Testament historiography, giving priority to the Jewish roots.[100]

The different literary influences can best be delineated as in the following table:

Feature	Gr.-Rom. biographies		Gospels	Jewish biographies	
	Cultivated	Popular		OT	Rabbinic
Independent genre	+	+	+	–	–
Anonymity	–	+	+	+	+
No authorial reflections	–	+	+	+	+
Unusual opening sentence	–	–	+	+	–
Prologue/epilogue	+	o	o	–	–
Simple prose	–	+	+	+	+
Semitisms	–	–	+	+	(+)
Parallelisms	–	–	+	+	+
Chiasms	–	–	+	+	+
Paratactic episodes	o	o	+	o	+
Much speech material	–	+	+	+	+
Mostly direct speech	–	+	+	+	+
Natural dialogues	–	+	+	+	+
Parables	–	–	+	o	+
Miracle stories	–	–	+	+	+
Call narratives	–	–	+	+	–
Didactic purpose	+	o	+	+	+

The symbol '+' means 'frequently' or 'always'; 'o' means 'sometimes'; '-' means 'rarely' or 'never'

98. D. Dormeyer, *Evangelium als literarische und theologische Gattung*, Erträge der Forschung 263 (Darmstadt: Wissenschaftliche Buchgesellschaft, 1989), 181–4.

99. Reiser, 'Alexanderroman', 131–63.

100. Idem, 'Stellung', 1–27.

The original audience of the Gospels may have noticed several generic features (column 4): They held independent biographies in their hands. These biographies were anonymous and offered no authorial reflections. They began with striking opening sentences, and two of them contained a technical prologue or epilogue. They were written in simple Greek prose that was permeated with lexical and syntactical Semitisms, parallelisms and chiasms. They largely consisted of more or less loosely connected episodes. Among them were parables, miracle stories, and call narratives. The books contained much speech material in direct speech and often in dialogues. They served a didactic purpose and were not meant for entertainment.

Ancient readers who were familiar with the Jewish and Graeco-Roman literature of their time could identify the following analogies:

1. There were relatively few close similarities between the New Testament Gospels and cultivated Graeco-Roman literature (column 2). Both groups of texts shared the use of the full biographical form, the use of prologues and a didactic purpose.
2. The Gospels had more in common with popular Graeco-Roman literature (column 3). Popular biographies, however, lacked comparable opening sentences, Semitic parallelisms, chiasms and lexical and syntactical Semitisms. They also did not offer close analogies to the smaller forms (parables, miracle stories and call narratives) that are so common in the Synoptic Gospels. Popular biographies did not, as a rule, serve the purpose of teaching but wanted to entertain.
3. The Gospels were even more similar to Old Testament historiography and the biographical material it contains (column 5). They began with opening sentences that had close parallels in Old Testament texts. And yet, in contrast to the New Testament Gospels, the Old Testament did not contain independent biographies, no technical prologues, fewer paratactic episodes and no akin parables.
4. The Gospels shared most features with the biographical material in rabbinic literature (column 6). Beyond those similarities shared with Old Testament historiography, the rabbinic tradition also contained similar parables and more paratactic episodes. The authors of rabbinic literature did not, however, produce full biographies of famous rabbis, nor did they use technical prologues.

The Gospel authors may have adopted the idea of full and independent biographies from Graeco-Roman popular or cultivated literature. It is not certain, however, that the authors of the New Testament Gospels needed these models in order to move from embedded biographical episodes to full and independent biographies. But the technical prologue in Luke's Gospel must clearly have been derived from the Graeco-Roman literary tradition.

In conclusion, the place of the New Testament Gospels in the manifold landscape of ancient biographical literature can be described as follows: the four New Testament Gospels are biographies of Jesus in Old Testament and rabbinic style with comparatively slight Graeco-Roman influences.

4

The Provenance of Jesus' Quotations of Scripture from a Social Memory Perspective

Thomas R. Hatina

The developing interest in social memory theory in biblical scholarship has been challenging long-held form-critical assumptions and explanations of how traditions, which eventually found their way into the Bible were transmitted and received. In Gospels studies and historical Jesus research the insights of social memory theory are becoming unavoidable and even threatening, challenging not only the way we have thought about the process of preservation, transmission and reception in the early church, but also the optimism of recovering and reconstructing the Jesus material.[1] Since the criteria of authenticity, which are grounded in the same historiography as form criticism, are likewise being threatened, it is not surprising to see a growing sentiment that we are on the precipice of either a renewed 'Quest' or another 'No Quest'.[2] While the theoretical

1. For an excellent summary of social memory theory in Gospels studies, see Chris Keith, 'Social Memory Theory and Gospels Research: The First Decade (Part One)', *Early Christianity* 6 (2015): 354–76; idem, 'Social Memory Theory and Gospels Research: The First Decade (Part Two)', *Early Christianity* 6 (2015): 517–42.

2. Jens Schröter, 'Jesus and Memory: The Memory Approach in Current Jesus Research', *Early Christianity* 6 (2015): 277–84; Anthony Le Donne, *Historical Jesus: What Can We Know and How Can We Know It?* (Grand Rapids: Eerdmans, 2011); Chris Keith and Anthony Le Donne, *Jesus, Criteria, and the Demise of Authenticity* (London: T&T Clark International, 2012). For an alternative position, see Tobias Hägerland, 'Jesus and the Scriptures: Problems of Authentication and Interpretation', in *Jesus and the Scriptures: Problems, Passages and Patterns*, ed. Tobias Hägerland,

challenges have been weighty, the appropriation of social memory theory to specific texts, as is the aim of this article, is in its infancy.[3]

In this contribution – which is but a small gesture of gratitude for John's influential mentoring and long-standing friendship – I focus on how social memory theory might re-direct our thinking about the provenance of the Scripture quotations attributed to Jesus in the canonical Gospels. Since new approaches are often clarified in light of existing ones, after an overview, the paper is divided into three parts. The first part briefly surveys how select form critics and historical Jesus scholars have understood the origins of these quotations. The second part summarizes the misuses and uses of the social memory paradigm in Gospels and Jesus studies. And the third part proposes that the quotations should be read as memory texts whose provenance is located in the commemoration process of the evangelists.

Quotations Attributed to Jesus: An Overview

It is striking how often in the Gospels Jesus quotes or alludes to the Scriptures.[4] The actual number of quotations attributed to Jesus in all four Gospels is difficult to establish because the distinction between quotation and allusion is sometimes blurred. According to Richard Longenecker's count, without the inclusion of parallels, Jesus quotes the Scriptures 39 times.[5] If we include allusions, the number skyrockets. Whatever the exact count, for the evangelists the Scriptures play an influential role in their presentation of Jesus' teachings.

There is little doubt that as a devout Jew living in 1st-century Palestine, Jesus would have been frequently exposed to the Scriptures and their

LNTS 522 (London: T&T Clark International, 2016), 3–32; Ernest van Eck, 'Memory and Historical Jesus Studies: *Formgeschichte* in a New Dress?', *HvTSt* 71 (2015), article 2837, 10 pages, http://dx.doi.org/10.4102/hts.v71i1.2837.

3. I leave aside the important discussion on the potential relationship between social memory theory and select form-critical insights. See Chris Keith, 'Memory and Authenticity: Jesus Tradition and What Really Happened', *ZNW* 102 (2011): 177; idem, 'Social Memory Theory and Gospels Research: The First Decade (Part Two)', 523–5; Anthony Le Donne, *The Historiographical Jesus: Memory, Typology, and the Son of David* (Waco: Baylor University Press, 2009), 38.

4. On the quotations in non-canonical sources, see Craig A. Evans, 'The Interpretation of Scripture in the New Testament Apocrypha and Gnostic Writings', in *A History of Biblical Interpretation*. Vol. 1, *The Ancient Period*, ed. Alan J. Hauser and Duane F. Watson (Grand Rapids: Eerdmans, 2003), 430–56.

5. Richard N. Longenecker, *Biblical Exegesis in the Apostolic Period*, 2nd edn (Grand Rapids: Eerdmans, 1999), 36, 42.

interpretive traditions through oral/aural media.[6] This inference seems reasonable, even innocuous. Though, interestingly, many prominent studies on the activities of Jesus rarely mention his use of Scripture. E. P. Sanders's groundbreaking study on the so-called facts (in comparison to the sayings) of Jesus locates him appropriately within Judaism, but does not include his use of Scripture as one of the eight facts that are most probable.[7] This may be an oversight or simply an assumption that does not require listing, much like the claim that Jesus was a Jew.[8] If we grant that Jesus was saturated within the political, social and religious matrices of Judaism, he surely would have used and engaged with the Scriptures of his faith on a regular basis whether he was literate or not. This is not the difficulty. Instead, the difficulty lies in the Gospels' representations of Jesus' quotations of Scripture. Determining their provenance depends on how one understands the relationship between the past and its reception. This is the crux of the divide between form critics and traditional historical Jesus scholars on the one hand and social memory theorists on the other.

I. *The Form Critical Paradigm*

Questions about the process, transmission and reception of isolated and fragmentary Jesus material within the oral period of the church have identified form criticism in New Testament studies.[9] More narrowly, form critics have not only attempted to identify the shape and function of Scripture quotations in the life of the early Christian communities, but have also attempted to explain why certain ones were chosen. While a small percentage of form critics have proposed that a number of the scriptural attributions go back to Jesus, the majority claim that they arose in the early church after Easter. Despite the wide range of conclusions, all form critics, like their historical Jesus counterparts, have shared an

6. On Scripture as the carrier of Judaean culture, see Tom Thatcher, 'Literacy, Textual Communities, and Josephus' Jewish War', *JSJ* 29 (1998): 123–42.

7. E. P. Sanders, *Jesus and Judaism* (London: SCM Press; Philadelphia: Fortress Press, 1985), 11.

8. E.g. in a later article, Sanders clearly states in passing that Jesus was rooted in the study of Scripture. E. P. Sanders, 'Jesus in Historical Context', *Theology Today* 3 (1993): 429–48.

9. See the insightful historical survey (in Czech) by Jiri Lukes, 'Osamostatneni, vyvoj a smerovani kriticke novozakonni exegeze od pocatku liberalismu do doby postmoderny – od J. P. Gablera k M. J. Borgovi', *Theologicka Revue* 1 (2014): 50–88, esp. 61–4.

optimism that the past can be retrieved and reconstructed if proper rules or criteria are applied. The optimism, which stems from Enlightenment principles, is more narrowly rooted within a modernist or positivist view of history and historiography, which is classically represented in the work of Ernst Troeltsch (1865–1923), who famously articulated linear principles of connectivity, such as causality of events and analogous relationships between past and present.[10]

Despite the appropriation of common methods and criteria, the differing results among form critics since C. H. Dodd's *According to the Scriptures* has been nothing short of staggering.[11] The provenance of the quotations attributed to Jesus cover the spectrum, from Jesus himself to his earliest followers. The differences are symptomatic of broader modernist or positivist views of history that have been critiqued for decades in other disciplines, but have only recently entered Gospels studies on a serious level.[12] One of the fundamental assumptions of form criticism and historical Jesus research is that the Gospels are archives whose layers can be successfully mined through the use of specific tools. While form criticism has contributed significantly to our awareness of the oral period and the Third Quest has contributed to the explosion of data about the 1st century, it has not achieved a consensus on the explanation and the relationship of the often-fragmented data. Despite attempts, the tools of form criticism and the criteria of authenticity in and of themselves have no inherent explanatory capacity. The varied explanations of the same data correspond to varied attempts to select and unify the data, which have often been theologically or ideologically motivated. This has particularly been noticeable in comparisons of data between Jewish and Graeco-Roman sources on the one hand and Christian ones on the other.[13] Selectivity of

10. See, for example, Ernst Troeltsch, *Religion in History*, trans. J. L. Adams and W. F. Bense (Edinburgh: T. & T. Clark, 1991).

11. C. H. Dodd, *According to the Scriptures* (London: Nisbet, 1952).

12. E.g. Hans-Georg Gadamer, *Truth and Method* (New York: Seabury Press, 1975); Hayden V. White, *Metahistory: The Historical Imagination in Nineteenth Century Europe* (Baltimore: The Johns Hopkins University Press, 1973). More recently, Robert Evans, *Reception History, Tradition and Biblical Interpretation: Gadamer and Jauss in Current Practice*, Scriptural Traces: Critical Perspectives on the Reception and Influence of the Bible 4, LNTS 510 (London: Bloomsbury T&T Clark, 2014).

13. See, e.g., Jonathan Z. Smith, *Drudgery Divine: On the Comparisons of Early Christianities and the Religions of Late Antiquity* (Chicago: University of Chicago Press, 1990); Geza Vermes, *The Authentic Gospel of Jesus* (London: Penguin Books, 2003), 280.

which sources constitute evidence and the imposition of narrative links between data points have been at the heart of the disagreements.[14]

The divergent views about Jesus' use of Scripture have been categorized by Steve Moyise into three approaches: minimalist, moderate and maximalist – each referring to the amount of Jesus material in the Gospels that can be traced back to the historical Jesus.[15] While these categories can be slippery, simplistic and presume a bias, they are nevertheless helpful in demonstrating how the same data can be interpreted in diverse ways. According to Moyise, minimalists like Geza Vermes, Marcus Borg and John Dominic Crossan arrive at the claim that all of the scriptural attributions were added by the early church because their interpretation of the data is ideologically guided by a suspicion of, and a personal sense of alienation from, institutional religion. On the other end of the spectrum are the maximalists, like Richard France and Charles Kimball, who are supposedly guided by theological convictions that require a strict continuity between Jesus and the Gospels. Moyise observes that both of these approaches oddly agree in not ascribing an alteration or shift in meaning to the quotations attributed to Jesus. For the minimalists, the texts and their meanings were established by the early church, and for the maximalists they were established by Jesus. Aligning himself with the moderate approach, Moyise believes that many of the quotations may go back to Jesus, but they could have been altered in the process of transmission. The operative assumption among many of Moyise's moderates is that whatever material can be explained as being consistent with 1st-century Judaism probably can be traced back to Jesus.

Moyise's assessment is an updated and digestible version of D. Moody Smith's more judicious summary of the problem some forty years earlier.[16] Since Smith is writing before the expansion of American evangelical contributions, he divides the approaches into conservative and radical positions, recognizing that such categories inherently lack precision.[17]

14. See, e.g., the layering of sources in John Dominic Crossan, *The Historical Jesus: The Life of a Mediterranean Jewish Peasant* (San Francisco: HarperSanFrancisco, 1991).

15. Steve Moyise, *Jesus and Scripture: Studying the New Testament Use of the Old Testament* (Grand Rapids: Baker Academic, 2010).

16. D. Moody Smith, 'The Use of the Old Testament in the New', in *The Use of the Old Testament in the New and Other Essays: Studies in Honor of William Franklin Stinespring*, ed. J. M. Efird (Durham: Duke University Press, 1972), 3–65, especially 20–5. Unfortunately, Moyise does not interact with Smith.

17. Smith's conservatives tend to reflect Moyise's moderates.

According to the conservative position, represented by Dodd, T. W. Manson and Edwyn Hoskyns, Jesus' mission and message was grounded in his reflection on Scripture and can be recovered from the Gospels. According to the radical position, represented by adherents of Rudolf Bultmann, Norman Perrin and Barnabas Lindars, the Scripture quotations are the product of the early church's reflection on the messianic identity of Jesus after Easter. Smith astutely points out that the two positions hinge on whether or not Jesus understood his ministry as messianic.[18] If he did, the influence of the resurrection is minimized. If he did not, then its influence is maximized.

Assessments like those of Steve Moyise and D. Moody Smith bring clarity to the problems of the historiographical presuppositions of form criticism and traditional historical Jesus research. Arguments for the continuity and discontinuity between the historical Jesus and the Gospels' representations of him are more tenuous than ever, and in my estimation have reached an impasse. Similar estimations are redirecting some scholars to look at the Gospels not so much as archives containing layers of tradition, but as social memory texts that are the imprints of complicated webs of communication.

II. *The Social Memory Paradigm*

To date, the main contribution of social memory theory lies in its critique of positivist historiographical presuppositions, which will either redirect or terminate our quests for Jesus and his earliest post-Easter followers, but as a hermeneutic it has yet to demonstrate how it aids in the interpretation of the Gospels without reconstructing them. Questions remain. If the Gospels are interpreted as works of memory that assume a past – which cannot be denied – what role do recognizable forms imbedded in the Gospels play? Does social memory serve as a tool for a redirected form criticism, especially if remembrances and micro forms/genres are linked?[19] Or does it no longer concern itself with the content of an assumed past, but rather with the literary present? If the latter is the case, how does the shift from the *Sitz im Leben* of the early church to the *Sitz im Leben* of the evangelist and/or his community provide new insights into the text? Presumably the evangelists' remembrances require explanations that include concrete spaces, times and uses of language, which require linking

18. Smith, 'The Use of the Old Testament in the New', 22.

19. See Ruben Zimmermann, *Puzzling the Parables of Jesus: Methods and Interpretation* (Minneapolis: Fortress Press, 2015), 77–8.

social memory theory with appropriate methods. Below, I attempt to do this by linking it with anthropology (especially studies in orality) and narratology in order to explain the reception process.

Since categories like 'social memory' and 'collective memory' are increasingly finding their way into New Testament scholarship for the wrong reasons, I offer some clarity by first addressing what they are not. In some cases, social memory has been adopted to convey the illusion of newness, much like the term 'intertextuality', which has been seized by scholars studying Scripture quotations and allusions in the New Testament. While the term conveys an air of freshness and sophistication, some of its users have rarely addressed the theoretical framework where it originated and where it is primarily used.[20] In most cases where social memory is inappropriately used, it refers to individual or psychological memory that assumes a process of communication whereby one person passes information to another person. Memory thus functions as a tool within the form-critical paradigm to demonstrate either the accuracy or inaccuracy of the oral transmission of Jesus material. Each side of the debate refers to studies of individual memory that corroborates its position.[21] Each tends to view social memory as a web of facts instead of viewing it as a cultural web of significance that shapes meaning.[22] And each side fails to distinguish tradition from memory. While studies in individual memory play a

20. See Thomas R. Hatina, 'Intertextuality and Historical Criticism: Is There a Relationship?', *BibInt* 7 (1999): 28–43.

21. For example, among those who appropriate memory to demonstrate the reliability of oral transmission include Richard Bauckham, *Jesus and the Eyewitnesses: The Gospels as Eyewitness Testimony* (Grand Rapids: Eerdmans, 2006); James D. G. Dunn, *Jesus Remembered*, Christianity in the Making 1 (Grand Rapids: Eerdmans, 2003); Robert K. McIver, *Memory, Jesus, and the Synoptic Gospels* (Atlanta: SBL, 2011). An example of those who propose that memory is generally unreliable includes, Bart Ehrman, *Jesus Before the Gospels: How the Earliest Christians Remembered, Changed, and Invented Their Stories of the Savior* (New York: HarperOne, 2016); John Dominic Crossan, *The Birth of Christianity: Discovering What Happened in the Years Immediately after the Execution of Jesus* (New York: HarperSanFrancisco, 1998), 61–3; Paul Foster, 'Memory, Orality, and the Fourth Gospel: Three Dead-Ends in Historical Jesus Research', *JSHJ* 10 (2012): 191–227; Zeba A. Crook, 'Collective Memory Distortion and the Quest for the Historical Jesus', *JSHJ* 11 (2013): 53–76.

22. E.g. Clifford Geertz, *Interpretation of Cultures* (New York: Basic Books, 1973), 5. Geertz's semiotic concept of culture is an important foundation for understanding social memory. Like Max Weber, he sees individuals suspended in 'webs of significance'. The analysis of these webs, which is culture, is not performed by experimental science in the search for meaning.

potential role in Gospels studies, they cannot do so in isolation apart from social and cultural concerns and they certainly cannot advance the field if they are guided buy apologetic concerns.[23]

Building on the work of Maurice Halbwachs, contemporary social memory theorists view memory as a sign (or effect) of communal affiliation. Psychological memory was not rejected by Halbwachs, but was viewed as an expression of the social patterning of individuals.[24] One of Halbwachs' key observations on the function of memory within religious frameworks is that recollections of the past are assimilated within the frameworks of the present. While the past is continually (re)shaped and (re)collected so as to have meaning in the present, the present is continually informed and guided by the past, especially if the tradition is older, is adopted by a large number of adherents and is widespread.[25] Halbwachs' focus on the present has undoubtedly been influential, but his ill-defined concept of 'the past' has left his theory deficient. While Halbwachs was not oblivious to the past as a prior cause of memory, it was not what we might call 'the actual past' or 'what really happened'.[26] Halbwachs' ambivalence toward the past has proven to be unsatisfying for social memory theorists working with ancient literature, notable Jan Assmann in Germany and Barry Schwartz in the United States.[27] Both have revived and modified Halbwachs' insights, but of the two, Schwartz, who has been labeled as 'the father of collective memory studies in contemporary American sociology', has been the most influential in Jesus and Gospels research.[28]

23. We are at the precipice of integrating studies in individual memory with social memory. Dale C. Allison's summary of the major insights into memory among psychologists is a good place to start for Gospels scholars. See his *Constructing Jesus: Memory, Imagination, and History* (Grand Rapids: Baker, 2010), 1–30. His assessment of wide-ranging studies leads him to conclude that over a period of time remembrances are guided by general impressions, which take various forms, but not specific words or conversations.

24. Maurice Halbwachs, *On Collective Memory* (Chicago: University of Chicago Press, 1992), 43, 50–1.

25. Ibid., 183.

26. Keith, 'Social Memory Theory and Gospels Research: The First Decade (Part One)', 361.

27. For a summary of Assmann's theory of the relationship between the present and the past, see ibid., 364–9.

28. Jeffrey K. Olick, Vered Vinitzky-Seroussi and Daniel Levy, eds, *The Collective Memory Reader* (Oxford: OUP, 2011), 242. While Schwartz's theory is dominant in Gospels studies, it has its detractors. See, e.g., Foster, 'Memory, Orality, and the Fourth Gospel'.

Schwartz compares the practice of social memory to public opinion as a filter through which the average person thinks about daily matters. In his words, social memory 'refers to the distribution throughout society of what individuals believe, know and feel about the past, how they judge the past morally, how closely they identify with it, and how they commemorate it'.[29] Social memory does not imply consensus, but a process or reception that contains variation among groups within the larger social group. As such it is not a resource or data bank of perspectives, but rather it is a 'cultural system' that reflects and illumines the broader culture and how it receives the past. Of particular importance for our study is Schwartz's modification of the presentist model, which he considers lop-sided. Like Halbwachs he preserves the emphasis on the present, but he sees the past playing a much more important role in how present memories are shaped. The actual past is neither mirrored in the present, nor is it entirely changed by the present. The former is to conceive of a fiction because it would deny not only how memory functions, but also how meaning of the past is determined by cultural shifts. The latter is to conceive of the present as the only relevant reality, which would render any notions of memory meaningless.[30] For Schwartz the past is important because that is where the object of commemoration is usually found, but it is pliable and subject to selection and change in the service of the present.[31] While the present can be affected by the actual past, it can also be affected by a stable image or tradition that did not originate in the actual past, but was simply accepted over time as true.[32]

III. *The Quotations as Memory Texts*

Applying Schwartz's continuity theory to the Gospels does not assume that the evangelists are necessarily 'pressured' by the past. The past, however, must remain in play and not be dismissed *a priori*. The difficulty that social memory theories present for positivist views of history is that the past cannot be authenticated because tradition and memory are collapsed.

29. Barry Schwartz, 'Where There's Smoke, There's Fire: Memory and History', in *Memory and Identity in Ancient Judaism and Early Christianity. A Conversation with Barry Schwartz*, ed. Tom Thatcher (Atlanta: SBL Press, 2014), 9–10.

30. Schwartz, *Abraham Lincoln and the Forge of National Memory*, 7.

31. Barry Schwartz, 'The Social Context of Commemoration', *Social Forces* 61 (1982): 395.

32. Keith, 'Social Memory Theory and Gospels Research: The First Decade (Part One)', 372.

Some traditions may correspond to the actual past (i.e. historical Jesus), whereas others may not. While we can postulate the probability of some traditions being older than others, authentication is not on offer. At best, social memory can inform us that the hermeneutical process of reception that led to the composition of the Gospels was continuously at play from the time of Jesus through the so-called ‘oral period’ of the early church to the Gospels, and beyond.[33] From this vantage point, the Gospels are viewed as the products of discourse within certain cultural frames that reflect and speak into the socially shared traditions that build group identity. To use more familiar categories, the Gospels blend tradition and redaction in the composition of a narrative.[34] Moreover, the evangelists would not have been able to distinguish between memories that correspond to reality and those that do not. There is no evidence in the Gospels that would suggest that some episodes or sayings were considered as corresponding to the actual past and others that did not.

So, how is social memory helpful for understanding the Scripture quotations attributed to Jesus? Its main contribution lies in its critique of positivist approaches by viewing these texts as hermeneutical products of reception. As such, it illumines how the attributions reflect the popular beliefs of the remembering communities and reveals the mnemonic processes that shaped those beliefs. Varied Scripture attributions to Jesus are not set against themselves as fodder for evaluating which one of them is ‘correct’, ‘true’, ‘late’ or ‘early’, but they are approached as products of varied beliefs that were shaped by their respective social frameworks.[35] To speculate, if narratives were composed about Jesus by the opponents of the evangelists’ communities, the attributions of scripture would have looked entirely different. Undoubtedly, the vast majority would not have

33. See the approach to the Mark, Q and *Thomas* as reception of common tradition in Jens Schröter, *Erinnerung an Jesu Worte. Studien zur Rezeption der Logienüberlieferung in Markus, Q, und Thomas*, WMANT 76 (Neukirchen-Vluyn: Neukirchener Verlag, 1997).

34. Sandra Huebenthal, ‘Luke 24.13-35, Collective Memory, and Cultural Frames’, in *Biblical Interpretation in Early Christian Gospels*. Vol. 3, *The Gospel of Luke*, ed. Thomas R. Hatina, SSEJC 16, LNTS 376 (London: T&T Clark International, 2010), 86–7. While ‘tradition’ can be a highly nuanced term, I understand it as the substance of memory.

35. Barry Schwartz, ‘Christian Origins: Historical Truth and Social Memory’, in *Memory, Tradition, and Text: Uses of the Past in Early Christianity*, ed. Alan Kirk and Tom Thatcher, Semeia 52 (Atlanta: SBL, 2005), 50; Jens Schröter, ‘The Historical Jesus and the Sayings Tradition: Comments on Current Research’, *Neot* 30 (1996): 151–68.

been placed on the lips of Jesus, but rather on the lips of the Jewish religious leaders accompanied by different meanings. Social memory theory places the clichéd perspectives of 'victor' and 'victim' in sharp relief.

My contention is that the Scripture quotations attributed to Jesus should be viewed as the products of commemoration, reflecting the discourse and identity of the evangelists' fellow Christians, and as the products of performance that formulate expectations of experience and behaviour. Since the commemoration process is always oriented toward relevance, and not the undiluted preservation of the past, it is not only impossible to trace these attributions to Jesus or to some stage during the oral period of the early church, but it also betrays how tradition is communicated and received at both the oral and written stages, to which I now turn.

Remembrance and Orality

To better understand how the remembrances of Jesus were intertwined with the Scriptures, it is important to consider the process of oral transmission, to which form critics have rightly drawn attention. Our understanding of the transmission process from oral traditions to written Gospels has been significantly advanced through anthropological and sociological studies. For social memory theorists, it is not an evolutionary or organic process as so many form critics have assumed.

The insights of Walter Ong have provided an entry way into the psychodynamics of oral culture. Despite apt criticisms that his chasm between orality and literacy is too broad, several of Ong's contributions into the assumptions and practices of orality continue to be useful.[36] One of his enduring insights is that the function of remembrances in oral cultures is oriented toward relevance. Instead of preserving analytical thought patterns, oral transmission favours practical and situational patterns.[37] The events selected for transmission may well have had a high degree of historicity, but they were not ultimately preserved for their own sake in an exact manner.[38] More recent studies that have moved beyond Ong propose

36. On the closer relationship between orality and literacy, see John Miles Foley, *How to Read an Oral Poem* (Chicago: University of Illinois Press, 2002), 37–8; idem, 'Memory in Oral Tradition', in *Performing the Gospels: Orality, Memory, and Mark. Essays Dedicated to Werner Kelber*, ed. Richard Horsley, John Draper and John Miles Foley (Minneapolis: Fortress Press, 2006), 83–96.

37. Walter J. Ong, *Orality and Literacy: The Technologizing of the Word* (London: Routledge, 2002), 52–3.

38. Ong challenged the form-critical assumption that transmission from oral to written tradition is not linear. See Werner H. Kelber, *The Oral and the Written Gospel:*

that the process of reception and communication overlap in both oral and written transmission.[39] In addition to relevance, the process of oral communication is also affected by time, which is best envisioned within Jan Assmann's concept of the fragmentation of tradition (*Traditionsbruch*), usually at the forty-year mark when communicative memory gives way to collective memory if a tradition is to endure.[40]

Some oral performance may have been structured, similar to literary performance. For some scholars, who agree that Mark, for example, was the product of oral convention, the potential for fluidity in the transmission process was almost certain since it was originally intended to be an oral (theatrical) performance that was repeated in varying forms prior to its written composition.[41] What is particularly important to note is that repetition implied change. Performances were fluid. Variance was expected. Yet, the plot would have remained intact. Fluidity would have also been limited by the confines of the host oral culture. For example, characters and their speech could have been altered in slight ways for the benefit of new audiences, especially when the plot is communicated to different ethnic groups, say from an audience that is only Jewish (in Galilee) to an audience that is predominantly Gentile (in Syria or Rome). If Scripture attributions were incorporated at this stage, they would have been rhetorically relevant for Jewish audiences, but not so much for Gentile ones – as is seen in the non-canonical gospels.[42]

It is also important to stress that the multi-layered communication process should not be conceived as links in a chain that originated with a single story.[43] The way forward, according to Schwartz and others, is

The Hermeneutics of Speaking and Writing in the Synoptic Tradition, Mark, Paul, and Q, Voices in Performance and Text (Bloomington: Indiana University Press, 1983), 90.

39. See the summary of recent studies in relation to the NT in Rafael Rodríguez, 'Reading and Hearing in Ancient Contexts', *JSNT* 32 (2009): 151–78.

40. Keith, 'Social Memory Theory and Gospels Research: The First Decade (Part Two)', 521–2; Jan Assmann, *Cultural Memory in Early Civilization: Writing, Remembrance, and Political Imagination* (Cambridge: CUP, 2011), 195–6.

41. Joanna Dewey, 'The Gospel of Mark as Oral Hermeneutic', in *Jesus, the Voice, and the Text: Beyond the Oral and the Written Gospel* (Waco: Baylor University Press, 2008), 71–87.

42. Joanna Dewey, 'The Gospel of Mark as an Oral-Aural Event: Implications for Interpretation', in *The New Literary Criticism and the New Testament*, ed. E. McKnight and E. S. Malbon (Valley Forge: Trinity Press International, 1994), 145–63. See also Whitney Shiner, *Proclaiming the Gospel: First-Century Performance of Mark* (Harrisburg: Trinity Press International, 2003).

43. Contra Ehrman, *Jesus Before the Gospels*.

to deploy communication models that may help us to understand how social remembrance functioned in ancient oral contexts. His model of choice is based on Edmund Leach's conception that single stories may have more than one original version. Thus, Schwartz argues that the transmission of the Jesus story occurred through a networking process whereby an individual (e.g. a disciple) transmitted it to his network, such as friends and relatives, who in turn passed it on to their networks. What is more, since contexts alter remembrances, individuals in the network potentially communicate data from different vantage points and for different purposes, with each retelling having a formative effect.[44] As a result, none of the renditions contained the truest meaning of the message. Rather the 'meaning' is found in the collective, when the networks are brought together.[45]

If this is a correct vantage point, then we are potentially faced with a multi-layered transmission process that further clouds our ability to see where scripture quotations first appeared during oral communication. No doubt that Scripture would have played a role in identifying and defending Jesus as the suffering Christ, but it is very difficult to claim that the quotations as they are found in the Gospels originated at this stage. Like literacy, orality does not separate, but confirms the integration of tradition and memory.

Remembrance and Narratology

While the use of Scripture would have been prevalent during the earliest decades of the early church, it is unlikely that the quotations, as we find them in the Gospels, would have been preserved in the oral communication about Jesus in some kind of linear process that defies our present models. It is far more likely that they were added at the time of writing.[46] There are three main reasons why I think it happened this way.

First, when we apply broader patterns of how social memory operates in oral cultures to the Gospels, we turn our attention to the media of premodern remembrance. Media are the vehicles of social memory that form a group's identity in relation to the past. They may include oral speeches, statues, shrines, rituals and even written texts.[47] One of the most effective and powerful forms of media for the early Christians was Scripture.

44. Susan Engel, *Context Is Everything: The Nature of Memory* (New York: W. H. Freeman, 1999), 12.

45. Schwartz, 'Where There's Smoke', 12–13.

46. I do not mean to suggest that the Gospels displaced oral tradition. They co-existed.

47. Schwartz, 'Where There's Smoke', 10.

The main function of social remembrance is the reception process, which is often called 'keying'. It occurs at both the oral and written levels, but it is more intentional in the latter. In Schwartz's words, 'Keying defines social memory's function, matching the past and present as (1) a model *of* society, reflecting its needs, interests, fears, and aspirations; (2) a model *for* society, a template for thought, sentiment, morality, and conduct; and (3) a frame within which people find meaning for their experience'.[48] What this means is that events or individuals that are the objects of a group's memory are placed within a familiar frame that activates meaning for its experience. In this manner, argues Schwartz, 'the Gospels key the activities and fate of Jesus to statements in the Hebrew Scriptures an estimated three hundred times, which affirms both the Gospel writers' mastery of Scripture and their listeners' identification with the history the sacred texts describe'.[49] One example of this process is found in Luke's story of the Emmaus road, which explicitly frames the unusual image of a crucified Messiah within the tradition of Israel's suffering in the Psalms.[50] The placement of Jesus' identification with the Scriptures on his lips (24.25-27) is an expression of the broader hermeneutic at play in Luke's community, which achieved relevance and meaning by framing the memories of Jesus within familiar sacred texts.

What we see in the Scriptures attributed to Jesus, as well as those about Jesus, is the process of the institutionalization of tradition.[51] Like ritual, the keying of Scripture to individual remembrances of Jesus leads to the stability of the social remembrances. In a sense, the stable collective of remembrances preserved in the Gospels becomes the new frame. Thus, it is not the social remembrances in and of themselves that remain stable or consistent, as if they comprise a data bank of knowledge that is passed on from person to person. Rather, if social remembrance approximates metaphor in the sense that it affects how people think about the information they receive, then the stability is found in both the process of keying and its result, which becomes the new contextual frame. Again, by keying the remembrances of Jesus into the Scriptures, which were a familiar social reference, Jesus became the (or part of the) frame within which new events were received.

48. Ibid., 16.

49. Ibid., 15–16.

50. Rafael Rodriguez, '"According to the Scriptures": Suffering and the Psalms in the Speeches in Acts', in Thatcher, ed., *Memory and Identity*, 241–62.

51. Schwartz, 'Where There's Smoke', 31.

Second, written narratives require much more information than oral transmission. Narratives grow and morph into more elaborate stories through the process of retelling. As the narrator retells his story, he interprets it, adding new details and information, which in turn requires more narrative, and so on.[52] When Mark, for example, dipped his stylus into his inkwell and began to write, Jesus as the object of communal remembrance required intentional analogous connections with the sacred history of Israel just as the plot of the narrative required connections between the events and the characters. Discourse about the past, ancient or modern, necessarily requires an imaginative element that brings coherence to preserved data. Without imagination, or the so-called fictional ingredient, the data cannot be understood and historical discourse cannot take place. Although the fictional component cannot exactly grasp the reality of the past, it attempts to represent it, albeit from the writer's vantage point.[53] This is precisely where keying takes place, in effect making the past and memory interdependent, though not identical. While the retelling of the past is malleable, past events still set limits on imagination that gives rise to narratives.

Likewise, characters require development through information. The process of writing turns agents that perform roles (e.g. 'helper', 'betrayer' or 'saviour') into complex characters possessing personality traits.[54] Frank Kermode explains that turning an agent into a character is a simple process: 'a few indications of idiosyncrasy, of deviation from type, are enough, for our practiced eyes will make up the large patterns of which such indications can be read as parts'.[55] Inferences that are guided by social remembrance fill in the rest. Agents receive names, actions and speech. Antagonists require a fuller development of their opposition, often through speech that can be easily refuted by the protagonist. Journeys require place names. Great deeds, such as healings and exorcisms, require specific contexts.

52. Frank Kermode, *The Genesis of Secrecy: On the Interpretation of Narrative* (Cambridge, MA: Harvard University Press, 1979), 81.

53. See especially the work of Hayden V. White, *The Content of the Form: Narrative Discourse and Historical Representation* (Baltimore: The Johns Hopkins University Press, 1987); *Metahistory: The Historical Imagination in Nineteenth-Century Europe* (Baltimore: The Johns Hopkins University Press, 1973); *The Fiction of Narrative: Essays on History, Literature, and Theory, 1957–2007*, ed. Robert Doran (Baltimore: The Johns Hopkins University Press, 2010).

54. Kermode, *The Genesis of Secrecy*, 81. See also Petri Merenlahti, *Poetics for the Gospels? Rethinking Narrative Criticism* (London: T&T Clark International, 2002), 77–97.

55. Kermode, *The Genesis of Secrecy*, 98.

Another important ingredient of information is the narrator's point of view, which requires an ideological or mythical basis. This is the heart of the imaginative element that draws lines of connection between the data. Point of view should not simply be equated with the persuasive manner in which the narrator presents certain norms, values and a general worldview within the story to the (implied) audience. Point of view is more complex than that. Boris Uspensky has been instrumental for narrative critics in identifying five 'planes' in which point of view can be expressed: the ideological (evaluative norms), the phraseological (speech patterns), the spatial (narrator's location), the temporal (time reference of the narrator) and the psychological (narrator's omniscience).[56] While each one of these 'planes' enables a more thorough definition of the narrator's point of view, it is the ideological 'plane' which is of foremost importance for understanding why Scripture quotations are so prevalent in the Gospel narratives.[57] The narrator's ideological viewpoint is essentially his conceptual view of the world – with its system of values and norms – which for the evangelists is largely founded on specific theological convictions about the identity and role of Jesus within God's scheme of salvation history. The ideological 'plane' drives the early Christian conviction that all Scripture points to Jesus.

The third reason why Scripture quotations attributed to Jesus were probably later additions is that the act of writing tends to be past-focused in contrast to oral communication, which tends to be present-focused. Werner Kelber explains this phenomenon in relation to early Christian Christology. Once Christology was committed to narrative, it was perceived as being past-focused, meaning that it looked back at the words and deeds of Jesus, in contrast to a present-focused Christology during the oral stage, which began with the presence of the exalted Christ in the community. Another way of putting this is that a past Christology is more

56. Boris Uspensky, *A Poetics of Composition: The Structure of the Artistic Text and Typology of a Compositional Form*, trans. V. Zavarin and S. Wittig (Berkeley: University of California Press, 1973), 6–7 and *passim*. See the use of Uspensky's multi-dimensional approach in David M. Rhoads and Donald Michie, *Mark as Story: An Introduction to the Narrative of a Gospel* (Philadelphia: Fortress Press, 1982), 35–42; R. Allan Culpepper, *Anatomy of the Fourth Gospel: A Study in Literary Design* (Philadelphia: Fortress Press, 1983), 21–34.

57. Rhoads and Michie, *Mark as Story*. See also the overarching importance of the ideological point of view in Robert R. Beck, *Nonviolent Story: Narrative Conflict Resolution in the Gospel of Mark* (Maryknoll: Orbis Books, 1996), 34; Thomas R. Hatina, *In Search of a Context: The Function of Scripture in Mark's Narrative*, JSNTSup 232, SSEJC 8 (London: Sheffield Academic Press, 2002).

reflective, whereas a present Christology is more experiential. Both past and present foci are inevitably symbiotic, but the emphasis of the one will impact the meaning of the other.[58] Here, Paul's letters provide an important touchstone since he is not at all interested in recalling the sayings of Jesus, let alone scriptural attributions, but rather the significance of the 'present' exalted Christ who guides his theological and ethical rhetoric. The Letters can be taken as imprints of remembrances at a pre-narrative oral stage, but not necessarily as the exact traditions received by the evangelists.

If Kelber is correct, then before a written Gospel was even conceived, it is easy to imagine that the primary reference in communication was the Christ of experience, which would not have required attributing Scripture to Jesus. Present experience, however, would inevitably affect reception by drawing conversations to the past, which would have invoked analogies with Scripture as part of the meaning-making process. Narrative necessarily reversed the process of reception because it placed Jesus in a plot whose story world was in the past. Since narrative is past-focused, then conceivably the evangelists would not only look back to the ministry of Jesus, but also to the sacred stories of Israel, which provided the frames for understanding that ministry. The Jesus of the past needed to be constructed in a way that adequately confronted the crises and objections that the evangelists were facing in their present. The intentional use of scripture, especially on the lips of Jesus, was the best rhetorical strategy and representation of the collective remembrance.[59]

Even if the temporal distinctions between the oral and written are not as stark as we once thought, they are still pertinent. Certainly there is overlap that distinctions can overshadow. The scribal activity of the evangelists represented oral performance much more than we once thought. It may have even been a variant of it. Scribal activity was not intended to preserve the remembrances that were assumed to be lost via orality. It was much more complex than that. Scribal activity may have even implemented forgetfulness.[60] All of this is to say that both oral performance and scribal

58. Kelber, *The Oral and the Written Gospel*, 184–226. By embedding the oral traditions in the medium of writing, Mark (as the first Gospel) shifted the authoritative location of Jesus from a present-focused Christology to a past-focused Christology that looked back at his life and death.

59. It may have even contributed to the evangelists' position of power over his opponents. On written texts as vehicles of power, see Rodríguez, 'Reading and Hearing in Ancient Contexts', 166–70.

60. Werner H. Kelber, 'The Works of Memory: Christian Origins as MnemoHistory – A Response', in Kirk and Thatcher, eds, *Memory, Tradition, and Text*, 228–9, 238 (221–48); Rodríguez, 'Reading and Hearing in Ancient Contexts', 163–4.

activity of writing narrative were dynamic processes prone to variance in the service of relevance in the mediator's present. Still, narrative required more deliberate keying and lines of connection.

Conclusion

The search for the provenance of the quotations attributed to Jesus, like so much of the material in Gospels, is intertwined with one's conception of the relationship between the past and its reception. For form critics the relationship is bifurcated, differentiated and even layered, emphasizing a present *Sitz im Leben/Jesu*, which has led to wide-ranging explanations of provenance. Since the Gospels are viewed as repositories of layered traditions that can be peeled back, reconstructions drive the agenda. For social memory theorists, the relationship between the past and its reception is integrated, collapsing tradition and memory. Since the Gospels are viewed as memory texts, provenance of the quotations attributed to Jesus are viewed as imprints of a post-Easter hermeneutical process. As such, they are the ideological/identity-formative points of reference that express the evangelists' present.

While my proposal of the provenance of the quotations coincides with the insights of several form critics and historical Jesus scholars, it is based on different reasons and on a different historiographical paradigm. Unlike form critics, social memory theorists do not try to 'prove' that the quotations are the products of the evangelists as opposed to the early church or even Jesus. Nor do they deny the value of the past. What the past actually was, however, can never be separated from its reception. We cannot arrive at a 'pure' past that was later 'contaminated' or even 'developed'. It doesn't work that way because social memory is not a method. Social memory does not tell us that Jesus quoted (or did not quote) scripture in the way that the evangelists describe, but it helps to explain why the evangelists thought he did. When social memory theory is coupled with anthropology (especially studies in orality), and narratology, as I have tried to do, then it is plausible that the provenance of the quotations resides at the compositional stage, without negating the assumption that Jesus would have known and used the Scriptures in the practice of his religion.

5

Son of Man – Lord of the Temple? Gospel Echoes of Psalm 8 and the Ongoing Christological Challenge

N. T. Wright

Introduction

Richard Hays's recent book, *Echoes of Scripture in the Gospels*, has already been hailed as a masterpiece which, like several of Hays's books, has opened up new vistas of exegetical and theological possibility.[1] I have elsewhere discussed some of the questions it raises, and in the present article I want to develop one point I mentioned there in passing.[2] Hays concentrates on the ways in which the biblical allusions and echoes in all four Gospels indicate that all of them, not only John as has so often been said, understand the Jesus they portray as the living embodiment

1. Richard B. Hays, *Echoes of Scripture in the Gospels* (Waco: Baylor University Press, 2015); see also *The Faith of Jesus Christ: The Narrative Substructure of Galatians 3:1–4:11*, 2nd edn (1983; Grand Rapids: Eerdmans, 2002); *Echoes of Scripture in the Letters of Paul* (New Haven: Yale University Press, 1989); *The Conversion of the Imagination: Paul as Interpreter of Israel's Scriptures* (Grand Rapids: Eerdmans, 2005). I offer these reflections with great respect to John Nolland, and with gratitude and admiration for his sterling contributions to NT scholarship. I am grateful to Dr Max Botner for his help in preparing this paper, and to Dr Michael Bird and Dr Crispin Fletcher-Louis for their comments on an earlier draft (though I have by no means always taken their advice, and they are not responsible for what follows).

2. 'Pictures, Stories, and the Cross: Where Do the Echoes Lead?', *JTI* 11, no. 1 (2017): 53–73.

of Israel's God. I will suggest that we can go further with this than Hays does, but that in order to do so we need to bring into play the question of Jesus and the temple.

As I proceed towards my opening exegetical observations, I note that these involve an initial acceptance of Hays's now well-known view of metalepsis: that a single line quoted from a biblical passage may constitute an invitation to the reader to supply at least some of the larger context, and that when this is done surprising and stimulating results often arise.[3] A measure of scepticism about all this has been common in some circles, but I shall put that to one side for the moment.[4] Like Hays in his recent book, I will allow the data, and the sense which a metaleptic reading might offer, to reflect back on method, rather than vice versa. I want to draw attention to two potential metaleptic echoes from Psalm 8. The use of this Psalm in Paul and Hebrews is well known; one might also discuss Acts 7.56 and 1 Pet. 3.22.[5] As others have shown, Psalm 8 was of considerable significance in Jewish thought both before and after the New Testament.[6] But for this study, I concentrate on Matthew and John.

Matthew 21

I begin with Mt. 21.16. Matthew, unique here among the synoptists, adds to the story of Jesus entering Jerusalem, and driving out the traders from the temple, a note about children singing 'Hosanna to the Son of David!' (21.15). The chief priests and scribes, who have been watching the remarkable things Jesus has been doing, object to this, and Jesus replies

3. See Hays, *Echoes of Scripture in the Letters of Paul*, 20; *Echoes of Scripture in the Gospels*, 11–12.

4. See, e.g., Paul Foster's contention that Hays's approach lacks the necessary criteria for weeding out spurious intertextual proposals ('Echoes without Resonance: Critiquing Certain Aspects of Recent Scholarly Trends in the Study of the Jewish Scriptures in the New Testament', *JSNT* 38 (2015): 96–111). See too R. W. Moberly's article in *JTI* 11, no. 1 (2017): Moberly is not sceptical about metalepsis in general, but warns against its over-use.

5. For Paul, see 1 Cor. 15.27; Eph. 1.22; Phil. 3.21; less obviously but still I think importantly, Rom. 8.18-30 (a point I owe to Dr. Haley Goranson). On the logic of Ps. 8 in Heb. 2 see D. M. Moffitt, *Atonement and the Logic of Resurrection in the Epistle to the Hebrews* (Leiden: Brill, 2011), 120–9. On 1 Pet. 3.22 see e.g. J. H. Elliott, *1 Peter: A New Translation with Introduction and Commentary* (New Haven: Yale University Press, 2000), 687.

6. See, for a start, F. J. Moloney, 'The Re-interpretation of Psalm VIII and the Son of Man Debate', *NTS* 27 (1981): 656–71.

with a reference to Ps. 8.3: 'Out of the mouth of babes and sucklings you have brought praise'.[7] No further comment is made. Jesus leaves the city and, as usual, goes out to Bethany.

The quote is clear, but Matthew's alert reader may already have spotted an echo of an earlier verse from the Psalm.[8] Matthew, again without parallel, speaks of people witnessing the remarkable deeds of Jesus, which he calls *thaumasia* (a New Testament *hapax legomenon*). This echoes the opening and closing of Psalm 8: 'O Lord our Lord, how remarkable (*thaumaston*) is your name in all the earth' (8.1, 9). Mention of that repeated line at once reminds a hearer of the more familiar Psalm echo, that of Ps. 110.1, where YHWH says to 'My Lord', 'sit at my right hand, until I make your enemies your footstool'.[9] Interestingly, when Matthew and Mark quote Psalm 110 they implicitly link it with Psalm 8. Both psalms speak of people being placed underfoot, Psalm 8 referring to 'all things' and Psalm 110 to 'enemies'. The LXX for the phrase in Psalm 8 is *hypokatō tōn podōn autou* whereas in Psalm 110 it is *hupopodion tōn podōn sou*, but Matthew and Mark, quoting Psalm 110, use the wording of Psalm 8 (while Luke reverts to *hupopodion* as in the LXX).[10] A further link between the two Psalms is provided by the mention in both of

7. NT quotations are from *The Kingdom New Testament: A Contemporary Translation* (New York: Harper Collins, 2011); OT quotations from NRSV. As John Nolland points out (*The Gospel of Matthew: A Commentary on the Greek Text* (Grand Rapids: Eerdmans, 2005), 848), Jesus' question, 'Have you never read…?' is echoed at 21.42 where Jesus quotes from Ps. 118.22, with the use of *thaumastē* there echoing *thaumasia* here (and see nn. 8 and 11 below).

8. So already W. D. Davies and D. C. Allison, Jr, *The Gospel according to Saint Matthew* (Edinburgh: T. & T. Clark, 1997), 3:142. Davies and Allison note the wider christological use of this psalm in the NT but not the specific point to be made below. R. T. France, *The Gospel of Matthew* (Grand Rapids: Eerdmans, 2007), 790, notes that *thaumasia* is unique in the NT but not its link with Ps. 8.

9. Quoted in Mt. 22.44 and par., alluded to in 26.64 at the climax of the hearing before Caiaphas. MT Ps. 8.2, 10 reads *yhwh adonēnu*; Ps. 110.1 reads *n'um yhwh laadonai*; LXX 8.2 is *kurios ho kurios hēmōn*, while Ps. 109.1 reads *eipen ho kurios tō kuriō hēmōn*.

10. Mt. 22.24 following Mk 12.36; Lk. 20.42. On the linking of Pss. 8 and 110 in early Christian texts, see David M. Hay, *Glory at the Right Hand: Psalm 110 in Early Christianity* (Nashville: Abingdon Press, 1973; repr. Atlanta: SBL, 1989), 35–7; Richard J. Bauckham, *Jesus and the God of Israel: God Crucified and Other Studies on the New Testament's Christology of Divine Identity* (Grand Rapids: Eerdmans, 2008), 173, 176. Bauckham points out that 'it is *in conjunction with Psalm 110:1* that these other texts [Dan. 7 and Ps. 8] play their principal roles in the New Testament' (173, his emphasis).

'enemies'. In Ps. 110.1-2, explained further in vv. 5-7, these appear to be foreign armies; in Psalm 8, unspecified 'enemies' who will be 'silenced' because of the 'bulwark' founded by what the 'babes and infants' will say. Already, therefore, a case can be made for seeing the quotation of Ps. 8.3 in Matthew 21 not simply as an explanation for the children's excited acclamation but, in company with Psalm 110, as a hint of a coming major theme, including part at least of the explanation for Jesus' action in the temple.

It is worth noting at this point a widespread Jewish tradition which linked Psalm 8, not least the mention of children singing God's praise, to the Exodus, and particularly to the Song of Moses and Miriam in Exod. 15.1-21. This is reflected in many sources, an obvious one being Wis. 10.21, where after the Exodus 'Wisdom opened the mouths of those who were mute, and made the tongues of infants (*glōssas nēpiōn*) speak clearly'. This tradition was developed in rabbinic and other writings from at least the 2nd century onwards.[11] Granted that Matthew, describing an incident at Passover-time, has put into the mouth of Jesus a line from the Psalm which points across to this theme, it seems quite possible that he, too, understands Psalm 8 as (among other things) a celebration of the Exodus. And, granted the main setting of Matthew 21 (Jesus' temple-action and its various explanations), we notice that Exodus 15 celebrates not only the rescue from Egypt but also the prospect of building the sanctuary in Zion (15.17) – a text linked at Qumran to the eschatological temple and the coming Davidic king.[12] It is also important to note that here Jesus uses a Psalm which speaks of praise offered to Israel's God to justify praise offered to himself.[13]

11. See e.g. Davies and Allison, *Matthew*, 3:142, with copious references; also Luz, *Matthew 21–28*, 13, and e.g. W. Horbury, *Messianism among Jews and Christians: Twelve Biblical and Historical Studies* (London: T&T Clark International, 2003), 261, citing Mekhilta, Shirata 1, on Exod. 15.1; Nolland, *Matthew*, 38, 848, pointing out that 'the relevant part of Ex. 15:2 is identical to Ps. 118:14, the psalm to which the children's acclamation relates, which was used in Mt. 21:9 and will be used again in v. 41 [*sic*: 42?] and 23:38 [*sic*: 39?]'.

12. 4Q174, linking Exod. 15 to 2 Sam. 7 and Ps. 2: G. Vermes, *The Complete Dead Sea Scrolls in English* (London: Allen Lane, 1997), 493–944. The Hebrew of Ps. 8.3 says that God has brought 'strength', *'oz*, from the children, echoing Exod. 15.2; but the word was frequently understood to mean, in some sense, 'praise': see the note in R. T. France, *Jesus and the Old Testament* (London: Tyndale Press, 1971), 251–2.

13. So France, *Matthew*, 789, and France, *Jesus and the Old Testament*, 152: 'Unless he is here setting himself in the place of Yahweh, the argument is a *non sequitur*'.

The possibility that Matthew has the whole Psalm in mind, not just the third verse, is further strengthened by exploring another echo, which takes us to the heart of my proposal. The Psalm goes on to raise the question: When I look at your heavens, the work of your fingers, the moon and the stars that you have established, *what are human beings that you are mindful of them, the son of man that you care for him*?[14] It goes on:

> Yet you have made them a little lower than God/the gods
> [or: angels, as LXX; Hebrew *Elohim*][15]
> And crowned them with glory and honour.
> You have given them dominion over the works of your hands;
> You have put all things under their feet… (8.3-6).

A moment's reflection on Matthew, never mind any other early Christian writers, will remind us that he does indeed exploit the idea of a 'Son of Man', first humiliated and then set in authority over all things. Matthew has already emphasized this in ch. 9. In 9.5, paralleled in Mark and Luke, Matthew's Jesus heals the paralysed man 'to let you know that the Son of Man has authority on earth to forgive sins'. Matthew then adds, in v. 6, that the crowds were frightened 'and praised God for giving authority like this to humans'. This is a clear thematic allusion to Psalm 8, though not a verbal one; Matthew's *exousia* is not used in the Psalm, but the question of the *exousia* claimed implicitly by Jesus in his temple-action is raised in Mt. 21.23, shortly after the quote from Psalm 8.[16] Then, to look at the most obvious passage, Matthew frames ch. 26 with just this theme. Unlike Mark or Luke, who cut straight into the plot against Jesus' life, Matthew gives Jesus an opening sentence: 'In two days' time, as you know, it'll be Passover! That's when the son of man will be handed over to be crucified' (26.1). Then, as the fast-paced scene reaches its climax, Jesus answers Caiaphas's (presumably scornful) question by declaring that 'from now on you will see "the son of man sitting at the right hand of the Power, and coming on the clouds of heaven"' (26.64). Matthew is presenting to his

14. Translating the last phrase literally: NRSV has 'mortals that you care for them' with a marginal note about the Hebrew original.

15. On the (relatively unimportant) distinction here between God and angels see J. R. Middleton, *The Liberating Image: The* Imago Dei *in Genesis 1* (Grand Rapids: Brazos, 2005), 58–60.

16. The word *exousia* occurs four times in Mt. 21.23-27, looking ahead to 28.18. The other obvious echo is Dan. 7.14, where (LXX, not Theodotion) the 'one like a Son of Man' receives *exousia*. The trouble with invoking Dan. 7 is that it can then drown out other echoes.

readers a 'Son of Man' who is betrayed and will be crucified, but who will then be vindicated, exalted, so that, as in 28.18, matching 9.6, he is given 'all authority in heaven and on earth'. This narrative has exactly the same trajectory as the small story of 'the Son of Man' in Psalm 8 and indeed Daniel 7. I suggest that the metaleptic echo in ch. 21 is already pointing in this direction.

The context of these passages offers a further echo and thereby a further interpretative clue. In ch. 21, the reference to Psalm 8 is part of Jesus' explanation of his violent action in the temple, or at least an oblique scriptural vindication of the acclamation he is receiving because of it.[17] In Mt. 24.2, Jesus declares that the temple will be destroyed (*kataluthēnai*). In ch. 26, his statement to Caiaphas (26.64) is part of his answer to the earlier charge (26.61; repeated at 27.40, again with a sneer, by the mockers at the cross), that Jesus had been threatening to destroy (*katalusai*) the temple and build it again in three days. Confrontation with the authorities, focused on suspicions about Jesus and the temple, provides a further resonance with Psalm 8 at the point mentioned a moment ago. In Psalm 8, the 'babes and sucklings' give perfect praise, 'because of your enemies' – which in Matthew's context would obviously be the temple and the chief priests – and the object of this is 'to silence the enemy and the avenger' (Ps. 8.3). 'Silence' translates the Hebrew *lehashbith*, which the LXX renders as *katalusai*, 'destroy', the same verb that is used in Matthew in relation to the Temple's imminent destruction. It looks as though language and themes from the Psalm have been woven surreptitiously into Matthew's account of Jesus' temple-action. Matthew's Jesus is indeed warning of the temple's downfall, and connecting that with his own vindication.

How might we explain this? And what contribution, however small, might the echo of Psalm 8 make towards such an explanation? There are three interlocking answers, and we must look briefly at each of them. Some see these as mutually exclusive alternatives; I think they are complementary.

The obvious answer from Matthew's Gospel as a whole, and particularly chs 21 and 22, is that Jesus is presented as the royal, Davidic Messiah; that this is reflected in the echo of Psalm 8; and that this

17. Some (e.g. U. Luz, *Matthew 21–28* (Minneapolis: Fortress Press, 2005), 13; earlier, e.g. B. Lindars, *New Testament Apologetic* (London: SCM Press, 1961), 166) have seen the unexpected 'children' in Mt. 21.16 as a reference back to the *nēpioi* to whom divine revelation is given in Mt. 11.25. That seems quite a stretch, though it is possible that Mt. 11.25, too, is a distant echo of Ps. 8.

sets Jesus in an adversarial relation with the temple and its hierarchy, expressed in dramatic symbol in his temple-action. The Davidic theme is clear all through. Matthew quotes the royal prophecy from Zechariah;[18] the procession with palm branches recalls the incipiently royal entry-processions of the Maccabees;[19] the crowds, and then the children, are shouting out 'Hosanna to the Son of David!';[20] the presence of the blind and the lame in the temple seems a deliberate and healing echo of David's decree in 2 Sam. 5.8;[21] Jesus' answer to the question about authority evokes the baptism of John, normally seen as a royal event;[22] the parable of the wicked tenants focuses on the owner's son, normally taken as messianic;[23] and the final dialogue in the sequence focuses on Ps. 110.1, an explicit evocation (not a denial, as is sometimes thought) of David and his son.[24] To this immediate context we can add the question of Caiaphas, whether Jesus is 'the Messiah, God's Son'; the charge before Pilate; the 'royal' overtones in the mocking; and the 'title' on the cross.[25] We need only add the worldwide authority claimed by the risen Jesus in Matthew 28, echoing the royal promises in the Psalms, Isaiah and (arguably) Daniel, and the picture is complete.[26] Matthew is not subtle. He sees Jesus as the Davidic Messiah. If we detect an allusion in his use of Psalm 8 to the humiliation and exaltation of 'the son of man', the most natural assumption is that Matthew is seeing that as a coded messianic reference.[27]

18. Zech. 9.9, cited in Mt. 21.5.

19. Both of Judas Maccabeus (2 Macc. 10.7) and later of Simon Maccabeus (1 Macc. 13.51).

20. 21.9, 15.

21. 21.14; this interpretation (as e.g. D. J. Harrington, *The Gospel of Matthew* (Collegeville: Liturgical Press, 1991), 295) is mentioned as an option by Davies and Allison, *Matthew*, 3:140; but see the cautionary note in Luz, *Matthew*, 3:13. France, *Matthew*, 788 points out the implied contrast between Jesus and David.

22. 21.23-27; cf. 3.17 (with 16.16).

23. 21.33-46.

24. 22.41-46; see Davies and Allison, *Matthew*, 3:254: 'neither the title nor its content is rejected or denigrated'.

25. 26.63; 27.11; 27.28-29, 42-43 ('He is the King of Israel'); 27.37.

26. Mt. 28.18; cf. e.g. Ps. 2.7-11; Isa. 11.1-10; Dan. 7.13-14.

27. This is taken for granted by e.g. Moloney, 'The Re-interpretation of Psalm VIII', 658: '[the children] have properly understood the messianic role of Jesus'. Moloney's article, though dated in some respects, is still important, not least for his Targumic explorations.

This is supported by the well-known Jewish interpretation of Psalm 8 in which, through its obvious echoes of Gen. 1.26-28, it is seen as a statement of kingly authority. This is simply assumed by many scholars.[28] Evidence sometimes cited includes *4 Ezra* 6.53 ('over all these you placed Adam, as ruler over all the works that you had made'); *2 En.* 30.12 ('I assigned him to be a king, to reign [over] the earth, [and] to have my wisdom'); and Philo, *Opif. Mun.* 136-50, especially 148:

> Quite excellently does Moses ascribe the bestowal of names also to the first man: for this is the business of wisdom and royalty (*sophias gar kai basileias to ergon*), and the first man was wise with a wisdom learned from and taught by Wisdom's own lips, for he was made by divine hands; he was, moreover, a king (*kai proseti basileus*), and it befits a ruler to bestow titles on his several subordinates.

We may also recall Wis. 10.2, where God gives Adam strength to rule all things (*kratēsai pantōn*); Sir. 49.16, where Adam is 'above every other created being', higher even than Shem and Seth who are 'glorified' (*edoxasthēsan*); *Jub.* 2.14, which more or less repeats Gen. 1.28; and the *Apoc. Mos.* 24.4, which speaks to Adam, after the fall, of the animals over which he had ruled. This catena is not massive, but it covers quite a spectrum of Jewish writings, and reveals a basic assumption that the first man is some kind of a king; or, to put it the other way round, that the true king will be in some sense the true Adam. This is strongly supported by the wider evidence from the Near Eastern world, and from Hellenistic philosophy.[29]

28. E.g. M. A. Fishbane, 'The Sacred Center: The Symbolic Structure of the Bible', in *Texts and Responses: Studies Presented to Nahum N. Glatzer on the Occasion of his Seventieth Birthday by his Students*, ed. M. A. Fishbane and P. R. Flohr (Leiden: Brill, 1975), 6–27, at 20 n. 34; A. Y. Collins and J. J. Collins, *King and Messiah as Son of God: Divine, Human and Angelic Messianic Figures in Biblical and Related Literature* (Grand Rapids: Eerdmans, 2008), 110; R. Middleton, *A New Heaven and a New Earth: Reclaiming Biblical Eschatology* (Grand Rapids: Baker Academic, 2014), 141; J. W. Jipp, *Christ Is King: Paul's Royal Ideology* (Minneapolis: Fortress Press, 2015), 104–6, citing copious primary and secondary sources. For rabbinic links between Ps. 8 and Gen. 2.19-20 see G. A. Anderson, 'The Exaltation of Adam and the Fall of Satan', in *Literature on Adam and Eve: Collected Essays*, ed. G. Anderson, M. Stone and J. Tromp (Leiden: Brill, 1997), 83–110, at 96.

29. For details see e.g. J. Marcus, 'Son of Man as Son of Adam', *RB* 110 (2003): 38–61, 370–86, e.g. 59 n. 82, with copious references; M. A. Fishbane, 'The Sacred Center: The Symbolic Structure of the Bible', in *Cult and Cosmos: Tilting Toward a Temple-Centered Theology*, ed. L. M. Morales (Leuven: Peeters, 2014), 402, citing the

How justified are we then in taking Psalm 8 as a whole, metaleptically referred to in Matthew 21, as a reference to Jesus as the true King, the Davidic Messiah? The link in thought might work like this:

1. Matthew 21 as a whole is about the kingship of Jesus, displayed in his dramatic action which claims authority over the temple and portends its doom;
2. when challenged, Jesus quotes Psalm 8;
3. Psalm 8 offers a poetic restatement of the human vocation to sovereignty as in Genesis 1 and 2 (especially 1);
4. that original human vocation was seen by some Jewish writers as explicitly 'royal';
5. elsewhere in Matthew 21 and 22 Jesus explains his temple-action in cryptic but converging language about his messianic vocation;
6. Matthew's denouement in chs 26 to 28 concerns the 'Son of Man' who is humiliated and killed but then exalted to a position of cosmic authority;
7. meanwhile the temple and its authorities are warned of imminent judgement.

It looks as though Matthew at least is trying to say, through this veiled but powerful echo, that in Jesus' temple-action we are to see the outworking of his vocation as Davidic Messiah, pointing forward both to his own humiliating death and to his vindication over his 'enemies', in this case the present temple (which will be 'destroyed') and its ruling authorities.

For some, the phrase 'Son of Man' would by itself be enough to sustain the weight of this argument, particularly because of Daniel 7. There, too, a strong case can be made for saying that in the 1st century at least the 'one like a Son of Man' in Dan. 7.13 was seen by some as a royal Messiah. That, at any rate, is the interpretation given by *4 Ezra* 11–12, explicitly

Enuma Elish and the Akinu festival; see too the Egyptian evidence in *New Documents* 9.15. From the Hellenistic world see e.g. Plutarch, *Princ. iner.* 780e5-f2. Once we add in wider biblical themes the royal and/or priestly echoes of Dan. 7 come naturally to mind. Among older literature see e.g. H. G. May, 'The King in the Garden of Eden: A Study of Ezekiel 28:12-19', esp. 170f., citing Bentzen, Mowinckel and Ringgren, saying that 'the royal terminology is evident and a kingly First Man at least implicit', referring to the king putting all his enemies under his feet in 2 Sam. 22.39 and 1 Kgs 5.3, and suggesting that Ps. 8 'may reflect an earlier form of the creation story than that now found in Gen. 1'; W. Brueggemann, 'From Dust to Kingship', *ZAW* 84 (1972): 1–18, esp. 12 (though focusing on Gen. 2, not on Gen. 1 and its echo in Ps. 8).

described as a fresh interpretation of Daniel (12.11-12) and focused on the 'lion' who is the coming Davidic Messiah (12.32). It is usual here as well to point out that Josephus's silence in interpreting Daniel 7, corresponding to his sudden coyness over the end of the vision of the statue in Daniel 2, indicates well enough that he sees both passages as indicating a coming Messiah.[30] When we then add Daniel 7 to the picture already built up, and see it quoted, along with Psalm 110, in Jesus' answer to Caiaphas in Mt. 26.64 – as part of the answer to a charge about conspiring against the temple! – the circle appears complete. Psalm 8 speaks of God overthrowing his 'enemies', and of the exaltation of 'the Son of Man'; Jesus, faced with the challenge of the chief priests and scribes in Matthew 21 and of Caiaphas in Matthew 26, quotes Psalm 8 to the first and Psalm 110 and Daniel 7 – both closely linked with Psalm 8 – to the second. Matthew's Jesus claims to be the Davidic Messiah who, as heir to David and Solomon, has authority over the temple. He will be exalted, while, according to 24.2, the temple will be overthrown.[31]

The circle appears complete; but perhaps appearances deceive. An alternative account of 'Son of Man' in Daniel, and by implication in Psalm 8, would shift the emphasis from a Davidic Messiah to a coming High Priest. Assuming that the phrase 'son of man' in the Second Temple world would carry at least a reference back to Adam, we note that there are certain texts in which Adam is seen not, or not only, as a king, but as a priest. It has frequently been pointed out that this emerges from, for instance, *Jub.* 3.26-27 (Adam offering sweet-smelling sacrifices), the *LAE [=Apoc. Mos.]* 29.3-6 (Adam taking spices from Eden with him at the expulsion so he can thereafter offer them to God) and several rabbinic sources.[32] The 1st-century *Liber Antiquitatum Biblicarum*, conscious of Adam's failure and the disasters which followed, holds back from making him a priest, but in doing so bears witness to a strong tradition which pointed in that direction.[33] In recent years the prime mover in

30. See the discussions in N. T. Wright, *The New Testament and the People of God* (London: SPCK, 1992), 312–17, and *Paul and the Faithfulness of God* (London: SPCK, 2013), 116f., 130f., 293. Josephus's exposition of Dan. 2 is at *Ant.* 10.206-9; the telling omission of what might have been an exposition of Dan. 7 is after 10.263.

31. The interpretation of Mt. 24, especially vv. 29-35, is beyond the scope of this paper. See N. T. Wright, *Jesus and the Victory of God* (London: SPCK, 1996), Chapter 8.

32. See the important article of C. T. R. Hayward, 'The Figure of Adam in Pseudo-Philo's Biblical Antiquities', *JSJ* 23 (1992): 1–20, here at 7.

33. Ibid., 19: *LAB* attacks the tradition, but thereby bears witness to its wide dissemination.

advocating a 'priestly' interpretation of Adam, and of 'the Son of Man', is Crispin Fletcher-Louis, whose case includes particularly a reading of the Hebrew version of Sir. 49.16 and a combined reading of the Day of Atonement liturgy of Leviticus 16 and the exaltation of 'one like a son of man' in Daniel 7. The 'son of man' is therefore the true Aaronic priest.[34] The jury is still out on this; but I find the most convincing argument in this direction to be the narrative arc from Genesis 1 to Exodus 40: if the tabernacle is the *microcosmos*, the small new working model of creation, against the day when Israel's God will complete the project and flood the whole world with his glory (Num. 14.21), then Aaron takes the place within this little world that was occupied by Adam and Eve in the garden.[35] This then, for me, makes sense of the possible link of Adam and the high priest in Sirach, rather than the other way round.

I do notice, however, that the key texts which stress Adam's role as priest come from periods either when there was no reigning king in Judaea or (since we cannot be sure of dates) only one that the writers might well disapprove of, such as the Hasmonaeans or Herodians. At such a time, and also because the writers might have been priests themselves, there may have been pressure to emphasize potential 'priestly' meanings of key texts and to downplay 'royal' ones. It is, of course, hard to say; and in many ways it does not matter so much for the interpretation of the New Testament, since the most important text for early Christology, Psalm 110, draws together priesthood and kingship. It is, of course, a subversive priesthood, 'after the order of Melchizedek': an originally Jerusalem-based priesthood, still powerfully evoked both in Genesis and in the Psalter.[36] It was a priesthood to which even Abraham owed allegiance, as the Letter to the Hebrews insists.[37]

The first option, then, is that Matthew is giving 'Son of Man' a royal connotation; the second, that he is understanding a priestly one. I do not regard these as mutually exclusive; and the use of Psalm 110 in the passage which concludes the sequence offers a way of combining them.

34. See, as the most recent example of this thesis (but not yet the end of the story), C. Fletcher-Louis, *Jesus Monotheism* (Eugene, OR: Cascade Books, 2015), with full bibliography of earlier studies. Fletcher-Louis's detailed arguments demand far more engagement than is possible here; as will become apparent, I believe his emphasis can and should be contained within a larger picture.

35. See e.g. L. M. Morales, *Who Shall Ascend the Mountain of the Lord? A Biblical Theology of the Book of Leviticus* (Downers Grove: InterVarsity Press, 2015), 39.

36. Gen. 14.17-20; Ps. 110.4.

37. Heb. 7.1-10.

But there is a third possibility for interpreting this incident and perhaps the phrase 'son of man'. If Matthew's Jesus is the 'Emmanuel',[38] he is already in person the one who *embodies* the reality to which the temple had all along pointed. That is why he performs an acted symbol of the destruction of the temple: not (as has been suggested by many, Jews as well as Christians) because the temple and its cult were primitive, representing an earlier stage of a putative religious evolution, but because the reality has appeared and the signpost is no longer necessary. The sense this makes is not one of comparative styles of religion, but of a *narrative* in which the divine purposes for creation's rescue and restoration, focused on a new Passover and new Exodus, were drawn together in the story of the archetypal human being who, it turned out, was also 'God with us'. This seems to me profoundly Matthaean, though obviously not unique to him.

From this quick survey of quotations, allusions and echoes to Psalm 8, in particular relation to Matthew 21, we might take a leaf out of Matthew 9 and apply it to the matter now in hand. In Matthew 9, Jesus, as Son of Man, is Lord of the Sabbath. Here in Matthew 21, I suggest, the echoes awoken by Psalm 8 indicate that he is also Lord of the temple. It is a commonplace of Jewish studies that the Sabbath is to time what the temple is to space. Jesus appears to be claiming authority over both, to be *embodying* both. He is bringing the long-awaited new day, the inauguration of God's reign. He, the Emmanuel, is now the place where heaven and earth come together at last.

Before asking where all this might lead us in terms of Christology and related issues, I turn to my second main text.

John 2

As is well known, the story of Jesus' temple-action, though found in the Synoptics at the close of his public career, is in John set very near the start, in ch. 2.13-22. So far as I can discover, no commentator has noticed that here, too, there is an echo of Psalm 8, albeit a more distant one. Jesus finds in the temple people selling oxen and sheep (*boas kai probata*), and also doves, and also the money-changes at their tables. Making a whip of cords, he drives them all (*pantas*) out of the temple, *ta te probata kai tous boas*, 'both the sheep and the oxen'. He overturns the tables and pours out the coins, and tells the dove-sellers to stop making 'my Father's house' a market-place.

38. 1.23; cf. 'I am with you' at 28.20.

The first fascinating thing here is that John, unlike any of the Synoptists, spells out twice which animals it is that Jesus is driving out, switching the order of the reference in the previous verse so that it corresponds exactly to Psalm 8, *ta probata kai tous boas*. Continuing the previous quotation from the Psalm,

> You have put all things under their feet:
> All sheep and oxen (*probata kai boas pasas*),
> Even the beasts of the field
> The birds of the air…

I would not wish to overplay this hand by suggesting that John has these psalmic birds in mind with his line about the dove-sellers, though with John it is hard to set limits. But I do think that the sheep and oxen, and the switching of the order to echo the Psalm, and the fact that this echo of Psalm 8 is placed, like that in Matthew, in relation to Jesus' action in the temple, ought to be taken into account in understanding John 2 and the temple-Christology to which it points. This might explain the surprising reference to oxen.[39] It would render unnecessary the various forced allegorical interpretations of the sheep and oxen that have been offered from time to time.[40] It would also help to explain the odd construction with 'all' (*pantas*): this echoes the repeated root in Psalm 8 (v. 7: you put all things [*panta*] under his feet; v. 8: all sheep and oxen [*probata kai boas pantas*]).[41] In other words, I suggest that some of the puzzles that have

39. J. Klawans, *Purity, Sacrifice and the Temple: Symbolism and Supersessionism in the Study of Ancient Judaism* (Oxford: OUP, 2006), 224, suggests that the idea of oxen being sold in the Temple is 'rather unlikely', citing S. Safrai, *Pilgrimage at the Time of the Second Temple* [in Hebrew] (Jerusalem: Akademon, 1985), 147; see too E. P. Sanders, *Judaism: Practice and Belief 63 BCE–66 CE* (London: SCM Press, 1992), 87–8. Sanders's arguments are important, though perhaps magnified by his polemic at this point against J. Jeremias. B. Lindars, *The Gospel of John* (Edinburgh: Oliphants, 1972), 138, cites Epstein, 'The Historicity of the Gospel Account of the Cleansing of the Temple', *ZNW* 55 (1964): 42–58, as arguing that the inclusion of oxen was an innovation by Caiaphas.

40. E.g. that Jesus was leading out his sheep (cf. 10.1); these and others noted by C. S. Keener, *The Gospel of John: A Commentary* (Peabody: Hendriksen, 2003), 521 n. 268.

41. See e.g. the debate noted in B. D. Chilton, '*[hōs] phragellion ek skoiniōn* (John 2.15)', in *Templum Amicitiae: Essays on the Second Temple presented to Ernst Bammel*, ed. W. Horbury (Sheffield: JSOT Press, 1991), 330–44, at 331–3. J. B. Lightfoot, in the recently discovered commentary, suggests that *pantas* refers to all the sellers, with *ta te probata* indicating '*and* the sheep…' (J. B. Lightfoot,

been observed in this text are best explained by detecting here another echo, albeit a fainter one, of Psalm 8 and of the 'Son of Man' in particular. And this gives added force to the proposal which I see emerging out of Matthew: that Jesus' claim to fulfil the son-of-man prophecies of Psalm 8 (linked with Psalm 110) and Daniel 7 lies behind his temple-action, seen as a coded prophetic warning of imminent destruction, and also points to the underlying explanation, in this case that Jesus himself is the true temple towards which the present Jerusalem temple is simply an advance signpost.

The larger context all points in this direction. John's temple-Christology is evident from the Prologue itself, with Jesus as the true *skēnē* where the divine glory is at last revealed. He, in other words, is the equivalent of the tabernacle at the end of Exodus, so that Jn 1.1-18 gives the christological version of the narrative arc from Genesis 1 to Exodus 40. This finds dramatic expression at the end of ch. 1, where Nathanael is assured that he will 'see heaven opened, and God's angels going up and down upon the son of man' (1.51). Like Jacob's ladder in Gen. 28.10-22, obviously echoed here, this is to be seen as a temple-image, with heaven and earth coming together 'upon the son of man'. As in 1.14, the human one is not simply the image at the heart of the new temple; he *is* the new temple in person, the place where and the means by which heaven and earth are now joined together.[42] This point is then glimpsed from another angle in the wedding at Cana (2.1-11), symbolizing the marriage of heaven and earth and the transformation of the Jewish cult (v. 6). And it then emerges in startling fashion as Jesus explains his temple-action: 'Destroy (*lysate*) this temple, and I'll raise it up in three days' (2.19); here Jesus says explicitly what he is accused of saying in Matthew and Mark. John explains: 'he was speaking about the "temple" of his body' (2.21). All these hints go together: Jesus, the Word made flesh, is the true tabernacle or temple, the one through whom heaven and earth are joined at last. And this will be put into decisive operation through his death and resurrection. He will act out, in his own death and resurrection, the humiliation and exaltation of the 'Son of Man' spoken of in Psalm 8.

The Gospel of St John: A Newly Discovered Commentary, ed. B. Witherington and T. D. Still (Downers Grove: InterVarsity Press, 2015), 122; so too C. K. Barrett, *The Gospel according to St. John: An Introduction with Commentary and Notes on the Greek Text*, 2nd edn (London: SPCK, 1978 (1955), 197–8, pointing out that many have seen the extra phrase *ta te probata kai tous boas* as an editorial addition.

42. Hays, *Echoes of Scripture in the Gospels*, 312–13, makes this clear, but without reference to Ps. 8.

For John, as for Matthew, this is seen as the vocation of the royal Messiah. Jesus is hailed by John the Baptist as 'the lamb of God' (1.29, 36); but the word that then goes around between Andrew and Simon, and between Philip and Nathanael, is that Jesus is Israel's Messiah, Israel's King, as foretold in Scripture (1.41, 45, 49). This opens a sequence of Johannine claims that Jesus is Israel's Messiah, claims which culminate in the sharp debate with Pilate and the 'title' on the cross.[43] There are of course many more obvious scriptural echoes in the temple-scene, not least Psalm 69 in 2.17. This is certainly one of the Scriptures to which John refers when he says that after Jesus' resurrection 'they believed the scripture' and the word that he had spoken. But John, like Matthew, seems to want us to have Psalm 8 in the mix as well, providing the implicit narrative of the humiliation and exaltation of the Son of Man and, with that, the further echo of Genesis 1 to go with the Prologue.

The implications of all this are clear enough in John. Jesus is himself the ultimate reality; the Jerusalem temple is indeed 'my father's house' but he is the Father's Son. Thus John is not, to use Klawan's term, 'antitemple'; nor does he have an anti-cultic 'attitude'.[44] He sees the temple as the God-given forward pointer to the new (but always intended) reality now unveiled in the Messiah.[45] As Christopher Rowland takes up the story from the end of John 1:

> The manifestation of divine gory exemplified by the sign at Cana in Galilee means that the locus of that divine glory is now focused pre-eminently, and perhaps exclusively, in the Word become flesh and in the demonstration of glory in the lifting up of Jesus on the cross (Jn 3.14; 12.32-33). As Jesus tells the Samaritan woman, Gerizim and Zion have had their day. True worship is worship in spirit and in truth (Jn 4.20-24). The Temple has to take second place to this definitive manifestation of divine glory.[46]

43. Jn 18.33-37 on Jesus' kingship; 19.3, 12, 14, 15, 19, 21-22. I regard the discussion about Jesus' Davidic ancestry in Jn 7.40-44 as Johannine irony, assuming his readers know the synoptic traditions of Jesus' birth at Bethlehem (so e.g. Barrett, *John*, 330).

44. See J. Klawans, *Purity, Sacrifice, and the Temple: Symbolism and Supersessionism in the Study of Ancient Judaism* (Oxford: OUP, 2006), 241–3.

45. On all this, see esp. G. K. Beale, *The Temple and the Church's Mission* (Downers Grove: InterVarsity Press, 2004).

46. C. C. Rowland, 'The Temple in the New Testament', in *Temple and Worship in Biblical Israel*, ed. J. Day (London: T&T Clark International, 2007), 469–83, at 472.

And for John at least the all-important connection seems to be the affirmation that Jesus is thus in some sense challenging or upstaging the temple precisely in his identity as 'Son of Man', the Messiah who perfectly expresses the human vocation as in Genesis 1 or Psalm 8. Caiaphas, saying more than he knew in Jn 11.48, warned that if Jesus went on doing what he was doing it might mean the end of both temple and nation, and that Jesus must therefore die instead of the nation (11.50) – which John (11.51-52) interprets as a true prophecy. But this is not a new point. John's whole Gospel is as much about temple as about people, claiming Jesus as the true 'tabernacle', the place where the divine glory has at last come to dwell in fulfilment of scriptural promises. And this extraordinary and far-reaching claim – a claim all but ignored in most New Testament theological writing over the last 200 years, a point to which I shall return – is to be made good through a *narrative*, a real-life story. The narrative in question is the *sequential story* in which the truly human one, the 'man' and 'Son of Man' of Psalm 8, is first humiliated and then exalted. The 'human one' of Psalm 8 obviously corresponds to the image-bearing human of Genesis 1, again strongly echoed in the Johannine Prologue. John is saying, among many other things but centrally among those other things, that the God of Israel is now made known, in the eschatological climax to which both temple and Scripture had pointed all along, in and as this God-bearing, God-imaging human called Jesus of Nazareth, Israel's Messiah, and that this makes the sense it makes not statically, as though in a tableau, but through the story of his humiliation and exaltation. John 2, in other words, is reinforcing what the end of John 1 had proposed in striking symbolic terms: we are to hear the story of the truly human one and to see it, exactly in line with the Prologue, as the story of the true, or ultimate, temple. The Johannine Son of Man, having claimed authority over the Sabbath, is Lord also of the temple.[47]

Here, then, are my two pieces of evidence: echoes of Psalm 8 in Matthew 21 and John 2, and both in connection with Jesus' messianic authority and his encoded warning against the temple. I am not of course suggesting that the reference I detect in both passages to Psalm 8 as concerning the humiliation and exaltation of the Son of Man in relation to the temple becomes the key to unlock all exegetical doors. But I think what we have seen raises questions that are worth following up. Along with the more obvious passages like Psalms 110 and 118, and Daniel 7, all of which have obvious links with Psalm 8, Psalm 8 itself should be given greater weight than usual as forming part of the very early christological

47. On Jesus and the Sabbath in John see e.g. 5.1-18, 27; 9.1-17.

reflection – so early that though it has left echoes it seems to have taken a step back and been squeezed out of more regular arguments. If I am right in detecting these echoes, it might appear that Psalm 8 was part of the very early Christian reflection on the meaning of Jesus' temple-action; and, since that action was seen by all the evangelists as decisive for understanding what Jesus was all about, the Psalm must be considered central to early Christology. One could suggest, of course, that Matthew and John have introduced it into a tradition where it was previously unknown. But the cryptic nature of the echo in both cases (along with the use of the Psalm in the rest of the New Testament) suggests rather that it was there earlier on and, being taken for granted, lost emphasis in the retelling. I am not much enamoured of hypothetical tradition-history, but there may be questions there still worth exploring. It may well be that others, contemplating the same evidence, will come up with different proposals to explain why this quiet but persistent hint should have appeared in the first place and why, having appeared, it should have stayed shyly in the background.

Concluding Reflections

All this raises wider issues, similar to those now evident in a range of writing which is rolling back an older tide and insisting that a Christology of 'divine identity' (as Richard Bauckham calls it)[48] is to be found not only in John and Hebrews but in the Synoptics as well. The combination of Jesus' temple-action and the explanatory use of Psalm 8 has something to add here, reinforcing the conclusions of Hays and others but offering a different dimension. Hays makes little of the temple, except when discussing John. Bauckham and Hurtado do not include it, or not in the way I think we should. But Mark opens his Gospel with two biblical quotations (Malachi and Isaiah) which speak explicitly, in their contexts, of the return of YHWH to Zion (Mal. 3.1; Isa. 40.3).[49] These are not what we think of as *messianic* predictions; they are about Israel's God coming back to the temple in power and visible glory. Mark, like John, is inviting us to see these predictions fulfilled in Jesus. But the Second-Temple

48. Bauckham, *Jesus and the God of Israel*, 18–59.

49. See Joel Marcus, *The Way of The Lord: Christological Exegesis of the Old Testament in the Gospel of Mark* (Louisville: Westminster John Knox Press, 1992), 12–47; Rikki E. Watts, *Isaiah's New Exodus in Mark* (Grand Rapids: Baker Academic, 2000; repr. WUNT 2/88 (Tübingen: Mohr Siebeck, 1997)), 53–90. For Hays's own discussion see *Echoes of Scripture in the Gospels*, 20–4.

question, faced with these prophecies, was: what will it look like when he does that? Will it be cloud and fire, a throne-chariot with whirling wheels, or what? The four Gospels answer: the revelation of the divine glory has been given, in and as *a human being*, the ultimate human of Genesis 1 and Psalm 8, Israel's representative, the Messiah. And this glory is revealed not in a static vision but in a *story*: the story of the humiliation and exaltation of the Son of Man and the overthrow and replacement of the temple. The Son of Man is Lord also of the temple.

John is the most explicit about how and why this makes sense, with his reprise of Genesis 1 and with Jesus as simultaneously the image-bearer (Jn 1.14 corresponds, within the Prologue, to vv. 26-28 within Genesis 1) and the ultimate tabernacle. Paul and the others add their own material. But Matthew and John, linking Psalm 8 with Jesus' challenge to the Jerusalem temple, seem to be saying that the humiliation and exaltation of the 'Son of Man' – his joining earth and heaven, perhaps – is the way to understand how it is that the God of Israel is appearing in paradoxical power and glory to accomplish the promised redemption. Jesus as temple; Jesus as Adam; the story of Adam as a descent followed by exaltation: I do not think that anyone prior to Jesus of Nazareth had put these elements of biblical narrative together in this fashion. But when Jesus' first followers, 'reading backwards', followed the biblical hints Jesus himself had given in deed and word, these great eschatological themes were ready to hand.

Jewish writers from early days to the present have seen the later christological formulae as unJewish, and they have a point. Some Christian theologians have seemed quite happy about this. But this does not mean that the earliest ways of speaking of Jesus, combining the narratives of temple and Adam, were unJewish. Far from it. Arguably, trying to do Christology without reference to those underlying narratives was bound to give hostages to fortune. Perhaps the exegete has, despite the common prejudice, something new to say to the systematic theologian.

Look at it like this. According to the received critical orthodoxy since at least Harnack – in fact, going back a long way behind him, but he was responsible for summing it up so clearly and launching it upon the 20th century – the New Testament was innocent of Trinitarian theology, and it was only when the early church forgot its original simplicity and went in for complex Greek philosophy that such ideas started to emerge, thereby falsifying an original faith which would have been shocked by such a distortion, or at least dilution, of basic monotheism.[50]

50. Adolf von Harnack, *History of Dogma*, trans. Neil Buchanan, 7 vols (London: Williams & Norgate, 1984–1989), 1:43–50.

At a superficial level Harnack was obviously right. Technical terms like 'substance', 'nature' and 'person' are not found in the first Christian century, or not (at least) in their later sense. But Harnack's view has bred a reaction in our own day, namely, that the 4th and 5th centuries did indeed develop the Trinitarian dogmas as we know them, *and that this was a right and proper development* to which the first Christians pointed forwards, if at all, in a semi-coherent, arm-waving fashion, seeing through a glass darkly and creating 'puzzles' for those who came after.[51] The New Testament, on this view, gave advance signposts towards later orthodoxy, but it is to the Fathers that we should look to see, in effect, what the early Christians had struggled to express with primitive and inadequate equipment. This view has picked up steam, I think, from the frustration of some systematicians with those exegetes who seem, from the theologians' point of view, stuck in a kind of reductionist historicism.[52]

A healthy corrective to all this can be found in a fresh christological focus on Jesus' temple-actions and temple-sayings, *combined with his Adam-actions and -sayings*; exactly the focus, in other words, of Matthew 21 and John 2. Jesus receives messianic acclamation and interprets it in terms of the mighty acts of Israel's God expressed through the humiliation and exaltation of the Son of Man. He embodies the divine Word and reveals the long-awaited divine Glory precisely through his human descent and his elevation to world sovereignty. As I said a moment ago, the untapped source of New Testament Christology is the expectation of YHWH returning to the temple.[53] The scriptural narratives of Genesis, Exodus, the Psalms and Isaiah – to look no further – provide a more than adequate account of how a Second-Temple Jew might hold a framework of thought within which it might make sense to see the returning divine glory in and as a human being, specifically the Messiah or the high priest.

51. This is how, for instance, I read W. Hill, *Paul and the Trinity: Persons, Relations, and the Pauline Letters* (Grand Rapids: Eerdmans, 2015); and see even Hays, *Echoes of Scripture in the Gospels*, 78, 189, speaking of 'puzzles' left – or even created! – by the NT writers which the later Fathers had to 'solve'.

52. I detect this reaction in the early pages of E. Radner, *Time and the Word: Figural Reading of the Christian Scriptures* (Grand Rapids: Eerdmans, 2016). Part of the problem there is methodological: exegetes are trained at least by implication to think that the only proper way to argue is by induction, while systematicians are trained to work by deduction. Each shakes its head sorrowfully at the other, neither realizing that *abduction* is different from both of those, and is in fact the best way to go – in fact, is always what really happens! – in both exegesis and systematics. But I think it goes a lot deeper as well.

53. See, e.g., N. T. Wright, *Jesus and the Victory of God* (London: SPCK, 1996), 612–53; *Paul and the Faithfulness of God* (London: SPCK, 2013), 644–56.

I am not saying that any pre-Christian Jews really did think like this; merely that we have here a framework, quite different from later patristic frameworks, within which the early Christians were able to explore their central beliefs. The rich, contoured and layered categories of earliest Christology were later flattened out into the categories of 'divinity' and 'humanity'. Those bare and static categories were always, arguably, attempts to put the wind of biblical narrative into the bottle of philosophically driven abstractions.

It is true (in other words) that the later technical language is missing from the New Testament. But this is not because the early Christians did not believe, in their own terms, pretty much what the later theologians worked their way round to saying. They did believe it – and they expressed it in concepts which, so far as I can see, were much less likely to result in giving hostages to fortune, much less likely to make the whole thing look like a confidence trick, much less in danger of being accused of trying to have one's theological cake and eat it. Harnack was right to say that the technical language was a later development, but wrong to suppose that the reality to which that language intended to refer was absent from early Christian reflection. The newer orthodoxy is right to affirm the positive relation between earliest Christian belief and Chalcedonian Christology, but wrong to suppose that the former consisted of fuzzy ill-formed early expressions and the latter of clear, untroubled truth. The difficulty is, I think, that from the 4th century onwards the Fathers, like many New Testament scholars until recently, seem to have ignored the tabernacle and the temple, on the one hand, and, on the other, the resources like Psalm 8 which offered the story of Adam as the vital interpretative grid. The words 'divinity' and 'humanity' are, at best, one-dimensional signposts pointing back to that three-dimensional reality. The early Fathers were trying to reconstruct in their own terms something the early Christians had done, far more easily and with far less ambiguity, in *their* own terms.

It is as though a generation, a thousand years from now, were to discover a box of piano music but, because of the spoiling of the planet, were unable to build pianos any more. They might succeed in making, out of the wrong materials, instruments that would produce a recognizable version of the music, though without the intended subtlety and resonance. The New Testament scholar, paying historical attention to the rich and dense biblical and Jewish context and especially to the symbolism of the temple on the one hand and the image-bearing human vocation on the other, may in fact still have a piano or two in a store room, and we might just be able to get them in tune once more. And when we do that I suspect that Psalm 8 will provide part of the resonance which the later instruments have never been able to match.

6

Authority and Accountability in Luke 11.24–13.9

Darrell Bock

One of the more enigmatic sections of Luke's Gospel is the Jerusalem journey section. This unit of mostly unique Lukan material is long, extending from the end of ch. 9 into ch. 19. It is diverse, being a combination of teaching material, events and parables. As such, the unit has perplexed interpreters because of its diversity of materials and the potpourri of topics it possesses. The essay's goal is modest. It seeks to look at a small portion of this material in Luke 11–13 and consider how it functions for the larger unit, as well as the Gospel as a whole. It is our view that the theme of this section involves a look at issues tied to authority and accountability to God. It also sends clues as to what the rest of this longer unit is seeking to achieve. For one indebted to John Nolland's work in Luke, a treatment of themes from this Gospel seems particularly apropos. He notes that the section we will examine has links into Lk. 12.54.[1] We will argue the conceptual theme extends into ch. 13. Our specification of that theme gives focus to the unit.

Authority and Accountability in Luke 11–13

We start in Lk. 11.14.[2] The scene comes after a sequence where Jesus has called for loving one's neighbour through the parable of the Good

1. John Nolland, *Luke 9:21–18:34*, WBC 35B (Dallas: Word Books, 1998), 635.

2. Joel Green, *The Gospel of Luke*, NICNT (Grand Rapids: Eerdmans, 1997), 450, sees a unit from 11.14-54 here. He calls it 'Jesus' Behavior Questioned'. This describes the contents of these verses well, but the theme of authority is driving the narrative at this point.

Samaritan, an exhortation to see Mary as a good example of a disciple who sits at Jesus' feet and a call to depend on God in teaching the Disciples' Prayer with an exhortation to be bold in our requests, trusting God's goodness (Lk. 10.25–11.13). From the focus on the disciple and his walk with God, the issue of Jesus comes centre stage.[3] The shift is important because it is often suggested that Jesus spoke about the kingdom and not so much about himself. However, the actions of Jesus precipitated a discussion of who he was showing himself to be in the midst of his kingdom message. Authority to both preach and claim the kingdom's arrival made Jesus part of the issue tied to the claims about the kingdom.

Luke 11.14-23 is a miracle story turned upside down. Where most miracles tell the story of the healing in some detail and then briefly mention any reaction, if discussing it at all, this miracle is told in one verse with the reaction dominating the account. The reversal of form tells us this is a major scene as the break in the normal pattern is designed rhetorically to get our attention. The goal is to have the reader of Luke ponder the story so far and what Jesus' activity means. In fact, a major way that Christology is presented in these Gospels is through contemplating the significance of what Jesus is doing.

Like the earlier response in Lk. 7.18-23, Jesus' work is to lead to reflection about what kind of time he brings and the source of his activity. So when his work is attributed to Beelzebul, while others sought to sit on the fence, Jesus responds. Luke notes Jesus knew their thoughts, a line that often means a challenge from Jesus follows (Lk. 5.22; 6.8; 7.40 – said less directly; 9.47; Mk 2.8). Jesus argues there are two options for his power: from above or from below. It is important to note all see something unusual is going on.[4] The issue is the source. Jesus contends if Satan is at work he is working with a house divided. That is not likely. But if God is at work, then the time of the kingdom has come. The miracles are seen as power points. They indicate that God and his authority are at work through Jesus. The allusion to the finger of God and Exod. 8.19 points to the time of salvation of the nation, a work Jesus now replicates with a new chapter in the book of deliverance.

3. In my commentary, I also denoted the section as extending to 11.54, calling it 'Controversies, Corrections, and Calls to Trust', while separating Lk. 12.1-48 as 'Discipleship: Trusting God'. I now see authority and accountability as a wider theme that allows an extension of the section as I hope to show here. Discipleship is possible and even demanded because of this more comprehensive theme. *Luke 9:51–24:53*, BECNT 3b (Grand Rapids: Baker, 1996), 1066.

4. Rightly observed in Nolland, *Luke 9:21–18:34*, 637.

The point provides an opportunity. So Lk. 11.24-26 deals with the fence-sitters. Here the issue is when a divine act of exorcism comes and cleans out the person, the choice is not to leave the abode empty and unfilled.[5] If that takes place, then the spirit returns with others and takes up renewed residence. The situation has not got better but worse. So the evidence of authority and opportunity calls for a response or else there is a worse result. God has worked and the act has gone unaddressed. Something of spiritual significance will fill the space. Make sure it is from God.

When a woman in the crowd gets nervous and blesses the mother who nurtured Jesus, the teacher does not back off (Lk. 11.27-28). He tells the audience that blessing comes to those who hear the word of God and keep it. This is the language of response in this context. The word is tied to the revelation in act and remark that Jesus has just made. With accountability comes responsibility to respond to the divine prompting.

The next scene makes the point that there is no other sign to be given to this generation than the one Jonah gave. The allusion to seeking signs goes back to the point of debate in 11.14-20.[6] That prophet brought a call from God to respond with a change of mind. The people are to embrace the wisdom of God as the queen of the south did or react as the people of Nineveh did when they repented at Jonah's word (Lk. 11.29-32). The activity of God through Jesus is the sign that is the word. A greater revelation is present than the king or that prophet. Response is the call; authority is the premise.

What Jesus is doing is like a light set on a stand (Lk. 11.33-36). One should see it correctly and have good sight. The eye is the lens that allows light to exist. One is to take it in so the body can be lit up, full of light. The light in this case is the word, the response to it is what lights the body. It may be overinterpreting to debate whether one takes in the light or whether the light comes from within.[7] Jesus is holding out the possibility

5. C. F. Evans, *Saint Luke*, TPINTC (London: SCM Press, 1990), 494, describes this unit as like 'an extract from a text book on demonology'.

6. Correctly Green, *Luke*, 463.

7. Many point to the common Graeco-Roman picture of the light going out through the eye from the person versus light going into the person; So Green, *Luke*, 464. In contrast, Nolland, *Luke 9:21–18:34*, 657, argues that the light is the message of Jesus (see vv. 34-36). A choice may not be required here. The idea of darkness inside is clearly related to not being responsive. So the image could well be to respond to the light so that you not only are light but have eyes that reflect the light now working from within.

the person can be full of light or darkness within. Jesus has a dialectic in mind here, the encounter with the light that also allows one to be light. As random as these scenes seem to be on the surface, there is a theme being traced in the middle of Luke's Gospel. With God's revelation of Jesus' authority comes accountability, and thus the need to respond.

Just as opportunity opens up the idea of choice, so opportunity missed also provides its lessons. So in a change of scene, we still do not get a major change of theme. As at many key points in Luke, we now have a major meal scene where important teaching takes place (Lk. 5.27-32; 7.36-50; 14.1-24; 22.1-38; 24.36-49). Luke 11.37-52 shows the need to think differently as Jesus challenges the spirituality of the Pharisees and scribes. Their choices point to the very need that Jesus' evoking of Jonah and Nineveh and the call about light also raised. Those who thought of themselves as paragons of righteousness actually were more like tombs of death and uncleanness. The challenge at dinner went unheeded. The result of Jesus' rebuke was not a turning back to God but a plot to hunt down the challenger (Lk. 11.53-54) – the expression for lying in wait being a term used for hunting down an animal.[8]

The warning about hypocrisy looks as if it has left our authority–accountability theme, but it has not (Lk. 12.1-4). It attaches to and assumes the previous long rebuke, given that the leaven of the Pharisees is noted.[9] Jesus goes on to warn about an exposure to judgement for the things done in the dark and things whispered in secret that will be disclosed. So accountability is still very much in view as Jesus raises the spectre of a judgement and justice to come.

Jesus quickly reaffirms that note about accountability in the call to fear the one who can cast into hell (Lk. 12.4-12). Jesus points to God's awareness of life's details with the remark about God knowing about the sparrows and the number of hairs on a person's head. The remark about blasphemy against the Spirit not being forgiven still means accountability is in view. Where blasphemy against the Son of Man (speaking against Jesus at a given point) can be forgiven, blasphemy against the Spirit cannot be forgiven as it is a resolve to reject how God's Spirit has shown who Jesus is. The remarks here hark back to the miracle in reverse of Lk. 11.14-20 and the settled judgement that Jesus acts using malevolent power. To decide Jesus' acts by the power of Satan is to substitute the wrong actor tied to Jesus' work and to miss the authority present in his activity. A subsequent exhortation about not fearing what to say under

8. BDAG, 455.
9. Green, *Luke*, 479.

pressure of persecution does turn the remark toward disciples, but a fear of men over a fear of God is raising a core allegiance question. It asks about one's loyalty to God and has as its premise seeing what God is doing through Jesus. So authority is still in view alongside accountability.

Accountability extends also to one's trust about resources and provision. The parable of the Rich Fool not only exhorts about how not to handle material provision but also about the accountability one has for how it is handled (Lk. 12.13-21). Of all the units in this section, this unit and the next one may be the two that look the most random and out of place in terms of our claim about a united theme, but the idea of accountability is still there, although it is applied with a fresh ethical concern.[10]

Responding to God and trusting him, including with the core provisions of life (Lk. 12.22-34), stands in contrast to the previous section where the rich fool took matters fully into his own hands. In a kind of reversal on the theme, the point here is that God will hold himself accountable for how the person who trusts in him is cared for and thus one need not be anxious about clothing and food. The assurance in 12.31 is that these things will be provided to the one who recognizes God's ability to provide and rests in it. The result is that one is to seek the treasure that comes from being responsive and trusting toward God. The authority of God and his own sense of caring for his own who trust him is in view here.

The next scene is a call to be watchful servants ready for the master to come home (Lk. 12.35-48).[11] Readiness is seen as a metaphor for faithfulness with reward for a job well done awaiting those who are ready. Peter's question about the audience leads Jesus to tell a parable about a servant who is faithful and those who are not. Accountability is certainly the theme here. The faithful slave is rewarded, while those who fall short have differing penalties depending on the degree of the lapse. One servant is cut to pieces and placed with the unfaithful. Another is whipped severely and a third is whipped lightly. This looks to distinguish between the person who does the opposite of what is asked from those who fail to follow through either with knowledge or out of ignorance. The whole shows that accountability is still present for all.

10. I failed to sense this connection in my earlier work, Bock, *Luke 9:51–24:53*, 1146.

11. In introducing this section, Nolland, *Luke 9:21–18:34*, 699, hints at what this essay as a whole is developing. There is a *leitmotif* running from 12.1–13.9 in the challenge of being ready for judgement. I am simply extending the scope of the motif not only to accountability because of coming judgement but also to the premise of the authority tied to Jesus it assumes, thus allowing us to go back to 11.14 as the starting point. This means about a third of the central section is concerned with this idea.

The choice offered means there will be division, even within families (Lk. 12.49-53). Jesus' presence is compared to a purging fire. Some will align and others will refuse. Choices are being made. The implication is to choose well. By associating Jesus with a purging fire,[12] we see authority is still in view.

So Jesus issues a warning that is also an implied rebuke (Lk. 12.54-56). People can tell the weather by the signs the sky gives. Clouds from the west mean rain coming from the Mediterranean. A southern wind means heat from the desert. But the risk is to miss reading the significance of the present time. Responding to the choice of authority and accountability Jesus' presence reflects is paramount. The danger is that the significance of what is going on around them will be missed.

Next Jesus gives an illustration about settling with one's accuser, paying the debt owed (Lk. 12.57-59). Failure to settle means one will pay every last coin owed. Now the context of all that has come before tells us this illustration, so similar to Mt. 5.25-26 in appearance, is actually making a distinct point from the example in Jesus' Sermon on the Mount. Whereas in Matthew one settles with a brother where there is a wrong that needs to be resolved, here one is to settle with God to whom ultimate debts are paid.[13] Everything about the context since 11.14 even as late as 12.54-56 points to the concern for our accountability to God and a response to Jesus.

Any doubt about the illustration applying to an accountability to God is removed with the following event in Lk. 13.1-5. Here Jesus deflects the issue of whether some are worse sinners with the observation that unless those asking the question repent, they also likewise will perish.

The final note of accountability now clearly extends to the nation in the parable of Lk. 13.6-9. Here we have the fig tree that after three years has yielded no fruit. The owner wants to chop it down, but the vinedresser asks for one more year to be given to it with the promise that if it fails to yield fruit then it can be cut down. Rhetorically this is presented as the more likely result, as the option of bearing fruit comes as a third-class condition, while the option of not producing fruit is a first-class condition.

12. On fire as a figure for judgement in Luke, see 3.9, 17; 9.54; 17.29.

13. On this idea, seeing the text too much in light of Mt. 5 or in terms of a source rooted in Q probably misreads the imagery as about how we treat our neighbour versus seeing it about how we respond to God. So I side here with Green, *Luke*, 512, who sees eschatological judgement as the point of a kind of symbolic remark versus the reading of Nolland, *Luke 9:21–18:34*, 714, who sees how we treat the neighbour as the point God will judge.

Conclusion

These three chapters represent a significant section of the central section of Lk. 9.51–19.27 (or 44).[14] The scenes from 11.14–13.9 set a tone for the choices the presence of Jesus' authority presents. There is an appeal to accountability that runs through scene after scene. Accountability will pop up now and again in the rest of the unit, but its concentration in this early portion of the central section lays the groundwork for what is at stake in Jesus' coming. The Gospel as a whole has shown Jesus' activity and presented it with notes of fulfillment about God's programme. As Jesus sets his face to go to Jerusalem in the opening of this largest unit in Luke's Gospel (Lk. 9.51, 53), the grounds for his presence and the importance of the options his presence creates become clear. Jesus presses for response in notes that alternate between points about Jesus' authority set next to points about ultimate accountability. This section shows that what might on the surface look like a series of random events and parables about Jesus actually does develop into a core storyline.

14. Whether to end the central section at 19.27 or 44 depends on how one links the transitional unit that is 19.27-44. In the perspective of the narrative, Jesus is still approaching the city in this unit and pronounces his judgement on it as he prepares to enter it and face his fate. This is a close call where I slightly prefer to see this as the wrapping up of his approach to the city.

7

Pharisees and Jesus' Power of Persuasion in Luke–Acts: Another Consideration of their Characterization

Robert L. Brawley

In the first three-quarters of the 20th century the Pharisees in Luke–Acts were taken as indications of tensions between Christianity and Judaism, and the Pharisees themselves were understood in terms of increasing anti-Judaism in the Synoptic tradition. In historical constructs supposedly lying behind Luke–Acts, the 'Way' had become a gentile movement that had written off Judaism.[1] Rudolf Bultmann interpreted the increased *presence* of Pharisees in Luke over against Mark as a tendency to increase their controversy with Jesus.[2]

Today the situation has changed remarkably. For one thing, post-Holocaust perspectives have sensitized interpreters to pejorative evaluations of both Judaism and the Pharisees. Thus in her recent monograph on the Pharisees in the Gospels and Acts, Mary Marshall judiciously resists presupposing that the Pharisees are 'wholly polemical'.[3] Second, literary

1. Hans Conzelmann, *The Theology of St. Luke*, trans. G. Buswell (New York: Harper, 1961), 145–8; Ernst Haenchen, *The Acts of the Apostles: A Commentary* (Oxford: Blackwell, 1971), 100–102.

2. *The History of the Synoptic Tradition*, trans. John Marsh (New York: Harper, 1963), 51–4.

3. *The Portrayals of the Pharisees in the Gospels and Acts*, FRLANT 254 (Göttingen: Vandenhoeck & Ruprecht, 2015), 15. So also John Nolland, *Luke*, WBC 35ABC, 3 vols (Dallas: Word Books, 1989–93), 1:233, 2:877. But see n. 19 below.

methodologies have demonstrated how characterization takes place. Third, sociological approaches especially regarding social identity and hierarchies of power, including the context of the Roman Empire, have opened new vistas.

Literary Methods

Pharisees appear as characters in Luke's narrative world. This narrative world has a fictive quality in the sense proposed by historiographers such as Hayden White, philosophers such as Paul Ricoeur, and biblical interpreters such as Jean Zumstein.[4] To use the term fictive is not to make judgements about what may qualify as factual on an ontic level. Indeed, all 'facts' exhibit this fictive quality, because 'statements of facts are always particular interpretations of circumstances, in which certain aspects are illuminated or selected'.[5]

To designate Luke–Acts fictive means that a narrator tells a story (διήγησις, Lk. 1.1) by constructing a *framework* for it and *filling* it in a certain fashion (καθηξῆς, 1.3) with time, space, affections, cultural presumptions, actions, speech, perspectives, evaluations, plots and characters. Consequently, what is true in narratives is always distanced from a supposedly ontic reality because narratives shape their visions of reality and create their own worlds.

Since the Enlightenment, biblical interpreters have largely been concerned with discovering a historical world behind the text. But because narratives present a world that they create, it is impossible to reverse the process and reify a supposedly ontic reality from the narrative. This has always been apparent with matters such as the virginal conception. As curious as interpreters may be, they cannot reconstruct a process in what is construed as ontic facticity. Nevertheless, the virginal conception exists in Luke's narrative world.

4. Hayden White, 'Historical Emplotment and the Problem of Truth', in *The Post-Modern History Reader*, ed. Keith Jenkins (London: Routledge, 1997), 392–6; P. Ricoeur, 'La fonction hermeneutique de la distanciation', in *Exegesis*, ed. F. Bovon and G. Rouiller (Paris: Neuchatel, 1975), 201–15; Jean Zumstein uses the term 'poetic narrative' (*Kreative Erinnerung: Relecture und Auslegung im Johannesevangelium*, trans. A. de Groot and E. Straub, ATANT 84 (Zurich: Theologischer Verlag, 2004), 2–3).

5. Chris Lorenz, *Konstruktion der Vergangenheit: Eine Einführung in die Geschichtstheorie*, Beiträge zur Geschichtskultur 13 (Cologne: Böhlau, 1997), 29 (author's translation).

Simultaneously, Luke's fictive narrative employs a cultural repertoire that interpreters cannot comprehend without knowing ancient history. Luke–Acts begins with a priest in the temple in the time of Herod without introducing client kingship in the Roman Empire or the priesthood in the temple cult. All such matters, the Greek language of Luke–Acts itself and common presumptions in virtually every sentence require historical studies in order for interpreters to know the cultural repertoire of the narrative world. When Pharisees appear as a known quantity in Lk. 5.17, they are part of the narrative's cultural encyclopaedia. But the narrative's fictive quality thwarts reversing the process as a means of determining a historical setting in early Christianity, because this puts the cart before the horse. The narrative world assumes cultural presuppositions from a historical world, but the narrative world portrays its own vision of reality rather than mirror ontic reality.

Nevertheless, Luke–Acts displays one way in which Pharisees were *remembered*. Historical memory is necessarily mediated through personal perspectives and configurations, which although based in experiences of the past, represents these as something viewed not in an objective sense but as it were in the way they are narrated.[6]

In addition, literary studies analyse how characterization takes place. Narratives present distinct clues, which Roland Barthes called 'semes' (elementary units of meaning),[7] which readers then construe into holistic characters. This entails viewing the characterization of the Pharisees holistically, sequentially and cumulatively. Characterization is especially complex because of overlapping grids of the narrative's ideological point of view, and the source and reliability of semes.[8] Interpreters violate sequence, for example, when they use thematic schemata to identify similar features of the Pharisees irrespective of the order in which they appear. Rather, readers encounter the semes for characterization in a progressive discovery of what is true in the narrative world. Progressive discovery is first of all a matter of readers' suspense when they anticipate how the narrative unfolds, but they are most intrigued not when their

6. Jens Schröter, *Von Jesus zum Neuen Testament: Studien zur urchristlichen Theologiegeschichte und zur Entstehung des neutestamentlichen Kanons*, WUNT 204 (Tübingen: Mohr, 2007), 108–9.

7. Roland Barthes, *S/Z: An Essay* (New York: Hill & Wang, 1974), 67, 191.

8. David Gowler, *Host, Guest, Enemy and Friend: Portraits of the Pharisees in Luke and Acts*, Emory Studies in Early Christianity 2 (New York: Lang, 1991); John Darr, *On Character Building: The Reader and the Rhetoric of Characterization in Luke–Acts*, Literary Currents in Biblical Interpretation (Louisville: Westminster John Knox Press, 1992).

anticipations are fulfilled but when they must revise them.[9] For instance, after intentions of some Pharisees to accuse Jesus (6.7), the antipathy of others (11.53) and some who ridicule his teaching (16.14), readers must revise their expectations when Pharisees do not participate in Jesus' crucifixion, Gamaliel advocates tolerance toward Jesus' disciples (Acts 5.34), some Pharisees become believers (15.5) and Pharisees in a Sanhedrin side with Paul (23.6-9).

Sociological Approaches

Sociological studies in particular have augmented knowledge of the cultural repertoire of the ancient Mediterranean world. In 1991 Jerome Neyrey edited a volume that based interpretations of Luke–Acts on wide-ranging sociological theory. It highlights the values of an honour/shame culture, especially as reflected in challenge–riposte interactions of interlocutors, as well as the relationship of individual identity to cultural socialization.[10] For example, in Luke 5 when Jesus tells a paralytic that his sins are forgiven, some Pharisees challenge him about the prerogative to forgive. They presume that he exceeds his ascribed social identity, and they act as social control agents and enter a challenge–riposte contest in which not only cognitive rationales are at stake but also the honour of both Jesus and his challengers. Perception of the relationship of personal identity to cultural socialization was developed more specifically with social identity theory, which gained prominence in Philip Esler's commentary on Romans.[11]

Further, French sociologist Pierre Bourdieu lucidly identifies hidden dimensions of hierarchies of social dominance.[12] Exhaustive socialization from early childhood produces cultural presumptions that are so internalized by both the dominant and sub-dominant that they appear to be

9. Wolfgang Iser, *The Implied Reader: Patterns of Communication in Prose and Fiction from Bunyan to Beckett* (Baltimore: The Johns Hopkins University Press, 1974), 278.

10. *The Social World of Luke–Acts: Models for Interpretation* (Peabody: Hendrickson, 1991).

11. *Conflict and Identity in Romans: The Social Setting of Paul's Letter* (Minneapolis: Fortress Press, 2003).

12. Pierre Bourdieu, *Distinction: A Social Critique of the Judgement of Taste*, trans. Richard Nice (Cambridge, MA: Harvard University Press, 1984); *La domination masculine* (Paris: Editions du Seuil, 1998). On hidden violence see also Luce Irigaray, *Sexes and Genealogies*, trans. Gillian Gill (New York: Columbia University Press, 1993), 109, 117.

natural, literally *common* sense, whereas they actually legitimate hierarchies of dominance – advantaged over disadvantaged, male over female, educated over uneducated, wealthy over poor, city populations over peasant farmers and so on. An immediate qualification is called for. To distinguish among people by such binary oppositions produces primarily masculine dominance. Humans actually share far more in common than sexual distinctions that are construed as gender, more in common than education or the lack thereof, more in common than the presence or absence of wealth, more in common than differences in languages and patterns of speech and so on. Thus distinctions among people run far more along a continuum than is the case with binary oppositions.[13] Nevertheless, masculine dominance prevails in that cultural divisions are made according to binary oppositions (rich/poor, male/female), and are thus culturally internalized as if natural.[14] For example, the debate about plucking and eating grain on the Sabbath (Lk. 6.1-5) is grounded not only in the law but also in cultural presumptions of the inviolability of the law, as if Sabbath conventions were the natural course of reality. But Sabbath norms regarding work related to food also support the dominance of the well-fed over the hungry such that hunger occasions few exceptions.

Clearly, imperial dominance is also legitimated by cultural presumptions. Granted, the legitimacy of the emperor to levy taxes comes into question in 20.22, but in everyday experiences, rather than the emperor, characters in Luke's narrative world encounter client kings, governors and the high priestly coterie (who were collaborators in imperial systems to maintain local order).[15] Thus, 3.1 is not merely the 'great synchronization' but an outline of Rome's well-defined hierarchy of imperial systems.[16] Further, everyone in the narrative world who is not a Roman citizen belongs to sub-dominant vanquished peoples, and Rome considered it their destiny as a superior culture to civilize inferior cultures, which the vanquished themselves internalized as superior and inferior classes.[17]

13. Phenomena such as genital ambiguity and individual identity undermine the binary construct of gender, including the cultural presumption that it is 'natural'. Bourdieu, *Domination*, 13–14; *Distinction*, 471. Irigaray, *Sexes and Genealogies*, 97–8, 101–2, 157–63. '[Nature] is in continuous becoming' (108), but dialectic is not binary opposition (111, 139–40).

14. Bourdieu, *Domination*, 8–9, 14.

15. Josephus, *Ant.* 20.251.

16. Similarly, Nolland, *Luke*, 1:139.

17. See the equation of cultural difference with class difference in Gayatri Chakravorty Spivak, *Other Asias* (Oxford: Blackwell, 2008), 58.

Luke's Characterization of Pharisees

In the context of John the Baptizer's ministry, which inevitably is the context of the collaborative imperial systems described in Lk. 3.1-2, Jesus inaugurates a mission as a prophet (4.16-30). He then assumes roles of a teacher who 'gospels', an exorcist who casts out demons and a healer who cures maladies. Demons name him God's Son, because they know that he is God's Messiah. Accordingly, he acquires status (honour), attracts crowds and calls disciples.

In this context Pharisees (anarthrous) come on the scene. In the first three episodes in which Pharisees are mentioned (5.17-26, 27-39), they are interlocutors with whom Jesus engages in reasoned dialogues. They even respond positively to Jesus' healing, and the narrative has implications that Jesus persuades them.

In 5.17 Pharisees appear among a crowd (spectators attracted to Jesus) but their title also singles them out. From the cultural repertoire readers know that they are esteemed and rate high in ascribed honour. John Nolland takes their provenance from all the towns of Judaea, Galilee and Jerusalem as Jesus' engagement with Pharisaism as a whole.[18] In contrast, the thesis is to show that those present, as on other occasions, represent themselves, not their entire sect. Here Jesus is impressed when some men *dramatize their faith*, which the paralytic is unable to do, by presenting the paralytic to Jesus through a hole in the roof of a house. Jesus shifts attention to the paralytic and 'gospels' him with the good news of forgiveness. At 5.21 definite articles specify some Pharisees as those who come with the crowd, not as opponents but as inquirers. Their affective mode is expressed by διαλογίζομαι: 'They began to reason carefully'. True, their premise is judgemental: 'Who is this who speaks blasphemies? Who can forgive sin except God alone?'. Jesus discerns their *reasoning* (διαλογισμούς), and presents an argument *in order to convince them* of his power to forgive sins: '*...so that you may know*' (5.24). Further, Jesus enables them to know. First, the former paralytic interprets the event by glorifying God (5.25). Then everyone is on the same page. Astonishment and awe seize them all,[19] and they also interpret the event: 'We have seen wonders today' (5.26).

18. *Luke*, 1:234.

19. So also Joel Green, *The Gospel of Luke*, NICNT (Grand Rapids: Eerdmans, 1997), 243. Nolland interprets 'all' as the crowds on the basis of Mark's parallel (*Luke*, 1:238). But on this first appearance of Pharisees in Luke, there is no prejudice to exclude them.

In quick succession Pharisees play the role of social control agents (5.27-39). On the occasion of Levi's banquet, which exemplifies his decision to follow Jesus, they grumble about the social propriety of Jesus' commensality with tax collectors and sinners. Their complaint implies hierarchical social distinctions between in-groups and out-groups, and inasmuch as tax collectors are local collaborators in imperial systems, the grumblers imply religious, social, economic and political dominance over them.[20] They reason that degrees of fidelity to God separate classes and legitimate hierarchies of dominance as if they are natural.[21] Although their interchange is with the disciples, Jesus' parable implicates himself: 'Those who are well need no physician but those with maladies' (5.31). The narrator provides no outcome. Nevertheless, the narration presumes that the parable convinces readers. What power of persuasion does it have for the interlocutors in the narrative world?

When an anonymous third person plural in 5.33 mentions Pharisees as if speaking of others, it is not clear that Pharisees are the ones who make observations about socio-religious distinctions between Jesus' disciples who eat and drink, and John's disciples and the Pharisees who fast. Jesus responds with *four* parables: the bridegroom, mending a garment, new wineskins for new wine and the appeal of new and old wine. Conventional interpretations emphasize the new over the old. All four actually build on *tensions* between the values of both old and new, especially apparent in the proper time for fasting, the preservation of the garment and wineskins and the value of old wine.[22] Again the reasoning speaks for itself. Is it persuasive for Jesus' interlocutors as well as for Luke's readers?

In 6.1-11 Pharisees are involved in conflict stories. In an incident involving plucking and eating grain, *some* Pharisees play the role of social control agents. They interrogate the disciples: 'Why are you doing what is not lawful on Sabbaths?'. Jesus reasons by analogy to what David and many more 'sons of humans'[23] did in the case of hunger. The enthymematic rhetoric leaves the conclusion unexpressed: hunger overrides law, they are hungry, so their hunger overrides law. But Jesus adds: 'The Son of Man is κύριος of the Sabbath' (6.5). In 5.24 'Son of Man' refers to Jesus and focuses on his power to forgive. Here disciples override the Sabbath,

20. Michael Wolter, *Das Lukasevangelium*, HNT 5 (Tübingen: Mohr, 2008), 228.

21. See nn. 12–14 above.

22. Contra Wolter, *Lukas*, 232–3. The issue is the proper continuity of old and new (Nolland, *Luke*, 1:249; Green, *Luke*, 250). But the continuity is not between Judaism and Christianity (so Nolland) but has to do with the arrival of God's commonwealth (Wolter correctly) in relation to redemptive history.

23. Wolter, *Lukas*, 235.

and so they act as if they are sons of humans (Ps. 8.5 LXX) who are κύριοι of the Sabbath. Inasmuch as Luke uses 'Son of Man' as Jesus' self-reference, in 6.5 he can only be one case of being κύριος of the Sabbath, along with his disciples. Exodus 20.11 and Deut. 5.14 give distinct rationales for keeping the Sabbath – a commemoration of creation, and a provision of rest. The unexpressed reasoning in the enthymematic rhetoric is that eating, like rest for the weary, satisfies hunger, and thus fulfils one purpose of the Sabbath. The narrative draws no conclusion, but once more if the reasoning is persuasive for readers, is it also for these Pharisees?

Luke 6.6 shifts to a synagogue on another Sabbath. Although the Pharisees are different from those in 6.1-5, there is continuity in issues and behaviour. Which takes precedence, relief of human need or a sacred commemoration? Jesus intuits what the narrator reveals to readers: these Pharisees are close observers in anticipation of accusing *him*. Crucially, in the narrative world these Pharisees are characterized differently from earlier cases where Pharisees are Jesus' interlocutors. Still Jesus responds as earlier with reasoning. The case is embodied in a man's withered right hand. Jesus expands the purpose of the Sabbath to a general proposition. Rather than stipulate negatively what one cannot do on Sabbaths, he asks in a positive way, what is it lawful to do? To do good? To save life? Initially these Pharisees watch closely (παρατηρέω), now Jesus turns his gaze toward them (περιβλέπομαι, 6.10), and restoring the man's hand – virtually a synecdoche for the totality of human existence[24] – dramatizes his answer. At this point these Pharisees respond quite differently from those who observed the healing of the paralytic and glorified God (5.26). Rather than celebrate with Jesus, they are 'without understanding' (ἄνοια, not 'fury'). Following honour/shame patterns of challenge and riposte, in 5.26 some Pharisees joined in sharing honour with Jesus and everyone else associated with the healing of the paralytic. Unlike them, these Pharisees experience loss of honour, and rather than dialogue with Jesus, they dialogue among themselves (διαλαλέω) what they might do with him (6.11), presumably to regain honour. Their deliberative question leaves the possibilities for what they might do indeterminate.

Pharisees next appear in a retrospective on John the Baptizer rather than as actors in Jesus' story (7.30). They are portrayed pejoratively as rejecting God's purpose by not being baptized. This analeptic recall is similar to Matthew's version of John's story, because although Pharisees are not mentioned in Luke's version of John's baptism, they appear in Matthew where John calls them and Sadducees 'offspring of vipers' (Mt. 3.7). But

24. François Bovon, *A Commentary on the Gospel of Luke*, trans. Christine Thomas, 3 vols, Hermeneia (Minneapolis: Fortress Press, 2002–2013), 1:204.

in Matthew they do not refuse John's baptism but accept it (ἐγὼ μὲν ὑμᾶς βαπτίζω). Luke, therefore, speaks not of a group that corresponds to Matthew's account in which Pharisees accepted baptism, but of others who did not. Thus, I translate Lk. 7.30: '*When* Pharisees and lawyers were not baptized by John, they rejected God's purpose for themselves'.[25]

Luke further differentiates among Pharisees by specifying the name and location of one of them (7.36-50). The hints that Simon is an urban householder whose dining posture is reclining distinguish him from people of the countryside and lower classes, who typically did not recline.[26] Simon is the first Pharisee to host Jesus,[27] and like others on previous occasions he presumes social hierarchies based on socio-religious norms.[28] He plays roles as both Jesus' interlocutor and a social control agent in relationship to a woman, who is a sinner in the city. Simon's internal monologue, which forms his side of the interlocution, puts Jesus' character as a prescient into question: 'If this man were a prophet, he would know who and what kind of woman is touching him.' With this Simon presumes not only a socio-religious hierarchy, but also a male/female hierarchy.[29] With her ointment, tears and hair the woman performs a parable and dramatizes what Jesus calls 'faith' (7.50). In contrast, Simon focuses not on her actions, which have the capacity to *acquire* status, but her *ascribed* status as a ἁμαρτωλός,[30] which marks her social caste and supposedly

25. Because Luke has been differentiating among Pharisees, the narrative has not given a totalizing evaluation of the Pharisees, which speaks against a concessive meaning for βαπτισθέντες (NRSV). Thus the temporal circumstance is preferable. These are certainly not 'the leaders of Israel' (as in Bovon, *Luke*, 1:285).

26. Lucian, *Sym.* 13; Athenaeus, *Deipn.* X.428B; Cicero, *De Sen.* 13.45–14.46.

27. In Luke only Pharisees host Jesus on multiple occasions.

28. Meals exaggerate similarities among an in-group and differences from an out-group. See M. Hogg and D. Abrams, 'Social Identity and Social Cognition: Historical Background and Current Trends', in *Social Identity and Social Cognition*, ed. M. Hogg and D. Abrams (Oxford: Blackwell, 1999), 9. Plutarch warns against mixing people of different classes and status at meals (*Quest. Conv.* VII.6.708).

29. Matthias Klinghardt demonstrates the impossibility of sorting meals into simple categories. They have social, religious, economic, gender and political dimensions (*Gemeinschaftsmahl und Mahlgemeinschaft: Soziologie und Liturgie frühchristlicher Mahlfeiern*, TANZ 13 (Tübingen: Franke, 1996), 99–109). On political critiques see 163–74. On male/female hierarchy see Irigaray, *Sexes and Genealogies*, 118, on the nonhierarchical difference of sexes, p. 144.

30. Clues to the nature of her sin are hopelessly ambiguous. See Charles Cosgrove, 'A Woman's Unbound Hair in the Greco-Roman World, with Special Reference to the Story of the "Sinful Woman" in Luke 7.36-50', *JBL* 124 (2005): 675–92. Further, the category 'sinner' is not determined by specific sins.

legitimates hierarchical social relationships. This thus reiterates Jesus' characterization as a friend of tax collectors and sinners. But readers now know that although Jesus eats with tax collectors and sinners, he also eats with Pharisees. In response to Simon's internal monologue, Jesus tells the parable of a creditor who cancels a large and a small debt. In contrast to Simon, he focuses not on the woman's social caste, but on her actions of gratitude, and announces the forgiveness of her sins. His benediction of peace vindicates her.

Roland Meynet[31] persuasively identifies Simon's prominence in the episode and Jesus' repeated endeavours to persuade him: (1) In the parable, the creditor takes the initiative for cancelling the debts both great and small; although quantitatively different, both debtors respond with gratitude. (2) When Jesus turns to the woman, he still appeals to Simon directly and invites him to turn to her also: 'Do you see this woman?'. Jesus therefore entreats the Pharisee to regard the woman anew as if a mirror in which to see himself. (3) Jesus relates the parable for Simon's sake: 'I have something to tell you'. (4) If the woman's love entails her pardon, Simon's pardon should entail his love. (5) Other guests declare the issue of the episode: 'Who is this who forgives sin?'. (6) The way the story is told compels Simon to include himself as one of the debtors, that is, as one whose sins are also forgiven.

The episode ends without confirming a revision of Simon's view of Jesus' identity and the dismantling of hierarchical social relationships. But the narrative presents the parable and Jesus' affirmation of the woman as persuasive for readers. Is Simon, who establishes criteria for Jesus' prophetic identity, also persuaded?[32]

Readers have a respite from Pharisees until 11.37 when another Pharisee hosts Jesus. Jesus' failure to purify his hands before eating scandalizes his host. Jesus presumes that his host's astonishment emerges from Pharisaic in-group norms, and this occasions a confrontational interchange. His direct address in the second person plural includes other guests but hardly the entire sect. Like a confrontational prophet of Israel,[33] he accuses those present of plunder and wickedness (11.39), marks them

31. This paragraph follows Roland Meynet, '"Celui à qui est remis peu, aime un peu…" (Lc 7.36-50)', *Greg* 75 (1994): 267–80.

32. See Robert Tannehill, 'Should We Love Simon the Pharisee? Hermeneutical Reflections on the Pharisees in Luke', *Currents in Theology and Mission* (1994): 424–33. Bovon mentions Jesus' desire to persuade (*Luke*, 1:291, 296). Green, *Luke*, 307–8, 312–15, rejects a negative evaluation of Simon in favour of an open ending.

33. Bovon, *Luke*, 2:154.

deviant by labelling them 'senseless' (11.40), and denounces them for hierarchical values that invert what is important,[34] while neglecting divine norms of judgement and love (11.42). Jesus' comments about pursuing honour address hierarchical social domination on an honour/shame scale (11.43). Further, his comparison of those present to unmarked graves (11.44) expresses what Bourdieu identifies as hidden cultural assumptions underlying hierarchies of dominance.[35]

A lawyer's protest that Jesus offends their honour reveals his hidden presumptions that legitimate hierarchies of dominance as normal (11.45). He partly characterizes Pharisees, because one clue to characterization is those with whom characters associate, as in the adage 'you are known by the company you keep'. Jesus unleashes another denunciation of lawyers, and disparages 'this generation' (11.51). In my view, *γενεά* is virtually universally misunderstood as the lifetime of contemporaries. The idiom rather concerns the *process of generation*, which for Jesus is the derivation of their behaviour from violent ancestors (11.47-51) – 'like father, like son'. Jesus condemns what Bourdieu calls hidden violence in hierarchical dominance.[36] Because matters such as tithing (v. 42) involve agricultural produce, I see no reason to exclude physical labours of sub-dominant classes from the 'burdens too difficult to bear' (11.46).

Pharisees respond to Jesus' unveiling of hidden violence underlying hierarchical dominance with the symbolic violence[37] of ill will (11.53). Their dialogue with Jesus abandons the possibility of being persuaded and takes the shape of cross-examination[38] in order to catch him in something he might say (11.53-54). Hidden cultural presumptions that legitimate domination carry over to 12.1. More than the difference between internal intentions and external reality, ὑπόκρισις is what underlies *social realities as if hidden behind a mask*, analogous to yeast. Here there is no direct address or further specification of the Pharisees. This time Jesus warns his disciples about their hidden cultural presumptions in general.

34. Wolter, *Lukas*, 431–3; Bovon, *Luke*, 2:160.

35. Bourdieu, *Distinction*, 471. Green refers similarly to institutions' as patterns of behaviour that are socially legitimated (*Luke*, 469 n. 61).

36. Invisible even for victims (Bourdieu, *Domination*, 7; *Distinction*, 471; also Irigaray, *Sexes and Genealogies*, 114).

37. That is, the effect of social presumptions that exploit the sub-dominant and leave the dominant supposedly innocent (Bourdieu, *Domination*, 40–4).

38. Joseph Fitzmyer, *The Gospel according to Luke: Introduction, Translation, and Notes*, AB 28-28a, 2 vols (Garden City: Doubleday, 1981–85), 2:952.

The next episode hardly paints some (τινες) Pharisees with the same brush. Instead of plotting against Jesus (11.53-54), they warn him to flee from Herod (13.31). Although they misunderstand the divine necessity underlying Jesus' itinerancy, he aims his response at Herod. This differentiates them from those who cross-examine him and indicates conspicuously that Luke distinguishes among Pharisees.[39] Further, Jesus' response rejects Herod's warrior way of dominance.

At 14.1 a Pharisee, personalized as a leader, again hosts Jesus. The healing of a man with oedema on the Sabbath and Jesus' reasoning with a parable reiterate previous Sabbath healings. His interlocutors' silence (14.4, 6) means at least that they offer no competing rationale and allows that Jesus' reasoning and dramatization may persuade them. This chapter highlights dialogue as in a symposium, and Jesus advises the guests not to seek places of honour – prominent features in Greco-Roman meals,[40] and his remarks undermine hierarchies of dominance. In 14.12-14 Jesus advises inviting those who cannot reciprocate, and ironically the host has invited Jesus, and he can hardly be expected to reciprocate. Second, when Jesus speaks of inviting the socially marginalized (14.12-14), he promises blessing in the resurrection of the 'just'. Presuming his participation in it, an interlocutor extols the blessedness of eating in God's commonwealth. But contemplating Jesus' parable, he must consider whether he is among those who are excluded.[41] Moreover, as Willi Braun demonstrates, this parable exhorts altering hierarchical social relationships.[42]

In 15.2 Pharisees again play the role of social control agents. Again they presume that commensality marks borders between hierarchical social groups and grumble about Jesus' table fellowship with tax collectors and sinners. Jesus responds typically with parables. The Lost Sheep and Lost Coin unveil a divine perspective of joy over repentance. Not until the parable of the Prodigal Son do issues of hierarchical classes and hidden assumptions underlying them surface. The first two parables presume that a shepherd and a woman act according to their established value systems. But the son inverts his value system. In squandering his property, he abandons his Abrahamic heritage of the inheritance of the land, and he

39. My reading is more generous to these Pharisees than Nolland's. Still he notes that Luke's presentation of the Pharisees is not 'entirely' 'monochrome' (*Luke*, 2:740). Also Wolter, *Lukas*, 495; Green, *Luke*, 537–8, 546.

40. See nn. 29–30 above.

41. So also Bovon, *Luke*, 2:369–71.

42. *Feasting and Social Rhetoric in Luke 14*, SNTSMS 85 (Cambridge: CUP, 1995), 113–31. See also Green, *Luke*, 553.

reverses his economic status. He exchanges his social identity as a son and heir for that of a hired hand. The older brother's presumptions of dominant status underlie his description of both his and his brother's identity.[43] He indicts his brother for wasting the father's assets with prostitutes and acts as a social control agent who wishes to maintain dominance (15.29-30). The father's invitation for the older son to join the party corresponds to a summons to adopt a divine perspective, analogous to the father's reversal of his brother's degraded status to son. Inasmuch as the parable duplicates the larger story in miniature, the father's affirmation that the older brother is always with him corresponds to a similar affirmation of the grumbling Pharisees (15.31). The parable ends with the father's declaration that the celebration is a necessity, presumably for everyone involved,[44] and is 'an implicit open-ended invitation' to adopt a divine perspective.[45] The history of interpretation demonstrates the power of these parables to persuade readers. Might the Pharisees in the narrative world also be persuaded? The answer rests solely with the readers.

The parable of the 'Unjust' Steward depicts a patron–client system – an economic delivery system stacked hierarchically, which Roland Boer categorizes as 'extractive' (16.1-9).[46] The interpretation is highly debated, often hinging on whether the speaker in 16.8-9 is the rich man or Jesus. However, it is clear to me that Jesus concludes the parable not by making the commendation of the steward the crux, but by contrasting the children of 'this age' with the children of 'light'.[47] *Everyone* in the parable operates on the basis of the extractive system of 'this age', and the conclusion in v. 9 is built on an oxymoron. The oxymoron is 'eternal tents'. That tents are temporary makes this scornfully sardonic, as if to say, 'Make friends with the mammon that derives from injustice, and see how long that lasts'.[48]

43. Wolter, *Lukas*, 540.

44. Ibid. But against Wolter, the affirmation that the older brother is always with the father shows that the reaction of the hearers is not irrelevant to the point of the narrative.

45. Green, *Luke*, 569.

46. *The Sacred Economy of Ancient Israel*, Library of Ancient Israel (Louisville: Westminster John Knox Press, 2015), 104–8.

47. Similarly Matthias Konradt, '"Macht euch Freunde aus dem ungerechten Mammon" (Lk 16:9): Ein Interpretationsversuch zum Gleichnis vom Verwalter und seiner besitzethischen Auslegung in Lk 16:1-13', in *Ethos und Theologie*, Festschrift Michael Wolter, ed. Jochen Flebbe and Matthias Konradt (Neukirchen-Vluyn; Neukirchener Theologie, 2016), 103–30, 112 and *passim*.

48. *Pace* Nolland, *Luke*, 2:801; see Stanley Porter, 'The Parable of the Unjust Steward (Luke 16:1-13): Irony is the Key', in *The Bible in Three Dimensions*, ed. David Clines et al. (Sheffield: Sheffield Academic Press, 1990), 127–53.

The steward anticipates that his favours will induce the debtors to receive him into their *houses* (οἶκοι, 16.4), mammon 'secures' eternal *bivouacs* (σκηναί, 16.9). Jesus' further comments in 16.10-13, grounded on the contrast of the children of this age with the children of light, confirm this: If 'you are not faithful with mammon that derives from injustice, who will entrust you with what is genuinely real?' Rather than genuine long-term security, patronage deriving from injustice produces no more than transient safety-nets.

Some Pharisees mock this. They also profit from patronage whether the hierarchical dominance is cultural (honour/shame) or economic. To clarify my reference to *some* Pharisees, these are specific Pharisees who overhear and mock Jesus. Thus the participial that describes them is restrictive: 'Those Pharisees who were lovers of money heard all these things' (16.14). Further, Jesus' direct address to them (16.15) indicates that he is speaking to certain ones. His comment that they justify themselves refers not to self-righteousness alone, because they legitimate themselves before others and thus over against them (16.16). Additionally, in an honour/shame context Jesus' comment that what is highly valued among humans is abominable before God reiterates the contrasts between children of this age and children of light, and between mammon and God.

At 17.20-21 some Pharisees are genuine interlocutors. They 'consult'[49] with Jesus: 'When is God's commonwealth coming?' Jesus' response is direct, but enigmatic: 'God's commonwealth cannot be substantiated by portents...indeed God's commonwealth is ἐντὸς ὑμῶν'. Given the narrative's dominant perspective ἐντὸς ὑμῶν hardly means that God's commonwealth is an interior personal experience. Rather, as elsewhere in Luke, Jesus announces the presence of God's commonwealth (e.g. 11.20).[50] There is no outcome for this short interchange. But these Pharisees are no more obtuse than Jesus' disciples to whom he immediately gives similar instructions (17.22-24; see Acts 1.6-8).

In 18.9-14 Jesus addresses auditors who claim hierarchical dominance over others, which is then replicated in a parable. A Pharisee appears not in Luke's primary narrative, but at an embedded level as a character in Jesus' story. The mere name 'Pharisee' confers status according to the cultural encyclopaedia. Although neither character typifies his group,[51] the Pharisee reiterates his hierarchical dominance over others such as the tax collector, and the tax collector likewise expresses his internalized sub-dominance. But he also appeals to God for approval. The parable

49. Bovon, *Luke*, 2:514.

50. Marshall, *Portrayal of the Pharisees*, 138.

51. Wolter, *Lukas*, 592.

overturns dominance resting on cultural presumptions, and a divine perspective legitimates the tax collector. Inversion of high and low overthrows hierarchical dominance (v. 14b).

In 19.39 some (τινες) Pharisees among a crowd in a specific location make a brief appearance as social control agents. They respectfully call Jesus 'teacher' but presume social dominance by commanding him (imperative) to rebuke his disciples. Nolland contends that this last appearance of Pharisees 'encapsulates all that has gone on before'.[52] Granted, characterization is cumulative, but readers must constantly revise their expectations, and these Pharisees play their own role in this incident. Jesus' response with its avowal of divine necessity rejects their attempt at dominance over his followers and legitimates them: 'I tell you, if these were silent, the stones would cry out' (19.40).

Pharisees appears on four occasions in Acts always with some positive connotations. In Acts 5.34, not only is the Pharisee Gamaliel part of a dominant political group (συνέδριον), but he also possesses high cultural dominance (honoured among all). He manifests dominance in the council by commanding that the apostles be put outside the chamber. But he then gives up his dominance. The council at large expresses its warrior way of dominance in the urge to kill (5.33), whereas Gamaliel abandons dominance and advises letting the divine course of history determine the (il)legitimacy of what the apostles are doing. His counsel takes a dramatically positive form. The condition that it might be from humans is stated with ἐάν plus the subjunctive (tentative), whereas the possibility that it is from God is expressed with εἰ plus the present indicative (probable). C. K. Barrett judges the forms of the conditional statements to be rhetorical variations that reflect not Gamaliel's mind, but Luke's.[53] But this is precisely the point; Luke characterizes Gamaliel as favourable toward the apostles' work.

Pharisees then appear in connection with the Jerusalem council. Given Jesus' attempts to persuade Pharisees in Luke, it is hardly surprising that some become believers (Acts 15.5). Here, however, they also reiterate the role of social control agents. But the course of the incident, like many of the episodes in Luke, overthrows their dominance. Rather Peter and James claim a divine perspective that undercuts ethnic dominance over gentiles (15.8-9, 14-18).

52. Nolland, *Luke*, 927.

53. *A Critical and Exegetical Commentary on Acts*, ICC, 2 vols (Edinburgh: T. & T. Clark, 1994–98), 1:296.

After these incidents, it is not totally unexpected that Paul twice claims to be a Pharisee. The first time he displays a strategy before a Sanhedrin to side with Pharisees against Sadducees with respect to the resurrection (23.6-10). Paul actually persuades the Pharisees, who declare him blameless (23.9). He makes a similar claim in a speech before King Agrippa. As a member of the strictest sect of 'our' religion, he defines his offence as fidelity to God's promises to Israel's ancestors, now manifest in the hope of the resurrection of the dead (26.4-8).

Conclusion

Methodological advances, new theoretical perspectives on narratives and the sociological expansion of the cultural encyclopaedia should enable discussion of the Pharisees in Luke–Acts to avoid two missteps. One is to consider them to be the same everywhere and the other is to consider them everywhere to be antagonists. From the cultural encyclopaedia they are honoured, which holds without question for Gamaliel in Acts 5. Their most common trait is that they play the role of social control agents and assert and struggle for hierarchical dominance. Jesus engages them repeatedly as competent interlocutors with whom he *reasons*, often in parables. Pharisees also have occasion to witness an alternative reality in characters who dramatize faith (5.20; 7.37-38). In at least the case of the healing of the paralytic, they are persuaded. By contrast, in 11.53 Pharisees bear extreme ill will. But they are 'never permanently closed – to the Gospel'.[54] On other occasions, such as in Simon's case in Luke 7 or the parables of Luke 15, Jesus' reasoning leaves readers to ponder whether Pharisees are persuaded. Clearly, however, Acts 15.5 confirms that some are persuaded. Never do Pharisees resort to force. Even in Lk. 19.39, when they act as social control agents and command Jesus to silence his disciples, they do not turn to the warrior way of control. The recall of Pharisees who rejected John's baptism in 7.30 is an analepsis that provides information external to the narrative and characterizes no specific players in Luke's story. Conversely, the leaven of the Pharisees in 12.1 warns the disciples against the hidden cultural assumptions of the Pharisees in general. Finally, with Roland Meynet and Robert Tannehill, I find the account of Simon the Pharisee to be a poignant appeal to him to embrace a new view of reality that Simon and virtually no reader can avoid.

54. Bovon, *Luke*, 2:324, but inconsistently Bovon takes the misstep of calling them Jesus' enemies, 2:340, and representatives of 'constant hostility', 2:403.

8

Jesus, Son of Adam and Son of God (Luke 3.38): Adam-Christ Typologies in Luke–Acts

Yongbom Lee

Introduction

Goppelt more than seventy years ago recognized, 'Adam-Christ typology seems to be back of the genealogy of Jesus in Luke 3:23-38'.[1] Luke traces Jesus' genealogy from Joseph all the way back to Adam (3.23-38). Luke ends his genealogy with a profound statement – [υἱός] τοῦ Ἀδὰμ τοῦ θεοῦ ('[Jesus] of Adam of God'). Nolland comments on Lk. 3.23-38:

> Luke, unlike Matthew, continues the genealogy on from Abraham to Adam and then God. Here Luke closely follows the Greek OT, except for the final listing of God which is quite distinctive. By extending the genealogy in this way, Luke makes his most important point in this section. Adam as son of God comes after the baptismal address of Jesus as Son of God (Luke 3:22) and before the tempter's beguiling suggestions to Jesus as Son of God (4:1-13, and esp. vv 3, 9). Thus both contrast and continuity is established between Adam as son of God and Jesus as Son of God. Jesus takes his place in the human family and its (since Adam's disobedience) flawed sonship;

1. Goppelt concludes, 'The result is as follows: Ἰησοῦς...ὢν υἱὸς...τοῦ Ἀδάμ = בן אדם (Heb.) = בר אנשא (Aram.) = υἱὸς ἀνθρώπου (LXX) ("Jesus…was the son…of Adam, that is, the Son of Man")'; Leonhard Goppelt, *Typos: The Typological Interpretation of the Old Testament in the New*, trans. Donald H. Madvig (Grand Rapids: Eerdmans, 1982), 97–8; *Typos: Die typologische Deutung des Alten Testaments im Neuen* (Darmstadt: Bertelsmann Verlag, 1939); cf. Yongbom Lee, *The Son of Man as the Last Adam: The Early Church Tradition as a Source of Paul's Adam Christology* (Eugene: Pickwick, 2012).

> but in his own person in virtue of his unique origin (1:35), and also as worked out in his active obedience (4:1-13), he makes a new beginning of sonship and sets sonship on an entirely new footing.[2]

While Luke does not develop explicit and sophisticated Adam-Christ typologies as Paul does in Romans 5 and 1 Corinthians 15, he exhibits subtle Adam-Christ typologies in the beginning of his Gospel and in Paul's speech at Areopagus in Acts 17.22-31. Luke compares and contrasts Adam's sonship and Jesus' Sonship, in order to support the universal scope of his soteriology in his two- volume work. The good news of Jesus Christ is for everyone, both Jews and Gentiles. Fitzmyer criticizes Jeremias who recognized Adam-Jesus typology in Lk. 3.21–4.13 and argues, 'it is far from certain that Luke is working with such a motif'. He claims, 'The genealogy ends in v. 38 with "son of God", and the typology is therefore not to be sought between Jesus and Adam, the next to last name in the list'.[3] C. F. Evans notes, 'Adam cannot be a son of God in the same physical sense in which the others were sons of their fathers. It is either a literary device to make the end of the genealogy match its beginning with Jesus, the Son of God, or it is a simple unreflective expression of the divine activity in creation and redemption through a man.'[4] When we consider the literary context of Lk. 3.21–4.13, however, C. F. Evans's claim for 'a literary device' or 'a simple unreflective expression' is unconvincing. Against Fitzmyer's and C. F. Evans's scepticism, I agree with Nolland that Luke hints at Adam-Christ typologies in support of his universal soteriology. In this study, I will explore Luke's subtle Adam-Christ typologies in four aspects: (1) creation and incarnation, (2) disobedient and obedient son, (3) unfaithful and faithful servant and (4) creation and resurrection.

Creation and Incarnation

Luke compares the creation of Adam and the incarnation of Jesus in Lk. 3.21–4.13. The phrase πλήρης πνεύματος ἁγίου ('full of the Holy Spirit') (4.1) implies an Adam-Christ typology in the context of Jesus' baptism and temptation (3.21–4.13). In ch. 1, Gabriel prophesizes the birth of

2. John Nolland, *Luke 1–9:20*, WBC 35A (Waco: Word Books, 1989), 175.

3. Joseph A. Fitzmyer, *The Gospel according to Luke I–IX*, AB 28 (New York: Doubleday, 1982), 498; cf. Joachim Jeremias, 'Ἀδάμ', *TDNT* 1:141–3.

4. C. F. Evans also comments, 'The peculiar argument of Acts 17.24-31 offers something of a parallel, whereas it is doubtful whether the Pauline conception of Jesus as the second Adam and Son of man (1 Cor 15:25-49) is present'; C. F. Evans, *Saint Luke* (London: SCM Press, 1990), 253.

Jesus to Mary, 'The Holy Spirit will come upon you, and the power of the Most High will overshadow you; therefore the child to be born will be called holy – the Son of God' (1.35).[5] In ch. 3, Luke describes the baptism of Jesus, 'Now when all the people were baptized, and when Jesus also had been baptized and was praying, the heavens were opened, and the Holy Spirit descended on him in bodily form, like a dove; and a voice came from heaven, "You are my beloved Son; with you I am well pleased"' (3.21-22). Immediately after calling Adam 'the son of God' (3.28), Luke begins narrating the temptation of Jesus with this statement, 'And Jesus, full of the Holy Spirit, returned from the Jordan and was led by the Spirit in the wilderness for forty days, being tempted by the devil' (4.1-2a). The devil tempts Jesus twice with the protasis 'If you are the Son of God' (4.5, 9). Jesus' victory over the devil's temptations confirms his identity as the Son of God. Therefore, it is not by accident that Luke portrays Jesus as being 'full of the Holy Spirit' (4.1), already having informed his readers about Jesus' Spirit-originated birth (1.35) and God's confirmation of Jesus as his beloved Son with the Holy Spirit's descent on Jesus like a dove (3.22). The phrase 'full of the Holy Spirit' specifically reminds Luke's readers of the fact that Jesus is the Son of God.

Luke's perceptive readers familiar with the Old Testament would have remembered the creation of Adam in Genesis. C. A. Evans acutely observes that Luke's pneumatology provides a key to unlock Adam-Christ typology in Lk. 3.21–4.13.[6] Evans raises an interesting question, 'On what ground could Jesus be called the "Son of God?"' in relation to Adam, the son of God.[7] He argues, 'If it was by virtue of his Spirit-generation that Jesus was regarded as the "Son of God", then Luke likewise must have regarded Adam as "son of God" by virtue of his generation by the Spirit (or breath) of God'.[8] This point becomes clear when we read Gen. 2.7, Ezek. 37.9 and Prov. 1.23 with the MT and the LXX side by side. First, Gen. 2.7 LXX attests the phrase πνοὴ ζωῆς (נשמת חיים) ('a breath of life') in association with the verb ἐμφυσάω (נפח) ('to breathe'), which clearly refers to God's Spirit in the creation of Adam in his image.[9] Second, Ezek. 37.9 LXX translates the Hebrew word הרוח as τὸ πνεῦμα

5. I use ESV as the primary English translation of the Scriptures, unless I indicate otherwise.

6. C. A. Evans, 'Jesus and the Spirit: On the Origin and Ministry of the Second Son of God', in C. A. Evans and James A. Sanders, *Luke and Scripture: Function of Sacred Tradition in Luke–Acts* (Minneapolis: Fortress Press, 1993), 36–45.

7. Ibid., 38.

8. Ibid., 39.

9. I use NETS as the English translation of the LXX.

('the breath') and uses it in conjunction with the verb ἐμφυσάω.[10] Third, Prov. 1.23 LXX translates the Hebrew word רוחי as ἐμῆς πνοῆς ῥῆσις ('the expression of my breath'). These linguistic observations show us that the semantic realm of πνοή and that of πνεῦμα in Greek overlap each other, just as the semantic realm of נשם and that of רוח in Hebrew overlap each other. Although Luke never cites Gen. 2.7 LXX in Lk. 3.21–4.13, he echoes the creation of Adam through the breath/Spirit of God and compares it with the incarnation of Jesus through the Holy Spirit. C. A. Evans concludes that Luke's pneumatology provides 'the basis for understanding why he calls both Adam and Jesus sons of God'.[11] On the basis of *De Virt.* 37.203-4 in which Philo associates Adam's sonship of God with being created through the breath of God, C. A. Evans claims, 'It is clear therefore that Luke's notion of the divine sonship of Adam was neither unique nor unintelligible to first-century readers of Scripture'.[12] Luke does not portray here what is known as 'adoptionistic' Christology later in early church history. As Gathercole's seminal study shows, Luke and the other Synoptic Gospels convey Christ's pre-existence in their own ways.[13] Luke compares the creation of Adam and the incarnation of Jesus in that both are closely associated with the work of God's Spirit. As Johnson comments, 'By placing the genealogy where he has, furthermore, Luke points less to Jesus' human ancestry and more to his status as "God's son", and this is to be understood above all as a "sonship", mediated by the Holy Spirit'.[14] Luke's subtle Adam-Christ typology here supports the universal scope of his soteriology in which God's salvation through Jesus is not limited to the descendants of Abraham (Jews) but extended to all the descendants of Adam (Jews and Gentiles).[15] While many commentators

10. Ezek. 37.9 echoes Gen. 2.7 in the vision of the valley of dry bones (Ezek. 37.1-14). God speaks to the prophet, 'Prophesy to the breath; prophesy, son of man, and say to the breath, This is what the Lord says: Come from the four winds, and blow into these corpses, and they shall live.'

11. Evans, 'Jesus and the Spirit', 40.

12. Ibid.

13. Simon J. Gathercole, *The Pre-existence Son: Recovering the Christologies of Matthew, Mark, and Luke* (Grand Rapids: Eerdmans, 2006); cf. Christopher Kavin Rowe, *Early Narrative Christology: The Lord in the Gospel of Luke* (Grand Rapids: Baker Academic, 2006).

14. Luke Timothy Johnson, *The Gospel of Luke*, Sacra Pagina 3 (Collegeville: Liturgical Press, 1991), 72.

15. Wolter relatedly notes, 'Jesus wird dadurch nicht zu einem neuen Adam, aber Lukas benutzt die Gottessohnschaft Adams als Modell, um den Bedeutungsrahmen für das Verständnis der Gottesshonschaft Jesu abzustecken'; Michael Wolter, *Das Lukasevangelium*, HNT 5 (Tübingen: Mohr Siebeck, 2008), 177.

acknowledge that the phrase [υἱός] τοῦ Ἀδὰμ τοῦ θεοῦ (3.38) signifies Jesus' identification with humanity, they overlook this important link between Luke's Christology and pneumatology in his description of the Sonship of Jesus.[16]

Disobedient and Obedient Son

Immediately after calling Adam 'the son of God' (3.38), Luke narrates the temptation of Jesus (4.1-13). To begin with, Luke alludes to the forty years of Israel's testing in the wilderness, when he cites three texts from Deuteronomy (8.3; 6.13, 16), which correspond with the forty days of Jesus' testing in the wilderness. As Pao and Schnabel point out, 'When the foundation story of Israel is evoked, Jesus does not simply embody Israel, but rather becomes the foundation of God's people in the eschatological era. As he did in the past, God is once again calling a "people for his name" (Acts 15.14).'[17] Considering the fact that Luke just compared Adam the son of God and Jesus the Son of God (3.21-38), however, I contend that Luke's contrast goes beyond Jesus and Israel. Matthew in his parallel passage (Mt. 4.1-11) alludes to Israel's disobedience in the wilderness and contrasts it with Jesus' obedience in the wilderness. Luke goes beyond this and echoes the first transgressor Adam in Genesis 3, when we consider the fact that his genealogy ends with Adam, the son of God (3.38). Luke indirectly contrasts Adam's disobedience – who provided the archetype of Israel's disobedience – and Jesus' obedience here. In response to the devil's temptations (4.1-13), Jesus cites Deut. 8.3; 6.13, 16, whose context concerns the temptations that Israel faced in the wilderness. Israel, God's firstborn son (Exod. 4.22), failed to overcome temptations like their ancestor Adam the son of God. In contrast, Jesus the son of Adam and the Son of God overcomes every temptation. While Matthew presents Jesus as a new Israel, Luke presents Jesus as a new Adam in God's new creation. As Pao and Schnabel note, 'Luke's genealogy…argues for the presence of thematic links on some

16. E.g. ibid., 175; Francois Bovon, *Luke 1: A Commentary on the Gospel of Luke 1:1–9:50*, Hermeneia (Minneapolis: Fortress Press, 2002), 137; Fitzmyer, *Gospel according to Luke I–IX*, 498; Joel Green, *The Gospel of Luke*, NICNT (Grand Rapids: Eerdmans, 1997), 189; I. Howard Marshall, *The Gospel of Luke*, NIGTC (Grand Rapids: Eerdmans, 1978), 161.

17. David W. Pao and Echhard J. Schnabel, 'Luke', in *Commentary on the New Testament Use of the Old Testament*, ed. D. A. Carson and G. K. Beale (Grand Rapids: Baker Academic, 2007), 287.

levels, and clearly the creation story often was linked with the exodus story (cf. Exod. 15; Deut. 32:7-14; Ps. 74:12-17; 77:12-20; 89:5-37; 114), especially when the new creative act of God is expected (cf. Isa. 43:15-21; 45:9-18; 51:12-16)'.[18] Jesus the obedient Son of God in the wilderness leads the way to God's salvation (a new exodus) and restores the corrupted image of God in Adam by his transgression (a new creation). Considering the universal scope of Luke's soteriology, it makes sense why Luke echoes the original temptation story of Adam, when narrating Jesus' temptation story. Israel's disobedience ultimately models after Adam's disobedience, who is the first human being and the progenitor of all human beings. This requires not a new Israel but ultimately a new Adam. As Goppelt notes, 'Israel is God's firstborn son (Exod 4:22; Hos 11:1)...he [Christ] is the firstborn of the new people of God'.[19]

Unfaithful and Faithful Servant

Luke contrasts Adam and Jesus as the unfaithful servant of the Lord and the faithful Servant of the Lord. This point is the most original contribution of this study and requires a careful intertextual investigation. Having overcome the devil's temptations in the wilderness, Jesus begins his public ministry in Nazareth with his manifesto. After reading Isa. 61.1-2 LXX, Jesus claims, 'Today this scripture has been fulfilled in your hearing' (Lk. 4.18-21). While Luke cites here Isa. 61.1-2 LXX, which many scholars identify with Trito-Isaiah (chs 56–66), he identifies Jesus with the Servant of the Lord in Deutero-Isaiah (chs 40–55) here (cf. Isa. 42.1) and elsewhere in his two-volume work (Lk. 22.37; Acts 8.32-33; 13.47; cf. Acts 3.13; 4.27, 30).[20] As Johnson notes, 'What was said by

18. Ibid.

19. Goppelt, *Typos*, 99.

20. As Koet observes, 'Luke 4 [vv. 10-19] and Luke 7 [vv. 18-29] together depict Jesus as somebody who fulfills a mission like that of the Servant as described in Isaiah 61. The fact that Luke 4 recalls the references to a Servant figure as in Isaiah 42 shows that this background is also important in Luke 4'; Bart J. Koet, 'Isaiah in Luke–Acts', in *Isaiah in the New Testament*, ed. Maarten J. J. Menken and Steve Moyise (London: T&T Clark International, 2005), 86; similarly, Peter Mallen, *The Reading and Transformation of Isaiah in Luke–Acts*, LNTS 367 (London: T&T Clark International, 2008), 199. In Deutero-Isaiah, the identity of the Servant of Yahweh (עבדי יהוה; παῖς/δοῦλος κυρίου) is multifaceted. Watts lists five referents for the Servant of Yahweh in Deutero-Isaiah: (1) Israel, (2) Cyrus, (3) the city of Jerusalem, (4) the prophet himself and (5) an unnamed individual leader; John D. W.

the prophet Isaiah about the "Servant of the Lord", Jesus declares to be "fulfilled" that day in him (4:21)'.[21] I propose that Luke contrasts Adam and Jesus as the unfaithful servant of the Lord and the faithful Servant of the Lord in the context of Lk. 3.1–4.30, in his extension of the earlier contrast between Adam and Jesus as the disobedient son of God and the obedient Son of God. In order to recognize this Adam-Christ typology, we must go back to the creation account in Genesis.

In the beginning chapters of the Hebrew Bible, the verb עבד is used in association with Adam (Gen. 2.5, 15; 3.23), which the LXX translates as ἐργάζομαι. The use of the verb in Gen. 2.15 is particularly interesting: וינחהו בגן-עדן לעבדה ולשמרה ('[God] put him [Adam] in the garden of Eden to work it and keep it'). Although the phrase עבדי יהוה is not attested in the MT, it is clear that Adam is the first and original servant of the Lord. Wenham comments on Gen. 2.15:

> עבד 'to serve, till' is a very common verb and is often used of cultivating the soil (2:5; 3:23; 4:2, 12, etc.). The word is commonly used in a religious sense of serving God (e.g., Deut 4:19), and in priestly texts, especially of the tabernacle duties of the Levites (Num 3:7-8; 4:23-24, 26, etc.). Similarly, שׁמר 'to guard, to keep' has the simple profane sense of 'guard' (4:9; 30:31), but it is even more commonly used in legal texts of observing religious commands and duties (17:9; Lev 18:5) and particularly of the Levitical responsibility for guarding the tabernacle from intruders (Num 1:53; 3:7-8). It is striking that here and in the priestly law these two terms are juxtaposed (Num 3:7-8; 8:26; 18:5-6), another pointer to the interplay of tabernacle and Eden symbolism already noted (cf. *Ber. Rab.* 16:5). It should be noted that even before the fall man was expected to work; paradise was not a life of leisured unemployment. Both *Enuma Elish* and the Atrahasis epic also speak of man being created to work to relieve the

Watts, *Isaiah 34–66*, WBC 25, rev. edn (Nashville: Thomas Nelson, 2005), 652–9. It goes beyond the scope of this study to discuss in depth the multidimensional identity of the Servant of Yahweh in Deutero-Isaiah. For our discussion here, it is sufficient for us to accept Beuken's thesis that the speaker in the first person in Isa. 61 identifies himself as a successor to the Servant in Isa. 40–55, with 'the coordinating themes of being moved by God's Spirit, good tidings and consolation, and ultimately the ascent of a righteous progeny'; W. A. M. Beuken, 'Servant and Herald of Good Tidings: Isaiah 61 as an Interpretation of Isaiah 40–55', in *The Book of Isaiah*, ed. J. Vermeylen, BETL 81 (Leuven: Leuven University Press, 1989), 438–40; similarly, Blenkinsopp, *Isaiah 56–66*, Anchor Yale Bible Commentaries 56 (New Haven: Yale University Press, 2003), 221; John N. Oswalt, *The Book of Isaiah Chapters 40–66*, NICOT (Grand Rapids: Eerdmans, 1998), 562–3.

21. Johnson, *Gospel of Luke*, 81; cf. Pao and Schnabel, 'Luke', 289–90.

> gods (EE 6:33-36; A 1.190-97). But the biblical narrative gives no hint that the creator is shuffling off his load onto man: work is intrinsic to human life.[22]

The garden of Eden represents a temple and Adam was the first priest serving and worshipping God. Genesis 1.26-27 tells us that, when God created Adam in his own image, God made Adam his servant/steward/representative to rule over all his creation on behalf of him.[23] However, Adam failed to be faithful to his identity and calling. Being tempted to become like God, Adam disobeyed God's command not to eat the fruit of the tree of the knowledge of good and evil (Gen. 3.5) and was expelled from the garden of Eden. Unlike Adam and Israel, Jesus the Son of God overcomes every temptation and proves to be faithful in his calling as the Servant of the Lord (cf. Lk. 22.42; Phil. 2.6-8). While Luke never mentions 'the Servant of the Lord' in Lk. 4.8-21, he clearly identifies Jesus with the Servant of the Lord in Deutero-Isaiah. There is no linguistic evidence that Luke has Adam in mind here; however, when we consider all the subtle Adam-Christ typologies that he has demonstrated up to this point, it is very possible. On the basis of these intertextual and thematic links, I contend that Luke echoes Adam as the first and original servant of the Lord in the garden of Eden (Gen. 2.15), and contrasts Adam the unfaithful servant of the Lord and Jesus the faithful Servant of the Lord.

Creation and Resurrection

Luke compares Adam and Jesus in Paul's speech to Areopagus in Acts 17.22-31, as the first human being created and the first human being resurrected. Paul's Areopagus speech often is associated with natural theology. Paul contextualizes the gospel into the Athenians' religious and philosophical context. Paul begins his speech with his mention of an altar with the inscription 'To the unknown god'.[24] Paul claims that the unknown god the Athenians worship is the God who created everything and the Creator 'does not live in temples made by man' (vv. 24-25). Then Paul mentions

22. Gordon J. Wenham, *Genesis 1–15*, WBC 1 (Nashville: Thomas Nelson, 1987), 67; similarly, J. Richard Middleton, *The Liberating Image: The Imago Dei in Genesis 1* (Grand Rapids: Brazos Press, 2005), 82–8; Eugene Carpenter, 'עבד', *NIDOTTE*, 304–5.

23. Similarly, Middleton, *Liberating Image*, 88–9.

24. Cf. Pausanias, *Descr.* 1.1.14; Philostratus, *Vit. Apoll.* 6.3.5; Diogenes Laertius, *Lives* 1.110.

God's creation of every nation from the first man, Adam (vv. 26-27a). As Pervo notes, 'The verse opens with a compressed assertion of the unity of the human race grounded in a common origin from God'.[25] Paul cites from a poem attributed to Epimenides and a Stoic philosopher Aratus and argues that God is not far from humanity (vv. 27b-28).[26] We are God's offspring (γένος ὑπάρχοντες τοῦ θεοῦ) (v. 29). Although God neglected the times of ignorance in the past, God now commands everyone to repent and will judge the world by an appointed judge (vv. 30-31). God has confirmed this by raising him from the dead. As Bock notes, 'The resurrection (Acts 2:24, 32; 13:33-34) is God's attestation about Jesus to all people'.[27] When Paul highlights God's creation of the world and God's judgement of the world through Christ, he mentions God's creation of the first human being Adam and God's raising of Christ from the dead, the firstfruits of resurrection (cf. 1 Cor. 15.20). In this way, Luke hints at a subtle Adam-Christ typology in Acts 17.22-31, in which he parallels the creation of Adam and the resurrection of Christ.

Conclusion

While we frequently encounter the statement that Jesus is the Son of God in the Gospels, the statement that Adam is the son of God is unique to Lk. 3.38. This study explores Luke's subtle Adam-Christ typologies in the beginning of his Gospel and in Paul's speech at Areopagus in Acts 17.22-31. While not fully developing Adam-Christ typology as Paul does in Romans 5 and 1 Corinthians 15, Luke employs subtle Adam-Christ typologies to support the universal scope of his soteriology in the following four aspects. First, Luke compares the creation of Adam and the incarnation of Jesus. Second, Luke contrasts Adam's disobedience and Jesus' obedience. Third, Luke contrasts Adam and Jesus as the unfaithful servant of the Lord and the faithful Servant of the Lord (cf. Gen. 2.5, 15; Isa. 42.1; Lk. 22.37; Acts 8.32-33; 13.47). Fourth, in Paul's speech to Areopagus in Acts 17.22-31, Luke compares Adam and Jesus as the first human being created and the first human being resurrected from the dead. These subtle Adam-Christ typologies support the universal scope of Luke's soteriology. God's salvation through Jesus is not only for Jews but also for Gentiles.

25. Richard I. Pervo, *Acts*, Hermeneia (Minneapolis: Fortress Press, 2009), 435–6.

26. Cited in F. F. Bruce, *The Book of Acts*, NICNT (Grand Rapids: Eerdmans, 1988), 339.

27. Darrel L. Bock, *Acts*, BECNT (Grand Rapids: Baker Academic, 2007), 570.

9

Identity and Christology: The Ascended Jesus in the Book of Acts

Steve Walton

I. *Introduction*

Luke[1] alone in the New Testament gives Jesus' exalted status narrative expression (Lk. 24.51; Acts 1.9-11), and thereby signals its significance for him. Nevertheless, Luke is far from alone in recognizing this status of Jesus to which the ascension points, as numerous scholars recognize.[2] Thus, Hebrews emphasizes Jesus' position of rule and authority in heaven (e.g. Heb. 1.3), Revelation highlights Jesus' reign as a key encouragement to beleaguered believers (e.g. Rev. 3.21; 5.6-14; 7.17) and Paul assumes Jesus' present rule in writing of Jesus' expected return (e.g. Rom. 8.34; Phil. 2.9; 1 Thess. 1.10; 4.16; cf. Eph. 1.20; 4.7-13; Col. 3.1; 1 Tim. 3.16). The Synoptic Gospels similarly speak of Jesus as 'ἐρχόμενον with the clouds' (e.g. Mt. 24.30; 26.64; Mk 14.62; Lk. 21.27), denoting either his 'going' to God to be given power and authority (Dan. 7.13) or his 'coming' from heaven to earth bearing divine power and authority[3] – for

1. I enter the usual caveat, that for the purpose of this paper I make no specific assumptions about Luke's identity, and use the name as a convenient and widely accepted shorthand.

2. See, e.g., the helpful collection of references in Douglas Farrow, *Ascension and Ecclesia: On the Significance of the Doctrine of the Ascension for Ecclesiology and Christian Cosmology* (Edinburgh: T. & T. Clark, 1999), 275–7.

3. For the former view, see N. T. Wright, *Jesus and the Victory of God*, Christian Origins & the Question of God 2 (London: SPCK, 1996), 360–5; for the latter, see, e.g. on Mk 13.26, Robert H. Stein, *Mark*, BECNT (Grand Rapids: Baker Academic,

our purpose, either option signals that Jesus is to be revered alongside God. John's Gospel speaks of Jesus' 'glorification' (e.g. 7.39; 8.54; 12.16; 14.13; 17.5), which denotes Jesus the son's journey back to his Father in heaven through death, resurrection and exaltation (3.13; 13.1-3; 16.5, 28).

Two questions focus our reflection on Luke's particular contribution in Acts to this widespread New Testament theme. First, we shall consider the portrait of Jesus as ascending and ascended by reflecting on the Acts account of the ascension (Acts 1.9-11), references to Jesus' status in speeches in Acts 2–7 (located in Jerusalem) and the ascended Jesus' engagement with the story of Acts, particularly in relation to Saul/Paul. This study will form the larger part of this essay.

Assembling the data to form this portrait will open up our second question, which is the extent to which Jesus is portrayed as having what has become known as 'divine identity', a category developed by Richard Bauckham and now used by a number of scholars working on New Testament Christology. This will allow us to engage with the discussion about whether Luke's Christology is accurately categorized as 'low' or 'high'.[4]

II. *Acts' Portrayal of Jesus as Ascending and Ascended*

Acts' portrait of the ascension event begins in 1.2 with the statement ἄχρι ἧς ἡμέρας...ἀνελήμφθη 'until the day when…he was taken up'. The verb is a 'divine' passive, denoting the actant as God. NRSV and NIV 2011 both add 'into heaven', although the equivalent words are not present in the Greek text. That said, Dupont rightly argues against van Stempvoort that the verb denotes the ascension of Jesus, rather than his passing from this world in death, and so those two English versions are making explicit a claim made implicitly by the verb choice.[5] A key argument for this interpretation is that the same verb in the passive voice is used in LXX for

2008), 613–15; Joel Marcus, *Mark*, AB 27, 27A, 2 vols (New Haven: Yale University Press, 1999, 2009), 2:908–89; Mark L. Strauss, *Mark*, ZECNT 2 (Grand Rapids: Zondervan, 2014), 591–2.

4. For a sketch of the debate with helpful references, see Christopher M. Tuckett, 'The Christology of Luke–Acts', in *The Unity of Luke–Acts*, ed. J. Verheyden, BETL 142 (Leuven: Peeters, 1999), 133–64, esp. 139–64.

5. P. A. van Stempvoort, 'The Interpretation of the Ascension in Luke and Acts', *NTS* 5 (1958–59): 30–42; Jacques Dupont, ''ΑΝΕΛΗΜΦΘΗ (Act. I. 2)', *NTS* 8 (1962): 154–7. For discussion, see my forthcoming commentary in the WBC series.

Elijah and Enoch passing from this world into heaven (4 Kgdms 2.9, 10, 11; 1 Macc. 2.58; Sir. 48.9; 49.14) and by Peter when speaking of Jesus' going to heaven (Acts 1.22, with wording very similar to this verse).[6]

II.a. *Luke's Description of the Ascension Acts 1.9-11*

The primary portrait of the event itself is in 1.9-11, and several points are crucial to note: the rich visual vocabulary, and the phrase εἰς τὸν οὐρανόν 'into heaven'; the verb voices; the cloud; the interpretive words of the two men in white; the implications suggested concerning Jesus' status; and the portrait of Jesus' presence.

II.a.1. *Visual Vocabulary and 'into Heaven'*. The rich visual vocabulary is frequently noted as a feature of this passage; there are five verbs of seeing in these two sentences: βλεπόντων 'as they were watching', ἀπὸ τῶν ὀφθαλμῶν αὐτῶν 'from their sight [literally, eyes]', ἀτενίζοντες 'as they were staring', ἰδού 'see!' and ἐμβλέποντες 'looking intently'.[7] This collocation of verbs of seeing is remarkable, and these terms are different from the terms generally used for visionary experiences.[8] Thus Barrett observes on βλεπόντων, that this verb 'places the Ascension in the same category of events as any other happening in the story of Jesus'[9] – indeed, this point is stronger than Barrett suggests, given the collocation of five such verbs.

Not only this, but Luke's account stresses the destination to which the ascending Jesus travels as εἰς τὸν οὐρανόν 'into heaven' (vv. 10b, 11), while playing on the dual reference of the phrase by having the two men in white ask why the onlookers are looking 'into heaven' (v. 10a), which could mean 'into the skies' or 'into the realm of God'.

6. Dupont, 'ΑΝΕΛΗΜΦΘΗ', 156.

7. Some ancient mss have the simple form βλέποντες 'looking', but that does not affect the argument here; for discussion see Bruce M. Metzger, *A Textual Commentary on the Greek New Testament*, 2nd edn (Stuttgart: Deutsche Bibelgesellschaft/ United Bible Societies, 1994), 245.

8. John B. F. Miller, *Convinced That God Had Called Us: Dreams, Visions, and the Perception of God's Will in Luke–Acts*, Biblical Interpretation 85 (Leiden: Brill, 2007), 8, notes that four words are most significant in Lukan dream-visions, ἐνύπνιον, ὀπτασία, ὅραμα and ὅρασις; he does not list any of the terms found here. Contra Rick Strelan, 'Strange Stares: ἀτενίζειν in Acts', *NovT* 41 (1999): 235–55 and John J. Pilch, *Visions and Healing in the Acts of the Apostles: How the Early Believers Experienced God* (Collegeville: Liturgical Press, 2004), 40–1, there is no evidence that ἀτενίζω denotes entering an altered state of consciousness through a self-induced trance.

9. C. K. Barrett, *A Critical and Exegetical Commentary on the Acts of the Apostles*, ICC, 2 vols (Edinburgh: T. & T. Clark, 1994, 1998), 1:81.

However, to notice these linguistic features is to raise the inevitable question: what actually happened? If we had been there with a video camera, what would we have recorded? David Strauss observes:

> The first impression from this narrative is clearly this: that it is intended as a description of a miraculous event, an actual exaltation of Jesus into heaven, as the dwelling-place of God, and an attestation of this by angels; as orthodox theologians, both ancient and modem, correctly maintain.[10]

Strauss is clear, of course, that no such event could have taken place. James Dunn (who quotes Strauss)[11] has for some years, and in several places, insisted that Luke cannot be describing events within space-time, but that Luke, because of his worldview, is compelled to express his belief in Jesus' location at the Father's right side and his consequent reign using 'concrete' imagery.[12] Dunn claims that the *only* worldview open to Luke is a 'three-decker' universe. He quotes from Bultmann's famous observation about what 'modern man' [*sic*] can believe:

> *Man's knowledge and mastery of the world* have advanced to such an extent through science and technology that it is no longer possible for anyone seriously to hold the New Testament view of the world – in fact, there is no one who does. What meaning, for instance, can we attach to such phrases in the creed as 'descended into hell' or 'ascended into heaven'? We no longer believe in the three-storied universe which the creeds take for granted. The only honest way of reciting the creeds is to strip the mythological framework from the truth they enshrine – that is, assuming that they contain

10. David Friedrich Strauss, *The Life of Jesus Critically Examined*, Lives of Jesus (London: SCM Press, 1973), 750.

11. James D. G. Dunn, 'The Ascension of Jesus: A Test Case for Hermeneutics', in *Auferstehung – Resurrection: The Fourth Durham-Tübingen Research Symposium: Resurrection, Transfiguration, and Exaltation in Old Testament, Ancient Judaism, and Early Christianity (Tübingen, September 1999)*, ed. Friedrich Avemarie and Hermann Lichtenberger, WUNT 135 (Tübingen: Mohr Siebeck, 2001), 301–22, here 308–9.

12. Dunn, 'Ascension'; see also his earlier dialogue with David Gooding, provoked by James D. G. Dunn, 'Demythologizing – The Problem of Myth in the New Testament', in *New Testament Interpretation*, ed. I. Howard Marshall (Exeter: Paternoster Press, 1977), 285–307; David W. Gooding, 'Demythologizing Old and New, and Luke's Description of the Ascension: A Layman's Appraisal', *IBS* 2 (1980): 95–119; James D. G. Dunn, 'Demythologizing the Ascension – A Reply to Professor Gooding', *IBS* 3 (1981): 15–27; David W. Gooding, 'Demythologizing the Ascension – A Reply', *IBS* 3 (1981): 46–54. His most recent statement is James D. G. Dunn, *Beginning from Jerusalem* (Cambridge/Grand Rapids: Eerdmans, 2009), 145–51, although this offers more questions than answers.

any truth at all, which is just the question that theology has to ask. No one who is old enough to think for himself supposes that God lives in a local heaven. There is no longer any heaven in the traditional sense of the word. The same applies to hell in the sense of a mythical underworld beneath our feet. And if this is so, the story of Christ's descent into hell and of his Ascension into heaven is done with.[13]

Dunn observes:

...this is not simply the way Luke conceived the ascension; it was the *only* way he could conceive of it... The departure of Jesus to heaven as narrative could not be conceptualized except as an ascension. And if we want to speak of the event behind the narrative, we have also to say that the event could not be experienced except as the witness of an ascension.[14]

This presents us, says Dunn, with 'the problem of a conceptualization of reality which we today do not, cannot share, but do not know how to reconceptualize'.[15] He goes on to argue that to ask what happened in any detail is to miss the point: what was important for the 'earliest tradents of the ascension tradition' was the *theme* of Jesus' exaltation to God's right side.[16] Dunn is considerably less clear – as he concedes – about the 'event-character' of the ascension.[17] Thus he concludes that the ascension is 'a story which clothes a still vivid metaphor'.[18]

I have reported Dunn's views at length because I judge that they are both widely held and deeply mistaken. The prime mistake Dunn makes, as does Bultmann, is the one from which others flow, and that is the claim that Luke had only one way of seeing the world open to him, a 'three-decker' universe in which heaven was 'up'. Two primary objections to this view may be lodged.

First, this is manifestly not so, for we know of a number of writers from the 6th century BCE onwards who held different views of cosmology, and the widespread nature of these views, temporally and geographically, means it is highly likely that Luke and others of his day knew of them.

13. Rudolf Bultmann, 'New Testament and Mythology', in *Kerygma and Myth: A Theological Debate*, ed. Hans-Werner Bartsch, trans. Reginald H. Fuller, 2 vols (London: SPCK, 1953, 1962), 1:1–44, here 4 (his italics). This is a fuller quotation than Dunn's.

14. Dunn, 'Ascension', 312 (his italics).

15. Ibid., 313.

16. Ibid., 317.

17. Ibid.

18. Ibid., 322.

Thus, prominent Greeks thinkers, notably Pythagoras and his followers, rejected the 'flat earth' view which was previously universal in our ancient sources, and conceived the earth as spherical.[19] In the 2nd millennium BCE, Babylonian and Chinese astronomers knew the planets Mercury, Venus, Mars, Jupiter and Saturn.[20] Astronomers thus faced the challenge of conceptualizing a universe with such bodies, and by the 1st century CE worked with models that included a spherical universe beyond which nothing physical existed, but beyond which an 'unmoved mover' – god – who brought the whole universe into being might exist, and who must be eternal (Aristotle, *Met.* 12.7.2=1073a). As far as we can see, such models did not necessitate picturing a realm outside the universe as 'up'. In Jewish thought, while 'heaven' is part of the merism denoting all of reality, 'heaven and earth',[21] the term is used both for the skies and for the realm of God. There does not seem to be agreement among Jewish writers of our period about the structure of reality: for example, apocalyptic writers described 'tours' of heaven from which visitors returned (e.g. *1 En.* 17–36; *2 En.* 3–66), although without precision about the location of heaven; Philo adapted Greek understanding in discussing creation (e.g. *Creation*, which synthesizes Genesis 1–3 and Plato's *Timaeus*), but again without precision about the relation of the heavenly realm to that of physical reality. There were people, and quite a number, in Luke's time who distinguished (in our terms) outer space from the divine realm.

Secondly, the use of 'up' in this context is necessary metaphorical and (as we would say) earth-centred, for ancients generally (but not exclusively)[22] held a geocentric view of the universe. Of course Luke describes things in the language of his day; but for him to speak of Jesus rising into the air and then being taken into heaven no more implies

19. See the masterly survey of Edward Adams, 'Graeco-Roman and Ancient Jewish Cosmology', in *Cosmology and New Testament Theology*, ed. Jonathan T. Pennington and Sean M. McDonough, LNTS 355 (London: T&T Clark International, 2008), 5–27. For what follows I am also in debt to my doctoral student, David Larsen.

20. A. Sachs, 'Babylonian Observational Astronomy', *Philosophical Transactions of the Royal Society of London. Series A, Mathematical and Physical Sciences* 276 (1974): 43–50.

21. See discussion in Jonathan T. Pennington, 'Dualism in Old Testament Cosmology: *Weltbild* and *Weltanschauung*', *SJOT* 18 (2004): 260–77, who argues cogently that OT cosmology is predominantly bipartite (heaven and earth) rather than tripartite (including an underworld).

22. Aristarchus of Samos (4th/3rd centuries BCE) proposed a heliocentric model; see Thomas Heath, *Aristarchus of Samos: The Ancient Copernicus* (Oxford: Clarendon Press, 1913).

that heaven is physically ‘up’ than a person today speaking of ‘sunrise’ should be taken to believe that the sun rotates around the earth – it is metaphorical, observer-centred language. To suggest that the ancients did not recognize that they used metaphorical language in speaking of the location of the divine realm in relation to the earthly is a rather flat-footed way of handling metaphor when we know the ancients discussed it with some sophistication.[23]

In addition, we may note that the line of thought that we know better than Luke because of our scientific discoveries, and thus his presentation of the ascension must be rejected, entails a modernist confidence in ‘objective’ knowledge which is untenable in a postmodern world where we recognize the necessarily perspectival nature of knowledge claims, including those of scientific knowledge.

Thus, unless we adopt an antisupernaturalist rejection of phenomena beyond our experience, Luke’s description of the event, that Jesus was elevated from the ground and passed into a cloud which obscured him from the sight of the onlookers, an act which was interpreted (probably through the lens of Dan. 7.13) as transferring him into the divine realm, is both coherent and consistent. Luke has recorded earlier post-resurrection accounts which portray Jesus as both disappearing and appearing (Lk. 24.31, 36), so the ascension account is not adding much to these descriptions. To take the description this way is in no way to deny that some of the features are *also* understood symbolically, but it is to reject the view that they are merely ‘apocalyptic stage props’ which are a way of speaking of Jesus’ exalted status without necessarily describing an event in space-time.[24] It is to say that the ascension of Jesus is portrayed as no less a space–time event than any other resurrection appearances of Jesus.

Why is this significant? As we shall see, Luke both implies theological claims about Jesus and his present status on the basis of the ascension story and presents that story as an event within the space–time universe. To deny the space–time-ness of the event is thus to deny the implications which Luke suggests flow from it – as so often in Scripture, history and

23. E.g. *Poet.* 21–22; *Rhet.* 3.2.6–4.4, 3.10.7–11.15. See the brief discussion in Michael S. Silk, ‘Metaphor and Simile’, in *Oxford Classical Dictionary*, 4th online edn (2012). Online: http://www.oxfordreference.com/view/10.1093/acref/9780199545568.001.0001/acref-9780199545568-e-4151 (accessed 13 January 2017).

24. E.g. Dunn, ‘Ascension’, 318: ‘The point is that such apocalyptic language would be widely recognized even then as having symbolic rather than literal force’. To say this is, of course, to concede that ancients could distinguish metaphor from literal description.

theology are not easily separable categories, and nor are historical and theological claims easy to split from one another. This may or may not be so elsewhere in the New Testament authors' language about Jesus' present exalted status alongside the God of Israel, but it seems to be so with Luke.

II.a.2. *Verb Voice, Subject and Object.* Luke's choice of verb voice, subject and object to describe Jesus' movement in this section stands out. There are a number of 'divine passive' uses, that is, uses of the passive voice where Jesus is the subject but with no stated actant, which imply that God is the one performing the action:[25] ἐπήρθη 'he was lifted up' (v. 9),[26] πορευομένου 'as [he] was going' (v. 10), ἀναλημφθείς '[who] was taken] and πορευόμενον '[who] was going' (v. 11). Further, Jesus is the object of the verb ὑπέλαβεν 'took him up' (v. 9), and the verb's subject is νεφέλη 'a cloud', which is not to be understood as acting with a will and mind of its own, but under the guidance of its Creator (see further below).

The significance of these features is that Luke thereby presents the God of Israel as acting to elevate Jesus, in both physical lifting and being raised in standing and esteem. As we shall see, this implication is made explicit in Peter's Pentecost speech (2.33-36).

II.a.3. *The Cloud.* A singular cloud ὑπέλαβεν Jesus from (ἀπό) their sight. Before discussing the echoes of the cloud with other clouds in Luke and elsewhere in Scripture, we should note the verb. The verb here is sometimes translated 'hid' (NIV 2011, 1984), whereas its more usual sense is 'take up' or 'receive up'.[27] Haenchen observes that the verb 'covers the moment of both concealment and separation, either of which may be expressed by ἀπό'.[28] None of this implies that the cloud is a means of transport to heaven.[29]

25. Note also the use of passive verbs when Luke speaks of Jesus' resurrection, again implying that God raised Jesus. For discussion, see my essay, 'Jesus, Present and/or Absent? The Presence and Presentation of Jesus as a Character in the Book of Acts', in *Characters and Characterization in Luke–Acts*, ed. Frank Dicken and Julia A. Snyder, LNTS 548 (London: Bloomsbury T&T Clark, 2016), 123–40, here 132.

26. With (e.g.) Joseph A. Fitzmyer, *The Acts of the Apostles: A New Translation and Commentary*, AB 31 (New York: Doubleday, 1998), 210.

27. BDAG s.v. So NRSV.

28. Ernst Haenchen, *The Acts of the Apostles* (Oxford: Blackwell, 1971), 149 n. 4; see BDAG, 105 ἀπό §§1.b, d.

29. Contra Fitzmyer, *Acts*, 210; with Eckhard Schnabel, *Acts*, ZECNT, expanded digital edn (Grand Rapids: Zondervan, 2012), ad loc.

What echoes might we hear when Luke mentions this cloud? Two passages in the Third Gospel resonate with this use, each with their own further biblical echoes. First, when Jesus speaks of the cloud (singular) in which the son of man comes or goes with power and glory (Lk. 21.27), the cloud portrays Jesus as (most probably)[30] going to God as the son of man in Dan. 7.13-14, to be given authority and rule over all things.

Secondly, at the transfiguration a (singular) cloud overshadows Jesus and his three disciples, and a voice from the cloud declares, 'This is my beloved son. Listen to him!' (Lk. 9.34-35). Here biblical echoes are multiple. There is Ps. 2.7, as at the baptism of Jesus (Lk. 3.22), although there the voice addresses Jesus directly, 'You are my beloved son'.[31] The description of the cloud in Lk. 9.34 as overshadowing (ἐπεσκίαζεν) them points to the cloud which overshadowed the tent of meeting and prevented Moses from entering (Exod. 40.35), and reverberates with the echo of the travelling cloud of God's presence with the wandering Israelites led by Moses (Exod. 13.21-22). These echoes invite readers to see the transfiguration cloud as marking God's presence and (thus) to hear the voice as God's voice.

Together, the Lukan and biblical echoes of this cloud mark the ascension scene as Jesus' exaltation by God to a divinely occupied place of universal rule and authority, which is confirmed by a divine voice – a voice which will come here through angels (v. 11, see below).

II.a.4. *The Words of the Two in White.* The two figures in white (v. 10), most probably angels, speak to interpret the disciples' experience (v. 11). Luke's ἰδού 'look!' (untranslated in many versions)[32] signals that readers should pay particular attention to the following words, which will give God's perspective on the ascension event. This interpretation provides a contrast to other heavenly journeys in Second Temple Jewish texts, which frequently involve a human travelling into the divine realm and then returning with a message for their earth-bound hearers and readers.[33] Here, rather, the angels bring the message, which promises the return of Jesus from heaven at a future date in a similar manner to his ascension.

30. For references see n. 3.

31. See discussion in Max Turner, *Power from on High: The Spirit in Israel's Restoration and Witness in Luke–Acts*, JPTSup 9 (Sheffield: Sheffield Academic Press, 1996), 197–201.

32. HCSB and CEV unsatisfactorily render it as 'suddenly'.

33. E.g. *1 En.* 17–36; Philo, *Spec. Leg.* 3.1-6; Rev. 1.10-11, 19; for brief discussion, see James D. Tabor, 'Heaven, Ascent to', *ABD* 3:91–4; James M. Scott, 'Heavenly Ascent in Jewish and Pagan Tradition', *DNTB* 447–51.

Contra the assumptions of Conzelmann and others, this passage neither says nor implies anything about a 'delay' of Jesus' future coming;[34] in fact, it says nothing about the timing of the event, in line with Jesus' statement that the disciples will not know (v. 7).

II.a.5. *Jesus' Presence as a Theme in the Ascension Scene.* Throughout the ascension scene and its immediate antecedent, the presence of Jesus is a significant theme. In his response to the question about the restoration of Israel, Jesus speaks of himself as represented by his witnesses, those with whom he speaks (v. 8, taking the genitive μου as 'on my behalf'). In the light of the way the Spirit's coming follows Jesus' ascension into heaven, it appears that Luke signals in the same verse that Jesus is present through the Spirit, who empowers his witnesses.

The threefold 'into heaven' (vv. 10, 11 [twice]), noted earlier, signals Jesus' presence in heaven, and Peter's Pentecost speech will clarify that Jesus now belongs in the position of power at God's right side (2.33), ruling over the universe. It is hard to accept Strelan's antithesis concerning the phrase εἰς τὸν οὐρανόν: 'This is not a spatial or locative description; it means that Jesus now participates in the rule of God'.[35] We do not have to choose between location as the denotation of the phrase 'into heaven' and rule as the connotation of the phrase – both are natural understandings of this phrase.

The presence of Jesus in heaven will not be permanent, however, for he will return to earth, promise the duo in white (v. 11). This will be the time which Peter will call the time of 'universal restoration' (3.21), when history is wrapped up and all things are restored to match the Creator's intentions.

This combination of Jesus' temporary presence in heaven with the Spirit's coming during that period, and then Jesus' return signalling and effecting the restoration of all things, portrays Jesus as having immense power and authority, of the kind which YHWH alone was understood to have in Second Temple Jewish thought.

II.a.6. *Jesus' Exaltation to the Place of Power.* Two other implications flow from the exaltation of Jesus, as we look back to Luke's account at the end of his Gospel, and forward into the narrative of the following chapters of Acts.

34. Hans Conzelmann, *The Theology of St Luke*, trans. Geoffrey Buswell (London: Faber & Faber, 1960), 95–136.

35. Rick Strelan, *Strange Acts: Studies in the Cultural World of the Acts of the Apostles*, BZNW 126 (Berlin: W. de Gruyter, 2004), 39.

Looking back, it is striking that Luke describes the disciples as *worshipping* (προσκυνήσαντες) Jesus after he is taken up to heaven (Lk. 24.52). The only other use of προσκυνέω in the third Gospel is where the devil invites Jesus to worship him, and Jesus rejects that invitation with a quotation from Deut. 6.13 which specifies that it is the Lord your God *alone* who should be worshipped (4.7-8).[36] Luke gives no indication that the disciples are misguided in 24.52 – rather the reverse – and thus that parallel indicates that it is appropriate to treat Jesus as YHWH alone should be treated.

Looking forward into the Acts narrative, Jesus' ascension opens traffic flow between heaven and earth. The Spirit will come (Acts 2), angels will appear in the narrative (e.g. 5.19; 8.26; 10.3; 12.7), signs and wonders will be performed, enabled by divine power (e.g. 2.43; 5.12; 6.8), people will be healed and delivered from evil spirits in the name of Jesus (e.g. healing: the sequence 3.6-7, 16; 4.10; cf. 9.34; deliverance: 16.16-18; cf., comically, 19.11-17). The entry of Jesus into heaven has opened the door, we might say, for heaven to come to earth.

II.b. *Interpretation of Jesus' Exaltation through Speech in Acts 2–7*

We turn from the account of the ascension to four passages in Acts 2–7 which both state and interpret Jesus' present exalted status: Peter's Pentecost speech (esp. 2.33-36), Peter's speech in the temple courts after the healing of the man at the Beautiful Gate (esp. 3.20-21), Peter and the apostles' speech to the Sanhedrin (esp. 5.31) and Stephen's dying words (7.56-60).

II.b.1. *Acts 2.33-36.* The key to understanding the Pentecost speech's claims about Jesus' status is v. 33. Jesus is now 'exalted (ὑψωθείς, a further 'divine passive') at the right hand of God' and in this position 'has received from the Father the promise which is the Holy Spirit'.[37] Thus the one who has 'poured out (echoing Joel 3.1-2 LXX [MT 2.28-29]) what you see and hear' is Jesus – he continues to be the verb subject throughout the sentence. 'What you see and hear' refers to the phenomena of vv. 1-4: the rushing wind, the tongues of fire, and the speaking in other languages, which are markers of the Spirit's coming (v. 4b).

36. I owe this observation to Richard B. Hays, *Reading Backwards: Figural Christology and the Fourfold Gospel Witness* (Waco: Baylor University Press, 2014), 69.

37. Taking the genitive τοῦ πνεύματος τοῦ ἁγίου as epexegetical.

The key to interpreting this verse is to ask, in Second Temple Jewish understanding, who pours out the Spirit.[38] The answer is YHWH and YHWH alone: no one else has this ability, for God's Spirit '*was a way of speaking of the active* (usually self-revealing) *personal presence of the transcendent God himself*'.[39] Luke prepares for this sentence by the presence of 'God declares' (λέγει ὁ θεός) in Acts 2.17. This phrase, absent from Luke's source text (Joel 2.28-32), presents God himself as speaking of the promise of the Spirit (Acts 2.17-21) – *God* will pour out the Spirit in the last days, not any human being or angel or other creature. So when Peter speaks in v. 33 to say that *Jesus himself* is the one who has poured out the Spirit at Pentecost – not even that Jesus *mediates* the Spirit from YHWH – this implies that Jesus, exalted to God's right hand, is Lord of the Spirit and the Spirit is his 'executive power'.[40] The Spirit is now related to Jesus as the Spirit has been related to God: 'God the Father grants Jesus *the same authority as himself* to pour out the Spirit'.[41] Indeed, Luke has Jesus say that he himself will send the Father's promise, i.e. the Spirit (Lk. 24.49, emphatic ἐγώ). Heaven is now 'open' for much greater traffic to earth as a result of Jesus' ascension – hence a sound comes from there (v. 2), and hence the Spirit comes from the exalted Jesus.

Peter wastes no time in spelling these implications out by contrasting Jesus with David, who did not ascend to heaven (v. 34) and identifying Jesus as the 'Lord' of Ps. 110.1 (a passage spoken by Jesus in a similar argument about David and the Messiah in Lk. 20.42-43). Thus Jesus is the one who now sits at God's right side awaiting his enemies being made his footstool: he is both Lord and Messiah (v. 36). As Barrett observes, '[h]e who shares the throne of God shares his deity; and he who is God is what he is from and to eternity – otherwise he is not God'.[42] In the setting of v. 33, Jesus is now in the same category as Israel's God as 'Lord', and that is why he is the one whose name people must call on to be saved (vv. 21, 38), for he is 'Lord of all', as Peter later says (10.36).

38. For what follows, see my essay Steve Walton, 'Whose Spirit? The Promise and the Promiser in Luke 12:12', in *The Spirit and Christ in the New Testament and Christian Theology*, ed. I. Howard Marshall, Volker Rabens and Cornelis Bennema (Grand Rapids: Eerdmans, 2012), 35–51, here 47–8.

39. Turner, *Power*, 277 (his italics).

40. Ibid., 278; cf. Douglas Buckwalter, *The Character and Purpose of Luke's Christology*, SNTSMS 89 (Cambridge: CUP, 1996), 194–6.

41. Buckwalter, *Character*, 195 (his italics); cf. *TDNT* 6:405 (Jesus is 'not a pneumatic, but the Lord of the Spirit').

42. Barrett, *Acts*, 1:152.

II.b.2. *Acts 3.20-21.* A key claim of Peter's speech in the temple courts (3.11-26), following the healing of the man at the Beautiful Gate (3.1-10), is about the present position and role of Jesus. He is now in heaven (v. 21), a (divinely) necessary (δεῖ) state of affairs.[43] From there he will be sent (by God) at the restoration of all things, the time when cosmic renewal and regeneration will take place. The echo of ἀποστέλλω (v. 20) from 1.11 makes this connection sure – it is Jesus' return which will coincide with (and probably trigger) cosmic restoration.[44] Jesus' status is signalled as one who not only restores Israel,[45] but the entire universe. In the absence of demiurges and the like in Judaism, this can only mean that Jesus is placed in a role which YHWH was expected to accomplish.[46]

II.b.3. *Acts 5.31.* Peter and the apostles respond to the Sanhedrin's reproach for continuing to speak in Jesus' name after being forbidden to do so (4.17-18; 5.28) with a theo- and Christocentric answer. Not only is God the one who must be obeyed rather than mere humans (v. 29; cf. 4.19), but this same God has reversed the Sanhedrin's verdict by raising Jesus from the dead (v. 30) and has exalted Jesus to his right side as ἀρχηγός and σωτήρ (v. 31). This passage echoes the themes of 2.33-35, which suggests that the ascension and its implications are also in view here. σωτήρ is predicated of Jesus in Lk. 2.11 (and not since in Luke–Acts) and the following reference here to repentance and forgiveness indicates what Jesus saves from. It is not widely noticed that σωτήρ is a common biblical designation of God, as well as (far less) human deliverers sent by God.[47] The following purpose clause indicates that God gives repentance

43. See the fine discussion in Charles H. Cosgrove, 'The Divine ΔEI in Luke–Acts: Investigations into the Lukan Understanding of God's Providence', *NovT* 26 (1984): 168–90.

44. Again we notice, contra Conzelmann, that there is no indication of the time – short or long – in which this return will take place, with Hans F. Bayer, 'Christ-Centred Eschatology in Acts 3:17-26', in *Jesus of Nazareth, Lord and Christ: Essays on the Historical Jesus and New Testament Christology*, in Joel B. Green and Max Turner (Grand Rapids: Eerdmans; Carlisle: Paternoster Press, 1994), 236–50, here 250.

45. See Richard Bauckham, *The Jewish World around the New Testament: Collected Essays I*, WUNT 233 (Tübingen: Mohr Siebeck, 2008), 325–70, esp. 361–6; Bayer, 'Eschatology'.

46. See the valuable discussions of OT and later Jewish 'restoration of Israel' themes in James M. Scott, ed., *Restoration: Old Testament, Jewish, and Christian Perspectives*, JSJSup 72 (Leiden: Brill, 2001).

47. God: e.g. LXX Deut. 32.15; 1 Sam. 10.19; Pss. 23.5; 24.5; 26.1 [MT 27.1]; 61.3 [MT 62.2]; 94.1 [MT 95.1]; Isa. 12.2; 17.10; 45.15, 21; 62.11; Bar. 4.22; Jdt. 9.11; 1 Macc. 4.30; *3 Macc.* 6.29, 32; 7.16. Human deliverers: Judg. 3.9, 15; Neh.

and forgiveness to the people as a consequence of Jesus' exaltation, or perhaps that Jesus himself is the one who does the giving: it is not completely clear who is the actant of the infinitive δοῦναι (v. 31).

II.b.4. *Acts 7.55-60.* Towards the end of Stephen's speech, he sees the exalted Jesus at God's right side (v. 55) and identifies him as the son of man, most probably alluding to Dan. 7.13, which is also in a martyr context.[48] In response to this sight, Stephen prays to Jesus: 'Lord Jesus, receive my spirit' (v. 59). Luke's specific expression is that Stephen 'calls on' (ἐπικαλούμενον), and this is 'cultic practice' language, as Hurtado notes.[49] Acts 9.14, 21 characterize the believers as those who 'call on the name (of Jesus)' (cf. 22.16). However, in (OT) Scripture, it is God alone who is the proper recipient of prayer,[50] so to include Jesus with God as one who is given 'public, corporate, cultic reverence'[51] is a remarkable innovation in a Jewish context which 'drew a sharp line between any such figure and the one God in the area of cultic practice, reserving cultic worship for the one God'.[52]

II.b.5. *Summary.* The passages we have considered provide a body of evidence that early believers understood Jesus to be exalted to the place of honour at God's right side in heaven, and that from there he exercised authority and rule to the extent that he took the God of Israel's distinctive role in both giving (the Spirit, phenomena, repentance and forgiveness) and receiving (prayer).

II.c. *Narrative Portrayal of Jesus as Acting and Appearing from Heaven*
Let us then turn to consider how Jesus is portrayed as acting and appearing from heaven in the narrative portions of Acts.[53] Because space is limited,

9.27. By NT times it may well have become a messianic designation (*1 En.* 48.7; 51.5a; see J. C. O'Neill, *The Theology of Acts in Its Historical Setting*, 2nd edn (London: SPCK, 1970), 144).

48. C. F. D. Moule, *The Origin of Christology* (Cambridge: CUP, 1977), 17. This is the only NT use of 'the son of man' outside the Gospels.

49. Larry W. Hurtado, *Lord Jesus Christ: Devotion to Jesus in Earliest Christianity* (Grand Rapids: Eerdmans, 2003), 198.

50. Cf. the uses of 'call on the name', which is the name of YHWH, in Ps. 80.19; Isa. 12.4; Zeph. 3.9; Zech. 13.9.

51. Hurtado, *Lord*, 199.

52. Ibid., 47–8.

53. See the more detailed study in Matthew Sleeman, *Geography and the Ascension Narrative in Acts*, SNTSMS 146 (Cambridge: CUP, 2009), *passim*.

we focus on Jesus' appearance to Saul of Tarsus, a highly significant event, for Luke tells it three times (Acts 9; 22; 26), and some examples – chosen from a number – where healing and deliverance come through Jesus or his name.

II.c.1. *Saul of Tarsus Acts 9; 22; 26.* Luke tells the story of Jesus' appearances to Saul of Tarsus on the road to Damascus three times. While there are differences among the stories, the core presentation of Jesus who appears is consistent among the three.[54] Here we observe factors signalling key features of the identity of Jesus.

First, the one who appears from heaven is Jesus himself, and he is characterized as 'Lord'. In response to Saul's question, he announces himself as 'Jesus, whom you are persecuting' (9.5; 22.8; 26.15). Ananias speaks of 'the Lord Jesus' as the one who appeared to Saul (9.17), and this interprets the uses of 'Lord' in vv. 10, 11, 13, 15. Further, he is the Lord 'who rescues' (ἐξαιρούμενος, 22.17), something predicated only of YHWH in LXX.[55]

Secondly, as we noticed above, the one who appears is identified with his suffering followers: *he* is being persecuted. This implies that Jesus now has multi-locational ability – he is not merely said to be identified with his people, but he himself is being persecuted in the persecution of his people.

Thirdly, the Jesus who appears stage-manages events by visiting Ananias and directing him to visit Saul (9.10-16). This much resembles the 'divine appointments' of Philip and the Ethiopian eunuch (8.26-40) and Peter and Cornelius (10.1–11.18) which surround this story in the Acts narrative. In both of those stories, it is clear that divine action brings the two protagonists together (8.26, 29; 10.3-7, 19-20, 30-33; 11.11-12, 17-18) and the same is true here – except that it is explicitly 'the Lord Jesus…[who] has sent me' (9.17).

Finally, Jesus strikes Saul blind and directs him to await instruction (9.6, 8-9; 22.10-11). Illness, including the removal of sensory powers – and even death – is frequently a divine action, or the action of a divine

54. For a detailed study, see Timothy W. R. Churchill, *Divine Initiative and the Christology of the Damascus Road Encounter* (Eugene: Pickwick, 2010), esp. 191–249.

55. Churchill, *Initiative*, 170–1, with the vast array of references in footnotes – 131 uses in the LXX. See also John J. Scullion, 'God in the OT', *ABD* 2:1014–48, here 1044 §3 'God Who Rescues'.

delegate in Scripture.[56] Direction from God to await instruction is similar,[57] as is commissioning to a divine task (26.16-18).[58]

II.c.2. *Healing and Deliverance.* Jesus himself acts in healing and deliverance in Acts. Healing can happen by Jesus explicitly being stated to be the actant, such as in the healing of Aeneas: 'Aeneas, Jesus the Messiah heals you' (9.34). It can also happen through the powerful effect of the name of Jesus, which stands for him in action, such as in the healing of the man at the Beautiful Gate: 'in the name of Jesus the Messiah the Nazarene, walk!' (3.6; cf. 3.16; 4.7, 17, 30).[59]

Deliverance from evil spirits similarly happens through the name of Jesus, illustrated positively by Paul's deliverance of the slave girl in Philippi (16.18), and comically in the failure of the Jewish exorcists in Ephesus, who are overcome by a demonized man because, although they use the name of Jesus, they are not in the kind of relationship with him which the believers are (19.13-17).[60] The conclusion of the episode states that 'the name of Jesus' is honoured (19.17).

II.c.3. *Acts 26.23.* Finally, in this necessarily selective discussion, the exalted Jesus is active in the world *himself*, for as Messiah he proclaims light to both Jews and Gentiles (26.23). This is a remarkable statement, as Beverly Gaventa notes: 'In Luke's understanding, it is entirely possible for Jesus to be at the right hand of God and simultaneously at work in Christian witness and work'.[61]

56. E.g. divine: 1 Cor. 10.1-5; divine delegate: Lk. 1.20; Acts 13.6-12; see valuable discussion of this theme in John Christopher Thomas, *The Devil, Disease and Deliverance: Origins of Illness in New Testament Thought*, JPTSup 13 (Sheffield: Sheffield Academic Press, 1998), *passim*, with summary on 297–301.

57. E.g. Exod. 24.12; Num. 9.8; Pss. 38.15; 106.13.

58. Churchill, *Initiative*, 245–6.

59. More fully, see my essay 'Jesus', here 133–4. On the name of Jesus in Acts, see John A. Ziesler, 'The Name of Jesus in the Acts of the Apostles', *JSNT* 4 (1979): 28–41.

60. See discussion in my essay 'Evil in Ephesus: Acts 19:8-40', in *Evil in Second Temple Judaism and Early Christianity*, ed. Chris Keith and Loren T. Stuckenbruck, WUNT 2/417 (Tübingen: Mohr Siebeck, 2016), 224–34, esp. 229–33.

61. Beverly R. Gaventa, 'Acts of the Apostles', in *New Interpreter's Dictionary of the Bible*, ed. Katharine Doob Sakenfeld, 5 vols (Nashville: Abingdon Press, 2006), 1:33–47, here 43.

II.d. *Summary*

This is a remarkable collection of data from Acts: we have seen that Luke locates Jesus after his ascension at the place of power at the Father's right side, that the apostolic message both proclaims and explains that status and that Jesus exercises authority from there by continuing to act within the earthly sphere. To what extent can we take the further step of seeing Luke as in some sense identifying Jesus with the God of Israel?

III. *Acts and 'Divine Identity' Christology*

'Divine identity Christology' has recently entered scholarly conversation about the early church's understanding of Jesus. Richard Bauckham introduces this category to answer the question what, according to Second Temple Judaism, makes God God. The failure to answer this question directly left older debate on Christology in ultimately sterile debates between ontology and function, or between 'high' and 'low' Christologies. I shall suggest that this category is a helpful lens through which to consider the data of Acts.

III.a. *What Is 'Divine Identity' Christology'?*

Bauckham first (to my knowledge) writes of how to recognize Israel's God as God in *God Crucified*, a superb short discussion of New Testament Christology.[62] His short answer is that God is known to be God because he is the sole creator and the sole ruler of all things.[63] Key examples include Nebuchadnezzar's recognition of God's rule: 'his sovereignty is an everlasting sovereignty' (Dan. 4.34) and the vision of YHWH as creator in Isaiah 40–55, such as 'The Lord is the everlasting God, the creator of the ends of the earth' (Isa. 40.28).

YHWH's sovereign status leads to monolatry – worship of this God alone. Second Temple Judaism mocked idolatry and the multiple gods of other nations (e.g. Isa. 44.9-20) because of the exclusive status of YHWH: 'I am the first and I am the last; besides me there is no god' (Isa. 44.6).

62. Richard Bauckham, *God Crucified: Monotheism and Christology in the New Testament* (Didsbury Lectures 1996; Carlisle: Paternoster Press, 1998), now incorporated into Richard Bauckham, *Jesus and the God of Israel: God Crucified and Other Studies on the New Testament's Christology of Divine Identity* (Grand Rapids: Eerdmans, 2008). References are to the 1998 edition.

63. Bauckham, *God*, 1–22; see my fuller summary in Walton, 'Jesus', 136–7, where I discuss a wider range of data from Acts.

Bauckham himself applies this line of thinking to Paul and John, very fruitfully,[64] and Richard Hays has recently used 'divine identity Christology' as a tool to interrogate how the four Gospels read Scripture.[65] Our question in relation to our ascension data in Acts is this: to what extent does Acts portray Jesus as sharing the divine identity of YHWH?

III.b. *To What Extent Does Acts Portray Jesus as Sharing the Divine Identity of YHWH?* Acts portrays Jesus as now exalted to the position of power at God's right side (1.9, 11; 2.33), and this means he is able to give the Spirit (2.33; 8.20), an ability which belongs to YHWH alone in Second Temple Jewish understanding. Jesus is given the divine name in consequence, 'Lord' (2.36), even 'Lord of all' (10.36), signalling his universal power and rule (and implicitly challenging any other 'lords' who claimed universal sovereignty).

The exalted Jesus is appropriately addressed in prayer, notably by Stephen (7.59), but also by implication in the phrase 'call on the Lord's name', where the 'Lord' is Jesus (2.21, 38; cf. 22.16).[66] This links into the question of monolatry, for Second Temple Judaism regarded YHWH alone as a proper object of prayer. Hurtado has further documented the early believers' devotional practices in relation to Jesus in Acts, and argues cogently that they bespeak a regard for Jesus as in the same category as YHWH.[67]

Jesus is not only exalted, but he is present with his followers: he is persecuted when they are persecuted (9.4; 22.7; 26.14). Acts is a record of what Jesus *continues* to do and teach (1.1). Thus Jesus acts from heaven on earth, in giving commands and instructions in divine fashion (9.6, 11, 15-16; 20.24) and in healing and deliverance (esp. 9.34, along with references to the 'name' of Jesus in such acts).

While there is thus no doubt that Jesus in Acts shares YHWH's sovereign position and rule, as well as YHWH's ability to be present in different places at the same time, the part of divine identity Christology which is missing in Acts is Jesus as Creator. There are clear mentions of God as Creator (e.g. 17.24), but not explicit statements that Jesus/the Son engaged in creating the universe, by contrast with such statements in

64. Bauckham, *God*, 25–69.

65. Hays, *Backwards*; more fully Richard B. Hays, *Echoes of Scripture in the Gospels* (Waco: Baylor University Press, 2016).

66. See Walton, 'Jesus', 133–4.

67. Hurtado, *Lord*, 177–216.

John, Colossians and Hebrews.[68] Nevertheless, the 'ascension evidence' in Acts for Jesus as sharing in the sovereign rule of YHWH is widespread and cogent – and this case can be expanded into other features of the narrative.[69]

One further point is worth noting. Bauckham observes that through the New Testament portrait of Jesus as sharing the divine identity a new feature of the God of Israel is made known, namely that God is a God who suffers in Christ.[70] Not only that, through Christ's suffering it becomes clearer that God identifies with the pain of his creation and enters into it, standing alongside people who are lowly, weak, poor or suffering. This novel feature of the understanding of Israel's God is present in Acts too, for the exalted Jesus is one who suffered in his earthly life, and especially in his passion at the hands of sinful people (2.23-24; 3.13-15). This Jesus is to be identified as YHWH's servant who suffers on behalf of the people of God to redeem them (8.32-35), and now suffers with his people (9.4).

68. Jn 1.3; Col. 1.15-17; Heb. 1.2.

69. See Walton, 'Jesus'.

70. Bauckham, *God*, 69–77.

10

The Jewish Saviour for Israel in the Missionary Speeches of Acts

Christoph Stenschke

I. *Introduction*

The many speeches of the book of Acts have a prominent place in the scholarly study of the book. In addition to queries regarding their literary character and their historical reliability, they have been mined for the theology of the author. According to many scholars, these speeches indicate the theological concerns of Acts particularly clearly.[1] Of the speeches, the so-called 'missionary speeches' have attracted most attention. We will focus on a neglected aspect of early Christian missionary preaching as portrayed in Acts, namely the *Jewish particularity in the presentation of the origin, ministry and significance of Jesus and of the salvation wrought by him.*[2] This aspect has received comparatively little attention, despite a number of recent monographs on the role and significance of Israel in Luke–Acts, in particular, on the motif of the restoration of Israel.[3] Studies

1. For criticism see R. I. Pervo, *Acts: A Commentary*, Hermeneia (Minneapolis: Fortress Press, 2009), 22.

2. This is a significant aspect of the particularism of Acts, but not the only one.

3. For examples, see G. Wasserberg, *Aus Israels Mitte – Heil für die Welt: Eine narrativ-exegetische Studie zur Theologie des Lukas*, BZNW 92 (Berlin: W. de Gruyter, 1998); D. P. Moessner, ed., *Jesus and the Heritage of Israel: Luke's Narrative Claim upon Israel's Legacy*, Luke The Interpreter of Israel 1 (Harrisburg: Trinity Press International, 1999); M. E. Fuller, *The Restoration of Israel: Israel's Re-gathering and the Fate of the Nations in Early Jewish Literature and Luke–Acts*, BZNW 138 (Berlin: W. de Gruyter, 2006); C. Schaefer, *Die Zukunft Israels bei*

of Acts and of its speeches often emphasize their universal scope. And indeed, Jesus is presented as universal Lord and Saviour.[4] Yet, these speeches also stress the Jewish nature of Jesus and his ministry and of salvation. For Luke–Acts, both aspects go hand in hand, as has rightly been emphasized by Bock.[5] Before we examine this aspect, a few general observations regarding the speeches are necessary. For several reasons the study of the missionary speeches of Acts is a challenging task.[6]

They are *summaries* of what was supposed to have been said on a particular occasion. For example, Acts 2.40 indicates that 'with *many other words* Peter bore witness and continued to exhort them, saying…'. It is also historically plausible that Peter's sermon on the Jewish Feast of Weeks lasted for more than about 90 seconds.[7] We are not dealing with complete speeches, but with *summaries*.[8]

Lukas: Biblisch-frühjüdische Zukunftsvorstellungen im lukanischen Doppelwerk im Vergleich mit Römer 11–9, BZNW 190 (Berlin: W. de Gruyter, 2012); and D. L. Bock, 'Israel in Luke–Acts', in *The People, the Land and the Future of Israel: Israel and the Jewish People in the Plan of God*, ed. D. L. Bock and M. Glaser (Grand Rapids: Kregel, 2014), 103–15.

4. According to M. L. Soards, *The Speeches of Acts: Their Content, Context and Concerns* (Louisville: Westminster John Knox Press, 1994), 204, the universal significance of God's salvation is found in many places and various ways in Acts, but is prominent in 1.8; 2.17-21, 39; 10.36, 43, 47; 11.17; 13.38-39, 47; 14.15; 15.8-9; 17.30; 18.6; 20.31; 22.14-15, 21; 26.12-18, 23, 25-26; 28.28. For a survey of Lukan Christology see H. D. Buckwalter, 'The Divine Saviour', in *Witness to the Gospel: The Theology of Acts*, ed. I. H. Marshall and D. Peterson (Grand Rapids: Eerdmans, 1998), 107–23.

5. 'Israel'.

6. On the missionary speeches, see C. H. Gempf, 'Historical and Literary Appropriateness in the Mission Speeches in Acts' (PhD diss., University of Aberdeen, 1988) and C. Stenschke, *Luke's Portrait of Gentiles Prior to Their Coming to Faith*, WUNT 2/108 (Tübingen: Mohr Siebeck, 1999). The strong emphasis on the speeches of Acts in the 1970s and 1980s (this is where Luke's theology was – almost exclusively – to be found!) has given way to a more balanced treatment of all of Luke–Acts in more recent research.

7. Acts 20.9, 11 suggest that Paul could speak for a long time. Even if one allows for generous literary revision, the speeches of contemporary orators such as Cicero give an indication as to the actual length of ancient speeches. The speeches that appear in the works of ancient historians differ in length.

8. See R. Bauckham, 'Kerygmatic Summaries in the Speeches of Acts', in *History, Literature and Society in the Book of Acts*, ed. B. Witherington (Cambridge: CUP, 1996), 185–217.

The missionary speeches in Acts are formulated with the *readers* of *all* of Luke–Acts in mind. After having read the Gospel, they are familiar with the aspects of God's salvation in Jesus that Luke chose to emphasize (Lk. 1.1-4).[9] There was no need for repetition in Acts. As M. Korn observes,

> The proclamation of Jesus in the missionary speeches presents only a skeleton in order to show their dependence on the past history of Jesus. For the readers of Acts, the flesh for this skeleton comes from the Gospel of Luke. For good reasons the beginning of Acts refers to the Gospel (Acts 1.1-2) as the presupposition for the following second volume.[10]

In addition, representative speeches before representative audiences (Jews in Jerusalem, Gentiles in Caesarea and Jews in the Diaspora) are reported in some detail.[11] For speeches on later occasions, short summaries suffice since the readers are familiar with the content of the earlier speeches. Some scholars have drawn far-reaching conclusions about Lukan theology from the alleged omissions in some speeches. For example, the fact that Jesus does not feature significantly in the speeches in Lystra and Athens caused U. Wilckens to conclude that Jesus was no longer relevant. In the words of Korn:

> Do these two sermons represent a new phase in the history of the church, i.e. the Gentile Christian mission, in which the past history of Jesus does not play a role any longer? Wilckens assumed this and concluded that, in Luke's own time, the Jesus-material was no longer relevant for the purposes of the missionary proclamation and that is was only in catechesis that this material still played a role.[12]

Given the nature of the missionary speeches in Acts and given that Acts is Luke's second volume and that Luke avoids repetition, such conclusions are highly questionable. In addition to the readers being familiar with

9. For detailed discussion, see I. H. Marshall, 'Acts and the "Former Treatise"', in *The Book of Acts in Its Ancient Literary Setting*, ed. B. W. Winter and A. D. Clarke, Acts in its First Century Setting 1 (Grand Rapids: Eerdmans; Carlisle: Paternoster Press, 1993), 163–82 and his discussion, 'Acts as Witness to the Gospel', in *The Acts of the Apostles*, NT Guides (Sheffield: JSOT Press, 1992), 43–6.

10. *Die Geschichte Jesu in veränderter Zeit: Studien zur bleibenden Bedeutung Jesu im lukanischen Doppelwerk*, WUNT 2/51 (Tübingen: Mohr Siebeck, 1993), 216.

11. Luke reports in some detail Paul's first missionary speech in Acts 13.16-41. See H. F. Bayer, 'The Preaching of Peter in Acts' and G. W. Hansen, 'The Preaching and Defence of Paul', in Marshall and Peterson, eds, *Witness*, 257–74, 295–324.

12. *Geschichte*, 216 (all translations from German sources).

Luke's Gospel, Jervell notes that 'Like Luke's Gospel, Acts presupposes that the life of Jesus was generally known to the people of God'.[13]

The narrative setting of the different missionary speeches needs to be considered carefully.[14] According to Luke's portrayal, some of the speeches in Acts were delivered before audiences of people who were familiar with the life of Jesus. This applies to the missionary speeches in Jerusalem in Acts 2 and 3 and to the defense speeches of the apostles before the religious leaders of Jerusalem. After all, the religious establishment kept a close eye on John the Baptist and Jesus from an early stage (cf. Lk. 5.17). When Jesus entered Jerusalem, he was no stranger. In addition, he spent several days in the city before his death. The disciples on the road to Emmaus rightly assumed that *everybody* in the city would be familiar with the recent events concerning Jesus (Lk. 24.18). If, as C. Gempf persuasively argues,[15] there is historical and literary appropriateness, it is not to be expected that the speeches of the early chapters of Acts present Jesus in much detail. There was no need to mention or even emphasize his Jewish origin as this was not contested. Instead, they focus on his *significance* and, in particular, on the resurrection, which proved him to be the Messiah and which was highly contentious (Acts 4.2).

II. *The Jewish Identity of Jesus and the Jewish Scope of His Ministry and of Salvation*

The *Jewish* scope of the missionary speeches becomes apparent in several areas. We separate here, for the sake of clarity, what is interwoven in the speeches.

II.a. *Jesus the Jewish Saviour*

The speeches leave no doubt about the Jewish origin of Jesus. He is an ἀνήρ from Nazareth (2.22; 3.6; 4.10; 6.14; 10.38; 22.8;[16] 26.9). In addition

13. *Die Apostelgeschichte*, KEK 3 (Göttingen: Vandenhoeck & Ruprecht, 1998), 145.

14. See the section 'Identifying the Speeches' in Soards, *Speeches*, 18–21. For a recent discussion of the sources of Acts, see Pervo, *Acts*, 12–14.

15. 'Appropriateness'.

16. E. J. Schnabel, *Acts*, ZECNT (Grand Rapids: Zondervan, 2012), 903: 'At the same time Paul's listeners may have noted that Jesus did not come from a famous city such as Tarsus (cf. v. 3), nor from Jerusalem, the center of the world for Jews, where they expected the Messiah to rule. Nevertheless, the fact that Nazareth is a quintessential Jewish town emphasizes the Jewishness of Paul's loyalties and convictions.'

to identifying the place Jesus comes from – according to Pervo – the title "Nazorean"...adds Israelite color'.[17] Jesus is presented as the ultimate fulfillment of the prediction of Deut. 18.15 of a prophet like Moses who is to be raised '*from your [fellow Israelite/Jewish] brothers*' (3.22).[18] The reference to 'David, the Patriarch' in Acts 2.29, a crucial figure in the history of Israel (2.30), explains who Jesus was and what happened to him, the Son of David (2.30-32: God 'would set one of his descendants on the throne...he foresaw and spoke about the resurrection of the Christ... This Jesus God raised up.'). The God of Israel glorified his servant Jesus (2.13). God has brought to Israel a Saviour, Jesus, from *David*'s offspring (13.22-23).[19] In this way it becomes clear that Jesus is the Son of David, the Messiah and Saviour of Israel, whom God promised in Scripture. Jervell comments as follows:

> The promise, ἐπαγγελία, 2.39; 13.32; 26.6, to David is, that a Saviour for Israel would come from his descendants... The Davidic descent of Jesus is presupposed, Lk. 1.32; 18.38-39; 20.41, in accordance with the prophecy of Nathan in 2 Sam. 7.12... What happened to Jesus was the fulfillment of the promise to David... As a matter of course Jesus is the Saviour of Israel... He is Israel's Messiah, also for non-Jews. Jesus belongs to the history of the people of God and is the ruler of Israel.[20]

With regard to Acts 13.17-23, he states: 'The history of the election of the Fathers onwards points to David and further beyond to Jesus... But it is decisive that in this manner Jesus becomes part of Israel's history';[21] see also Acts 13.32-33. Through his resurrection, Jesus becomes the king of Israel (13.32). Given these references and the characterization of Jesus in Luke's Gospel, it was thus not necessary to identify Jesus explicitly as a Jew.

II.b. *Judaea and Jerusalem as the Stage of the Ministry of Jesus*

The ministry of Jesus (and its results in the early church) happened throughout all Judaea, beginning from Galilee after the baptism that the

17. *Acts*, 564.
18. For detailed description see Schnabel, *Acts*, 217–18.
19. Jervell, *Apostelgeschichte*, 358: 'Through the resurrection the promise of a Saviour for Israel from the lineage of David was fulfilled'. Jesus' origin is known. This is a matter of honour in the ancient world; see K. C. Hanson and D. E. Oakman, *Palestine in the Time of Jesus: Social Structures and Social Conflicts*, 2nd edn (Minneapolis: Fortress Press, 2008), *passim*. His humble earthly origins are not denied.
20. *Apostelgeschichte*, 356.
21. Ibid., 355–6.

Jewish prophet John proclaimed in the entire region around the Jordan (10.37). The setting of Jesus' ministry was all of Judaea.[22] John the Baptist, mentioned in this context, proclaimed a baptism of repentance to *all the people of Israel* (13.24). Jesus' deeds occurred 'both in the country of the Jews [that is in Galilee and in Judaea] and in Jerusalem' (10.39).[23] The disciples and others who had come with Jesus *from Galilee to Jerusalem* are witness to his ministry in Galilee and to his crucifixion, burial and resurrection in Jerusalem (13.31; see Lk. 9.51; 18.31; 19.28; 23.49; Acts 1.21-22; 10.39, 41). The inhabitants of Jerusalem and their rulers did not recognize Jesus but condemned him (13.27). The Roman officer Pontius Pilate was involved as judge in the death of Jesus in his function as *praefectus Iudaeae* (according to an inscription bearing his name discovered in Caesarea,[24] see Lk. 3.1 ἡγεμονεύοντος; Acts 3.13; 13.28). This also firmly places the events in Judaea. The resurrection appearances of Jesus took place in Jerusalem (13.32; cf. 13.31). All of that happened as a fulfilment of Jewish Scripture (13.29, a fulfilment of everything that the prophets had predicted about him). 'The saving message was sent first to the Jews, through Jesus, who – although universal sovereign – labored and died in Judea'.[25]

II.c. *The Jews as Primary Recipients of Salvation in References to Jesus*

The *actual first addressees* of the Gospel are the people of Israel (2.14, 22, 29, 'again it is emphasized that the audience belongs to Israel…in this way the addresses are identified as members of the ancient people of God.').[26] In Acts 2.14, Peter's audience consists of Judaeans from the surrounding region and of inhabitants of Jerusalem and thus of people from the Roman province of Judaea. In Acts 2.22, the audience is addressed as 'men of Israel', 'using the honorific name of Abraham's descendants, which underscores their status as members of God's people'.[27] Acts 2.36 identifies them with a biblical phrase as 'all the house of Israel', stressing corporate responsibility and the relevance of God's making Jesus both

22. 'The term Judaea…includes here Galilee; as the formulation "beginning in Galilee" demonstrates', Schnabel, *Acts*, 501.

23. These geographical references need to be seen in view of the recent assessment of the cultural identity and significance of Judaea in the 1st century CE.

24. Pontius Pilatus *praefectus Iduaeae*, full text, translation and discussion in W. Eck, *Rom und Judaea: Fünf Vorträge zur römischen Herrschaft in Palaestina*, Tria Corda 2 (Tübingen: Mohr Siebeck, 2007), 16, 34–43.

25. Pervo, *Acts*, 279.

26. Jervell, *Apostelgeschichte*, 144.

27. Schnabel, *Acts*, 141. Acts 2.29 refers to them as 'dear brothers'.

Lord and Christ for *all* of Israel. The royal status of Jesus as the Son of David

> ...is of utmost significance for all of God's chosen people, for the entire Jewish people. If Jesus is indeed the Messiah, the promised king who is expected to restore Israel and bring salvation, then all Israel must consider the consequences of this truth, acknowledge Jesus' messianic dignity and find salvation by submitting to his lordship.[28]

Peter answers to the people (πρὸς τὸν λαόν) and again addresses them as men of Israel (3.12).[29] Although the members of the Sanhedrin are directly addressed, the good news of God's saving presence in Israel through Jesus the Messiah concerns *all Jews*, irrespective of where they live: 'let it be known to all of you and all the people of Israel' (4.10). In Acts 13.16, Paul addresses the audience as 'Men of Israel and you who are God-fearers...' The audience is placed in Jewish history: 'The God of this people Israel chose *our fathers*' (13.17).

However, the people of Israel are not only the first addressees of a universal message. Through Jesus, God acted among them. What they experienced was unique: *Jesus was attested to Israel* ('you') by God with mighty works and wonders and signs that God did through Jesus ἐν μέσῳ ὑμῶν (2.22): '...the miracles of Jesus happened for the benefit of the Jews, and they happened in public. God's accrediting demonstration of Jesus' identity took place for and among the Israelites, that is among God's people.'[30] No stranger, but the God of Abraham, the God of Isaac, and the God of Isaac, the God of our fathers glorified his servant Jesus (3.13).

Not only from a chronological perspective, but also from a salvation-historical point of view, Israel has a *prominent position*: God sent Jesus first *to the Jews* (3.26). Schnabel writes:

> God sent Jesus, his Servant, 'to you [the Jews] first' (ὑμῖν πρῶτον). In the Greek, 'to you first' is placed first, in prominent position. The dative in ὑμῖν can be interpreted as a dative of advantage linked with the participle 'raised up' (ἀναστήσας), or as the indirect object of the main verb, 'sent' (ἀπέστειλεν). The continuity of the fulfillment of God's covenant promises from Abraham to the peoples of the earth is firmly connected with present Israel. The blessing of the nations is tied to Israel.[31]

28. Ibid., 150.

29. On the significance of λαός in Luke–Acts see H. Frankemölle, 'Λαός', *EDNT* 2 (1991): 339–44.

30. Schnabel, *Acts*, 141.

31. Ibid., 220.

The God of the Jewish fathers has raised Jesus from the dead (5.30). Again Schnabel: 'This means that his death, resurrection, and exaltation are not merely historical events of the recent past, but events that belong to the history of salvation that God initiated with his revelation to Abraham, Isaac, Jacob, Moses, David, and the other prophets (cf. 2.30; 3.13, 18, 21-25)'.[32] God first gives repentance *to Israel* and grants her forgiveness of sins (5.31), before God also grants to the Gentiles repentance that leads to life (11.18). On 'the word that God sent to the *children of Israel*' (10.36),[33] Schnabel comments aptly:

> God has fulfilled his promise of salvation to the people of Israel through Jesus, Israel's Messiah... The term translated as 'message'...is the good news that the peace the Messiah was expected to bring has arrived with Jesus. Jesus is the one through whom God sent his message to Israel... God sent the message and the reality of messianic salvation through Jesus to Israel first, implying that the new mode of salvation in which God accepts people from every nation does not invalidate the salvation-historical priority of the people of Israel.[34]

The reference to John the Baptist in Acts 10.37 emphasizes the importance of him as the one who prepared the Jewish people for the one who would come after him and who would baptize with the Spirit. Before Jesus' coming, John proclaimed a baptism of repentance to all the people of Israel (13.24).

The disciples were commissioned to preach to *the people [of Israel]* (10.42, the Jewish people, v. 37). They are to be witnesses to the people of Israel (13.31): 'These were the witnesses, not regarding the world, but regarding the people, which means Israel. The mission of the Twelve was therefore a mission to Israel.'[35]

From David's offspring God has brought *to Israel* a Saviour, Jesus, as he promised (13.23).[36] Jesus is first and foremost Israel's Saviour

32. Ibid., 311.

33. The deep conviction that God's Christ is first and foremost for Israel is reflected in Peter's reaction of surprise in Acts 10.34-35 (in the only *missionary* speech in a narrow sense before a predominantly Gentile audience). While Peter proclaims Jesus as *Lord of all* (10.36) and as the judge of *(all) the living and the dead*, and while he speaks of forgiveness of sins through his name for *everyone* who believes in Jesus (10.42f.), the presentation of this Jesus is distinctly Jewish.

34. *Acts*, 500.

35. Jervell, *Apostelgeschichte*, 358.

36. According to Schnabel, *Acts*, 577, the specific promise can hardly be any other text than 2 Sam. 7.12: 'Israel's prophets interpreted Nathan's oracle in terms of

according to divine promise. The good news is that God's promise to the Jewish ancestors has been realized. What God had promised to *the fathers* of Israel, he fulfilled *for their children*, the Jews, by raising Jesus (13.32-33). The present Jewish audience is portrayed as children of the biblical recipients of promises. Paul proclaims the fulfillment of the promises to Israel.

Paul had to testify about Jesus in *Jerusalem*, before also testifying in Rome (23.11). Although he was sent to the Gentiles, this announcement implies Jesus' acceptance and commendation of Paul's past witness in Jerusalem. 'Jesus would proclaim light both to *our people* and the Gentiles' (26.23): while the Gentiles are clearly in view, Israel comes first.

Peter calls his Jewish audience to repent so that their sins would be forgiven and that times of refreshing would come from the presence of the Lord (3.20). Jesus, the Messiah, will come to Israel: 'The…result of the repentance of the Jewish people is the culmination of the "times of refreshing" in the return of Jesus, the Messiah… Jesus is the Messiah, the Saviour of Israel, whom biblical tradition and the Jews of the Second Temple period expected for the future.'[37]

This would be time for the restoration of all the things about which God spoke by the mouth of his holy prophets long ago (3.21).[38] Bock concludes his survey of Israel in Luke–Acts: 'Jesus' story is Israel's story, as well as a story that blesses the world. It anticipates a future time when Israel responds to Jesus and God restores the nation as the prophets promised.'[39]

Thus *the Jewish origin of Jesus, the scope of his ministry in all of Judaea and of the Jews as the primary recipients of Jesus the Saviour play a prominent role in the missionary speeches of Acts*. After salvation has come to Israel, after Israel has been re-gathered and restored in the

a future "David", an expectation understood in terms of a coming messianic king who would save and restore Israel. The references to Israel in vv. 23-24 create an *inclusio* with v. 17: Jesus and John the Baptist are part and parcel of God's intervention in the history of Israel in which God acts for the salvation of his people.'

37. Schnabel, *Acts*, 215.

38. Regarding ἀποκατάστασις, Jervell, *Apostelgeschichte*, 167, refers to the occurrence of the verb in Acts 1.6, 'where clearly the same matter is addressed as here, for the restoration of the kingdom for Israel, the matter under concern see also Acts 15.16-17'. On p. 168, he notes that 'the topic is the restoration of all things. This can only mean "the kingdom for Israel", Acts 1.6, which according to Acts 1–2 did not coincide with the coming of the Spirit'. In contrast, Pervo, *Acts*, 107, speaks of 'universal restoration'.

39. Bock, 'Israel', 112.

ministry of Jesus and in the early Jerusalem community, this salvation may venture forth to the Gentiles.[40]

II.d. *Christological Titles with Jewish Background/Implications*

The missionary speeches are peppered with christological titles which also emphasize the Jewish identity of Jesus and the Jewish nature of the salvation. Jesus as *the Christ* and other titles attributed to him embody conclusions that were drawn from his ministry and express his significance. Jesus is repeatedly called the Christ (χριστός), the Jewish Messiah (Acts 2.31, 36; 3.18, 20; 4.10; 5.42, etc.). As the Messiah, Jesus is Israel's Saviour, the eschatological agent of God who came to restore Israel and bring salvation. Jesus is *Israel's* Messiah.[41] To these occurrences one must add the passages in which the early Christian proclamation is mentioned (e.g. 5.42: 'they did not cease teaching and preaching *Jesus as the Christ*', or 9.22; 10.36). Jesus as the *Christ* implies his Jewish/Davidic roots and other aspects of his life and ministry which, in themselves, provided the evidence for his being the Messiah. The Jewish *Messiah* also implies the Jewish understanding of the kingdom of God which is closely linked to this figure. While there was no agreement on the details, expectation of one or more Messianic figures was a significant feature of early Jewish eschatological expectation. In view of Jesus and his fate, Lukan Christology redefines the concept of Jewish Messianism.

In addition to the *Christ*, other titles are used for Jesus. Some are distinctively Jewish; others also appear in other contexts: Jesus is called the *Lord* (2.36), the *Author of life* (3.13), the servant (παῖς in 3.13, 26; 4.25, 30), the *Holy and Righteous One* (3.14; 7.52) and the leader to life (3.15; 5.31). Jesus is identified as the *prophet* announced by Moses (3.22). As the stone that was rejected by the builders, Jesus has become the *cornerstone* (4.11). Jesus is the Saviour (5.31; 13.23). He is the *Son of God* (9.20). God preached the good news of peace through Jesus Christ, who is *Lord of all* (10.36) and the judge of the living and the dead (10.42; 17.31). Jesus is proclaimed as the Lord (11.20). Paul's summary

40. See J. Jervell, 'The Divided People of God', in *Luke and the People of God: A New Look at Luke–Acts* (Minneapolis: Augsburg, 1972), 41–74.

41. See Schnabel, *Acts*, 239, and Jervell, *Apostelgeschichte*, 93–5. Jervell writes regarding Luke's use of titles: 'where the proximity to OT–early Jewish concepts can be more clearly recognized than elsewhere in the NT'. Luke uses Christ as a title 'that is determined by the history of Israel in the pattern of promise and fulfillment, Jesus fulfills the promises to the people of God… The Messiah is a thoroughly OT–early Jewish figure.'

of his proclamation as 'testifying to both Jews and Greeks of repentance toward God and of faith in our *Lord* Jesus *Christ*' (20.21) encapsulates the significance of Jesus.[42] The Jewish emphasis not only applies to the Christology of Acts but also to other aspects of the salvation which Jesus came to bring.

II.e. *Other Jewish Aspects in the Missionary Speeches*

Through the references to the patriarchs ('the God of *Abraham*, the God of *Isaac*, the God of *Jacob*, the God of our fathers, glorified his servant Jesus…'; 3.13) to *Moses* (3.22; 13.39; 26.22) and to *David* (2.25, 29, 34; 13.22, 34, 36),[43] to important figures in the history of Israel, in the context of references to Jesus, he is placed in the larger context of God's dealing with Israel (see above). Jesus is part of the history of Israel. Jervell noted that Luke 'did not write the history of a religious movement or sect, but the final part of the history of the people of the God of Israel'.[44] To play on his words: Luke did not write a life of Jesus and an account of early Christianity but further chapters on and of the history of the people of Israel.

In addition to these references to Israel's past, Jesus is also placed in a particular Jewish *chronology*. What God accomplished through Jesus for his people Israel happened not only at particular places and for a particular people (see above), but also at a particular time, namely 'after the baptism that John proclaimed' (10.37) and during the time of Pilate, governor of Judaea (see above): 'whom you delivered and denied in the presence of

42. On Jesus as Lord in Acts see J. D. G. Dunn, 'KYRIOS in Acts', in *The Christ and the Spirit I: Christology* (Grand Rapids: Eerdmans, 1998), 241–53. For surveys of Lukan Christology (in which the titles given to Jesus are an important ingredient) see D. Buckwalter, 'The Divine Saviour', in Marshall and Peterson, eds, *Witness*, 108–23; J. A. Fitzmyer, *The Gospel according to Luke I–IX*, 2nd edn, AB 28 (Garden City: Doubleday, 1986), 192–219; J. B. Green, *The Theology of the Gospel of Luke*, NT Theology (Cambridge: Cambridge University Press, 1995), 55–68; J. Jervell, *The Theology of the Acts of the Apostles*, NT Theology (Cambridge: CUP, 1996), 25–34; P. Pokorny, *Theologie der lukanischen Schriften*, FRLANT 174 (Göttingen: Vandenhoeck & Ruprecht, 1997), 110–20.

43. See Y. Miura, *David in Luke–Acts: His Portrayal in the Light of Early Judaism*, WUNT 2/232 (Tübingen: Mohr Siebeck, 2007).

44. Quoted from J. D. G. Dunn, 'The Book of Acts as Salvation History', in *Heil und Geschichte: Die Geschichtsbezogenheit des Heils und das Problem der Heilsgeschichte in der biblischen Tradition und in der theologischen Deutung*, ed. J. Frey, S. Krauter and H. Lichtenberger, WUNT 248 (Tübingen: Mohr Siebeck, 2009), 385–401 (401); see also J. Nolland, 'Salvation-history and Eschatology', in Marshall and Peterson, eds, *Witness*, 63–81.

Pilate' (3.13); '...they asked Pilate to have him executed' (13.28). The references to Pontius Pilate serve to date the events to a specific period of time, namely the period between 26 and 36 CE.[45] Jesus came at a determined time in Israel's history (cf. also Lk. 1.5; 2.1-2; 3.1-2).

It is also noteworthy that the missionary speeches are thoroughly based on the Old Testament. They are based on the prophets and Moses who predicted that the Christ must suffer and be the first to rise from the dead and that he would proclaim light both to our people and the Gentiles (26.22-23).[46] In addition, the proclamation of the apostles is expressed throughout in biblical terms, giving evidence of and underlining its Jewish nature. Three examples suffice. In very Jewish terms – drawing on the Old Testament and early Judaism – Peter announces messianic 'refreshment' (3.20-21), the 'definitive age of salvation'.[47] The rejection of Jesus is expressed in Old Testament language in Acts 5.30: by 'hanging him upon a tree', the leaders treated Jesus as a dangerous criminal, as someone who is under God's curse and who must be eliminated from God's people.[48] The gospel is presented as the good news of peace (10.36). Schnabel notes: 'This peace corresponds to the Hebrew concept of "well-being" associated particularly with the messianic age (cf. Lk. 2.14; 10.5; 19.42) and with the freedom from hostile powers, whether spiritual or temporal, that this state involves (Lk. 1.78, 71)'.[49] Even when distinctly Graeco-Roman notions are employed to communicate aspects of Jesus and the Gospel to non-Jewish audiences, the Jewish sub-structure of the message is apparent: the Graeco-Roman theme of benefaction appears in the summary of Acts 10.38-39 (Jesus 'went about doing good', εὐεργετῶν). Pervo rightly notes that Jesus' activities as benefactor are 'nonetheless portrayed in language more at home in apocalyptic: Jesus was at war with the devil...

45. See also Acts 4.27 ('for truly *in this city* there were gathered together against your holy servant Jesus...both *Herod* and *Pontius Pilate*'). For a detailed discussion, see Frey et al., eds, *Heil*, in particular Dunn's essay, 'Acts as Salvation History'.

46. Pervo, *Acts*, 635. For detailed treatment see D. L. Bock, *Proclamation from Prophecy and Pattern: Lucan Old Testament Christology*, JSNTSup 12 (Sheffield: JSOT Press, 1987); D. L. Bock, 'Scripture and the Realization of God's Promise', in Marshall and Peterson, eds, *Witness*, 41–62; and I. H. Marshall, 'Acts', in *Commentary on the New Testament Use of the Old Testament*, ed. G. K. Beale and D. A. Carson (Grand Rapids: Baker Academic; Nottingham: Apollos, 2007), 513–606.

47. Bock, 'Israel', 112, including brief discussion of the OT and early Jewish conceptions.

48. See Schnabel, *Acts*, 312, and D. W. Chapman, *Ancient Jewish and Christian Perceptions on Crucifixion*, WUNT 2/244 (Tübingen: Mohr Siebeck, 2008), 14–26.

49. *Acts*, 500.

Luke does not "replace" apocalyptic concepts with Hellenistic categories. He rather presents them in terms that Greeks can comprehend.'[50]

The references to the Jewish nature of Jesus and of salvation end with the missionary speech in the synagogue of Pisidian Antioch in Acts 13.[51] This is probably not a question of geographic proximity, temporal distance or change in audience, because such references do appear in speeches before Gentiles in Caesarea and in Pisidian Antioch. Rather, this speech is the last missionary speech in the narrow sense of the term. It is therefore not surprising that later speeches do not contain references to the Jewishness of Jesus or of salvation. This lack does not imply that this emphasis lost its importance.

III. *Implications*

Despite their universalistic perspective which has often been noted, the missionary speeches of Acts are also characterized by distinctly Jewish elements: Jesus, the Jew, ministered in Judaea; the salvation he came to bring in fulfillment of Israel's Scriptures first and foremost concerns the Jewish people; the gospel is thoroughly Jewish and cannot be understood apart from this foundation.[52]

Assessment of the portrayal of Acts depends on decisions regarding its historical reliability and date. To what extent does Acts, and in particular its speeches, provide a reliable picture of the early apostolic preaching? If Acts is to be dated to the early sixties of the 1st century CE (immediately after the last events narrated in Acts 28), the likelihood of reliable information is higher, although a later date does not necessarily preclude it. A reliable presentation of the early apostolic preaching in Acts would allow us to draw some conclusions regarding the understanding of Jesus and of salvation (-history) and the self-understanding of the early Jewish Christian community vis-à-vis its relationship to other Jews and to the nascent Gentile mission.[53]

If Acts primarily reflects the concerns of the third generation of Christians, then the *Jewish* portrayal of Jesus and salvation sheds light

50. Ibid., 280. Pervo offers a brief summary of ancient notions of benefaction.

51. Cf. Acts 16.22; 19.33-34; 22.8, 14, 17; 23.11. Paul proclaims *Christ* Jesus to Felix (24.24). The adequate proclamation and explanation of Jesus as Christ is impossible without reference to Israel.

52. For the Jewish character of the soteriology of Acts see the summary in Jervell, *Apostelgeschichte*, 104–5.

53. Lack of space does not allow detailed interaction with Jervell's seminal essay, 'Divided People'.

on the ambiguous process of what is commonly called 'the parting of the ways'.[54] Why would an apology for Paul and the Law-free Gentile mission (so the purpose of Acts) emphasize the Jewishness of the gospel? Is this Jewish emphasis due to traditional material which the author merely adopted or is it part of the author's strategy of emphasizing the fulfillment of Scripture and continuity with Israel?[55] If so, how does it serve this function?

The Jewishness of Jesus has been examined and emphasized in Jesus research of the past three decades, in particular in studies of the Gospels. This has become one of several areas where Jewish and Christian scholars work hand in hand.[56]

In addition to its implications for understanding the history and theology of early Christianity, the portrayal of Acts serves as an antidote to – often philosophically influenced – one-sided universalistic readings of the New Testament, in particular in the wake of the European Enlightenment,[57] which overlook or ignore its particularism and thoroughly Jewish nature. The emphasis of Acts on Jesus the Jew and the Jewish character of salvation and the gospel also serves as a necessary corrective to ideological interpretations that strip Jesus of his Jewish identity.[58] An extreme case in this regard has been the 'Aryan' Jesus of Nazi theology where the stripping of Jesus and the gospel's Jewish identity reached its all-time low.[59]

54. For surveys of the issues see D. Boyarin, *Border Lines: The Partition of Judeo-Christianity* (Philadelphia: University of Pennsylvania Press, 2004); J. D. G. Dunn, ed., *Jews and Christians: The Parting of the Ways: AD 70–135* (Cambridge: CUP, 1999); and J. M. Lieu, *Christian Identity in the Jewish and Graeco-Roman World* (Oxford: OUP, 2004).

55. See Jervell, 'Divided People'.

56. For examples see A.-J. Levine, *The Misunderstood Jew: The Church and the Scandal of the Jewish Jesus* (New York: HarperOne, 2006) and D. A. Hagner, *The Jewish Reclamation of Jesus: An Analysis and Critique of Modern Jewish Study of Jesus* (Eugene: Wipf & Stock, 1997); for a survey see C. Brown, 'Quest for the Historical Jesus', *DJG* (2nd edn): 718–56 (741–5).

57. For an astute early analysis see M. Meinertz, *Jesus und die Heidenmission*, 2nd edn, NTA I.1–2 (Münster: Aschendorff, 1925), 2–19.

58. The early Luther rightly emphasized the Jewish identity of Jesus; see his treatise *Dass Jesus ein geborener Jude sei* of 1523; for a summary and analysis see Thomas Kaufmann, *Luthers 'Judenschriften': Ein Beitrag zu ihrer historischen Kontextualisierung* (Tübingen: Mohr Siebeck, 2011).

59. P. von der Osten-Sacken, ed., *Das missbrauchte Evangelium: Studien zu Theologie und Praxis der Thüringer Deutschen Christen* (Berlin: Institut Kirche und Judentum, 2002); and S. Heschel, *The Aryan Jesus: Christian Theologians and the Bible in Nazi Germany* (Princeton: Princeton University Press, 2008).

The portrayal of Acts must not be ignored in the witness of the church. If the portrayal of Acts is not only merely interesting for historical reasons (i.e. understanding early Christianity) but also of abiding significance for later generations, then without the *Jewish* Saviour and salvation for *Israel*, there is no Christian gospel. Here we focus on Jesus and leave other aspects aside. Acts is a strong reminder that neither the Jesus of Western philosophies or ideologies nor the distinctly African, Asian, Latino or 'Whatever-else-Jesus' in all kaleidoscopic interpretations is the Saviour of the world, but the descendant of David, Jesus of Nazareth, sent first by the God of Israel to the Jewish people.[60] Jesus does not need to be and cannot be incarnated in African, American, Asian, Australian or European soil as has sometimes been demanded. He is not the helpless babe whom the peoples of the earth can adopt and make into one of their own. He was incarnated into *Jewish* soil, born in Bethlehem (Lk. 2.4-7) as God's Son. He was 'born of a woman, born *under the Law*' (Gal. 4.4). As such and only with and because of his identity as God's Saviour for Israel, he is and can be the universal Saviour and Lord of all, which is why the peoples of the earth can and must adopt him. The Jewish identity of Jesus and the Jewish context of his mission is *not merely the cultural form* in which the biblical message is clothed and which is not part of the essential message to be reproduced in every culture. However, because of the universal lordship of Jesus and the universal offer of salvation, *the good news can be and should be incarnated in the different soils of this world*[61] so that people hear and understand what has happened 'in Judaea, beginning in Galilee' (Acts 10.36-43) and appreciate how it applies to them: 'everyone who believes in him receives forgiveness of sins through his name' (10.43).

60. For surveys of the different interpretations of Jesus see V.-M. Kärkkäinen, *Christology: A Global Introduction* (Grand Rapids: Baker Academic, 2003); J. Levison and P. Pope-Levison, 'Christology 4. The New Contextual Theologies: Liberation and Inculturation', in *Global Dictionary of Theology: A Resource for the Worldwide Church*, ed. W. A. Dyrness and V.-M. Kärkkäinen (Grand Rapids: IVP Academic; Nottingham: IVP, 2008), 175–86. See also K.-S. Tan, 'Christ/Christology', in *Dictionary of Mission Theology: Evangelical Foundations*, ed. J. Corrie (Nottingham/Downers Grove: IVP, 2007), 47–51.

61. Often the incarnation of Jesus has been understood as a model for Christian mission; for a survey see S. Mondithoka, 'Incarnation', in Corrie, ed., *Dictionary*, 177–81. He further notes: 'Incarnation has important implications for "critical contextualization", which means applying God's truth in a culturally relevant and sensitive manner and yet without compromising its meaning. Here again the incarnation is our model' (p. 180).

11

'A Tale of Two Cities'? Jerusalem in the Gospels of Matthew and Luke

Daniel M. Gurtner

I. *Introduction*

'It was the best of times, it was the worst of times'. One might appropriate the famous first line from Dickens's *A Tale of Two Cities* to describe the situation faced by the Jewish-Christian communities of the 1st century. Though their Messiah had come at last, the disaster of the First Jewish Revolt against Rome (66–73 CE) threatened to suffocate that hope in a cloud of despair. And, if Josephus's accounts of the atrocities within the city of Jerusalem during the Roman assault are any indication of the realities experienced, the gloom of 18th-century Paris depicted in the opening pages of Dickens's classic pales in comparison.

The concern here, however, is not two cities, but one: Jerusalem – specifically, the dual portrayals of Jerusalem in the Gospels of Matthew and Luke. Professor Nolland's important and extensive work in both of these Gospels amply demonstrates that they are ideal testing grounds for comparative work on early Christian perspectives on Jerusalem, its temple and its cultic worship. Some time ago Professor Nolland and I co-edited a collection of essays drawn from a 2005 Tyndale Fellowship conference.[1] In that volume I explored the subject of Matthew's presentation of Jerusalem in general and its temple in particular.[2] The impetus

1. Daniel M. Gurtner and John Nolland, eds, *Built upon the Rock: Studies in the Gospel of Matthew* (Grand Rapids: Eerdmans, 2008).

2. 'Matthew's Theology of the Temple and the "Parting of the Ways": Christian Origins and the First Gospel', in Gurtner and Nolland, eds, *Built upon the Rock*, 128–53.

for that essay was to provide a careful and close reading of the distinctively Matthaean presentation of these subjects in order to consider his perspective on the legitimacy of the temple and its cult. Though the first Gospel is often caricatured as 'anti-Jewish', we offered an alternative reading with specific regard to Jerusalem and its temple. The scope of the present essay is to revisit that conclusion with fresh eyes, after a ten-year absence, and to put it in dialogue with the Gospel of Luke.

Naturally this discussion has been utilized in other contexts, most notably in the ongoing debate regarding the 'parting of the ways' between Christianity and Judaism. Both Richard Bauckham and James D. G. Dunn,[3] for example, recognize the importance of the temple as a defining element of 'Jewish self-identity'.[4] It stands to reason, then, that the presentation of the temple within these two Gospels speaks to early Christianity's understanding of its own relation to Jerusalem, its temple and its cultic worship. The most striking obstacle we face is that it is difficult to reconstruct a clear portrait of the temple from Matthew and Luke. Statements *about* the temple are present and important, but scant. They must, then, be pieced together to arrive at each Gospel's coherent presentation. At a surface level, however, both Matthew and Luke's portrayals of the temple might seem to be internally contradictory. Is it a place to be 'cleansed' and preserved for prayer (Mt. 21.13; Lk. 19.46)? Or is it a place to be left desolate (Mt. 23.38; Lk. 13.35) and ultimately destroyed (Mt. 24.2; Lk. 21.2)? Apparently it remained an appropriate place for Jesus to teach (Mt. 21.23; Lk. 20.1) and was *still* a place to offer sacrifices (Mt. 8.4; Lk. 5.14). Addressing these tensions may lead us to a more comprehensive picture of Matthew's and Luke's understanding(s) of the temple.

II. *The Temple in Matthew: Matthew's Temple from Beginning to End*

In light of Matthew's infamous 'anti-Jewish polemic', scholars frequently conjecture that he is likewise anti-temple. Some underscore its destruction as God's ultimate rejection of Israel[5] and as the end of the mission to

3. James D. G. Dunn, *The Partings of the Ways: Between Christianity and Judaism and Their Significance for the Character of Christianity*, 2nd edn (London: SCM Press, 2006), 49–129.

4. R. J. Bauckham, 'The Parting of the Ways', *ST* 47 (1993): 141.

5. Daniel Marguerat's *Le jugement dans l'évangile de Matthieu*, 2nd edn (Geneva: Labor et Fides, 1995). Though, for a corrective, see Anders Runesson, *Divine Wrath and Salvation in Matthew: The Narrative World of the First Gospel* (Minneapolis:

Israel.[6] Further, some contend that Matthew's Jesus seems to replace the function of the Jerusalem temple[7] as he immediately provides healing for the lame and blind within its courts (21.14). Others have claimed that this 'cleansing' text illustrates that the Herodian temple was 'judged inadequate as the place of God's presence and authentic worship'.[8] Yet careful analysis of the entirety of Matthew's narrative reveals a more complicated picture.

At the beginning of his Gospel, Matthew makes no mention of Luke's episode with Zechariah in the temple. Instead his temple interests begin in his 'temptation' narrative (4.1-11), where the devil (ὁ διάβολος) takes Jesus into the 'holy city' and places him 'on the highest point of the temple' (ἐπὶ τὸ πτερύγιον τοῦ ἱεροῦ, 4.5).[9] In the next chapter Matthew makes reference to the temple cult (5.23-24), where the worshipper brings his gifts (προσφέρω + δῶρον, 8.4; 2.11) upon the altar (ἐπὶ τὸ θυσιαστήριον).[10] That the gift is given at all seems to presume the validity of this sacrifice, though it is subservient to reconciliation, which must occur first (πρῶτον, 5.24). Regardless, participation in the cultic worship is neither replaced nor mooted, but 'presupposed'.[11] Likewise, after healing a man (Mt. 8.1-4) Jesus tells him to tell no one of his healing, but to go to the high priest. As in 5.24, Matthew alone records that the man is to offer a 'gift' (τὸ δῶρον, 8.4) *after* the cleansing, again presuming the legitimacy of offering the appropriate sacrifice.

Fortress Press, 2016), esp. 11–12. Cf. also E. Lohmeyer, *Das Evangelium des Matthäus*, 4th edn (Göttingen: Vandenhoeck & Ruprecht, 1967), 184; D. Andreoli, 'Il velo squarciato nel Vangelo di Matteo', *BSW* 1 (1998): 35–40.

6. U. Luz, *Das Evangelium nach Matthäus*, 4 vols, EKK (Zurich: Benziger Verlag, 1985–2002), 1:54–5, 211; W. G. Thompson, 'An Historical Perspective in the Gospel of Matthew', *JBL* 93 (1974): 243–62. See Matthias Konradt, *Israel, Church, and the Gentiles in the Gospel of Matthew*, trans. K. Ess (Waco: Baylor University Press, 2014), 11.

7. J. D. Kingsbury (*Matthew as Story*, 2nd edn [Philadelphia: Fortress Press, 1988], 30) declares '…Jesus himself supplants the temple as the "place" where God mediates salvation to people'.

8. J. P. Heil, *The Death and Resurrection of Jesus: A Narrative-Critical Reading of Matthew 26–28* (Minneapolis: Fortress Press, 1991), 85.

9. This may hint at Matthew's developing notion of authority confrontations that occur in the ἱερόν.

10. This is probably the altar of burnt offering in Jerusalem. W. D. Davies and D. C. Allison, *Matthew*, 3 vols, ICC (Edinburgh: T. & T. Clark, 1988, 1991, 1997), 1:517.

11. Ibid., 1:518.

Later in Matthew Jesus asserts that God desires 'mercy and not sacrifice' (ἔλεος θέλω καὶ οὐ θυσίαν, 9.13; also 12.7; cf. Hos. 6.6). It is largely accepted that Matthew's καὶ οὐ is not a starkly contrastive assertion but a Hebraic idiom of 'dialectical negation' meaning 'I desire mercy *more* than sacrifice'.[12] Luz further asserts that Matthew 'did not abolish the cultic law but made it inferior to the love command (5:18-19; 5:23-24; 23:23-28)'.[13] Likewise Jesus later subordinates the temple and its cult to mercy, but he does not negate them (Mt. 12.5-7).[14]

Mention of the temple tax (Mt. 17.24-29) is unique to Matthew. Here Jesus pays the tax not out of obligation, but 'so that we may not offend them' (17.27). It seems that here Matthew affirms the temple cult but questions the role of taxation in maintaining it.[15] In any case, Davies and Allison support Matthew's positive view of the temple when they suggest the payment is made to 'prevent others from inferring that Peter or Jesus has rejected the temple cult'.[16]

At the outset of Matthew's Passion Narrative (Mt. 21.1-27), Jesus enters Jerusalem (21.1-11) and the temple (ἱερόν, 21.12), where he performs his notorious 'cleansing'. It is common for this scene to be read as Jesus nullifying the temple's cultic function and replacing the temple with himself.[17] But the text emphasizes the temple as a house of prayer, and Jesus says or does nothing to counter the sacrificial cult. Calling the temple 'a house of prayer' suggests that the temple has a purpose, but that purpose is being frustrated by corruption and exploitation within the temple precincts.[18] Jesus' 'cleansing' of the temple serves to 'purge it of practices that mocked its divinely intended purpose'.[19]

12. U. Luz, *Matthew 8–20*, Hermeneia (Minneapolis: Fortress Press, 2001), 34. *Pace* G. Strecker, *Der Weg der Gerechtigkeit: Untersuchung zur Theologie des Matthäus* (Göttingen: Vandenhoeck & Ruprecht, 1962), 32.

13. Luz, *Matthew 8–20*, 34; Davies and Allison, *Matthew*, 2:104–5.

14. Konradt, *Israel, Church, and the Gentiles*, 145.

15. R. J. Bauckham, 'The Coin in the Fish's Mouth', in *Gospel Perspectives 6: The Miracles of Jesus*, ed. D. Wenham and C. Blomberg (Sheffield: JSOT Press, 1986), 219–52.

16. Davies and Allison, *Matthew*, 2:746.

17. W. Carter, *Matthew: Storyteller, Interpreter, Evangelist* (Peabody: Hendrickson, 1996), 221.

18. R. J. Bauckham, 'Jesus' Demonstration in the Temple', in *Law and Religion: Essays on the Place of the Law in Israel and Early Christianity*, ed. B. Lindars (Cambridge: James Clarke, 1988), 84.

19. D. A. Hagner, *Matthew*, 2 vols, WBC 33A–B (Dallas: Word Books, 1993, 1995), 2:598; cf. R. Beaton, *Isaiah's Christ in Matthew's Gospel*, SNTSMS 123 (Cambridge: CUP, 2002), 183.

Next the 'blind and lame' (τυφλοὶ καὶ χωλοὶ) come to Jesus and he heals them *there* (ἱερόν, 21.14),[20] presumably in the outer courts, where they were permitted. It seems that, rather than abrogating the Law, Matthew recounts Jesus' healing of them so as to remove the issue that forbade them entrance in the first place: their disabilities.[21] Matthew, then, is concerned that the temple be restored to its intended function as a 'house of prayer'.

For the ensuing cursing of the fig tree pericope (21.21-22),[22] Telford demonstrates that Matthaean redaction of the Markan pericope lays emphasis on the power of Jesus and resulting faith,[23] rather than associating the miracle of the cursed fig tree with the temple. In other words, the story in Matthew 'has been removed from the sphere of judgment and eschatology, and is treated as if it were a normal miracle story'.[24] We find, then, that Matthew, while clearly escalating Mark's polemic against the Jewish leaders, softens his polemic against the temple. Thus when Jesus again enters the temple courts (ἱερόν, 21.23), there is no hint that the temple's legitimacy is in question; rather, the focus is simply Jesus' 'authority' (ἐξουσία).[25]

In Matthew 23, Jesus chastises the 'blind guides' for thinking that swearing by the temple (ναός) means nothing, but swearing by the gold of the temple (ναός) is binding (23.16). They are criticized for making distinctions between oaths taken 'by the temple' (ἐν τῷ ναῷ, 23.16) and 'by the gold of the temple' (ἐν τῷ χρυσῷ τοῦ ναοῦ, 23.16) on the one hand, and 'by the altar' (ἐν τῷ θυσιαστηρίῳ, 23.17) and 'by the gift upon it' (ἐν τῷ δώρῳ

20. He has seen them before in Matthew and healed them (15.30), apparently in ironic contrast to the 'blind' Pharisees who refuse to be healed and whom Jesus commands his disciples to leave (15.14). Cf. M. Knowles, *Jeremiah in Matthew's Gospel: The Rejected-Prophet Motif in Matthean Redaction*, JSNTSup 68 (Sheffield: JSOT Press, 1993), 234–5, who associates this text with the Davidic Messiahship of Jesus.

21. Cf. B. Gerhardsson, *The Mighty Acts of Jesus according to Matthew* (Lund: Gleerup, 1979), 30 n. 16.

22. Cf. D. Duling, 'The Therapeutic Son of David: An Element of Matthew's Christological Apologetic', *NTS* 24 (1978): 393.

23. Cf. W. Telford, *The Barren Temple and the Withered Tree: A Redaction-critical Analysis of the Cursing of the Fig-Tree Pericope in Mark's Gospel and its Relation to the Cleansing of the Temple Tradition*, JSNTSup 1 (Sheffield: JSOT Press, 1980), 81.

24. Ibid., 80. Thus the saying regarding the throwing of the mountain into the sea (Mk 11.23; Mt. 21.21) is no longer suggestive of the temple mount, as it is in Mark. Ibid., 79. Cf. Davies and Allison, *Matthew*, 3:152–3.

25. For potential allusions to the temple in Mt. 21.33-46; 22.1-14, see Gurtner, 'Matthew's Theology of the Temple', 141–3.

τῷ ἐπάνω αὐτοῦ, 23.18; cf. 5.23) on the other.[26] Both the gold and the gift, he states, have significance because of the altar with which they are associated.[27] Furthermore, Jesus insists that the value of such gold is found in the *temple* (ναός, 23.17), and swearing by this temple (ναός) is the same as swearing by the one who dwells in it (23.21, 22). Though the subject here is surely the use of oaths, Matthew explicitly cites the Pharisees' misappropriation of their oaths with respect to the temple and its sacrifices. As before, this suggests a concern not with the temple but the misuse of it,[28] and Matthew presumes God is still in it (ἐν τῷ κατοικοῦντι αὐτόν, 23.21).[29] Similarly, in Matthew's curious account of the murder of Zechariah between the temple (ναός) and the altar (θυσιαστηρίον, 23.35),[30] the point of contention is, perhaps in typical prophetic (Jeremiah) fashion, misuse of the temple.[31] The pericope culminates in two further 'judgement' texts, first (23.38) where Jesus declares the desolation (ἔρημος) of their 'house'. While this is typically seen as God's abandonment of the temple, hinting at its subsequent destruction, the abandonment is clearly the result of the sins of God's people.[32] Like Josephus (*Ant.* 20.166; cf. *War* 5.19), Matthew may envision God's departure from the temple[33] and Jesus' departure as a similar act of abandonment.[34] Again, though, fault lies with the misuse and corruption of an otherwise perfectly legitimate temple. In

26. Hagner, *Matthew*, 2:669.

27. Davies and Allison, *Matthew*, 3:292. Cf. Luz, *Das Evangelium nach Matthäus*, 3:326–8.

28. Davies and Allison (*Matthew*, 3:292–3) rightly observe that they are chastised precisely for disobeying the *cultic* law.

29. On potential implications for the dating of the Gospel in light of this observation, cf. Davies and Allison, *Matthew*, 3:293; R. T. France, *Matthew: Evangelist and Teacher* (Downers Grove: IVP, 1989), 88.

30. Although which Zechariah is in view has been disputed, it seems probable that the one in 2 Chron. 24.20-22, who was stoned to death in the courtyard of the temple, is the best choice.

31. This point is most explicitly seen in Matthew's allusion to Jer. 7.11 (Mt. 21.13; cf. Isa. 56.7; Knowles, *Jeremiah in Matthew's Gospel*, 188).

32. Ezek. 8.6, 12; 9.3, 9; 11.23; cf. 12; 1 Kgs 9.6-9; Isa. 64.10-11; Josephus, *War* 5.412-13; 6.295-300; Tacitus, *Hist.* 5.13; *2 Bar.* 8.2; 64.6-7; *Paraleipomena of Jeremiah* 4.1.

33. Cf. France, *Matthew: Evangelist and Teacher*, 215; P. Luomanen, *Entering the Kingdom of Heaven*, WUNT 2/101 (Tübingen: Mohr Siebeck, 1998), 227–8. Knowles, *Jeremiah in Matthew's Gospel*, 267.

34. D. C. Kupp, *Matthew's Emmanuel: Divine Presence and God's People in the First Gospel*, SNTSMS 90 (Cambridge: CUP, 1996), 93–4; Davies and Allison, *Matthew*, 3:333.

the second judgement text Jesus emphatically predicts that 'not one stone here [of the temple] will be left on another; every one will be thrown down' (Mt. 24.2; cf. Mk 13.1; Lk. 21.5). Jesus' implicit and explicit statements regarding the destruction of the temple do not themselves 'question the legitimacy of the cult', as some seem to presume.[35] Instead, as is the case in other prophetic foretellings of the destruction of Jerusalem and its temple,[36] destruction is the direct and immediate consequence of the sins of Israel's leadership in mismanaging the temple. This culminates when Jesus goes to the Mount of Olives (Mt. 24.3), where he sees the temple which will be destroyed, and indicates a return to the Mount of Olives (cf. 27.53; Acts 1.9, 12).[37] This resonates with Zech. 14.4, which asserts that the Lord will stand on the Mount of Olives at the great day of judgement upon Jerusalem (14.1-21). The prophetic judgement is announced.

Matthew's account of the 'abomination that causes desolation' (τὸ βδέλυγμα τῆς ἐρημώσεως) standing in the holy place (24.15) draws from Daniel (9.27; 11.31; 12.11). Regardless of the precise referent,[38] Matthew seems to identify the defilement of the temple with some eschatological 'sign'. Olmstead contends this 'signals God's judgment on rebellious Israel for the rejection of his servants which spans her history' for which the 70 CE tragedy is a 'precursor'.[39] Similarly the mismanagement of Israel's leadership is underscored in Jesus' illustration of a servant 'whom the master has put in charge of the servants in his household' (Mt. 24.45) and who is expected to be found faithful upon the master's return (24.46-51).

At his arrest Jesus objected that '[e]very day I sat in the temple courts (ἱερόν) teaching, and you did not arrest me' (Mt. 26.55), which seems to point back to the events in 21.1-27. Then at his trial before Caiaphas (Mt. 26.57-66) Jesus is accused of speaking against the temple (ναός). Here Matthew identifies the temple (Mk 14.58) as 'God's temple' (τὸν ναὸν τοῦ θεοῦ, Mt. 26.61), perhaps emphasizing the illegitimacy of accusations that Jesus betrayed animosity toward the divinely instituted temple (Mt. 26.59-60). Next, what Mark renders as a prediction of Jesus' destruction of the temple (καταλύω, Mk 14.58) Matthew presents in terms of Jesus'

35. See Davies and Allison, *Matthew*, 3:334.

36. Ibid., 3:335, citing Micah (Mic. 3.12), Jeremiah (Jer. 7.8-15; 9.10-11; 26.6, 18), and Jesus bar Ananias (Josephus, *War* 6.300-309).

37. Davies and Allison, *Matthew*, 3:347.

38. It may allude to the attempted desecration by Caligula (40 CE), to the destruction of the temple itself (as in Lk. 21.20), or to a future 'eschatological defilement' associated with the antichrist. Davies and Allison, *Matthew*, 3:345–6.

39. W. Olmstead, *Matthew's Trilogy of Parables: The Nation, the Nations and the Reader in Matthew 21.28–22.14*, SNTSMS 127 (Cambridge: CUP, 2003), 116.

ability (δύναμαι καταλῦσαι, Mt. 26.61), which may underscore Matthew's concern that Jesus not speak directly against it.[40] Regardless, Matthew is explicit in indicating that the charges are false (ψευδομαρτυρία, Mt. 26.59). Even at his crucifixion the same (false) charges are repeated: 'You who are going to destroy the Temple (ναός) and build it in three days, save yourself! Come down from the cross, if you are the Son of God!' (27.40; cf. Mk 15.29-30).[41] The final reference to the temple in Matthew is the rending of its veil at Jesus' death (τὸ καταπέτασμα τοῦ ναοῦ ἐσχίσθη, Mt. 27.51). While it is likely readers of Matthew's Gospel understood this event in close connection to the tragedies of 70 CE, it seems difficult to reduce this event to a cryptic reference to the temple's destruction as a primary meaning.[42]

This overview of Matthaean texts related to the temple and its cult demonstrates that Matthew seems quite deliberate, even strategic, about his presentation. Even where Matthew includes statements about the temple's destruction (e.g. Mt. 27.1-2), they are countered by lament (Mt. 23.37-39). For Matthew the demise is certain, but regrettable. He assumes its propriety and perceives no need to attack it.[43] Instead, Matthew is an author 'emphasizing the sovereignty of Jesus over the Temple rather than one reflecting an antagonism towards it'.[44] A similar lament was pronounced by Jeremiah (Jer. 2.30; cf. Neh. 9.26). That the destruction of Jerusalem is depicted on the heels of this account leads us to conclude that the destruction is necessitated not because of fault with the temple but because of the unrepentance of the Jewish leaders.[45]

40. Telford, *Barren Temple*, 83. At least it may indicate that Jesus' ability to destroy the temple underscores his power as the Son of God (Mt. 4.3, 6; 26.53; 27.40-42) to do so, but his obedience as Son of God not to (cf. 27.43). Luz, *Matthäus*, 4:176.

41. On Judas throwing his ill-gained money into the temple (ναός; Mt. 27.5), see Gurtner, 'Matthew's Theology of the Temple', 149–50.

42. Cf. Daniel M. Gurtner, *The Torn Veil: Matthew's Exposition of the Death of Jesus*, SNTSMS 139 (Cambridge: CUP, 2007). Though see, more recently, Matthias Konradt, 'Die Deutung der Zerstörung Jerusalem sim Matthäusevangelium', in *Josephus und das Neue Testament. Wechselseitige Wahrnehmungen. II. Internationales Symposium zum Corpus Judaeo–Hellenisticum*, ed. C. Böttrich and J. Herzer, WUNT 209 (Tübingen: Mohr Siebeck, 2007), 195–232.

43. Davies and Allison, *Matthew*, 3:143, cf. n. 64; 2 Kgs 21.10-15.

44. R. A. McConnell, 'Law and Prophecy in Matthew's Gospel' (PhD diss., University of Basel, 1964), 72–5, esp. 75. Telford, *Barren Temple*, 83–4.

45. Cf. Davies and Allison, *Matthew*, 3:324; cf. Olmstead, *Trilogy*, 83; D. C. Allison, 'Matt. 23.39 = Lk 13.35b as a Conditional Prophecy', *JSNT* 18 (1983): 75–84; C. Deutsch, 'Wisdom in Matthew: Transformation of a Symbol', *NovT* 32 (1990): 13–47.

III. *The Temple in Luke*

With this presentation from Matthew in mind, we now turn to Luke first to consider how scholars assess his presentation of the temple and then to provide our own examination of Luke's Gospel in its entirety. We will see that while Luke has a number of unique readings, his perspective toward the temple and its cult is similar to that of Matthew.

a. *Luke's Temple in Scholarly Discourse*

Scholarly discussion on Luke's presentation of the temple is complicated. As far back as 1981 Weinert lamented that much work done in this area[46] either reads other New Testament texts into the Lukan account or fails to account for the breadth of the evidence in Luke–Acts.[47] The results are necessarily tenuous and ultimately unsatisfactory. In his estimation, only four Lucan texts suggest criticism of the temple (13.34-35; 19.45-46; 21.5-7; 23.45), but, he contends, the criticism is muted by Luke's editing of his sources.[48] Weinert's own work seeks to elucidate the redactional interests of Luke in both Luke and Acts. He observes that in Luke alone the temple references are found primarily in the first two chapters (1.9, 11, 21-22; 2.22, 27, 37, 46, 49) or in the last six (19.45-47; 20.1; 21.l, 5, 37-38; 22.52-53; 23.45; 24.53), whereas in the 'intervening two thirds of the Gospel such references are relatively rare and often indirect' (4.9; 6.4; 11.51; 13.1, 35; 18.10).[49] For Weinert, the central section (Luke 19–24) provides clearly identifiable Markan material which Luke has redacted, and therefore provides a point of entry.[50] From this he finds that the temple is presented positively as 'the preeminent religious sanctuary in Israel'.[51] It is the site of 'God's intimate personal presence among his

46. For him, this mainly involved M. Bachmann, *Jerusalem und der Tempel. Die geographisch-theologischen Elemente in der lukanischen Sicht des judischen Kultzentrums* (Stuttgart: Kohlhammer, 1980); K. Baltzer, 'The Meaning of the Temple in the Lukan Writings', *HTR* 58 (1965): 263–77; L. T. Brodie, 'A New Temple and a New Law: The Unity and Chronicler-based Nature of Luke 1:1–4:22a', *JSNT* 5 (1979): 21–45; F. X. Reitzel, 'St. Luke's Use of the Temple Image', *Review for Religious* 38 (1979): 520–39; C. Van der Waal, 'The Temple in the Gospel according to Luke', *Neot* 7 (1973): 44–59.

47. Francis D. Weinert, 'The Meaning of the Temple in Luke–Acts', *BTB* 11, no. 3 (1981): 85–9. See also his more extensive, 'The Meaning of the Temple in the Gospel of Luke' (PhD diss., Fordham University, 1978–1979).

48. Weinert, 'Meaning of the Temple', 85.

49. Ibid.

50. Ibid., 86.

51. Ibid.

people',[52] 'a place of communication between God and Israel',[53] 'a place for giving and receiving testimony of God's presence among his people'[54] and a place 'of God's revelatory communication with his people'.[55] This Weinert finds throughout the other sections of Luke as well (Luke 1–2; 3–18). Furthermore, he demonstrates that in Luke's account Jesus 'does nothing…to upset the worshipers who are their customers, or the other traffic of the Temple cult'.[56] Conflict with Jesus within the temple is presented in such a way that the opposition is 'embodied in Israel's leaders rather than in the Temple or the people at large'.[57] In Luke's presentation of the destruction of the temple, 'he avoids Mark's tendency to make the Temple the object of God's apocalyptic wrath' and 'carefully plays down any suggestion that Jesus is opposed to the Temple itself'.[58] In general, Weinert argues that '[i]n Luke's hands any suggestion that Jesus directed this saying against the Temple itself disappears'.[59] Where there is judgement and destruction, he finds that this is 'because of the irresponsibility of Israel's leaders'.[60] Weinert's work is helpful for a variety of reasons, as we will see below. Initially, from a methodological standpoint, he is careful to differentiate Lukan presentation of the temple from his presentation of Jesus' opponents.

In a 1988 monograph, J. Bradley Chance[61] argues that the significance of the temple in Luke is found in the eschatological age of salvation that comes with the arrival of Jesus. Contrary to the assertions of Conzelmann,[62] Chance finds no evidence of 'spiritualizing' the temple.[63] Instead, it is a legitimate place for receiving prophecies for Israel (at least, in Luke 1–20), but is taken over by the Messiah (Lk. 19.45–21.38) so that it may be the setting for him to teach all nations. In this regard

52. Ibid.
53. Ibid.
54. Ibid.
55. Ibid.
56. Ibid.
57. Ibid.
58. Ibid., 87.
59. Ibid.
60. Ibid.
61. J. Bradley Chance, *Jerusalem, the Temple, and the New Age in Luke–Acts* (Macon: Mercer, 1988). This is a revision of the author's PhD dissertation (1984) from Duke University under Franklin W. Young.
62. Hans Conzelmann's *Die Mitte der Zeit*, ET *The Theology of St Luke*, trans. G. Buswell (New York: Harper & Brothers, 1960).
63. Chance, *Jerusalem*, 5–46.

both Jerusalem and its temple become the location not for a 'true Israel' but for the 'renewed Israel'.[64] Jerusalem, then, is the setting for Gentile mission and so becomes the 'place of the nations' salvation'.[65] Luke's depiction of the destruction of the temple is not simply the result of Jerusalem's rejection of Jesus, but also its rejection of his *mission.*[66] But Chance argues that this does not suggest Luke's rejection of Judaism, for apparent statements about rejection – such as Jerusalem not seeing Jesus again until they say 'Blessed is he who comes in the name of the Lord' (Lk. 13.35) – include hope of restoration.[67] Chance holds to this argument despite the fact that, as he concedes, Luke never explicitly claims a restoration for Jerusalem or the temple, but merely implies it.[68] Whatever one makes of such conclusions,[69] Chance makes headway methodologically in considering the presentation of Jerusalem and its temple in Luke as a whole. Like Weinert, his approach counters some of the previous atomistic assessments.

A more recent discussion by Joel Green suggests that Luke's primary interest in the temple 'lies in its role as a "cultural center"'.[70] Here is where Green detects a conscious subversion by Luke, who first acknowledges this central role and then develops an 'increasingly negative characterization of the temple'.[71] For him this Roman political world is more than a mere 'backdrop' to Luke's Gospel, and temple depictions must be read against a larger rubric of subversion.[72] Additionally, the presence of the temple in Luke underscores 'importance *of the piety of Israel* in Luke's account'.[73] In the end, the temple will present itself 'as antagonist to Jesus

64. Ibid., 83.
65. Ibid., 112–13.
66. Ibid., 122.
67. Ibid., 129.
68. Ibid., 133–5.
69. See Neil Elliott, 'Review of Chance, *Jerusalem, the Temple, and the New Age in Luke–Acts*', *JAAR* 58, no. 4 (1990): 695–8; Darrell L. Bock, *A Theology of Luke and Acts: God's Promised Program, Realized for All Nations* (Grand Rapids: Zondervan, 2012), 401 n. 38.
70. Joel B. Green, *The Theology of the Gospel of Luke* (Cambridge: CUP, 1995), 5, drawing from Clifford Geertz, 'Centers, Kings, and Charism: Reflections on the Symbolics of Power', in *Local Knowledge: Further Essays in Interpretive Anthropology* (New York: Basic Books, 1983), 121–46.
71. Green, *Theology*, 6. This, he contends, results in 'the eventual and thoroughgoing theological critique of the temple to follow in Acts' (ibid.).
72. Ibid., 8.
73. Ibid., 12 (emphasis original).

and his message'.[74] Green seems to capture Luke's sense more clearly when he indicates that the scribes, lawyers and teachers of the law 'are consistently portrayed in a role antagonistic toward Jesus'.[75]

In his theology of Luke–Acts, Bock gives sparse attention to Jerusalem and its temple except in the context of Lukan eschatology.[76] The fall of Jerusalem in 70 CE, in Bock's view, 'guaranteed the coming reality of the end-time judgment of the world' and declared that 'God's program was on track'.[77] Presumably this means that the judgement upon Jerusalem anticipates a more universal judgement upon those who reject Jesus. Bock rebuffs Chance's thesis as viewing the temple activity 'too positively'.[78] For him, the 'temple is hardly renewed when Israel is seen as under exiliclike judgment until she recognizes her Messiah' (Lk. 13.34-35; 19.41-44).[79] Jerusalem too falls under the same indictment, since in it 'God's program is a highly contentious issue and believers are persecuted' and 'the presence of conflict shows that Luke does not see these sacred locales so positively'.[80] Therefore, for Bock, 'Jerusalem is no longer the hub of divine activity'.[81]

Bovon's claims differ. He contends that for Luke the temple 'stands in the center of Jerusalem, the holy city, by God's will'. And in Luke–Acts it 'becomes the site of revelation (Lk. 2.46, 49) and of Jesus' teaching (19.45-47), and, later, the first arena of activity for the Twelve (Acts 3.1, 11). After that, however, it loses its function in salvation history to Christ and the congregation, in a shift determined by providence.'[82]

These are some complicated and conflicting statements. Many scholars argue that Luke provides a negative assessment of Jerusalem and the temple. But while Luke is indeed clear that the Jewish leaders are antagonistic toward Jesus, it is less clear that the same could be said about the temple itself, its cult or even Jerusalem. Conflating the hostility toward Jesus that occurs *within the temple* with Luke's perception of the *temple itself* is problematic, and falls short of the contours of Luke's presentation.

74. Ibid.
75. Ibid., 70.
76. Bock, *Theology of Luke and Acts*, 77–9, 400–402.
77. Ibid., 401.
78. Ibid., 401 n. 38.
79. Ibid.
80. Ibid.
81. Ibid.
82. François Bovon, *Luke 1*, Hermeneia (Minneapolis: Fortress Press, 2002), 34 n. 31. Citing Michael Bachman, *Jerusalem und der Tempel: Die geographisch-theologischen Elemente in der lukanischen Sicht des jüdischen Kulzentrums*, BWANT 39 (Stuttgart: Kohlhammer, 1979).

From a methodological standpoint, we will place the Acts discussion to one side for the sake of brevity. We aim to compare *bios* with *bios* in Luke and Matthew. Moreover, while attention to demonstrably redactional activity by Luke seems like a sensible starting point (Weinert), it risks privileging alleged Lukan redaction at the expense of Lukan composition. In other words, Luke's distinctive handling of source material is not the only or even the best means of ascertaining his perspective on the temple. For one must presume that even where he utilizes a source with little or no evidence of redaction, his mere preservation of that source unaltered should be understood as 'Lukan' in the sense that he adopts it. We can and must presume that his preservation of the *entirety* of the evidence in the third Gospel was a sensible decision of the mind that last preserved it in its final form.

b. *Luke's Temple: From Beginning to End*

At the outset Luke portrays both a unique and positive depiction of the temple and its cult.[83] He alone records the narrative of Zechariah (Lk. 1.5-23), who carries out the duties of his priestly office within the temple (Lk. 1.9). It is here that he offers the incense and has a vision (Lk. 1.11-20, 22) while the pious pray outside (Lk. 1.10, 21). The presumption is that the morning and evening incense (Exod. 30.7-8) were being offered within the temple (ναός),[84] and there is no evidence of criticism toward the temple, its function or its priesthood.[85] Also unique to Luke is his account of Mary's and Joseph's concern for purification (αἱ ἡμέραι τοῦ καθαρισμοῦ; cf. Lev. 12.6) in accordance with the law of Moses (κατὰ τὸν νόμον Μωϋσέως, Lk. 2.22) and their observance of the requisite sacrifices (Lk. 2.23-24; Exod. 13.2; Lev. 12.8; cf. Neh. 10.35-36).[86]

83. Bovon (*Luke 1*, 101) observes that in Luke τὸ ἱερόν is the 'holy enclosure' whereas the temple itself is ὁ ναός or τὰ ἅγια.

84. John Nolland (*Luke 1:1–9:20*, WBC 35A (Dallas: Word, 1989), 28) observes that Luke's ναός is used of the holy place, whereas Luke typically employs the broader word ἱερός. See also Bovon, *Luke 1*, 34 n. 31.

85. So also Bovon, *Luke 1*, 32. Even though Zechariah soon will prophesy (Lk. 1.67 προφητεύω) that his child will prepare a way of salvation (σωτηρία) in the forgiveness of sins (ἐν ἀφέσει ἁμαρτιῶν; Lk. 1.77) – presumably a cultic function – no critique of the temple or its cult is evident.

86. Luke even notes the curious indication of 'their' (αὐτῶν) purification, whereas only the mother was subject to impurity. Nolland, *Luke 1:1–9:20*, 118; Joseph A. Fitzmyer, *The Gospel according to Luke I–X*, AB 28 (Garden City: Doubleday, 1979), 424.

Simeon and Anna within the temple precincts yield no evidence of hostility. Simeon is righteous and devout (δίκαιος καὶ εὐλαβὴς, Lk. 2.25), and, not by his own initiative but led by the Spirit (ἐν τῷ πνεύματι, Lk. 2.27), enters the temple (εἰς τὸ ἱερόν) where he meets Jesus' parents who are careful to adhere to the law on his behalf (κατὰ τὸ εἰθισμένον τοῦ νόμου περὶ αὐτοῦ, 2.27). Whereas Simeon must enter into the temple precincts (2.27), Anna (Lk. 2.36-38) is already there,[87] and in fact never leaves (οὐκ ἀφίστατο τοῦ ἱεροῦ, Lk. 2.37). In both instances these devout figures are within the temple, awaiting the 'consolation of Israel' (παράκλησιν τοῦ Ἰσραήλ, Simeon; Lk. 2.25) and 'the redemption of Jerusalem' (λύτρωσιν Ἰερουσαλήμ, Anna; Lk. 2.38). Throughout, the temple is affirmed as a legitimate place for prophecy, even though the ultimate consolation and redemption, presumably, is to be sought elsewhere. As a youth Jesus travels to Jerusalem (Lk. 2.41-50) to observe the Passover with his family (cf. Exod. 23.14-17; Deut. 16.16), as was their custom (κατὰ τὸ ἔθος, 2.41). Jesus remains in Jerusalem (2.43), only to be found in the temple (2.46)[88] where he explains to his bewildered parents that they should have known he had to be in his father's house (Lk. 2.49).[89] The setting seems so affirming of Jewish cultic practices that Bovon posits a *Sitz im Leben* as an apologetic to 'Jewish aspersions about Jesus' miserable origins'.[90] Luke even goes so far as to use the high priesthood of Annas and Caiaphas as temporal markers (Lk. 3.2), which seems unnecessary since he has already employed the reign of Tiberias Caesar, Pontus Pilate, the tetrarchies of Herod, Philip and Lysanias for the same purpose (Lk. 3.1).[91] Later Luke will identify the temple as 'the house of God' (τὸν οἶκον τοῦ θεοῦ, Lk. 6.4; cf. Mt. 12.4; Mk 2.26; Lev. 24.9; 1 Sam. 21.1-6), without polemic, not even about the propriety of entering the temple.

87. Bovon, *Luke 1*, 106.

88. Perhaps the portico of Solomon (Acts 3.11; 5.12, 21, 25; Bovon, *Luke 1*, 112).

89. Even these 'teachers' (διδάσκαλοι) are not portrayed in a negative light. Nolland (*Luke 1:1–9:20*, 69) observes that this term is unique in Luke. Elsewhere the author uses terms such as νομικός, γραμματεύς, νομοδιδάσκαλος ('lawyer', 'scribe', 'teacher of the law') with decidedly negative connotations.

90. Bovon, *Luke 1*, 110.

91. Notice the naming of two persons – Annas and Caiaphas – for a singular high priesthood. Nolland observes that Annas (6–15 CE) was the father-in-law of Caiaphas (18–36 CE), and the former retains considerable stature even during the reign of the latter (cf. Jn 18.13, 24; Acts 4.6). Nolland (*Luke 1:1–9:20*, 140) acknowledges the possibility that there may be an implicit refusal to acknowledge the deposition of Annas, and to render the passage, 'in the time of the high priest Annas, and of Caiaphas' (cf. Acts 4.6). Perhaps more likely is Bovon's contention that, like in

Other similar instances of the temple and its cult are also found in Luke, such as the parable of the Good Samaritan (Lk. 10.30-37), where nothing ill is said of Jerusalem, the temple or the institution of the priesthood. Yet the *behaviour* of both the priest (10.31) and Levite (10.32) fails to exhibit the obedience to Torah expressed by the Samaritan (10.33-37). The reference to the blood of Abel and that of Zechariah, killed 'between the altar and the house' (μεταξὺ τοῦ θυσιαστηρίου καὶ τοῦ οἴκου, Lk. 11.51), merely uses cultic items as a point of reference. The same can be said for the blood of the Galileans that Pilate mixed with their sacrifices (Lk. 13.1), which, though puzzling,[92] seems to connote violence done to people within the temple precincts[93] with little said about the temple itself.

A dramatic turn in Luke's view of Jerusalem occurs in 13.33-35, where Luke prefaces the lament over Jerusalem[94] with Jesus saying, 'it cannot be that a prophet should perish away from Jerusalem' (Lk. 13.33; cf. Lk. 4.24; 6.23).[95] This entails a litany of allusions to the Hebrew Bible (cf. Deut. 13.1-5, 10; 32.11; 2 Chron. 24.20-22; Isa. 54; 62.1, 4; Pss. 17.8; 36.7; 147.2), most importantly Jer. 22.1-8[96] from which the language of a desolate house is drawn (cf. Jer. 22.5 LXX: εἰς ἐρήμωσιν ἔσται ὁ οἶκος οὗτος).[97] This is followed by the lament over Jerusalem

Josephus, the NT identifies the officiating high priest and his predecessors as a sort of college of the highest religious authorities' (Bovon, *Luke 1*, 120). Luke's account of the temptation (Lk. 4.1-13; cf. Mt. 4.1-11; Mk 1.12-13) places Jerusalem at the end, perhaps in connection with Jesus' life as a whole which ends in Jerusalem. Bovon, *Luke 1*, 139. Again Bovon (*Luke 1*, 40) posits a *Sitz im Leben* in controversy with Judaism. Whereas Matthew identifies Jerusalem simply as 'the holy city' (τὴν ἁγίαν πόλιν, Mt. 4.5) Luke more properly identifies it by name (Ἰερουσαλήμ, Lk. 4.9). And in his wording of Jesus at the 'pinnacle of the temple' (τὸ πτερύγιον τοῦ ἱεροῦ, Mt. 4.5; Lk. 4.9), the devil challenges Jesus to throw himself down 'from here' (ἐντεῦθεν, Lk. 4.9), perhaps inferring his presence with Jesus at that location.

92. Bock lists no fewer than five options from both Josephus and Philo alone in terms of historical identification (cf. esp. Philo, *Spec. Leg.* 3.91). Darrell L. Bock, *Luke 9:51–24:53*, BECNT (Grand Rapids: Baker Books, 1996), 1205. See also François Bovon, *Luke 2*, Hermeneia (Minneapolis: Fortress Press, 2013), 267.

93. Bovon, *Luke 2*, 268.

94. Bovon (ibid., 322) identifies the lament as a 'judgement oracle' in which the good done by God is contrasted with the evil done by the people.

95. See further Fitzmyer, *Luke*, 1032.

96. John Nolland, *Luke 9:21–18:34*, WBC 35B (Dallas: Word Books, 1993), 741–3.

97. Bovon, *Luke 2*, 329.

(Lk. 13.34-35; cf. Mt. 23.37-39)[98] and then the condemning pronouncement: 'Behold, your house is left to you desolate' (ἰδοὺ ἀφίεται ὑμῖν ὁ οἶκος ὑμῶν, Lk. 13.35). The 'house' may be the temple (cf. Ezek. 8.14, 16) or Jerusalem as a whole (cf. Jer. 12.7 LXX).[99] Even here the desolation of the 'house' makes no critique of the institution of the temple, and the condemnation spoken is toward the people who, as in prior generations, seek the demise of one of God's prophets.[100]

Soon Luke records a parable – again unique to him – which is explicitly said to confront contemptuous self-righteousness (Lk. 18.9-14) in which two men – a Pharisee and a tax collector – go to the temple to pray (ἀνέβησαν εἰς τὸ ἱερὸν προσεύξασθαι, Lk. 18.10). The latter rather than the former goes home justified (δεδικαιωμένος, Lk. 18.14a) not because of any cultic activity but because of his pious demeanour (ὁ...απεινῶν ἑαυτὸν ὑψωθήσεται, Lk. 18.14b). The presumption, though, is that prayer at the temple is perfectly suitable, though the achievement of a right relationship with God entails no participation in sacrificial worship.

Presumably readers are to infer that the advent of the 'kingdom of God' would occur upon Jesus' arrival in Jerusalem, so he tells a parable pre-emptively (Lk. 19.11; cf. 19.28). Perhaps this was because Jerusalem 'was the place where the Messiah was supposed to arrive' (cf. Zech. 9.9-10),[101] but Jesus indicates that the kingdom would not appear immediately (παραχρῆμα, 19.11b). Later in the same chapter Jesus weeps over Jerusalem (Lk. 19.41-44) prior to the 'cleansing' (Lk. 19.45-48). He laments that the things that make for peace are now hidden from them (19.42), and anticipates days that will come upon Jerusalem,

> when your enemies will throw up a barricade against you, and surround you and hem you in on every side, and they will level you to the ground and your children within you, and they will not leave in you one stone upon another, because you did not recognize the time of your visitation (Lk. 19.43-44, NAS).

98. The accounts are nearly identical, though Luke does not include Matthew's addition of desolation (ἔρημος, Mt. 23.38). Luke renders Matthew's γάρ (Mt. 23.39) with καί (Lk. 23.35), and lacks the Matthean ἄν (Mt. 23.39).

99. The translation is ambiguous, and may well connote simply God's abandonment of the temple, and leaving it to them. In that case, it does no good and will not last. Bovon, *Luke 2*, 330.

100. For Bovon, the 'protective wings [over Jerusalem] would no longer be those of the temple but those of Christ'. Ibid., 333–4.

101. Ibid., 610. Nolland (*Luke 18:35–24:53*, WBC 35C (Dallas: Word Books, 1993), 913–14) sees Jerusalem as a 'throne city' and contends the corrective by Jesus is to avert the misconception of military intent.

Nolland observes points of correspondence from the Old Testament (e.g., LXX 1 Kgdms 23.8; 2 Kgdms 12.28; 4 Kgdms 6.14; Isa. 29.3; Ezek. 4.1-3) with greater affinity than Josephus's description of the assault of Titus (Josephus, *War* 5.466, 508). The cumulative effect of Luke's evocation of the texts from the Hebrew Bible is 'to call to mind strongly the role of these conquests as judgments of God upon the sin of his people',[102] the specifics of which in judgement unfold in Luke 21.

Luke's account of the 'cleansing of the temple' scene (Lk. 19.45-46; cf. Mt. 21.10-17; Mk 11.15-17) contains no material unique to him, though his is much more concise than that of either Matthew or Mark.[103] He shares Mark's 'began to drive out' (ἤρξατο ἐκβάλλειν, Lk. 19.45; Mk 11.15), but only those who sold are driven out. Luke says nothing about those who bought, the overturning of the tables of the money-changers, or the seats of those who sold pigeons. Nor does he mention Mark's account that Jesus prevented people from carrying things through the temple (Mk 11.16) or his designation that Jesus 'taught' (Mk 11.17). Luke also does not mention the blind and lame coming to Jesus to be healed in the temple, as Matthew does (Mt. 21.14-17). Finally, in the quotation about the house of prayer – which again all three share – Luke does not include Mark's 'for all the nations' (Mk 11.17). For Luke the poignancy is expressed with brevity. Jesus drives out the sellers (Lk. 19.45), telling them that they have turned what is intended to be a house of prayer (cf. Isa. 56.7) into a robbers' den (σπήλαιον λῃστῶν, Lk. 19.46). Though some reckon the 'cleansing of the temple' in Mark's account to be a proleptic destruction of the temple, Nolland observes this is unlikely in Luke's case, where it is 'difficult to find more than a protest and a token putting of things to rights'.[104] Indeed any sense here in which Jesus may be seen as critical of the Jerusalem temple is minimized by Luke.[105] Instead, Luke, invoking Jeremiah (7.11) indicts not the temple but the people and the 'pious show of things' they make within the temple.[106]

Perhaps this dichotomy between the affirmation of the temple and the behaviour of those in supervision over it is underscored in the next scene (Lk. 19.47-48), where Luke alone says that Jesus was teaching daily in the temple (ἦν διδάσκων τὸ καθ' ἡμέραν ἐν τῷ ἱερῳ, Lk. 19.47; cf. Mk 11.18-19). The chief priests and scribes seek to destroy him, as in

102. Nolland, *Luke 18:35–24:53*, 932–3.

103. Nolland (ibid., 937) calls it a 'severe abbreviation'.

104. Ibid. Similarly, François Bovon, *Luke 3*, Hermeneia (Minneapolis: Fortress Press, 2012), 19.

105. Nolland, *Luke 18:35–24:53*, 937.

106. Ibid.

Mark (Mk 11.18), though he adds that 'the principle men of the people' (καὶ οἱ πρῶτοι τοῦ λαου, Lk. 19.47) do so as well. Nolland goes so far as to say:

> The prominence that Luke gives to the temple location of Jesus' ministry in Jerusalem is part of his contention that Jesus, and therefore Christians (despite anticipating its fall in a divine judgment), had the highest of regards for this central point of Jewish reverence. Luke will make it clear in 24:52–53 and in Acts with the continued Christian orientation to the temple that not even the execution of Jesus at the instigation of those who control the temple can dislodge this Christian loyalty.[107]

Nolland's observation is important, for it seems indicative of the entirety of Luke's Gospel. Later in Luke (20.1-8 // Mt. 21.23-27; Mk 11.27-33) the temple is an appropriate place for Jesus to teach and preach (Lk. 20.1). Presumably also the temple treasury (Lk. 21.1-4; cf. Josephus, *War* 5.200) is an appropriate place for giving gifts, large or small (cf. Mk 12.41-44).[108]

Climactic discussion of the destruction of the temple commences while on the subject of its adornments (Lk. 21.5-6; cf. Mt. 24.1-2; Mk 13.1-2)[109] utilizing language that recalls Jeremiah (Jer. 7.1-14; 22.5; cf. 52.12-13).[110] More explicit language of destruction (Lk. 21.20-24) requires careful attention to Luke's synoptic counterparts (cf. Mt. 24.15-22; Mk. 13.14-20). Luke shares with the others the seeing and desolation (ἴδητε...ἡ ἐρήμωσις, Lk. 21.20; Mt. 24.15; Mk 13.14), the warning to 'let those who are in Judea flee to the mountains' (Mt. 24.16; Mk 13.14; τότε οἱ ἐν τῇ Ἰουδαίᾳ φευγέτωσαν εἰς τὰ ὄρη, Lk. 21.21), and concern for those with child and nursing (Mt. 24.19; Mk 13.17; Lk. 21.23). Luke does not include several features found in Matthew and Mark, such as the setting up of the sacrilege where it should not be and the parenthetical 'let the reader understand' (Mt. 24.15; Mk 13.14). He makes no mention of imploring those on the housetops not to go down or those in the field not to take his mantle (Mt. 24.17-18; Mk 13.15-16). No mention is made of the concern that the events not occur in winter (Mt. 24.20; Mk 13.18), it

107. Ibid., 940.

108. Nolland (ibid., 979) observes that Luke's τὰ δῶρα, 'the gifts', suggests 'nonobligatory contributions'.

109. See Josephus, *Ant.* 15.391-402; *War* 5.184-226; cf. 2 Macc. 3.2; 9.16. Whereas previously he spoke of the fall of Jerusalem (19.43-44), here (v. 6) he specifies the temple. The fate of the city and temple are one and the same (Bovon, *Luke 3*, 109).

110. Nolland, *Luke 18:35–24:53*, 988.

being the greatest tribulation since the beginning of the world (Mt. 24.21; Mk 13.19), or of the shortening of these troubled days for the sake of the elect (Mt. 24.22; Mk 13.20).

Luke alone indicates that Jerusalem will be surrounded by armies (κυκλουμένην ὑπὸ στρατοπέδων Ἰερουσαλήμ) and provides an exhortation that they should know that its desolation has come near (τότε γνῶτε ὅτι ἤγγικεν ἡ ἐρήμωσις αὐτῆς). His wording is unique with respect to those inside the city not departing, nor those in the country seeking to enter the city (Lk. 21.21b). His reason (ὅτι) also is unique: 'these are the days of vengeance, to fulfill all that is written' (ἡμέραι ἐκδικήσεως αὗταί εἰσιν τοῦ πλησθῆναι πάντα τὰ γεγραμμένα, Lk. 21.22; cf. Hos. 9.7; Jer. 28.6 LXX). Rather than 'tribulation' (θλῖψις, Mt. 24.21; Mk 13.19), Luke describes these days as ones of 'distress' (ἀνάγκη, Lk. 21.23). Again uniquely, Luke calls this 'wrath upon this people' (ἐπὶ τῆς γῆς καὶ ὀργὴ τῷ λαῷ τούτῳ, Lk. 21.23). They will fall by the sword, be taken captive and Jerusalem will be trodden down by the Gentiles 'until the times of the Gentiles are fulfilled' (ἄχρι οὗ πληρωθῶσιν καιροὶ ἐθνῶν, Lk. 21.24).[111] Nolland observes[112] that, as before (Lk. 19.41-44), the vocabulary throughout the pericope is drawn from LXX depictions of the prior threat to Jerusalem (e.g., Isa. 29.3; Jer. 41.1 [MT 34.1]; 51.6, 22 [MT 44.6, 22]) and resembles the early stages of Rome's assault on the city (Josephus, *War* 4.486-90). Later Luke alone records Jesus' exhortation to the daughters of Jerusalem to weep for themselves and their children (Lk. 23.28), indicating they will experience the judgement of God that awaits the city[113] and may connote the need for repentance.

Despite its impending destruction, the temple remains a place where Jesus teaches (Lk. 21.27), after which he spends the night on the Mount of Olives, only to return to the temple to teach the next morning (Lk. 21.38). This is underscored later at the arrest, where the officers of the temple (στρατηγοὺς τοῦ ἱεροῦ, a reading unique to Lk. 22.52) are among those arresting Jesus, who points out that he was daily in the temple for them to arrest him there (καθ' ἡμέραν ὄντος μου μεθ' ὑμῶν ἐν τῷ ἱερω, Lk. 22.53).

Luke's account of the preparation for the day of Unleavened Bread (Lk. 22.7-14; cf. Mt. 26.17-20; Mk 14.12-17) alone indicates it as the day 'on which the Passover lamb had to be sacrificed' (ᾗ ἔδει θύεσθαι τὸ

111. Nolland (ibid., 1002) asserts the verse 'is a pastiche of allusions to OT descriptions of judgment upon Jerusalem (see esp. Jer 20:4–6; 28:14; and the Greek text of Zech 12:3)'.

112. Ibid., 1000.

113. Ibid., 1137.

πάσχα). The indication here by Luke is the necessity of following the appropriate procedures (δεῖ; cf. Exod. 12.6, 18; Lev. 23.5; Num. 9.3, 5; Deut. 16.6-7).[114]

The rending of the temple veil (τὸ καταπέτασμα τοῦ ναοῦ) occurs in all three Synoptics (Lk. 23.45; Mt. 27.51; Mk 15.38). Bovon is typical of many scholars who see here 'a prelude to the destruction of the temple'.[115] But nothing in the context supports this reading. Nolland is more attuned to the Lukan context in his understanding of the event as an indication of access to heaven through the death of Jesus (cf. Lk. 3.21; Acts 7.55-56).[116]

More affirmations of Jerusalem, the temple and its affiliated institutions are found in the end of Luke's Gospel. Luke (alone) records the women refraining even from caring for Jesus' body on the Sabbath, underscoring his concern that things be done according to the command of Scripture (cf. Lk. 23.56; Exod. 20.10; Deut. 5.14). Luke presumes news of events surrounding Jesus were known throughout Jerusalem, as the query of Cleopas suggests (Lk. 24.18). The disciples then return to Jerusalem (Lk. 24.33) where the eleven and other disciples were apparently stationed. For Bovon, 'Jerusalem remains the center of salvation history'.[117] In Luke's unique account of Jesus' ascension (Lk. 24.45-53) one encounters, as before, forgiveness of sins, but without recourse to the cult (Lk. 24.47a). Instead, this salvation is to be proclaimed, beginning in Jerusalem (Lk. 24.47b). And so Jesus instructs them to return to that city (Lk. 24.49) and, after his ascension (Lk. 24.51), they do (Lk. 24.52). It is in Jerusalem where they are continually in the temple praising God (ἐν τῷ ἱερῷ εὐλογοῦντες τὸν θεόν, Lk. 24.53).

Luke's Gospel starts in Jerusalem and ends there; the temple is the setting here (v. 53) and in the beginning (1.9, 21; 2.27, 46).[118] Naturally Jerusalem as the starting point for the ongoing mission will be developed

114. See also 2 Chron. 35.13-14; Josephus, *War* 6.9.3 §523; *Jub*. 49.10-12. With Nolland (ibid., 1032–3) the contention that this necessity (ἔδει) is tied to the passion predictions (Lk. 9.22; 17.25; 22.37; 24.7, 26; Joel Green, 'Preparation for Passover (Luke 22:7–13): A Question of Redactional Technique', *NovT* 29 (1987): 312) is tenuous.

115. Bovon, *Luke 3*, 325. He adds that this 'entails the end of the sacrificial cult, the end of divine revelation, the end of immediate and henceforth access to God, and the end of separation between Israel and the nations'.

116. Nolland, *Luke 18:35–24:53*, 1157–8. Following Dennis D. Sylva, 'The Temple Curtain and Jesus' Death in the Gospel of Luke', *JBL* 105 (1986): 239–50.

117. Bovon, *Luke 3*, 376.

118. Ibid., 412.

in Luke's second volume (Acts 1.8; cf. Acts 3.1, 12-16). For Green, Luke's presentation is an acknowledgement of '*the centrality of the Jerusalem temple* to the social world of Jesus'.[119] For Nolland, the symbolism is important: 'though it is for all the world, the gospel emerges from the very heartland of Jewish faith'.[120]

But perhaps the notion of a social world and even the heartland grasps only part of Luke's concern. The temple is not simply the setting of key events – though it is that. It is also an institution ordained by God, and the directives of its cultic practices laid out in the Hebrew Bible are presumed to be valid and are to be observed. Absent are the conjectures of negativity and condemnation about Jerusalem, the temple and its cultic functions that are espoused among some scholars. Condemnation and judgement ensues, of course, but a close reading of Luke reveals the care with which the evangelist distinguishes the temple from its inept leadership. It is the leadership and Jesus' opponents in general who, as with other prophets before Jesus, reject the work of God in Jesus and incite God's judgement upon Jerusalem and its temple. What becomes interesting is that its function is affirmed and, while not critiqued explicitly, seems to fade with respect to Jesus. Forgiveness of sins is acquired without the temple cult (Lk. 5.20). Even here objections are not raised with regard to cultic practices but with respect to God's prerogative (cf. Lk. 7.48-49; 8.37-39; 11.4).

IV. *Conclusion*

We have seen that the evangelists have a remarkably consistent and positive portrayal of the temple. No negative word is uttered by either the evangelists or Jesus about the temple *itself*. Indeed, Matthaean and Lukan redaction seems to stifle texts where Mark's Jesus could be understood as anti-temple, and negative statements about it, such as its impending (or past?) destruction, are centred on confrontations with the religious leaders who mismanage it. Destruction allusions and statements about the temple also resonate with language and theodicy found in Jeremiah, where God's displeasure with those managing the Solomonic temple finds expression in judgment executed against the temple itself. Fault lies with *them* and, as in Jeremiah's time, the temple, so to speak, took the fall.

There remain two ancillary matters to consider in this synthesis. First, we notice that Jesus conducts healings at times without reference to the temple or its cult. Similarly, as Matthias Konradt observes, as we have

119. Green, *Theology*, 12 (emphasis original).

120. Nolland, *Luke 18:35–24:53*, 1221.

seen above, Jesus' atoning death (e.g., Mt. 26.28) renders the temple obsolete.[121] This is an important corrective to alleged anti-temple rhetoric in Matthew that may work just as well in Luke. A second implication of the present discussion is its contribution to questions raised by Dunn and others regarding the 'parting of the ways'. Dunn devotes considerable attention to the temple and, in his estimation, Jesus' words and actions in the Gospels as a whole 'could be said to contain implicit critique in regard to purity issues'. This is not so different, though, from what one encounters in the *Psalms of Solomon* or sectarian documents from Qumran.[122] Davies and Allison concur, finding that Matthew falls in line with late 1st-century Jewish thought. *4 Ezra*, *2 Baruch* and the *Apocalypse of Abraham*, for instance, likewise attribute Jerusalem's tragic demise and the leveling of its sanctuary to Jewish failing.[123] These findings suggest that the evangelists Matthew and Luke, like some of their contemporaries and their prophetic influences from the Hebrew Bible, exhibit a deep concern for the propriety of God-ordained cultic worship as well as the piety of those charged with its oversight. The authors exhibit no hostility to these institutions; instead, they face destruction because of their leaders' hostility toward the plan of God in Christ. Moreover, the cultic functions of the temple as a means of communion with the one true God of Israel is ultimately achieved in the sacrificial death of Christ. While it remains a place from which missions will spread unto the ends of the earth (Acts 1.8), its cultic function no longer has a place in God's redemptive plan. Though Matthew's and Luke's portrayals of Jerusalem, the temple and its cult are in some ways distinct, they offer not a tale of two cities, but one.

121. Konradt, *Israel, Church, and the Gentiles*, 145 n. 309.

122. Dunn, *Partings of the Ways*, 73.

123. *Matthew*, 3:143, cf. nn. 65–7.

12

Insisting on Easter: Matthew's Use of the Theologically Provocative Vocative (κύριε) in the Suppliant Narratives

Douglas Sean O'Donnell

I. *Introduction*

While the titles used for Jesus in the Gospel of Matthew do not embody Jesus' whole identity and mission, they do summarize accurately central aspects of the evangelist's storyline and theological vision. Each title – Christ, son of David, Son of Man, Lord and so on – adds its own unique colour to the narrative tapestry Matthew has masterfully woven together. The last strand listed is not the focus of this study because its word-count outnumbers Christ, Son of David and Son of Man (although it does)[1] or because I render it higher status than those key christological titles (although an argument can be made). Rather, the motive behind this study is simple. I seek to shed light on an important but surprisingly overlooked word,[2] especially as it is set within the context of the suppliant

1. 'Christ' (17 times), 'Son of David' (10 times) and 'Son of Man' (30 times).

2. To my knowledge, there are no monographs on the theme and only two articles: Jack D. Kingsbury, 'The Title "Kyrios" in Matthew's Gospel', *JBL* 94 (1975): 246–55, and Laurence Culas, 'The Title "Lord" in the Gospel according to Matthew and Its Implications for the Evangelist and His Church', *Indian Theological Studies* 48, no. 3 (2011): 215–32. Both articles cover the material on the suppliants sparingly, and the suppliants find almost no role in Kingsbury's thesis that 'Matthew employs *kyrios*...[as] an "auxiliary christological title", the purpose of which is to attribute divine authority to Jesus in his capacity as the "Christ", "Son of David", "Son of God" or "Son of Man"' (p. 248). In scholarly commentaries on Matthew and Matthaean theologies the theme is also covered thinly.

narratives – those outsiders who cry out in faith, calling Jesus 'Lord'. As scholars agree that κύριος is a key christological title in Matthew,[3] then this theme deserves fuller treatment than it has been given. Moreover, as the role of the suppliants offers a valuable contribution to Matthean theology, then what follows will hopefully demonstrate an aspect, or various aspects, of their contribution.

In this essay, I do not set out to answer the question, 'In what ways does Matthew use the word κύριος?' The answer to that question is simple enough. Matthew uses κύριος, as the other Graeco-Roman, Jewish and Christian authors do, in three ways – as an honorific title ('sir'), a designation of authority ('master') and a theological indicator ('Lord'). Rather, the question I will tackle is, 'What does Matthew want his intended readers to understand by the term "Lord" when used on the lips of the suppliants?' I will answer this question by showing three clues from the context that support the view that Matthew intended the ἐκκλησία to understand the suppliants' κύριε to Jesus as a christologically charged title, representing Jesus' divine lordship, or in Matthew's own climatic terminology, representing Jesus as the Lord who, like κύριον τὸν θεόν (4.7, 10; 22.37), has 'all authority in heaven and on earth' (28.18). While Matthew's use of 'Lord' is not that of Paul's or the post-resurrection church (namely, as a title to designate the position of the risen Lord, e.g., Acts 7.59; Col. 1.15-20), nevertheless, each suppliant in the Evangelist's narrative insists on Easter before Easter – that Jesus' power over death be made available to them immediately.

II. *Matthew's 'Lord' Language*

Before we examine the three clues, we begin with an overview of the language in the whole Gospel, including brief synopses of the suppliant pericopes where the title is used. Spread in balanced proportions, throughout twenty-eight chapters, are eighty occurrences of κύριος in the first Gospel. The term is used in a variety of genres, including historical narrative (1.20, 22, 24; 2.13, 15, 19; 28.2), Old Testament quotations or allusions (3.3; 4.7, 10; 5.33; 21.9; 22.43, 44, 45; 23.39), instructions (6.24; 10.24, 25; 11.25; 21.3; 24.42; 27.10), authoritative self-declarations (7.21, 22; 9.38; 12.8), parables (13.27; 18.25, 27, 31, 32, 34; 20.8; 21.30,

3. It is reasonable to side with Georg Strecker and W. D. Davies that κύριος ranks along with 'Son of David' (see *Der Weg der Gerechtigkeit*, FRLANT 82 (Göttingen: Vandenhoeck & Ruprecht, 1962), 118–20, 123–6) and 'Son of Man' (see *The Setting of the Sermon on the Mount* (Cambridge: CUP, 1964), 96–9, 360) as one of the most significant titles in Matthew.

40; 22.37; 24.45, 48, 50; 25.11, 18-24, 26, 37, 44), pleas for deliverance (8.2, 6, 8, 25; 14.30; 15.22, 25; 17.15; 20.30, 31, 33), a seemingly sincere confession from an apparently uncommitted disciple (8.21) and half-informed confessions from committed disciples (e.g., 14.28; 26.22). It is also found in Peter's honorific but ignorant announcements (16.22; 17.4; 26.22) and honest but careless question on the mathematics of forgiveness (18.21).

'Lord' is applied twenty-five times to God,[4] fifty-one times to Jesus (or in relation to Jesus),[5] once to a character in a parable who symbolizes neither God nor Jesus (21.30), and Pilate (with the secular 'sir' as an appropriate translation, 27.63).[6] Those using the word include the narrator, Jesus, the disciples and the suppliants. As it relates to the focus of this study, the suppliants use the title for Jesus eleven times (8.2, 6, 8; 9.28; 15.22, 25, 27; 17.15; 20.30, 31, 33). Every occurrence has Jesus as its object and is communicated in the vocative.

II.a. *The Leper (Matthew 8.1-4)*

The first character to use the term is the leper in Mt. 8.2. In Mt. 8.1-4 'great crowds' follow Jesus as he comes down from 'the mountain' (v. 1). Matthew highlights one face in the crowd – 'a leper' (v. 2a). Matthew uses two verbs to describe this man's movements and posture (v. 2a):

4. This includes references to characters connected directly with God, such as 'the angel of the Lord' (1.20, 24; 2.13; 28.2), as well as the 'lord' of the parable of the Unforgiving Servant (18.22-35), who is clearly God (v. 35) and 'the lord of the vineyard' in 21.40 and possibly 20.8. However, regarding 20.8, it is possible that Jesus is 'lord of the vineyard' (see 19.28 for the closest contextual connection to Jesus as eschatological judge). I find Daniel Johansson's thesis for Mark can also be applied to Matthew, namely, that Matthew's 'ambiguous use of κύριος is intentional and serves the purpose of *linking Jesus to the God of Israel*, so that they *both share the identity as κύριος*', '*Kurios* in the Gospel of Mark', *JSNT* 33 (2010): 102–3.

5. I take Jesus to be 'the lord of the harvest' (9.38), 'the lord of the Sabbath' (12.8), 'the lord of the house' (13.27; see vv. 37, 41 for clear designations), and the 'lord' of 10.24, 25 (see Günther Bornkamm, 'End-Expectation and Church in Matthew', in *Tradition and Interpretation in Matthew*, ed. Günther Bornkamm, Gerhard Barth, and Heinz Joachim Held, NTL (Philadelphia: Fortress Press, 1963), 41) and in the parables of ch. 25.

6. Some have taken the 'lord' in 21.3 to be the owner of the donkey and colt (e.g., see M.-J. Lagrange, *Evangile selon Saint Matthieu*, 7th edn (Paris: Gabalda, 1948), 397). The more likely reading is that it refers to Jesus (e.g., see W. D. Davies and Dale C. Allison, *Matthew*, ICC (Edinburgh: T. & T. Clark, 1997), 3:117 and Grant R. Osborne, *Matthew*, ZECNT 1 (Grand Rapids: Zondervan, 2010), 754).

προσελθὼν [αὐτῷ]	Having approached him
προσεκύνει αὐτῷ	He worshipped him

Directly following this, the leper addresses Jesus (κύριε) and makes his request ('if you are willing, you are powerful [enough] to cleanse me', v. 2b). The miracle immediately follows. Jesus touches the unclean man, and the man's 'leprosy was cleansed' (v. 3). This short narrative concludes with Jesus' admonishment to silence and command to keep the Mosaic regulations concerning cleansing (v. 4).

II.b. *The Centurion (Matthew 8.5-13)*

In the second suppliant narrative Matthew records the healing of the centurion's slave (8.5-13). The setting, however, shifts to Capernaum and the next character is not an outcast Jew but an establishment Gentile. However, like the leper, the centurion comes to Jesus in humility seeking healing (v. 5).

προσῆλθεν αὐτῷ	He approached him
παρακαλῶν αὐτὸν	He was begging him

His first word is 'Lord' (κύριε) and his supplication (v. 6) is similarly short. Again, as Jesus did for the leper, he immediately responds. He promises to come to the man's house and heal the servant (v. 7). A dialogue ensues about the appropriateness of a Jew coming into a Gentile's house. Part of the debate centers on the centurion's admission of unworthiness (οὐκ εἰμὶ ἱκανὸς, v. 8). That admission follows his second 'Lord' (κύριε). The centurion argues that a mere word should suffice (v. 8). Jesus marvels at this man's faith, bestowing upon him one of the highest commendations and promises in the Gospel (see vv. 10-12). Jesus then gives his word, presumably speaks a word and immediately 'the servant was healed' (v. 13).

II.c. *The Blind Men (Matthew 9.27-31; 20.30-34)*

The third suppliant κύριος narrative is about the healing of the blind men (9.27-31). There are two stories of healings of blind men in Matthew, the second coming in 20.30-34. Both are worth considering here, as the similarities highlight well the theme of our study. First, both stories use the verb of discipleship (ἀκολουθέω): one at the start (9.27), the other at the end (20.34). Second, both employ the verb κράζω (κράζοντες // ἔκραξαν) – a verb laced with a mix of desperation and hope – followed by the redundant λέγοντες (9.27; 20.30). Third, and most significant to this study, both share the terminology of 'Lord', 'Son of David' and 'have mercy on us'. The relationship between the titles 'Son of David' and 'Lord' (which is beyond the scope of this study) is significant, as is the appeal 'have mercy on us', which will be explored below. For now, it is simply worth noting both the irony – that the blind men *see* Jesus as the royal Messiah before the disciples do! – as well as the emphasis on *κύριος*. The first set of blind men call Jesus 'Lord' once (9.28), and the second set thrice (20.30, 31, 33). Fourth, both express faith, not only in the manner in which they address Jesus, but also in direct response to questions he asks (see 9.28; 20.32-33). Finally, both conclude with the same mode of healing (Jesus touched) and result (they saw) (9.29-30; 20.34).

II.d. *The Canaanite Woman (Matthew 15.22-27)*

Another suppliant narrative employing *κύριος*-terminology is that of the Canaanite woman (15.22-27). Of all the interesting, unexpected and odd array of outcasts who call Jesus 'Lord' and ask him to save, she ranks first. She also ranks first for *κύριος* references in Matthew (4×). While she uses *κύριος* to describe 'the master of the house', whose table she seeks to sup at (or under!), it is clear that this 'master' symbolizes Jesus, whom she addresses in every sentence as *κύριος*: 'Have mercy on me, O Lord' (v. 22); 'Lord, help me' (v. 25); 'Yes, Lord' (v. 27).[7] These declarations, like those of the other suppliants, are supplemented by her movements and posture (*ἐλθοῦσα προσεκύνει αὐτῷ*, v. 25), her expressive emotions (*ἔκραζεν* ['she was crying out'] + *λέγουσα*, v. 22; cf. *κράζει*, v. 23), and her acknowledgment of Jesus' identity ('Son of David', v. 22).

II.e. *The Father of the Demon-Possessed Boy (Matthew 17.14-21)*

The final narrative where *κύριος* is featured in a suppliant's cry comes in the story of the healing of the demon-possessed boy (17.14-21). As Jesus comes down from the mount of transfiguration he walks into a valley infested with evil. A desperate father asks his help for his 'epileptic' (*σεληνιάζεται*) son, who is tortured (v. 15) by overpowering demonic-induced (*δαιμόνιον*, v. 18) seizures. The apostles are impotent to assist. We are not given the reason for their failure, only Jesus' prophetic vexation with unbelieving Israel (v. 17), followed by his prompt and complete exorcism (v. 19) and private rebuke of his disciples (v. 19a). It appears

7. Mark also uses the vocative for this story, but only once (7.28). In fact, it is the only occurrence in his Gospel.

that the only person in this narrative who expresses genuine faith in Jesus is the boy's father,[8] whose request is seemingly as impossible as moving a mountain from Jerusalem to Jericho (v. 20). And like the other faith-filled suppliants who cry out 'Lord', he expresses his faith with the same motion (προσῆλθεν αὐτῷ),[9] posture (γονυπετῶν[10] αὐτὸν), confession (κύριε) and plea (ἐλέησόν μου, vv. 14-15).

II.f. *Two Summary Observations*

In section III that follows, I will explore further the significance of each character's actions as it pertains to his/her κύριος confession. For now, two key observations should be noted. First, there is the diversity of characters (a leper, a centurion, a mother, a father and four blind men), along with who they represent (a slave, a demon-possessed girl, a demon-possessed boy). There are seven Jews, four Gentiles; nine males, two females; one slave, presumably ten free. Is this Matthew's narrative portrayal of Paul's pronouncement in Gal. 3.28? Second, there is the similarity of situations. They all face life-threatening dilemmas. With that, they all come to Jesus (προσελθὼν αὐτῷ) because they believe he can deliver them from the evils of disease, demons and death. Moreover, and most importantly for our study, their postures (προσεκύνει αὐτῷ; γονυπετῶν αὐτὸν) and pleas (κύριε, often along with ἐλέησόν μου, and/or υἱὸς Δαυίδ) provide nearly identical faith-filled expressions. Matthew's literary/theological artistry is perhaps nowhere more apparent.

III. *Clues for Reading the Suppliants' κύριε as Christologically Charged*

Next we turn to consider the clues for reading the suppliants' 'Lord' as Christologically charged. As we are considering the issue of whether the term κύριος should be read as weakly as 'sir' or as strongly as deity, or somewhere between those extremes, the stronger view becomes more probable once we consider how Matthew uses κύριος-language throughout his Gospel, especially before the first suppliant's 'Lord' is voiced.

8. See Akta Ogawa, 'Action-Motivating Faith: The Understanding of "Faith" in the Gospel of Matthew', *Annual of the Japanese Biblical Institute* 19 (1993): 66.

9. In Matthew, προσέρχομαι can take on an ominous undertone, as when Satan came (προσελθὼν, 4.3) to tempt Jesus and Judas came (προσελθὼν, 26.49) to betray him. However, it can also be a faith-filled word, as made explicit throughout chs 8–9. Most often those who trust in Jesus *come to him* – including the suppliants (8.2, 16; 9.2, 18, 20, 28, 32), the disciples (8.25) and even tax collectors and sinners (9.10).

10. For a discussion on γονυπετῶν, see n. 44.

In Matthew 1–7, κύριος is used in three ways: for YHWH; for Jesus, seemingly as YHWH; and by Jesus as a self-designation that communicates the highest christological connotations.

III.a. *The Suppliants' 'Lord' in Context*

Regarding Matthew's first application, the term 'Lord' is used of God in two ways in chs 1–7. First, it refers to his messenger – 'an angel of the Lord' (1.20, 24; 2.13, 19). Second, it appears in the Old Testament quotation formulas (e.g., 2.15, 17) and Old Testament quotations (3.3; 4.7, 10; 5.33), the last three spoken by Jesus.

As nearly all the references to the 'Lord' in Matthew 1–7 refer to YHWH, Matthew makes plain to his readers the identity of κύριος. The God of their Bibles (the LXX in some form)[11] is the κύριον τὸν θεόν (Deut. 6.13, 16 LXX; Mt. 4.7, 10) first introduced in Matthew. This Lord sends his angels (ἄγγελος κυρίου, e.g., 1 Chron. 21.18 LXX; Mt. 1.20) to communicate his will and his prophets to prepare his way (τὴν ὁδὸν κυρίου, Isa. 40.3 LXX; Mt. 3.3).

With this context in mind, the two places where κύριος-language refers to Jesus in these opening chapters would have been confusing, if not shocking, to first-century monotheistic Jews. First, without hesitation, in Mt. 3.3 the evangelist applies the term for the sacred tetragrammaton (יהוה) to Jesus. The allusion is clear that when John the Baptist speaks of preparing 'the way of the Lord' (v. 3) it is in reference to the coming of Jesus (v. 11).[12] Second, following the Baptist's lead, when Jesus arrives on the scene he concludes his first discourse by using the double vocative (κύριε κύριε) as a self-designation (7.21-24). Here Jesus not only affirms that 'Lord' is the proper title for him,[13] but he sets his first self-designated

11. In the LXX the title 'occurs over nine thousand times, and in some 6,156 occurrences it is used in place of the proper name of God, "Yahweh"', B. Witherington and L. Yamazaki-Ransom, 'Lord', *DJG*, 527. In post-OT Greek Jewish literature κύριος 'frequently appears as a term of God (e.g., c. 200 times in Sirach)', *NIDNTTE*, 3:773. Moreover, Andy Johnson notes that the LXX's use of κύριος 'as a reverential circumlocution for Yahweh' was 'a widespread practice among religious Greek-speaking Jews', 'Lord', *NIDB*, 3:687.

12. What C. Kavin Rowe said of Lk. 3.4-6 is true of Matthew: 'Because 3:4-6 is an Old Testament quotation the κύριος in 3:4 is unquestionably the κύριος of the Old Testament; because John the Baptist in Luke's narrative literally does prepare the way for Jesus structurally, sequentially, and as his prophet, the κύριος indubitably refers to Jesus', *Early Narrative Christology: The Lord in the Gospel of Luke* (Grand Rapids: Baker Academic, 2009), 71.

13. Even for those professing Christians, whose charismatic credentials are impressive, calling Jesus 'Lord' will not suffice to gain entrance into the kingdom.

use within the context of himself serving as the eschatological judge,[14] which is not the only time in Matthew where he claims to exercise this authority. Even though κύριος is used of Jesus sparingly in chs 1–7, the uses therein make clear that Matthew has intentionally blurred 'the lordly identity of Jesus and of Yahweh in the OT'.[15] As he makes increasingly clear as the narrative progresses, for Matthew 'there is one κύριος, and yet two figures, God and Jesus, share this name and title'.[16]

These patterns in Matthew 1–7 repeat often throughout chs 8–28, as 'Matthew employs *kyrios* in order to attribute an exalted station to Jesus'.[17] Jesus is acknowledged as the one who comes 'in the name of the Lord' (21.9; cf. Ps. 118.26; Mal. 3.1). He is seemingly labeled 'the lord of the vineyard' (see Mt. 20.1; 21.33),[18] and perhaps even 'the lord of the harvest' (9.38).[19] He is understood as the coming κύριος, notably in the Olivet Discourse where the double vocative is again used (25.11).[20]

That does not mean, however, that the title is not the appropriate designation. 'To address Jesus as "Lord, Lord" implies a serious level of engagement with him, as illustrated by the episodes in ch. 8 to follow', John Nolland, *The Gospel of Matthew*, NIGTC (Grand Rapids: Eerdmans, 2005), 339.

14. On the theme of Jesus as the coming Lord and judge in early Christian literature, see esp. 1 Cor. 4.4-5; 1 Thess. 4.15-17; 2 Thess. 1.9-10. In Rabbinic Judaism the title 'Lord' was used of God in the sense of God as 'the Lord and Governor of the whole world and its history' and as 'the Lord and Judge of the individual' (e.g., 'Lord of judgement', *Ethiopic Apocalypse of Enoch* 83.11). W. Foerster, 'κύριος', *TDNT*, 1085.

15. Simon J. Gathercole, *The Preexistent Son: Recovering the Christologies of Matthew, Mark, and Luke* (Grand Rapids: Eerdmans, 2006), 245. This is said in reference to Mt. 22.43-45. But the same can be said of 3.3 and 7.21, 22.

16. Robert L. Mowery, 'From Lord to Father in Matthew 1–7', *CBQ* 59 (1997): 643. Mowery also notes how 'the four references to an angel of the Lord are in passages which lack Synoptic parallels'. Similarly, in his study in Luke, Rowe comments: 'Luke positions κύριος within the movement of the narrative in such a way as to narrate the relation between God and Jesus as one of inseparability, to the point that they are bound together in a shared identity of κύριος (*Verbindungsidentität*)', *Early Narrative Christology*, 27.

17. Kingsbury, 'The Title "Kyrios" in Matthew's Gospel', 249.

18. Alluding to Isa. 5.7 LXX/MT, God is 'the lord of the vineyard' in Mt. 21.40 and likely Jesus in 20.8, as the context seems to indicate (see 19.28).

19. See Douglas Sean O'Donnell, *Matthew: All Authority in Heaven and on Earth*, Preaching the Word (Wheaton: Crossway, 2013), 279.

20. The double vocative 'appears eighteen times in the Septuagint' and 'every single occurrence is an indisputable reference to Yahweh', Charles L. Quarles, *A Theology of Matthew: Jesus Revealed as Deliverer, King, and Incarnate Creator*

He is the 'lord of the Sabbath' (12.8).[21] Finally and climatically, in Mt. 22.41-45, he reveals his true identity through his Pharisee-stumping riddle: he is one of the two κύριοι of Ps. 109.1 (LXX), a being who shares enthronement with YHWH.[22]

With that text in particular, along with the host of others above, perhaps the closest theological explanation of Matthew's narrative is Paul's declaration, 'There is one God, the Father…and one Lord, Jesus Christ' (1 Cor. 8.6). Whatever explanation or analogy one may give, it is certain that Birger Gerhardsson's view of κύριος as a term that had 'not yet received any proper Christological connotation' for Matthew or his community is wrong,[23] and that Charles Quarles's thesis hits closer the mark: 'The context…of several of Matthew's descriptions of Jesus as Lord strongly suggests that "Lord" functions [or, *can* function] as a title of deity'.[24]

With all this in mind, when Matthew's readers arrive at the suppliant narratives, they are shaped by how Matthew uses his 'Lord' language elsewhere. This theocentric use beforehand provides readers with a fitting context within which to understand the term christologically in the ensuing narrative. For example, then, as the reader moves from the end of the Sermon on the Mount to the first two suppliants, she should see in the leper's 'Lord' and centurion's double 'Lord' a direct connection to how Jesus should be approached. Jesus should be called κύριος and anyone approaching him in faith should be willing, as these two were, to stand wholeheartedly upon his sure and powerful word to save.

This perspective is reinforced by the other suppliants whose petitions to Jesus echo the language of Old Testament prayers to YHWH. Of the four evangelists, Matthew uses three unique expressions that correspond directly with Old Testament supplications: the Canaanite woman's 'have

(Phillipsburg: P&R, 2013), 142. For 'people to call on Jesus as "Lord" in the judgment scenes (Matt. 7.21; 25.37, 44)…is a distinctly Matthean phenomenon' (Gathercole, *The Preexistent Son*, 246).

21. The OT 'clearly attributes' not the specific title, but certainly the authoritative role κύριος of the Sabbath (12.8) to God (see Johansson, '*Kurios* in the Gospel of Mark', 112). Anthony J. Saldarini views Jesus' 'the Lord of the Sabbath' as an allusion to Lev. 23.3, 'a Sabbath to the Lord', *Matthew's Christian-Jewish Community* (Chicago: University of Chicago Press, 1994), 129.

22. The Messiah is more than David's offspring ('son'), he is also David's 'Lord'. That is, the one seated next to YHWH is both a divine and human figure.

23. Gerhardsson, 'The Christology of Matthew', in *Who Do You Say That I Am? Essays on Christology*, ed. M. A. Powell and D. R. Bauer (Louisville: Westminster John Knox Press, 1999), 19.

24. Quarles, *A Theology of Matthew*, 142.

mercy on me, O Lord' (15.22),[25] the father's 'Lord, have mercy on my son' (17.15) and the blind men's 'Lord, have mercy on us' (20.31;[26] cf. 'Have mercy on us', 9.27). These same expressions are found in the Psalms (singular, 6.2; 9.13; 30.10; 41.4, 10; 86.3; cf. 40.11; plural, 123.3 LXX) and prophets (plural, Isa. 33.2 LXX). In fact, in the LXX when ἐλεέω (in the second-person-singular imperative) is combined with κύριε, YHWH is always the object of the petition. Thus, it is reasonable to conclude from both the Old Testament context and that of the context of the first Gospel as a whole that Matthew intends to assist his scripturally informed readers in seeing the suppliants' κύριος as Christologically charged. He desires that they understand that the odd array of outcasts, who sound like the psalmists, approach Jesus in some sense as YHWH alone would be approached.[27]

III.b. *The Suppliants' Requests*

This Christologically charged reading is further confirmed when we examine an additional element of the suppliants' language. As we will see next, when pleading with Jesus, the suppliants not only sound like Old Testament saints pleading with YHWH but they also ask him to do what only God in the Old Testament can do.

The centrality of the theme of authority in Matthew has been duly noted by scholars. It has also been long observed how the disciples acknowledge Jesus' authority, in part, by consistently labeling him 'Lord', rather than 'teacher' or 'rabbi' which are the common titles used by enemies and strangers. In Matthew, among οἱ δώδεκα (with the notable exception of Judas, who calls Jesus 'rabbi' in 26.25, 49), only the title 'Lord' seems fitting. However, what is often neglected is how, of all the characters in Matthew, the suppliants exemplify what it means to embrace Jesus' divine

25. Her cry in 15.25 ('Lord, help me') is an echo of Pss. 44.26 and 109.26. 'These two verses are the only combinations of the vocative "Lord" with the second-person-singular imperative "help!" in the Septuagint. Although Matthew's account is paralleled in Mark 7:24–30, this phrase is unique to Matthew', Quarles, *A Theology of Matthew*, 144–5.

26. Matthew replaces Mark's 'Son of David' (Mk 10.47) with κύριος, one of many redactions that highlight the importance of this title to Matthew's theology.

27. The suppliants foreshadow prayer to Jesus – 'those who call upon the Lord Jesus Christ' (1 Cor. 1.2), 'a regular Old Testament formula for worship and prayer offered to God (Gn. 4:26; 13:4; Ps. 105:1; Je. 10:25; Joel 2:32; *etc.*', R. T. France, 'The Worship of Jesus: A Neglected Factor in Christological Debate?', in *Christ Is Lord: Studies Presented to Donald Guthrie*, ed. H. H. Rowdon (Leicester: IVP, 1982), 30.

authority. They grasp that even 'the blind [can] receive their sight[28]... lepers [be] cleansed[29]...and the dead [or those on their deathbeds, be] raised up' (11.5).[30] They even grasp that Jesus has heaven-sent power on earth over the underworld.[31] Thus, they direct their trust to Jesus' authority and experience his divine healing power.

With this, while some might consider it a stretch to claim that those 'in Matthew's Gospel who approach Jesus uttering the word κύριε are acknowledging that he is a figure not merely of human, but lordly or divine, dignity',[32] surely considering what they ask Jesus to do moves the meaning of their expression beyond a polite greeting. 'Sir' will not suffice! With the working assumption that Jesus possesses divine power to conquer disease, demons and death, they ask him to act like God.

28. 'The two blind men had no historical reason to suppose they could be healed; it had never happened before. Yet their belief that Jesus was the Davidic Messiah led them to believe that Isa 35:1 could finally come true, and they came to him', Osborne, *Matthew*, 356.

29. The same can be said of leprosy, as Nolland notes: 'An account of the miraculous cure of leprosy does not seem to be included among the Jewish and pagan miracle accounts that have survived from antiquity', *Luke 1–9:20*, WBC 35A (Dallas: Word Books, 1989), 226.

30. The Bible gives examples of the prophets (e.g., 2 Kgs 5) and apostles (e.g., Mt. 10) performing similar miracles. The major differences are that when the needy approach them they (1) do not call them 'Lord', (2) the prophets or apostles are not asked for direct help from them, but through them from God and (3) the miracle does not occur immediately by or under their own direction or authority. Moreover, the OT recognizes that such miracles are from the hand of YHWH (e.g., 2 Kgs 5.7; Ps. 146.8a). Regarding leprosy, 'there is a rabbinic tradition that says, in reference to the "law of the leper" (Lev 14:2), that in the world to come "all the deformed [including lepers] will be healed" (Midrash Tanhuma, Mesora'§7; cf. Mesora'§9 "in the world to come I [God] am the One who will cleanse you from on high")', Craig A. Evans, *Matthew*, NCBC (Cambridge: CUP, 2012), 236. Perhaps to Matthew, John the Baptist's reference to 'the coming One' (ὁ ἐρχόμενος, Mt. 1.3) is more than Jesus as the one 'who comes in the name of the Lord' (Ps. 118.26) but Jesus as the Lord God who will come (see Zech. 14.5).

31. Matthew makes clear that Jesus – as the saving 'Lord' (8.25) and 'Son of God' (v. 29) – has the power to control the chaotic seas and conquer a legion of demons (vv. 23-34). In curing leprosy and blindness, and expelling demons, Jesus is doing what only God can do, namely, reversing the curse (Gen. 3) and binding the strong man (Mt. 12.28-29).

32. Kingsbury's summary ('The Title "Kyrios" in Matthew's Gospel', 246) of Bornkamm's 'Enderwartung', in *Überlieferung und Auslegung im Matthäus-evangelium*, 39.

This point is especially clear in the centurion's supplication.[33] The centurion could have brought his 'paralytic' (παραλυτικός, 8.6; cf. 9.2) to Jesus. But he did not because he believed that Jesus could heal from a distance without the patient present, or, as far as we know, without that patient trusting in Jesus to save. He expressed, as Luz put it, 'unlimited confidence in the authority of Jesus who can make sick people whole by means of his own word'.[34] The centurion's request, 'Lord...only say the word, and my servant will be healed' (Mt. 8.8), is remarkable. For his εἰπὲ λόγῳ surpasses even Martha's admission, 'But even now I know that whatever you ask from God, God will give you' (Jn 11.22), since he makes no mention of God. He believes Jesus himself has such divine authority.[35] As Wilkins says, 'This centurion pays homage to an even greater authority in Jesus, whose word alone, like God's word (cf. Ps. 107:20), can heal'.[36] In fact, this centurion asks the man Jesus to perform, without heaven's help, an unprecedented miracle.

In his study *Faith in the Synoptic Gospels*, Edward O'Connor categorizes the centurion's faith under his chapter heading 'Faith as Understanding'. This is an important insight. Especially important is the centurion's perception of the person of Jesus. While O'Connor doubts that the centurion had 'a clear perception of Christ's divinity', he rightly observes that his declaration demonstrates that 'this gentile had spontaneously attributed to Christ the power which had long been for the Jews paramount to the attributes of God – that of acting through His mere word'[37] (e.g., Ps. 33.9a).

33. Let it be noted, however, that the centurion's supplication, in the flow of Matthew's narrative, builds on the leper's request, which sets 'the will of Jesus... on par with that of God' (Nolland, *Matthew*, 349). Thus, as Nolland points out, 'The address, "Lord", is not significant by itself, but in the light of what follows [the request] we perhaps hear echoes of the use of "Lord" in the worship of God as exalted Lord' (ibid.).

34. Ulrich Luz, *Matthew 8–20*, trans. J. E. Crouch, Hermeneia (Minneapolis: Fortress Press, 2001), 10.

35. 'Here the christological motivation is...certainly present: here is a "Lord" with authority analogous his own, but operating in quite another league', Nolland, *Matthew*, 355. This is likewise true for the blind men of 9.28. 'In giving their answer ["Yes, Lord"] the blind people are drawn into the circle of those who address Jesus as Lord... They believe not just that Jesus is some mediating channel for the power of God, but that he is in himself and by right God's plenipotentiary' (401).

36. Michael J. Wilkins, *Matthew*, NIV Application Commentary (Grand Rapids: Zondervan, 2004), 342.

37. O'Connor, *Faith in the Synoptic Gospels: A Problem in the Correlation of Scripture and Theology* (South Bend: University of Notre Dame Press, 1961), 71–2.

In light of the preceding analysis, we may agree that the centurion, along with the other suppliants, did not 'realize anything like the whole truth about Jesus'.[38] We may also agree that Jerome's claim 'beneath the covering of the body he saw the concealed divinity'[39] is an exegetical exaggeration. However, such convictions do not dismiss the fact that the one who acts with *God-like authority* in chs 8–9 is presented as divine throughout much of Matthew 1–28. And, seemingly, the centurion grasps (or, the readers are to understanding him as grasping) something of this. He may not have viewed Jesus as the ultimate fulfillment of the Isaianic 'Immanuel' (1.23),[40] but he wholeheartedly trusted that Jesus possessed and exercised God-like supernatural powers. He may not have seen Jesus as saviour from his sins (see 1.21), but he certainly saw him as saviour from the powers of death. He may not have prayed to Jesus as the Lord God of the Hebrew Scriptures as Matthew and his first readers did, but he certainly asked Jesus to act as only YHWH could.

III.c. *The Suppliants' Postures*

A third clue for reading the suppliants' κύριε as a Christologically charged designation relates to the previous two. Beyond sounding like Old Testament saints pleading with YHWH when they plead with Jesus and asking him to do only that which YHWH can do, their posture before Jesus resembles an appropriate physical deportment before deity.

In Pablo Veronese's (1528–1588) painting 'Jesus and the Centurion' (1581) the Italian artist paints the Roman military leader on one knee with two soldiers attempting to lift him from this embarrassing position. However, in Matthew, the centurion is one of the suppliants whose posture is not recorded. Yet, as that narrative especially focuses on *words*, his unique confession οὐκ εἰμὶ ἱκανὸς perhaps symbolizes his bended knee. Whatever the case, like John the Baptist he approaches Jesus in utter humility (see 3.11; 8.8), and perhaps, if there is any tinge of his

38. Birger Gerhardsson, *The Mighty Acts of Jesus according to Matthew* (Lund: LiberLäromedel/Gleerup, 1979), 86.

39. Jerome, *Commentary on Matthew*, trans. Thomas P. Scheck, FC 117 (Washington: Catholic University of America Press, 2008), 100.

40. Matthew might have used the title Ἐμμανουήλ and explanatory phrase μεθ' ἡμῶν ὁ θεός (1.21) as 'Jesus = God'. However, Nolland's translation of μεθ' ἡμῶν ὁ θεός as 'God is/will be with us' and explanation that the christological focus of 1.18-25 is 'upon the initiative of God in the incorporation of Jesus into the line of David' is a more plausible reading. See 'No Son of God Christology in Matthew 1.18–25', *JSNT* 62 (1996): 10, 11.

unworthiness beyond racial and religious distinctions (i.e., his personal unworthiness due to sin), then the tenor of his speech resembles that of Isaiah before the throne of God (Isa. 6.5).

That said, I do not want to posit physical posture in the centurion narrative where none is portrayed. The same is true for the miracles of the blind men. I will not claim that their 'sitting by the roadside' (Mt. 20.30) was a significant gesture. Instead, our attention will centre on the one, repeated, gesture that Matthew centres on – the act of kneeling before Jesus. Using two verbs for the suppliants (προσκυνέω and γονυπετέω) Matthew records three of the eight suppliants kneeling before Jesus.

The word προσκυνέω expresses 'in attitude or gesture one's complete dependence on or submission to a high authority figure' – either a transcendent being [i.e., God][41] or a human being [but to a human 'recognized as belonging to a superhuman realm'[42]] and it can be translated '(fall down and) worship, do obeisance to, prostrate oneself before, do reverence to, welcome respectfully' (BDAG, 882–3). The other word, the somewhat rare γονυπετέω, is best rendered 'kneel down' or 'fall on one's knees' before someone in petition. Thus, the verbs are almost synonymous. The word γονυπετέω might connote 'kneeling in entreaty'[43] while προσκυνέω connotes 'kneeling in worship'.[44] That division fits, for Matthew reserves προσκυνέω for key christological narratives – the adoration of the magi (2.2, 8, 11), the temptation in the wilderness (4.9, 10), the synagogue ruler who requests Jesus to raise his dead daughter (9.18), the disciples' response to Jesus walking on water (14.33), the mother of Zebedee's

41. For 164 of the 171 instances of the hithpalel form of שחה, the LXX uses προσκυνέω (e.g., 'Oh come, let us worship and bow down; Let us kneel before the Lord our maker', Ps. 95.6).

42. Considering the data, this part of the definition might be too strong or precise.

43. So Osborne, *Matthew*, 655.

44. The word πίπτω is used 19 times, with only four verses relevant to our study (i.e., verses on falling before God or Jesus). None of them implies merely deferential respect to another human being. They all reflect homage before a supernatural superior. First, the magi 'fell down and worshipped' (πεσόντες προσεκύνησαν) Jesus (2.11). Second, in the temptation narrative, Satan promises Jesus 'all the kingdoms of the world' if Jesus will fall down and worship him (πεσὼν προσκυνήσῃς, 4.9), with the προσκυνέω/πίπτω combination in play again. Third, Peter, James and John 'fell on their faces' (ἔπεσαν ἐπὶ πρόσωπον αὐτῶν) before the transfigured Jesus (17.6). Fourth, when Jesus prays to the Father at Gethsemane, 'he fell on his face and prayed' (ἔπεσεν ἐπὶ πρόσωπον αὐτοῦ προσευχόμενος, 26.39). Thus, Matthew's use of πίπτω reinforces his use of προσκυνέω, as kneeling, or falling prostrate, before a divine being.

misguided but astounding faith in Jesus' future glorious kingdom (20.20) and the resurrection appearances (28.9, 17).[45]

We can read too much into Matthew's use of προσκυνέω, just as we can of his use of κύριος. However, the combination of κύριε and προσεκύνει is rare enough (only Mt. 8.2; 15.25 in the NT) that it is worth considering its potential significance. Only Matthew uses these words for the leper (cf. Mk 1.40; Lk. 5.12) and the Canaanite/Syrophoenician woman (cf. Mk 7.25). As Hurtado observes, 'Whereas Mark uses the term προσκυνέω solely in two ironic scenes where Jesus is reverenced by demons and his tormentors, and Luke uses the term solely to characterize the reverence given to the risen Jesus, Matthew repeatedly employs προσκυνέω to describe the homage given by disciples and supplicants (and by them alone) to the earthly Jesus'.[46] In light of this, it seems most probable that all thirteen uses of προσκυνέω should be translated 'worship'[47] and that every use in reference to coming before Jesus (10×) suggests someone who prostrates himself/herself before him in the same way they would before God. In other words, agreeing with Held, when it comes Matthew's use of προσκυνέω with those who encounter Jesus (2.2, 8, 11; 8.2; 9.18; 14.33; 15.25; 20.20; 28.9, 17) it is used 'only in the sense of genuine worship'.[48] Or, as Hurtado summarizes: 'This pattern of preference for προσκυνέω, with its strong associations with cultic worship, suggest that Matthew has chosen to make these scenes all function as foreshadowings of the exalted reverence of Jesus familiar to his Christian readers in their collective worship'.[49]

This view is further supported when Matthew adds the word 'Lord'. Matthew uses κύριε thirty-three times more than Mark (34 to 1) and προσκυνέω eleven times more (13 to 2).[50] He uses these two terms more

45. While the NT does use προσκυνέω to depict people bowing before other people (e.g., Rev. 3.9), the typical Jewish reaction to someone doing this is to rebuke them (see Acts 10.25; Rev. 19.10).

46. Larry W. Hurtado, *How on Earth Did Jesus Become a God? Historical Questions about Earliest Devotion to Jesus* (Grand Rapids: Eerdmans, 2005), 148.

47. See Richard Bauckham, 'The Throne of God and Worship of Jesus', in *The Jewish Roots of Christological Monotheism*, ed. J. R. Davila, C. C. Newman and G. S. Lewis (Leiden: Brill, 1999), 67–8.

48. H. J. Held, 'Matthew as Interpreter of Miracle Stories', in Bornkamm, Barth and Joachim, eds, *Tradition and Interpretation in Matthew*, 229.

49. Hurtado, *How on Earth Did Jesus Become a God?*, 146.

50. 'The net effect of Matthew's numerous omissions and insertions of προσκυνέω in cases where Jesus is the recipient of homage is a consistent pattern' (ibid., 147).

than any other New Testament author,[51] and together they paint a picture of an appropriate posture before the one to whom 'all things have been handed over' (Mt. 11.27; cf. 28.18). For Matthew, it is only right, as Paul said, that 'every tongue confess that Jesus is Lord' and 'every knee…bow' before the humble one whom God has highly exalted (Phil. 2.9). Indeed, with Matthew's use of προσκυνέω, especially in combination with κύριος, he has made an obvious effort to amplify the homage given Jesus so that his Christian readers might identify with those characters who prefigure their own post-Easter devotion to their risen and exalted Lord.

IV. *Conclusion*

In the Gospel of Matthew, the suppliants join Jesus' disciples in consistently calling Jesus 'Lord'. This essay has explored the significance of this Matthaean emphasis, arguing that the suppliants' κύριος is a Christologically charged designation that demonstrates their acknowledgement of Jesus' divine authority. In answering the question 'What does Matthew want his intended readers to understand by the term "Lord" when used on the lips of the suppliants?' I have provided three reasons for embracing this reading. First, we have seen that Matthew's use of κύριος-terminology throughout his narrative favours this view. Matthew does not explain how Jesus became 'Lord', he simply uses his theologically subtle narrative artistry to assume such is the case (that God and Jesus are both κύριος). Second, we have explored how the suppliants echo the cries of Old Testament saints to YHWH when they pleaded with Jesus to have mercy and save. In other words, they ask Jesus to act like God. Third, we have highlighted how their posture before Jesus resembles an appropriate attitude and approach before deity. They kneel before Jesus, just as someone would before God. With all this in mind, it is apparent that Matthew intends for their vocative – κύριε – to be theologically provocative! His suppliants, who are always presented (above the often obtuse and sometimes ὀλιγόπιστοι twelve) as exemplars of faith, are exhibited to the reader as examples of post-resurrection κύριος Christology. To them, even before Easter, 'Jesus is Lord'.

51. The vocative (κύριε) is used 33 times in John and 27 times in Luke. The total number of uses of προσκυνέω in the other NT writings are: 'Mark (2), Luke (3, of which two refer to worship of God), John (10, all but one of which refer to the worship of God), Acts (4, three of which designate worship of God), 1 Corinthians (1), Hebrews (2)', and Revelation (24) (ibid., 146 n. 21).

13

How Do the Beatitudes Work? Some Observations on the Structure of the Beatitudes in Matthew

David Wenham

Introduction

The Beatitudes that open the Sermon on the Mount in Matthew's Gospel are some of the best known and most loved sayings in the Bible. But, although they are full of great phrases and attractive resonances, aren't they a bit of a mess, a rather jumbled-up collection of blessed thoughts?[1]

1. The literature on the Beatitudes is vast. The subtitle of this article 'some observations' is an acknowledgement that its focus is on Matthew's understanding, without going into the question of the meaning in Jesus' own context. We are also not exploring Matthew's own church background and context, but focusing on the text within the Gospel as we have it. Footnoting and cross-referencing will be kept to a minimum; major resources continue to be Robert Guelich, *The Sermon on the Mount: A Foundation for Understanding* (Waco: Word Books, 1982); H. D. Betz, *A Commentary on the Sermon on the Mount, including the Sermon on the plain [Matthew 5:3–7:27, and Luke 6:20-49]* (Minneapolis: Fortress Press, 1995); also the monumental French work of Jacques Dupont, *Les Beatitudes*, Vol. 1 (Paris: J. Gabalda, 1958). Notable among more recent treatments is Charles Quarles, *Sermon on the Mount: Restoring Christ's Message to the Modern Church* (Nashville: B. & H. Publishing, 2011). There are also major commentaries on Matthew, to which I am indebted, including notably W. D. Davies and D. C. Allison, *The Gospel according to Saint Matthew* (Edinburgh: T. & T. Clark, 1988), U. Luz, *Matthew 1–7: A Commentary* (Minneapolis: Augsburg, 1989), also John Nolland's outstanding *The Gospel of Matthew* (Bletchley: Paternoster Press, 2005). I am grateful to John not only for his writings, but also for his support, friendship and sharing of ideas and resources which I experienced as a colleague in Trinity College, Bristol.

There are nine of them: there is repetition with two of them having the identical promise 'for theirs is the kingdom of heaven' – did the author run out of promises? The promise with those two is in the present tense, but in all the others is future, e.g. 'they will be comforted'. There is duplication, with two of the Beatitudes speaking of the same group – the persecuted. Most of the Beatitudes are in the third person, e.g. 'theirs is the kingdom of heaven', 'they will be comforted', but the last is in the second 'Blessed are you when others revile you and persecute you'. Some of them seem to be encouragements to people under pressure (e.g. the persecuted), others to be commendations of the righteous (e.g. the pure in spirit).[2]

A common view that may help explain these things is that Matthew and Luke are drawing on their common Q source: Luke is closest to the original Q, with all his Beatitudes being encouraging ones, not ethical, with all the promises being in the second person, and all them with a future tense.[3] Matthew has modified the Q form, adding some extra promises, all of them ethically oriented (e.g. blessed are the pure in heart), and altering others of them in an ethical/spiritual direction (hence 'blessed are the poor in spirit…those who hunger and thirst for righteousness' vs. Luke's more original 'blessed are the poor…and those who hunger'). On this view an explanation of Matthew's messiness is that he has modified his source, but not very well, leaving us with a somewhat ragged result.

The argument of this article is that this does an injustice to Matthew, and that his version of the Beatitudes is very coherent and very carefully edited.[4] It is a parallel case to that of the Lord's Prayer, later in the sermon,

2. 'Blessed' is not the ideal translation of the Greek *makarios* (Latin *beatus*), which means 'happy'. Beatitudes are found in the Old Testament and in later Jewish literature, some of them identified by scholars as wisdom sayings describing wise ways of living, some of them as eschatological, promising future blessing. Matthew's and very clearly Luke's Beatitudes in Lk. 6.20-23 fall into the second category, though Matthew's could be seen as having some of the characteristics of wisdom sayings.

3. Luke follows his four Beatitudes with four corresponding woes, which have themselves evoked plenty of scholarly discussion.

4. This is not to question the usefulness of source critical approaches, but, if Matthew has been editing Q or any other source, he has done it very expertly and effectively. See Neil McEleney's 'The Beatitudes of the Sermon on the Mount/Plain', *CBQ* 43 (1981): 1–13: he concludes with a similar analysis of the Matthaean Beatitudes to what I am proposing, but he reaches it via a useful discussion of various source-critical possibilities and options. He and others could be right in advocating some form of the Q hypothesis, but it is clear from his discussion how uncertain and speculative some of the source-critical ideas are. There are of course alternatives to Q, with a good number of scholars preferring to think of Luke using Matthew,

where Matthew's form of the prayer is very carefully almost poetically arranged with its seven petitions having a 3-1-3 structure.[5]

The argument depends on viewing the first eight Beatitudes as a group. What then of the ninth second person plural Beatitude: 'blessed are you when others revile you and persecute you', which might appear to undermine the argument? The answer to that, I suggest, is that it should be seen separately: it is not a clumsy repetition of the eighth 'blessed are those who are persecuted for righteousness' sake', but it is a transitional saying that develops the thought of the eighth but also takes us from the opening declarations (the third person Beatitudes) into the rest of the Sermon which is mostly addressed to 'you' the hearers.[6] It links the prelude, i.e. the first eight Beatitudes, to the main symphony of the Sermon. That it should be seen as such a transition (rather than a half-cooked bit of editing) is confirmed by the striking coherence of the preceding eight.

The Structure Explained

The thesis of this article is that the eight should be viewed like this:

1.Blessed are the poor in spirit,
for theirs is the kingdom of heaven.

> 2 Blessed are those who mourn, *for they will be comforted.*
> 3 Blessed are the meek, <u>*for they will inherit the earth.*</u>
> 4 Blessed are those who hunger and thirst for **RIGHTEOUSNESS,**
> *for they will be filled.*
>
> 5 Blessed are the merciful, *for they will be shown mercy.*
> 6 Blessed are the pure in heart, <u>*for they will see God.*</u>
> 7 Blessed are the peacemakers, *for they will be called sons of God.*

8 Blessed are those who are persecuted because of **RIGHTEOUSNESS,**
for theirs is the kingdom of heaven.

others emphasizing the importance of oral tradition in the early days of the church, and suspecting that the sort of teaching of Jesus preserved in Matthew's and Luke's Sermons will have been well known in various versions.

5. I argued for this in 'The Sevenfold Form of the Lord's Prayer in Matthew's Gospel', *ExpTim* 121 (2010): 377–82, where I also introduce my reflections on the Beatitudes, which I develop in this article. Again in the case of the Lord's Prayer, if Matthew has been drawing on a Q version closer to Luke's version, he has done an impressive editorial job.

6. Scholars have often seen Beatitude 8 as Matthew's creation, with no. 9 as the more original based on Q. If that is true, our argument is not undermined, and indeed might possibly be enhanced.

Μακάριοι οἱ πτωχοὶ τῷ πνεύματι,
ὅτι αὐτῶν ἐστιν ἡ βασιλεία τῶν οὐρανῶν.
μακάριοι οἱ πενθοῦντες, *ὅτι αὐτοὶ παρακληθήσονται.*
μακάριοι οἱ πραεῖς, ὅτι αὐτοὶ *κληρονομήσουσιν τὴν γῆν*.
μακάριοι οἱ πεινῶντες καὶ διψῶντες τὴν ΔΙΚΑΙΟΣΥΝΗΝ,
ὅτι αὐτοὶ χορτασθήσονται.

μακάριοι οἱ ἐλεήμονες, *ὅτι αὐτοὶ ἐλεηθήσονται.*
μακάριοι οἱ καθαροὶ τῇ καρδίᾳ, ὅτι αὐτοὶ *τὸν θεὸν ὄψονται*.
μακάριοι οἱ εἰρηνοποιοί, *ὅτι αὐτοὶ υἱοὶ θεοῦ κληθήσονται.*
μακάριοι οἱ δεδιωγμένοι ἕνεκεν ΔΙΚΑΙΟΣΥΝΗΣ,
ὅτι αὐτῶν ἐστιν ἡ βασιλεία τῶν οὐρανῶν.

We notice a number of points:

1. *Two balanced stanzas*
The eight Beatitudes can be viewed as two stanzas: the first four Beatitudes are 36 words in the Greek (and all begin with the letter pi), the second four are also 36 words.[7]

2. *A bracketing inclusion*
The first Beatitude has a promise in the third person 'For theirs is the kingdom of heaven' and so does the last Beatitude. It is wholly unlikely that this repetition is the result of editorial fatigue with the writer having run out of promises, and very likely that it is deliberate, creating an *inclusio*. This suggests the not very surprising conclusion that the Beatitudes and indeed the Sermon on the Mount, to which they are a prelude, are about the kingdom of heaven.

3. *The present and future tenses*
The other six Beatitudes have a variety of promises with a future tense, so that we have in the first half one present tense + three future tenses, and in the second half the mirror image with three future tenses + one present tense. This makes sense given what we have already suggested about the first and the last forming an *inclusio*. It also suggests that in fact

7. Lots of scholars have observed this, e.g. Charles H. Talbert in his very useful *Reading the Sermon on the Mount: Character Formation and Decision Making in Matthew 5–7* (Columbia: University of South Carolina Press, 2004), 47–58. See also the excellent discussion of this and the Beatitudes generally in Quarles, *Sermon on the Mount*, 35–70. It is interesting to speculate as to whether Matthew has worded any of the Beatitudes with the word count in mind. 'Poor *in spirit*' could be partly explained thus.

all the Beatitudes are promising the kingdom of heaven to people, with Beatitudes 1 and 8 making the promise in general terms, and Beatitudes 2-7 unpacking that general promise in concrete ways appropriate to the people concerned (hence most clearly 'those who mourn...will be comforted', 'the merciful...will receive mercy').[8]

As for the present and the future tenses, Beatitudes 1 and 8 make it clear that the kingdom of heaven belongs now in the present to those whom Jesus describes – it is their inheritance; but fully entering into the inheritance and experiencing the practical blessings of the kingdom, i.e. the comforting, the seeing God, etc., still lie in the future.

4. *The righteousness theme*

It makes good sense to argue that the eight Beatitudes comprise two stanzas. In both stanzas the kingdom of heaven features as a key theme, occurring explicitly in stanzas 1 and 8, as we have seen; in addition both stanzas end with a beatitude that describes people with an interest in 'righteousness' – 'hungering for righteousness' in no. 4, being 'persecuted for righteousness' in no. 8. This is going to be another of the key themes in the Sermon on the Mount, here anticipated in the Beatitudes. Beatitude 8 explicitly links the theme of righteousness with that of the kingdom of heaven, and this is precisely what the Sermon on the Mount is going to be about, as it expounds the way of Christian discipleship; see, for example, two key texts: 5.20 'Unless your righteousness exceeds that of the scribes and Pharisees, you will not enter the kingdom of heaven' and 6.33 'Seek first the kingdom and his (i.e. God's)[9] righteousness'. It is clear enough that the Beatitudes are carefully constructed and are a prologue and introduction to the Sermon that is to follow.[10]

8. Of those future promises, nos 2, 4, 5 and 7 are future passives. They are so-called divine passives referring to an action of God. The two other promises, nos 3 and 6, are future active/middle; 'they shall inherit the land/earth', 'they shall see God' also imply divine gift, and they are if anything the most striking of all the promises.

9. Some ancient manuscripts have a feminine, and so it means 'seek first the kingdom and its righteousness'.

10. It hardly needs saying that both kingdom of heaven and 'righteousness' are important themes to Matthew outside the Sermon, with 'righteousness' being especially significant for Matthew's Jesus (see Jesus' first recorded words in 3.15, and also 5.20, 6.33). See also my 'The Rock on Which to Build: Some Mainly Pauline Observations about the Sermon on the Mount', in *Built upon the Rock: Studies in the Gospel of Matthew*, ed. D. Gurtner and J. Nolland (Grand Rapids: Eerdmans, 2007), 187–206.

5. *The different focus of the two stanzas*

Despite what unites the two halves, they do have a different focus. The conditions described in Beatitudes 1-4 – poor in spirit, mourn, meek, hungry and thirsty for righteousness – all suggest need of some sort, with the possible exception of no. 3, 'the meek', which could be seen as more ethical; the conditions described in Beatitudes 5-8 all suggest people living positive kingdom lives – being merciful, pure in heart, peace-makers and righteous. The one possible exception is no 8, since it refers to persecution, a situation of need; and yet the emphasis is on the righteousness of those described not just on the persecution that has resulted. Despite the two possible exceptions the difference between the two halves is notable, and is illustrated from Beatitudes 4 and 8, with 4 speaking of people 'hungering and thirsting for righteousness' and 8 of people being persecuted for righteousness. In the first case the righteousness is something longed for, in the second something attained and lived out.

Some scholars have disputed the argument that the first four describe need and longing, the second righteousness in action, and some have argued that Matthew has reinterpreted the Q Beatitudes which were conspicuously about people suffering, and made them ethical/spiritual, hence his additional Beatitudes, numbers 5-7, about mercy, purity and peace-making, but hence also his modifications to his first four Beatitudes with 'poor' in Q (and Luke) becoming 'poor in spirit', meaning humble, and 'those who hunger' becoming 'those who hunger and thirst for righteousness'; in addition Matthew has imported 'blessed are the meek', using the language of Ps. 37.11, thus giving an unmistakably ethical tone to the first four Beatitudes.

But, although this sounds plausible at first glance, especially in the light of a comparison with Luke, it is not obvious that this is the conclusion if Matthew's Beatitudes are considered for themselves. All of numbers 1-4 feel very much as though we are in the 'not yet' of mourning and hungering. Beatitude 1 'Blessed are the poor in spirit' is often taken ethically to mean 'humble'; but it may just as well be understood as something like 'dispirited'.[11] The link of that Beatitude with no. 8 about those who are persecuted for righteousness, which we noted above, might point in that sort of direction, as may the possible echoes of Isaiah 61, which we will consider shortly. As for 'Blessed are the meek' this

11. The phrase is paralleled in the Dead Sea Scrolls, 1QM 14.7. Unfortunately the exact meaning of the Hebrew phrase is not entirely clear, with some scholars arguing that it means faint-hearted, but others arguing for humility.

does have a claim to being an ethical Beatitude, with 'meekness' being close to gentleness; but in the context (of the other opening Beatitudes, and of the accompanying promise 'they shall inherit the land') it arguably means being 'still before the Lord and waiting patiently for him', to quote words from Psalm 37 just a few verses before the reference to the meek in inheriting the earth (37.7).[12] The meek are those waiting quietly for God to act. The Beatitude is akin to the one that follows about people hungering and thirsting for righteousness/justice. It is therefore not clear that Matthew has ethicized the first four Beatitudes. He might be said to have 'spiritualized' them, clarifying that the poverty and hunger of which Jesus speaks is not just physical poverty and hunger; but still there is a big shift of focus between the first four Beatitudes describing people waiting hungrily for the kingdom, and the second four Beatitudes describing people living the righteousness of the kingdom, being merciful, pure in heart, etc.

The one possible exception is Beatitude 8: 'Blessed are those who are persecuted for righteousness' sake, for theirs is the kingdom of heaven'. Does this really belong with the second group of Beatitudes that have an ethical focus – the merciful, the pure in heart, the peace-makers? It certainly has a good claim to be in that group, if that group is identified as describing the righteousness of the kingdom lived out: no. 8 people's righteousness is such that they are persecuted, and the persecution is because they have lived it out. But it is true that no. 8 also has some claim to belong with the first group, since it speaks of a group who are suffering and needing help. This is not perhaps as surprising or complicating a conclusion as we might think, since Beatitude 8 is different from 5-7 because of its 'for theirs is the kingdom of heaven', and it does have strong links with Beatitude 1 'Blessed are the poor in spirit'. But this in no way spoils the argument about the distinction between the two groups. Rather Beatitude 8 could be said to have loyalties in both groups, which is perhaps appropriate given its end position: it links together the themes of

12. The Greek words for 'poor' (*ptōchos*) and for 'meek' (*praus*) are both used in the Septuagint's Greek translation of the Old Testament for the Hebrew word *anī*, the word used in Isa. 61.1 'good news for the poor/afflicted'. People have speculated that Beatitudes 1 and 2 could be different translations of the same original, and they have also noted the textual uncertainty with 'Blessed are the meek' coming second in some texts. (C. Michaelis discusses some of the issues in 'Die Π-Alliteration der Subjecktsworte der ersten 4 Seligpreisungen in Mt. v 3-6 und ihre Bedeutung für den Aufbau der Seligpreisen bei Mt., Lk. und in Q', *NovT* 10 (1968): 148–61.) The questions do not significantly affect the argument of this article, though the similarity of the two words in terms of their Hebrew background is interesting.

the first group, i.e. people in need and suffering, and of the second group, i.e. those living righteously. Beatitude 8 turns out to be a most effective conclusion to the eight Beatitudes: it forms an *inclusio* with Beatitude 1 and reminds us that the Beatitudes are all about who the kingdom of heaven is for; it links together the kingdom of heaven with 'righteousness' flagging up the themes of the Sermon which is to follow; and it links together the themes of the first four and the last four Beatitudes.

The conclusion of all these observations must be that the Beatitudes are carefully constructed and are a prologue and introduction to the Sermon that is to follow.

Further Observations: The Importance of Isaiah 61

The argument for the two-stanza structure has been made, and is strong. But still how do the two stanzas relate to each other? They are both about people to whom the kingdom of heaven is given and belongs. The first stanza portrays them as people who are under pressure and hungry for God's righteousness and justice to come, i.e. for his kingdom to come and his will to be done; the second portrays them as people whose lives are already demonstrating the kingdom and the will of God being done – by being merciful, pure and peace-making. The relationship of the two stanzas has often been explained in terms of dependence on God and his grace on the one hand, the starting-point of kingdom of heaven membership, and of transformation and kingdom living in love on the other. The Sermon on the Mount will develop and explain the second theme at length – living kingdom righteousness – but before that it is important to recognize the starting point of grace.

This explanation has a lot going for it, even if it could sound a little like a Protestant reading of Paul – i.e. salvation by grace preceding good works. But does it fully explain what these stand-alone third-person statements about those who are blessed inheritors of the kingdom are doing in Matthew's Gospel? They are not commending grace as the starting point for kingdom membership, not directly anyway. They are, at least in the first four Beatitudes, statements encouraging people in need that the kingdom of heaven is for them. That is also true of Beatitude 8, with its reference to those who are persecuted for righteousness. Given the *inclusio* formed by Beatitudes 1 and 8, it looks as though the Beatitudes as a whole are good news and great encouragement for people under pressure.[13]

13. Interestingly this is one respect in which Matthew and Luke agree, since Luke starts with 'Blessed are you poor', and ends with 'Blessed are you when people

An important supporting point has to do with Isaiah 61, which has often been identified as likely background to the Beatitudes.

> 61.1 The Spirit of the Lord GOD is upon me, because the LORD has anointed me to bring good news to the poor; he has sent me to bind up the broken-hearted, to proclaim liberty to the captives, and the opening of the prison to those who are bound; [2] to proclaim the year of the LORD's favour, and the day of vengeance of our God; to comfort all who mourn;[3] to grant to those who mourn in Zion – to give them a beautiful headdress instead of ashes, the oil of gladness instead of mourning, the garment of praise instead of a faint spirit; that they may be called oaks of righteousness, the planting of the LORD, that he may be glorified.

The importance of this passage to Luke is undeniable, since the very first preaching of Jesus in Luke is in the Nazareth synagogue, where Jesus reads this passage, and says 'Today this Scripture is fulfilled in my hearing' (4.16-21). For Luke it is as though this passage from Isaiah defines Jesus' ministry (see also 7.22). And it is only logical to assume that Luke has this in mind in his version of the Sermon on the plain, with its references to the poor and those who mourn.

It is not quite so clear with Matthew, but it is likely for him as well. In favour of this we note (a) that already in his Gospel very shortly before the Sermon on the Mount Matthew has explained Jesus' ministry in terms of Isaiah, quoting Isa. 9.1, 2 as fulfilled by Jesus' coming into Galilee:

> [15] Land of Zebulun, land of Naphtali, on the road by the sea, across the Jordan, Galilee of the Gentiles – [16] the people who sat in darkness have seen a great light, and for those who sat in the region and shadow of death light has dawned.

(b) Matthew later in his Gospel has Jesus explain his ministry to John the Baptist on the basis of Isaiah 61 and its reference to the good news being proclaimed to the poor:

> [4] Jesus replied, 'Go back and report to John what you hear and see: [5] The blind receive sight, the lame walk, those who have leprosy are cleansed, the deaf hear, the dead are raised, and *the good news is proclaimed to the poor*' (Mt. 11.4, 5).

persecute you'. Scholars have argued that Matthew has lost or even deliberately changed this Lukan take on the Beatitudes as promises to the needy, transforming them into ethical injunctions. In fact it is nothing like as simple as that, as our observations on Matthew's structure have shown.

(c) Jesus' explanation to John echoes not just Isaiah 61, but also Isa. 35.5, 6: 'Then the eyes of the blind shall be opened, and the ears of the deaf unstopped; then shall the lame man leap like a deer, and the tongue of the mute sing for joy'.

Not only does this make clear the importance of Isaiah in Matthew's thinking about Jesus,[14] but it is striking how in the words to John the Baptist Jesus' healing ministry and the proclaiming of the good news to the poor go together (see also Mt. 10.7). This is relevant to the Sermon on the Mount, since it is immediately preceded by a description of Jesus proclaiming 'the good news of the kingdom' and healing (4.23-25). Then Jesus begins in the Beatitudes to speak of the blessedness of the 'poor in spirit, for theirs is the kingdom of heaven'.

In the light of these connections and in particular of the immediate context with the reference to Jesus 'proclaiming the good news of the kingdom' that comes straight before the Sermon, we may conclude that Matthew sees the Beatitudes as Jesus proclaiming the good news of the kingdom, and specifically as Jesus bringing the good news to the poor, of which Isaiah 61 spoke. Before he launches into the main body of the Sermon with its instructions to his disciples (in the second person) on how to live in the kingdom, Jesus is portrayed by Matthew as the herald announcing the good news to the poor (in the third person). This is an important part of the answer to the question about the function of the Beatitudes in Matthew.

But does the argument about Isaiah 61 only help explain the first four Beatitudes, since it is those that most obviously fit the description of Jesus proclaiming good news to the poor? Perhaps. But it is notable that Isaiah 61 is not just a vision of Yahweh rescuing his oppressed people; it is also a vision of righteousness being established in and for the people of God. So in v. 3 those who now mourn will be called 'oaks of righteousness', in v. 8 we are told of Yahweh's love for justice and hatred of robbery and wrongdoing and the chapter concludes climactically with the beautiful vision of vv. 10, 11:

14. Werner Grimm emphasizes the importance of Isaiah and specifically Deutero-Isaiah arguing that Jesus in Matthew combines reflection on Isa. 61 with reflection on Isa. 52, where the one 'bringing good news' is the herald on the mountain. Jesus is such a herald. (See his 'Die Hoffnung der Armen Zu den Seligpreisungen', *TBei* 11 (1980): 100–113.) The mountain context of Jesus' sermon has all sorts of OT resonances: Moses on Mount Sinai is very likely background, and Isa. 2.2-4 is also striking with its reference to the mountain of the Lord and to the Lord teaching us his ways and with its call to 'walk in the light of the Lord'.

> [10] I will greatly rejoice in the LORD, my whole being shall exult in my God; for he has clothed me with the garments of salvation, he has covered me with the robe of righteousness, as a bridegroom decks himself with a garland, and as a bride adorns herself with her jewels.[11] For as the earth brings forth its shoots, and as a garden causes what is sown in it to spring up, so the Lord GOD will cause righteousness and praise to spring up before all the nations.

This focus on restored righteousness and justice especially in the second half of Isaiah 61 makes perfect sense, as an integral part of the joyous salvation which Yahweh's anointed one has been announcing. And it may not be coincidental that the Matthaean Beatitudes (with their very joyful dimension) move from an emphasis on salvation for the needy, in the first four, to a focus on transformed lives in the second four. We could indeed sum up the second four as a mini-summary of righteousness in action: Beatitude 4 spoke of people hungering and thirsting for righteousness, and Beatitudes 5-8 describe what righteous kingdom living will look like. The parallels are not total, but there is what we could call an Isaianic logic to the shift of focus in Beatitudes 5-8, which also prepares us for the Sermon on the Mount, which is going to describe much more fully what kingdom righteousness and following Jesus look like.[15]

Conclusions

We are now in a position to answer our question about the purpose of the Beatitudes: what are these blessed sayings doing? What does Matthew think Jesus is doing? The answer is threefold: first, he is proclaiming the good news of the kingdom, identifying and congratulating those who are coming to him and coming into the kingdom and who will receive its amazing blessings. Jesus is thus fulfilling Isaiah 61 with its description of the Spirit-filled one proclaiming good news to the poor and to those of God's people who mourn. Secondly, he is describing those to whom the kingdom of heaven is given, and their characteristics. The Beatitudes highlight first their need, their sadness and their longings for justice, but then sum up what their lives as disciples and kingdom people will (and should) look like – merciful, pure in heart, peace-makers. Thirdly, the Beatitudes form a brilliant preface to the Sermon, putting it in the context of the good news, introducing us to the key themes of kingdom of heaven and of righteousness, which the sermon will then expound.

15. These observations could help with the question that scholars have discussed about Jesus' audience, as described by Matthew. Clearly disciples are addressed (5.1, 9, 13, 14), but the crowd is also listening in with interest (7.28).

The Beatitudes are thus not just a collection of wonderful and beautiful sayings that move the heart. They are extraordinarily carefully crafted, introducing Jesus' preaching of the good news and his teaching, which is so important in Matthew's Gospel, as the rock on which human lives need to be built.

14

The Holy Spirit in Matthew's Gospel

Roland Deines

When it comes to the Holy Spirit in the Bible, few people would turn to Matthew's Gospel for inspiration. In studies dealing with the Holy Spirit Luke's is the Synoptic Gospel taking pride of place, not least because of the prominence of the Spirit in Acts.[1] Matthew is seldom studied on its own, and the question of whether he has something specific to contribute is rarely addressed. What follows is therefore an attempt to listen to Matthew's voice and to try to understand how he weaves the topical 'thread' of the divine Spirit into the fabric of his Gospel.[2]

Matthew, i.e. the author of the Gospel which bears this name, seems to have been a patient teacher, in places perhaps prone to pedantry, and it usually pays off to monitor the ways by which he guides his readers

1. Two recent examples include Anthony C. Thiselton, *The Holy Spirit – In Biblical Teaching, through the Centuries, and Today* (Grand Rapids: Eerdmans, 2013) and various contributions to *The Holy Spirit and the Church according to the New Testament: Sixth International East–West Symposium of New Testament Scholars, Belgrade, August 25 to 31, 2013*, ed. P. Dragutinović, K.-W. Niebuhr and J. Buchanan Wallace, WUNT 354 (Tübingen: Mohr Siebeck, 2016). One of the editors, Karl-Wilhelm Niebuhr, specifically mentions the lack of any discussion of Matthew in the volume in the 'Introduction', concluding that 'the Holy Spirit in Matthew deserves more attention than it actually receives in New Testament scholarship' (p. 14).

2. I do this in close interaction with John Nolland's rich commentary *The Gospel of Matthew: A Commentary on the Greek Text*, NIGTC (Grand Rapids: Eerdmans, 2005), as a personal greeting for John's birthday.

step by step to a fuller understanding of a given topic. Taking his narratological structure into account often provides an additional element for the understanding of this gospel as a unified composition, which is, at least to my mind, didactically the most thorough of the four.[3] The task is therefore to explore how the topic of the Holy Spirit is made part of the unfolding narrative, where the topic surfaces and which other themes or 'threads' Matthew connected with it. A comparison with Mark and Luke is another part of this investigation, as by this the distinctive voice of Matthew becomes more discernible. No signature under any proposed solution of the Synoptic Problem is required to make this a rewarding task, because independently of all assumed usage of sources it is evident that he wrote about the same events in a very similar way as Mark and Luke. So if he refers to the Holy Spirit in places where the others do not, or avoids this language in places where they do, the question, 'Why is this so?' is on the table and invites some guesses about the theological mindset of Matthew.

One has to admit from the outset, though, that the Holy Spirit does not look like a dominant theological thread in Matthew. This is perhaps evidenced most obviously by what is lacking, namely a formulaic language for issues related to the Spirit. His usual method of connecting separated parts of a topical thread is the use of repeated formulae or phrases to alert his audience to the other passages with the same syntagm. No obvious phraseology comes to mind regarding the Spirit but that means not that he is not interested in it as the differences between the Synoptics reveal. It is therefore best to start with some statistics and comparisons to find out about Matthew's particular nuances.

Some Statistics to Start With

Based solely on the numbers, it seems that the Holy Spirit is not a major topic for Matthew or for Matthew's Jesus. Statistics for πνεῦμα can demonstrate this very easily, this being the only term used for the Holy Spirit in Matthew (though not every use of πνεῦμα refers to the Holy Spirit). Matthew has all together 19 occurrences of the word, which is very few compared to 23 in Mark, 36 in Luke and 24 in John (and 70 in Acts). From those 19 only 12 clearly refer to the Holy Spirit (1.18, 20; 3.11, 16;

3. See my *Die Gerechtigkeit der Tora im Reich des Messias: Mt 5,13–20 als Schlüsseltext der matthäischen Theologie*, WUNT 177 (Tübingen: Mohr Siebeck, 2004), 81–90, 95–101.

4.1; 10.20; 12.18, 28, 31, 32; 22.43; 28.19); in 5.3 ('the poor in spirit') the spirit is ambiguous but most likely an anthropological quality[4] as in 26.41 ('the spirit is willing') and 27.50 ('Jesus gave up his spirit'; Mk 15.37 has simply ἐξέπνευσεν; Lk. 23.46 combines the Markan verb with a quotation of Ps. 31.6 εἰς χεῖράς σου παρατίθεμαι τὸ πνεῦμα μου).[5] In 8.16 τὰ πνεύματα are the powers afflicting those who are called 'demon-possessed'. They are called πνεύματα ἀκάθαρτα in 10.1 and 12.43 (singular), and are regarded as 'evil' (πονερόν, 12.45).[6]

Table 1 presents all references to the Holy Spirit in the Synoptics, following Matthew's order. In cases where in a parallel the Holy Spirit is not mentioned it is bracketed; if an alternative term is mentioned, it will be mentioned. References from the mouth of Jesus are printed in bold. Texts that are usually attributed to Q are marked with 'Q'; if there are disputes about the attribution Q is put into brackets (Q), but no further discussion will be provided. A passage that is regarded as part of Q but the mentioning of the Spirit as part of Q is disputed, will be indicated by $Q^?$.[7]

4. Nolland, *Matthew*, 198–9, provides a helpful list of proposed interpretations, and suggests that the reference is to those 'who sense the burden of their present (impoverished) state, and see it in terms of the absence of God' (200–201). As Matthew connects the presence of the kingdom with the Spirit by which Jesus casts out demons (12.28), one could argue that those who feel spiritually 'impoverished' and therefore long for the coming of the kingdom will receive the Spirit as a sign of the kingdom. This is supported by the underlying text Isa. 61.1 about the Spirit-filled servant bringing good tidings; see also D. A. Hagner, *Matthew*, WBC 33A-B (Dallas: Nelson, 1993–95), 91–2.

5. On the last two references see Nolland, *Matthew*, 1101–2; on 27.40 see his comments *loc. cit.* 1210–11 (πνεῦμα is here used synonymously with ψυχή).

6. In general, Matthew prefers to talk about demons and demon-afflicted persons (see Nolland, *Matthew*, 410), but no differentiation from the language of evil spirits seems to be intended. In both cases healing is achieved by 'casting them out'. Whether his use of 'unclean spirits' is solely the result of 'following sources' as Nolland suggests, seems to me less clear.

7. See Burton L. Mack, *The Lost Gospel: The Book of Q and Christian Origins* (San Francisco: HarperSanFrancisco, 1993), 69–102 (the redactional layers he and Kloppenborg identified are marked as Q^1-Q^3); James M. Robinson, Paul Hoffmann and John S. Kloppenborg, eds, *The Critical Edition of Q*, Hermeneia (Minneapolis: Fortress Press, 2000); H. T. Fleddermann, *Q: A Reconstruction and Commentary*, Biblical Tools & Studies 1 (Leuven: Peeters, 2005).

Table 1

Matthew	**Mark**	**Luke**	
		1.15 (17, 80) about John the Baptist	
		1.41 Elizabeth	
		1.67 Zechariah	
1.18, 20		1.35	
		2.25-27 Simeon	
3.11 Q John about Jesus	1.8 (without fire)	3.16 Q (but for Mack only Q^2)	cf. Acts 1.4-5; 11.16 (both times presented as a saying of Jesus)
3.16 (Q)	1.10	3.22 (Q)	cf. Jn 1.32
4.1 Q	1.12	4.1 Q (Mack: Q^3)	
(4.12)	(1.14)	**4.14**	
cf. 12.14 Isa. 42.1-4 is fulfilled in Jesus		**4.18** Jesus reads Isa. 61.1-2	
(7.11)		**11.13** $Q^?$	
(9.4)	2.8 Jesus by his spirit	(5.22)	
No equivalent for this part	8.12 (like 2.8)	Like Matthew	
10.20	**13.11**	**12.12** Q, see also 21.15	cf. Jn **14.26**
(11.25)		**10.21** $Q^?$	
12.18 (Isaiah)			
12.28 $Q^?$		**11.20** Q (finger)[8]	
12.31, 32 Q (only v. 32)	**3.29-30**	**12.10** Q	
22.43 (ἐν πνεύματι)	**12.36** ἐν τῷ πνεύματι τῷ ἁγίῳ	20.42 (in the Psalter)	
		24.49	cf. Acts 1.4
28.19			

8. Usually, 'finger of God' is regarded as the original reading in Q (in Mack's reconstruction this is part of Q2). For a powerful (and in my view convincing) defence

Some comments about what the table indicates:

1. *Matthew*: The first three usages 1.18, 20; 3.11 are anarthrous; in 12.32 and 28.19 the article is used but no difference in meaning is attached to it.[9] In addition Matthew employs 'the Spirit of God' in 3.16 (article textually uncertain); 12.28 (anarthrous); 'the Spirit of the Father' (10.20, with article), and 'my Spirit' in 12.18 in a divine speech quoting Isa. 42.1. In Mt. 4.1 πνεῦμα is without further qualification ('...driven into the wilderness by the Spirit'), but the context makes it likely, that the same spirit is meant as in 3.16; the same goes for 12.1 ('blasphemy of the Spirit...'). The last reference is 22.43, Jesus' question to the scribes in Jerusalem about David, who spoke about his 'Lord in the Spirit' (anarthrous, referring to Ps. 110.1).

The distribution of the references for the Holy Spirit is uneven. The *beginning* of Jesus' life (1.18, 20) and ministry (3.16; 4.1) is marked by the Spirit acting as divine agent (1.18, 20; 3.16; 4.1); the *ministry* of Jesus itself, announced by the Baptiser as a baptism 'with Holy Spirit and fire', reveals Jesus' insights with regard to the Spirit and his authority over the spirits: he knows about the inspiring power of the Spirit in the past (David in 22.43) and the future (10.20; the tense used is present but the situation described is in the future), he connects – uniquely in the synoptic tradition – his own power over the demons to his ability to act 'in the Spirit of God' (12.28), and he teaches authoritatively on the Holy Spirit (12.28, 32-33) and evil spirits (12.43-45). Jesus is further able to give his *disciples* authority over the 'unclean spirits' (ἔδωκεν αὐτοῖς ἐξουσίαν πνευμάτων ἀκαθάρτων, 10.1), which in light of 12.28 can mean that they are somehow enabled by the Spirit and therefore in the possession of it, although this is never addressed properly in the first Gospel (see below). It concludes with the commandment of the risen Jesus to baptise 'in the name of the Father, and the Son, and the Spirit' (28.19), and this triadic formula, which appears only here in the New Testament, is perhaps best explained with reference to Mt. 3.11-16, where all three divine actors were described as active in Jesus' baptism (see below).

The majority of references in all three Synoptics and so also in Matthew are from the mouth of Jesus (in Matthew six out of twelve, 10.20; 12.28, 31, 32; 22.43; 28.19), or comments made by the evangelist (1.18, 20;

of the originality of the 'Spirit of God' see Fleddermann, Q, 483–4 (and p. 231 on the Holy Spirit in Q).

9. The first four instances are prepositional clauses and Matthew tends to omit the article more often in such cases but, as 12.32 shows, there is no consistency. In 12.32 the reason for the article in κατὰ τοῦ πνεύματος τοῦ ἁγίου might be the close parallelism with κατὰ τοῦ υἱοῦ τοῦ ἀνθρώπου.

3.16; 4.1; 12.18). The only other person who talks about the Spirit – but only as a future experience – is John the Baptist (Matt 3:11 parr.). This may indicate that for Matthew the Spirit is an element of the new age that John could only announce.[10] He could not inaugurate it because the new experience of the Spirit, i.e. the 'baptism with the Holy Spirit', is bound to Jesus and the salvation that comes with him. If this is a valid observation, it has some important implications for the question of whether or not Matthew's Gospel has a different understanding of the presence of the Spirit in the believer than the Johannine and Pauline tradition (see below): it would mean that Matthew's intention here was to pinpoint a salvation-historical difference in the way the Spirit was experienced up to and during Jesus' lifetime (like in 22.43) and the time after his death and resurrection. This implies that he was aware something 'more' was to happen to those who belong to Jesus and were able to experience this post-Easter baptism (which is based on Jesus' death, see Lk. 12.50). This new experience, however, one has to assume, was in the time of Matthew's writing already in action.

2. The *differences from Mark*, when it comes to details, are quite remarkable, even if the general picture is similar: Jesus has power over the unclean spirits (1.23, 26-27; 3.11; 5.2, 8, 13; 6.7; 7.25; 9.17, 20, 25 (twice)), after he himself became equipped with the Spirit in his baptism (1.10, 12) as announced by the Baptist (1.8).[11] Jesus' own 'spirit' in the anthropological sense is mentioned in 2.8 (Jesus 'discerned in his spirit';

10. On the twofold division of salvation history in Matthew with John as transitional figure see Deines, *Gerechtigkeit*, 50–1, 148 n. 150, 279; Nolland, *Matthew*, 458–9. That John should be understood as standing on the side of 'prophecy and preparatio' and not yet 'fulfilment' is argued convincingly by Mervyn Eloff, 'ἀπό... ἕως and Salvation History in Matthew's Gospel', in *Built upon the Rock: Studies in the Gospel of Matthew*, ed. Daniel M. Gurtner and John Nolland (Grand Rapids: Eerdmans, 2008), 85–107 (96–101).

11. In Mark and Luke, the first miracle of Jesus – which is not in Matthew – is the healing of a person with an unclean spirit (Mk 1.23-28 par. Lk. 4.33-37); the demon recognizes Jesus as 'the holy one of God' and acknowledges Jesus' superior power ('you have come to destroy us'). Matthew consistently avoids giving the demons any voices which might be why he omitted this story. In the healing of the Gerasene demoniac(s), Mt. 8.28-34 parr. Mk 5.1-20; Lk. 8.26-39, Matthew shortens drastically the conversation between Jesus and the demon(s); Jesus says only one word: 'Go!' (ὑπάγετε, v. 32). The same is true for the very short exorcisms in 9.32-33; 12.22, and even more in the healing of Mt. 17.14-21 parr. Mk 9.14-29; Lk. 9.37-43a. In Matthew it is initially not made clear that the boy's symptoms are caused by a demon or evil spirit (cf. Mt. 17.15 with Mk 9.17; Lk. 9.30). Only 17.18 makes this clear.

both Mt. 9.4 and Lk. 5.22 omit τῷ πνεύματι αὐτοῦ) and 8.12 ('he sighed in his spirit'), where, again, Matthew and Luke avoid the term (Mt. 12.39; 16.2; Lk. 11.16). On the other side, Mt. 27.50 has no close equivalent in Mk 15.37 or Lk. 23.46 (both have ἐξέπνευσεν instead of the Matthaean ἀφῆκεν τὸ πνεῦμα). The proverbial sentence about the 'willing spirit' and the weak flesh is identical in Mark and Matthew (Mk 14.38 par. Mt. 27.50) but missing in Luke (and John). The accusation against Jesus of having 'an unclean spirit' (πνεῦμα ἀκάθαρτον ἔχει) in Mk 3.30 is presupposed in Matthew but not repeated, whereas Jesus' saying about the unforgivability of blasphemies against the Holy Spirit is preserved in all three Synoptics (Mk 3.29 parr. Mt. 13.31-32; Lk. 12.10), with Matthew having the longest version of the saying.[12] Both Matthew and Mark promise the inspiration of the Spirit to the disciples when they are accused and brought to court (Mk 13.11 par. Mt. 10.19-20); Luke omits the Spirit and replaces it with δώσω ἡμῖν στόμα καὶ σοφίαν, so differing from the passive forms δοθήσεται (Matthew) or δοθῇ (Mark) and turning Jesus into the subject of the inspiration.

3. In Luke the pattern is similar to Matthew: the first four chapters display a wide array of active agency of the Holy Spirit, with promises given about John the Baptist being filled with the Holy Spirit (πνεύματος ἁγίου πλησθήσεται, 1.15) from the womb, and having the 'spirit and power of Elijah' (1.17; the last comment on John as a child is in 1.80: he grew and became strong in the spirit ηὔξανεν καὶ ἐκραταιοῦτο πνεύματι[13]); the angel Gabriel tells Mary that she will get pregnant by the Holy Spirit (1.35; πνεῦμα ἅγιον stands in parallelism to δύναμις ὑψίστου; in both cases the designation for the Spirit is subject of the verb); Elizabeth is 'filled with the Holy Spirit' upon uttering her greeting to Mary and the unborn Jesus (1.41) (so also Zechariah [1.67] before he 'prophesied' the Benedictus); in Jerusalem the righteous man Simeon, upon whom was the Holy Spirit (2.25), waited for the Messiah to come because he had once received a revelation by the Spirit that he would live to see him (2.26);

12. On Matthew's particular interest in this topic see Nolland, *Matthew*, 505 n. 84.

13. This reference can be taken as referring to the Holy Spirit but not necessarily so, see Thiselton, *Holy Spirit*, 37. Luke also uses πνεῦνα anthropologically (1.47; 8.55) and it is most likely that in 23.46, where Jesus hands over his spirit to the Father, his life's spirit is meant, not the Holy Spirit; see, e.g., M. Wolter, *Das Lukasevangelium*, HNT 5 (Tübingen: Mohr Siebeck, 2008), 762. See also Lk. 2.40, where a well-attested manuscript reading (including Alexandrinus) adds πνεύματι before the verb as in 1.80; it is again difficult to decide whether this was understood as meaning the Holy Spirit or the human spirit.

so when the 40-day-old Jesus was presented to God in the temple by his parents, he came 'by the Spirit' (2.27) to be there and to praise God for fulfilling his promises in another inspired hymn (2.28-32).

Luke shares with Matthew and/or Mark (with the 'usual' minor differences) the mentions of the Spirit in the baptism and temptation of Jesus (3.16, see also Acts 1.5; 11.16; 3.22; 4.1), and the teaching of Jesus about the Spirit in a similar context (12.10, 12). The same is true for unclean spirits (4.33, 36; 6.18; 7.21; 8.2, 29; 9.39, 42; 10.20; 11.24, 26; 13.11). Both Matthew and Luke also share a tradition about an Isaianic prophecy about the future Spirit-bearer being fulfilled (cf. Mt. 12.17-21 with Lk. 4.17-21), only Matthew has it as a fulfilment quotation, whereas in Luke Jesus reads and interprets the text himself in the Nazareth synagogue. In 4.1, 4.14 and 10.21 Luke alone highlights that Jesus was filled with the Holy Spirit, though Matthew and Mark offer close parallels. Similarly Lk. 11.13 refers to the gift of the Holy Spirit, where Matthew has 'good gifts' (7.11).

Luke only uses πνεῦμα for the 'ghost' the disciples feared to encounter when the risen Christ suddenly appeared (24.37, 39). A further Lukan particularity is his use of synonyms for the Holy Spirit, like δύναμις in 1.35 and 24.49 (compare 3.16 and Acts 1.4).[14] A possible substitute is also χάρις in 2.40, where Jesus was 'filled with wisdom' and the 'grace of God was upon him'. Especially the use of 'upon' (ἐπί) could be seen as evidence in favour of such an understanding.

The Spirit-thread in Matthew

The Spirit's Agency in Jesus' Birth, Baptism and Temptation

We have already noticed that the distribution of the references for the Holy Spirit is uneven: from the twelve references five appear between 1.18 and 4.1 (no saying of Jesus among them). Here the Spirit is – with the exception of John's announcement in 3.11 – acting on its own initiative and not even bound back to God (none of the early references use 'the Spirit of God', which appears in 3.16 for the first time), being related from the beginning to Jesus. The Spirit is the agent of Mary's pregnancy and not his human father Joseph (1.18-21). Up to this point, God is not

14. Of the 15 references for δύναμις in Luke's Gospel, some could be understood as a reference to the Holy Spirit (4.36; 5.17; 6.19; 9.1; 19.37; 21.27). In 1.17; 4.14 δύναμις is used together with the Holy Spirit (but not in parallelism like in 1:35). The remaining evidence refers to Jesus' healing powers (8.46; 10.13), evil power (10.19), powers of nature (21.26) and God (22.69).

even mentioned as Jesus' father (unlike Mk 1.1).[15] All forty generations that preceded him were fathered by men of flesh and blood, as is made clear by the 39-times repetition of ἐγέννησεν in 1.2-15. In the case of Jesus it is not male activity but female receptivity (ἐξ ἧς ἐγεννήθη) that led to his birth. Whereas men can beget sons 'out of' a woman (cf. ἐκ τῆς in vv. 3, 5, 6), Mary became pregnant 'out of the Holy Spirit' (1.18, 20 ἐκ πνεύματος ἁγίου). The reluctance to write more boldly about the topic of Jesus' divinely induced conception (which Matthew shares with Luke) might be explained by the danger of misconception, especially when taken out of its immediate Jewish setting, where God is not conceived of as a sexually active being, contrary to the Greek and Roman pantheon. It is therefore clearly against the intention of Matthew to speculate about any gendered role of the Holy Spirit in this process.[16] God reveals himself as Jesus' father clearly for the first time only in the baptism scene, but is not addressed as such in these early chapters aside from the veiled proclamations in 1.23 quoting Isa. 7.13 as a word 'spoken by the Lord' and identifying Jesus as 'Emmanuel', and equally in 2.15, quoting Hos. 11.1.[17] Matthew's restraint could again be in order to avoid any sexual or gendered understanding of the divine fatherhood.

The announcement of John in 3.11 about the future baptism 'with the Holy Spirit and fire' points towards the ministry of Jesus, which starts in 4.12 with the arrest of John. The baptism itself brings together for the first time all three 'characters' to whom Matthew gives the highest authority in his Gospel, with the father making himself heard in a heavenly voice, and the Spirit (now for the first time identified as the 'Spirit of God') becoming visible in the likeness of a dove. Both divine beings relate to Jesus, who is identified by the heavenly voice as God's Son (and 'God' is thus revealed as father in a new way) and by the dove as bearer of the

15. The difference from Lk. 1.28-32 is notable. In Matthew God is alluded to, first, and only in passing, in 1.20, in 'the angel of the Lord'.

16. However, in what Origen calls the gospel 'according to the Hebrews', a saying of Jesus is quoted where he calls the Holy Spirit 'my mother'. Since the Jewish Christian gospels in general are closest to Matthew's Gospel, it is at least possible that 1.18, 20, were read in this way. See J. K. Elliott, ed., *The Apocryphal New Testament* (Oxford: Clarendon Press, 1993), 9. Nolland, *Matthew*, 92–3, helpfully discusses the issue of gendered language in these verses, mentioning Job 33.4; Ps. 104.30 and the idea of the Spirit's role in the formation of a child in the womb.

17. Hosea clearly had Israel as a people in mind. On Matthew's use of the passage see Richard B. Hays, *Echoes of Scripture in the Gospels* (Waco: Baylor University Press, 2016), 114.

fullness of the Spirit. In Matthew's description this revelatory experience happened for the sake of Jesus: 'For *him* the heavens opened', and the slightly awkward αὐτῷ, whose text-critical authenticity is not beyond doubt,[18] serves as a counterbalance to the proclamation of the heavenly voice, which is – differently from Mark und Luke – not addressed directly to Jesus ('*You are…*') but to an unspecified audience ('*This is* my son, the beloved, in whom I take delight').[19] What Jesus saw is described with two participles depending on εἶδεν, namely that the Spirit 'came down' (καταβαῖνον), i.e. from the opened heaven 'like a dove',[20] and 'it came to him' (ἐρχόμενον ἐπ' αὐτον, cf. 3.7). Whereas Mark and Luke both employ καταβαίνω, Matthew is the only one who adds the second verb. I am not sure whether this is 'nothing more specific than to give greater weight to this scene', as Nolland comments.[21] The personal pronoun at the end, αὐτόν, mirrors the initial αὐτῷ and underlines the sole focus on Jesus: for *him* the heavens were opened, and to *him*, from heaven, came the Spirit. The biblical allusions in this scene, most obviously Isa. 11.1-5, 42.1 and 61.1, identify Jesus as the Messiah, who is expected to come empowered by God's Spirit.

Except the agency of the Spirit does not stop here but takes an unexpected turn. Instead of leading Jesus to glory[22] he led him into the desert to be tested by the devil. All three Synoptics provide this information, but in distinctly different expressions. In Mark the Spirit is the subject of the active verb ἐκβάλλω, the technical term for exorcisms (Mk 1.12), and it is understandable why Matthew and Luke wanted to avoid the impression of Jesus being 'exorcised' into the wilderness. Luke gives Jesus more agency, because he, now filled with the Spirit, makes the

18. For its originality see Hagner, *Matthew*, 1:54, Nolland, *Matthew*, 150.

19. Whereas many commentators assume the change in wording to indicate a 'public divine affirmation of Jesus, directed towards the crowds standing nearby', Nolland, *Matthew*, 156–7, and Matthias Konradt, *Das Evangelium nach Matthäus*, NTD 1 (Göttingen: Vandenhoeck & Ruprecht, 2015), 53, rightly caution against this understanding. It is a proclamation for the sake of the reader, made in heaven for the sake of the heavenly ones to whom Jesus belongs as well.

20. On the dove symbolism see W. D. Davies and D. C. Allison, *A Critical and Exegetical Commentary on the Gospel according to Saint Matthew*, 3 vols, ICC (Edinburgh: T. & T. Clark, 1988–97), 1:331–4; Nolland, *Matthew*, 156. There is a debate about whether Matthew implies that Jesus saw the Spirit in the visual form of a dove (so clearly Luke; Nolland, *Matthew*, 155–6, favours it also for Matthew), or rather the movement, as e.g. Konradt, *Matthäus*, 53, argues.

21. Nolland, *Matthew*, 156.

22. Cf. Exod. 33.12, on 'leading away', see also 33.1-3.

first move by returning from the Jordan (Jesus is subject of ὑπέστρεψεν), before the Spirit leads him (ἤγετο) away (4.1-2). Matthew is closer to Mark, when he describes Jesus as the passive subject of the Spirit's lead, expressed by ἀνάγω, a composite verb used only here in Matthew but 20 times by Luke (e.g. in 4.5).

With 4.1 the Spirit disappears as an active agent within the Gospel narrative. What the reader of the Gospel learns about the Spirit from now on is – with the exception of 12.18 – exclusively based on Jesus' words about the Spirit.

2. *Jesus' Teaching about the Holy Spirit*

The sayings of Jesus about the Spirit can be divided into two groups: the first, made up of 10.20 and 22.43, talks about the activity of the Spirit in the chosen messengers of God in the past (the prophets, with David as example, who spoke 'in the Spirit' about him) and the future (the disciples in their future trials will receive the help of the Spirit). As the inspiration of the Holy Scriptures can be assumed as the generally held opinion in the time of Matthew (see already Zech. 7.12), there is nothing surprising to the first element. But it is worth remembering that when the Spirit allowed David to see Jesus sitting at the right hand of the Father in heaven (that this is Matthew's understanding of Ps. 110.1 is without doubt), then Jesus and the Spirit have had already a longstanding 'history' together.[23]

The other group, concentrated in ch. 12 and introduced by the quote of Isa. 42.1-4, focuses on Jesus and the Spirit. This concentration of Spirit-related sayings at this point in the narrative is no coincidence but part of the dramatic events that led to a change in Jesus' attitude. Up to 11.6 the message of God's kingdom is addressed to Israel as a people. With 11.7 the tone changes: Jesus addresses the lack of faith on behalf of Israel's crowds very clearly, and the conflict with the Pharisees and other Jewish leaders intensifies. Even John the Baptist and the family of Jesus are placed on the doubting side (11.2-4 and 12.46-50 respectively frame this decisive shift in the Gospel's overall perspective). As a result, Jesus is

23. Commentators often fail to discuss whether Matthew thinks of David seeing Jesus prophetically on the throne of God in the future, so U. Luz, *Matthew 21–28: A Commentary*, trans. James E. Crouch, Hermeneia (Minneapolis: Fortress Press, 2005), 89, or whether, as I take Matthew to mean, the thought is of David seeing 'his son' Jesus sitting on the throne as something that had taken place already at the time of his vision. From Mt. 23.37 par. Lk. 13.34 it seems likely that Matthew, like Paul, presupposes the Son's participation in God's history with his world and his chosen people from the beginning (cf. 1 Cor. 10.4; 8.6; Col. 1.16; Jn 1.1-3).

described as forming a community within Israel in his name (most clearly expressed in 16.18; 18.20), which will exist until the Parousia.

It is within this swing from an Israel-centred to a community-centred perspective that Jesus addresses his Father directly for the first time in 11.25-27, and he will do so thereafter only once again in Gethsemane (26.39, 42[24]). Seen in relation to 3.17 and 17.5, 11.25-27 can be taken as the Son's answer to the Father's declaration. Hence it is not just God who confirmed the sonship of Jesus and his delight about him at two crucial points of his ministry, but in return also Jesus acknowledged his sonship and what it involves.[25] This relationship between Jesus and his Father is characterized by a 'uniqueness of mutual knowledge',[26] and the palpable immediacy of Father and Son might also be the reason why Matthew, unlike Lk. 10.21, does not present this praise as inspired or mediated by

24. The only other verse where Jesus is talking directly to his heavenly father is 27.46, Jesus' cry on the cross. There he addresses his father with words from Ps. 22.2 as 'my God' and not as in the three cases mentioned above as 'Father'. Of the 51 occurrences of θεός in the first Gospel, the personal pronoun is used only in 4.7, 10; 22.37 ('your God'), which are all OT quotations (see also 1.23, translating Emmanuel as 'with us is God'). It is possible, therefore, that the singularity of Jesus' '*my* God' (seen in combination with the many references to Jesus talking about 'my father'), is Matthew's deliberate highlighting of the unique relationship between Jesus (often referred to as 'Son of God') and God his father.

25. The phrase ἐξομολογοῦμαί σοι, πάτερ in v. 25 (par. Lk. 10.21) is in English exegetical tradition often translated as 'I thank you, Father' (e.g. NRSV, REV, defended also by Nolland, *Matthew*, 470), whereas German translations tend to translate 'Ich preise dich, Vater' (e.g. Luther's Bible; Zürcher Bible, 2007; see Luz, *Matthew 8–20*, 155: 'I praise you, Father'). It is widely accepted that the expression resembles closely traditional Jewish prayer language (see A. Schlatter, *Der Evangelist Matthäus: Seine Sprache, sein Ziel, seine Selbständigkeit*, 6th edn [Stuttgart: Calwer Verlag, 1983], 381), but this should not cloud the fact that the content for what praise is given has no clear parallel in Jewish sources. Nolland, *Matthew*, 472, points towards Exod. 33.12-13 as 'the closest parallel in the OT' to such a mutual knowledge between God and a human, but rightly asserts that despite a possible influence of Moses' distinctive relationship with God this 'specific father/son relationship remains distinctive'. Accordingly, ἐξομολογέω might be translated in such a way as to express the distinctive 'confessional' element in it more strongly (as in Matthew's only other usage, in 3.6 par. Mk 1.5, where it describes the confessing of sin, and is closer to the use of ὁμολογέω as in 7.23; 10.32). See Phil. 2.11 where Jesus' obedience and honouring of his Father precedes and anticipates what all will one day do to him (namely ἐξομολογήσηται); similarly Mt. 11.26 is testimony to Jesus' willing acceptance of and confession of the Father's plan of salvation.

26. Nolland, *Matthew*, 470.

the Holy Spirit (ἠγαλλιάσατο [ἐν] τῷ πνεύματι τῷ ἁγίῳ).[27] Also in Mt. 11.27 the reciprocal knowledge of Father and Son is expressed more intimately compared to Lk. 10.22, with both, the Son and Father, forming for each other mutually subject and direct object.[28]

After this self-identification of Jesus as the Son, there follows immediately the conflict with the Pharisees in 12.1-8 over the Sabbath (a key element of the 'yoke of the Torah', mentioned in 11.29-30). The subsequent dispute (12.9-14) climaxes in the Pharisees' decision to kill Jesus (v. 14). But before the first direct verbal confrontation between Jesus and the Pharisees in front of the crowds (12.23-37) takes place, Matthew has Jesus withdraw, which allows him to reveal Jesus as the (still hidden) servant of God by quoting Isa. 42.1-4. In this quote, Jesus is proclaimed as the bearer of God's spirit (12.18c = Isa. 42.1c), whose work points beyond the boundaries of ethnic Israel (cf. vv. 18d, 21 = Isa. 42.1d, 4b). The transition between this unusually lengthy quote and the debate with the Pharisees about the power that is at work in Jesus' healing ministry, is an equally unusually short description of a healing, which needs to be seen in conjunction with the quote from Isaiah.[29] This healing of a person who is blind, deaf and possessed by a demon demonstrates that Jesus is indeed the Servant of God as the previous quote of Isa. 42.1-4 has already indicated. Reading on, God declares himself as the giver of the spirit of life for all (Isa. 42.5, which needs to be seen in relation to Mt. 12.18, where Jesus is described as the one who possesses God's Spirit), and then continues (vv. 6-7): 'I am the LORD, I have called you in righteousness…; I have given you as a covenant to the people, a light to the nations, to (1) *open the eyes that are blind*, to (2) *bring out the prisoners from the dungeon*, (3) *from the prison* those who sit in darkness'. A threefold liberation is here announced by Isaiah (see also 61.1), and Matthew presents Jesus as the one, who can heal a person with three afflictions by the power of the Holy Spirit vested in Jesus, as the ensuing debate makes clear.

27. Cf. Lk. 1.47 (also 1.14, in a context where the Spirit is mentioned in 1.15, and again 1.44 together with 1.41).

28. Nolland, *Matthew*, 473; cf. 24.36 and 28.19.

29. Nolland (ibid., 492–3) sees in this 'longest of the formula quotations…the least extensive linkage with its immediate context'; also Hays, *Echoes of Scripture*, 179, seems to be unhappy with Matthew's decision and judges it an 'odd prooftext for Jesus ordering the crowds not to make him known'. He himself, however, points out that the 'surplus of cited material' is Matthew's way 'to draw the reader's attention to the broader literary and theological context'. From this wider context it becomes clear that God himself wants to be the one who introduces his servant and makes him known among the people (42.6, 8-9).

In reaction to this, the crowds are able to make the connection and are on the point of accepting that Jesus is indeed the Son of David, the Messiah, the servant of God, who is equipped with the Spirit by God himself.[30] But the Pharisees immediately douse the fire before it actually blazes, repeating the charge – see 9.34 – that Jesus' healings are not by the power and spirit of God (which 12.18c implies) but by a demonic power (12.24).

The fact that Jesus perceives their thoughts (ἐνθυμήσεις, v. 25) without being told (as in 9.4), can be seen as a hint of his messianic possession of the Spirit. As Otto Betz in his study of the trial of Jesus has argued, the request of members of the high priest's council that Jesus prophesy after his blindfolding must be understood as the direct consequence of his messianic confession (Mk 14.65 parr. Mt. 26.68; Lk. 22.64-65).[31] Based on Isa. 11.2-4 (in the LXX the Holy Spirit features more than in the MT) it was expected that the Messiah would judge not on the basis of what his eyes see and ears hear but on what the Spirit allows him to see and to hear. Matthew omits the blindfolding but otherwise has the most intelligible account of this mock messiah-test: Jesus is addressed as Χριστέ, and the challenge to prophesy is framed as a question: 'Who is it, who hits you?' Nolland rejects Betz's suggestion on the basis of the missing blindfolding in Matthew's version (only Mark records this). But the blindfolding may be seen as a Markan exaggeration and not necessary for the understanding and application of the Isaiah-text as a messianic test-case. One can easily imagine a prisoner being bound in such a way that he could be beaten from behind without being able to see his torturer. Especially when seen in conjunction with Mt. 12.25, the possible objections against the interpretation of Betz are not unsurmountable.[32]

But Matthew does present Jesus not only in such a cryptic way as the one who acts in the power of the Spirit. Against the charge that he healed the man and expelled his demons with the help of Beelzebul, Jesus insists on his empowerment by the Spirit (Mt. 12.28): 'If I cast out the demons with God's Spirit, then the Kingdom of God has come upon you'.[33] The presence of the Spirit is a sign of the kingdom of God (in the OT the coming of the Spirit is a hallmark of the eschatological

30. Readers in the 1st century would not differentiate between God's servant and the messianic Son of David, because for them the book of Isaiah is a unified narrative, and the gift of the Spirit is promised to both, see Deines, *Gerechtigkeit*, 482. The Isaiah Targum is a good example of such a harmonizing interpretation.

31. Otto Betz, 'Probleme des Prozesses Jesu', *ANRW* II 25.2 (1982): 566–647 (638–9).

32. Nolland, *Matthew*, 1135 n. 261.

33. For the Lukan parallel, see above n. 8.

future, see Isa. 4.4; 32.15-17; 44.3; Ezek. 11.19; 36.26-27; 39.29; Joel 3.1-2; Zech. 4.6; 12.10), which means the inauguration of the kingdom takes place wherever Jesus is (or those whom he allows to participate in his Spirit-empowerment, as Mt. 10.1 presupposes, see below). Two further observations are noteworthy: first the way the agency of the Spirit, which was so dominant until 4.1, has changed. The Spirit who previously led Jesus into the wilderness so that he might be tested, is now the 'instrument' of Jesus (ἐν πνεύματι is an instrumental dative). The second point is that here as in 3.16 the expression 'Spirit of God' is used, which brings the three divine characters in close proximity again (compare 11.25-27; also 12.18, where παῖς can be understood as son).

But Jesus is not only aware that his exorcisms in the power of the Spirit mean the inbreaking of the kingdom of God, he also adds a caution, which is primarily addressed to the Pharisees, though it surely includes the audience of Matthew's Gospel as well. Jesus makes clear that the Pharisees crossed the red line with their accusations. To declare someone to be in collaboration with the devil when he is doing the will of God with the help of the Spirit is unforgivable. This is a new teaching that perhaps has its closest parallel in *1 En.* 67.8-10,[34] but there the context is the generations before the flood. What makes the saying of Jesus so distinctive is the authority with which he presumed to know precisely which sins can be forgiven and which cannot,[35] and the elevation of the Holy Spirit over the Son of Man: 'Therefore I say to you, every sin and blasphemy will be forgiven people, but the blasphemy against the Spirit will not be forgiven. And whoever speaks a word against the Son of Man will be forgiven but whoever speaks against the Holy Spirit, will not be forgiven, neither in this age nor in the coming one.' The first apodictic statement in v. 31 is followed by a relative clause with conditional meaning in v. 32 (introduced with ὅς ἐάν), a pattern that can be found regularly in Matthew

34. Nolland, *Matthew*, 86; he himself regards Isa. 63.10 as the closest parallel, but there the Israelites 'only' upset (παρώξυναν, the verb παροξύνω appears in the NT only in Acts 17.16 and 1 Cor. 13.5) God's Spirit but nothing is said about this being unforgivable, quite the opposite. What follows in Isa. 63.11ff. is a prayer of repentance, which God answers with the promise to be again with his people (65.1). The other parallel Nolland mentions, Damascus Document CD 5.11-12, most likely does not concern God's Spirit but the human spirit (which is here regarded as holy, to be sure). Strack-Billerbeck 1:637–8, provides not even any close parallels.

35. Nolland, *Matthew*, 504–5, helpfully connects this passage with the Matthaean emphasis on forgiveness: 'The possibility of forgiveness for people is fundamental to what Jesus came to do'. God's 'forgiveness project' is jeopardized by the Pharisees as they 'exclude people from participating in what God is doing in Jesus'.

(e.g. 5.18-19; 16.24-25; 18.3-6). In each case the relative clause functions as an application or example of the rule stated before.[36] From the context it becomes clear that Matthew understands this unforgivable sin as deliberate attribution of the good, salvific work of God's Spirit (namely the exorcism Jesus has performed in fulfilling Isaiah's – and therefore God's – promise) 'to his ultimate enemy, Satan'.[37] Equally strong language can be found in Mt. 16.21-23 (Peter as Satan) and 23.33 (against the scribes and Pharisees). The reason for this ultimate warning is in both cases that salvation is at stake: without Jesus accepting his way to the cross, no forgiveness of sin would be possible, and the guilt of the Pharisees is that they are preventing people's belief in the divinely guided mission of Jesus (see esp. 23.13). The attack on the Pharisees is so forceful because they are recognized as champions in doing God's will by the people and they have the authority to teach (Mt. 23.2; cf. Jn 3.10). They more than anyone should be able to distinguish God's Spirit from demonic powers. But it is one thing that they cannot recognize that Jesus brings forth good fruits (v. 33), and another to speak against it and to attribute it to the devil, so putting the salvation of others, or what John Nolland calls the 'forgiveness project', at risk. They are culpably responsible for what they say (vv. 36-37, compare Jas 3.1).

What Matthew does here, therefore, is to connect the Spirit-thread with the forgiveness-thread, which stretches from its first mention in the programmatic 1.21 (Jesus 'will save his people from their sins') to 26.28 ('my blood of the covenant, which is poured out for many for the forgiveness of sins'). The latter marks the inauguration of the fulfilment of the initial promise, and 27.4 adds a powerful postscript: whereas Jesus is prepared to take away sin by giving up his life (26.45), the priestly elite ignored Judas's confession ('I have sinned…') and sent him away without compassion: 'What is this to us? See to it yourself!' They cannot forgive sins, as Jesus claimed to do (cf. 9.2-6) and is now going to fulfil.[38] It is within this wide arc that the debate in ch. 12 needs to be seen.

36. Cf. Deines, *Gerechtigkeit*, 372–4; idem, 'Not the Law but the Messiah: Law and Righteousness in the Gospel of Matthew – An Ongoing Debate', in Gurtner and Nolland, eds, *Built upon the Rock*, 53–84 (77–8).

37. R. T. France, *The Gospel of Matthew*, NICNT (Grand Rapids: Eerdmans, 2007), 483. See also Thiselton, *Holy Spirit*, 42–4.

38. After 1.21, the topic of sin is taken up again in 3.6, with Matthew carefully avoiding the impression that John's baptism would forgive sins (as Mk 1.4 implies more clearly); in 6.12, 14-15, the plea for forgiveness of sins in the Lord's Prayer is the only one which is related to a reciprocal, precedent action (v. 12b 'as we also have forgiven our debtors'), and the only one which is exemplified immediately after in 6.14-15 (par. Mk 11.25), and again in 18.23-35. In 9.10-13 Jesus is to be found in

As a result, the Pharisees seem to back down momentarily, asking Jesus for a sign. They do not accept what he has done and said so far as a sufficient enough sign (cf. 11.4-6, the answer Jesus gave to the envoys of John). Jesus' reply is no longer an invitation, which is why he starts now to talk in riddles and in a veiled way about himself and his identity: Jonah's three days in the belly of the fish is the first hint pointing towards Jesus' death and resurrection; the repentance of the Ninevites is a sign for the future repentance of non-Jews; the queen from the south who visited Solomon (the 'first' son of David) points to the foreigners, who in the future will be willing to learn from Jesus (cf. 8.10-12).

Matthew 12.43-45 is not closely related but might be an explanation in line with 12.30. The question must be asked: who or what is it that Jesus (or Matthew) expects to be the new occupant of the house after the previous owners are driven away? Should one see the Holy Spirit as the new owner?

3. *The Holy Spirit and the Disciples of Jesus*

This question leads back to the beginning of Jesus' ministry and the announcement of John that the one coming after him will 'baptise with the Holy Spirit and fire' (3.11). Nowhere in Matthew's Gospel can this be seen, nor indeed the passing on of the Holy Spirit to anybody else (contrast Jn 20.22[39]). The disciples are at best indirectly described as being connected to the Spirit in 10.1 (if seen in light of 12.28) and 10.20, but in neither case is there any clear indication that the Spirit lives or dwells within the disciples in a permanent way.[40]

the company of tax-collectors and sinners, but this is *after* he has demonstrated that he can forgive sins (9.2-7). According to 18.15-17, 21-22, looking forward to the community that is about to be formed in the name of Jesus, sin remains an issue even there (18.20, cf. ἐκκλησία in 16.18; 18.17); the parable in 18.23-35 is about forgiving each other as illustration and explanation of 18.21-22 as well as 6.12, 14-15.

39. See also Jn 14.17, 26; 15.26; 16.13, where Jesus renews the promise of the Spirit (see 1.33) for his disciples shortly before his death. But also before this we find constant reminders to the gift of the Spirt, which can only be given subsequent to Jesus' glorification (7.39, see also 4.23-24).

40. The same goes for Mark, where the last reference to the Spirit is in 13.11 (the parallels in Matthew and Luke are placed much earlier in their Gospels). In this promise to the disciples Jesus assures them that in situations of persecution the Holy Spirit will speak through and for them. This indicates clearly the work of the Spirit in the disciples, but without explaining how the disciples and the Spirit were conjoined initially. In Luke the situation is rather different, with the empowerment of the disciples and of later believers being a key topic, especially in Acts. It is noteworthy that Luke made a real effort finally to present Jesus as the giver of the Spirit at Pentecost.

This conspicuous difference between John's Gospel and Pauline literature on one side and the Synoptics on the other has been understood as evidence for a dichotomy in early Christianity with regard to the Spirit. The assumption is that the Synoptic tradition (Matthew and Mark especially, with Luke preparing the way for the Pauline understanding in 11.13 diff. Mt. 7.11), represents the Palestinian Jewish-Christian tradition, in which the experience of the Spirit is not connected to baptism and a subsequent indwelling of the Spirit in the believer, but is seen as a temporary support for the witness of the gospel in times of distress and persecution only.[41] The key witness for such an understanding of the Spirit is Mt. 10.20 par. Lk. 12.12 and Mk 13.11.

It is disputed among those who hold to this interpretation, whether the disciples' participation in the exorcistic authority of Jesus (Mk 6.7 parr. Mt. 10.1; Lk. 9.1) should also be understood as a delegation of the Holy Spirit, whether permanent or temporary. In Mark the situation is described in some detail, which creates the impression that Jesus gave them the authority over the unclean spirits as a particular, singular event now in the past. The imperfect ἐδίδου could suggest an action which started in the past and is still in progress. However, Mark in 6.30 describes the end of the action which started in 6.7. In contrast to Mark, Matthew gives no hint that the commissioning of the disciples in 10.1-42 is meant as a one-off action. He omits the details and uses the aorist tense instead: ἔδωκεν αὐτοῖς ἐξουσίαν πνευμάτων ἀκαθάρτων...[42] Understood as an ingressive aorist, focusing on the beginning, he creates the impression that the disciples, listed immediately after by name (10.2-4), still possess the authority Jesus has given them. Looking back from 12.28, where Jesus relates his own power over the demons to his ability to act 'in the Spirit of God', this can only mean that Jesus is able to share his Spirit-induced authority over the 'unclean spirits' with his *disciples*. This would imply that they are in a similar way to Jesus – at least for a clearly defined task – enabled by the

In Joel's prophecy quoted in Acts 2.16-17, it is God who is the one who will pour the Spirit. But in describing the resurrection and subsequent ascension of Jesus to 'the right hand of God', he explains in detail that Jesus, after receiving the Holy Spirit from the Father, poured it out for all to hear and to see (Acts 2.33). On this passage see Thiselton, *Holy Spirit*, 56–7; A. W. Zwiep, 'Luke's Understanding of Baptism in the Holy Spirit', in *Christ, the Spirit and the Community of God: Essays on the Acts of the Apostles*, WUNT 2/293 (Tübingen: Mohr Siebeck, 2010), 100–119.

41. See Friedrich Avemarie, *Die Tauferzählungen der Apostelgeschichte*, WUNT 139 (Tübingen: Mohr Siebeck, 2002), 387–94.

42. Lk. 9.1 also uses the aorist tense.

Spirit and therefore – again, at least for this task – in the possession of it, even if this is never addressed properly in the first Gospel.[43] This task-focused possession of the Holy Spirit, which enables a person for a certain undertaking or office is perhaps the most prominent motive of the Spirit's agency within humans in the Old Testament,[44] and Matthew's Gospel is describing aptly and truthfully the transitional period of Jesus' ministry, when the new fullness is already looming but not yet fully achieved as long as Jesus' task is not yet completed.[45] Extrapolating from the saying about the wedding guests who cannot fast as long as the bridegroom is with them (Mt. 9.14), but will do so when he leaves, one could argue that the Spirit is treated by Matthew similarly: as long as Jesus the Spirit-bearer par excellence is with his disciples, they have no need of the Spirit as they are with the one who is Emmanuel.

Instead of explaining the obvious differences between the Gospels in terms of different theologies based on their provenance, the reticence of Matthew (and Mark and Luke) can be seen as further evidence for the often made observation that the synoptic tradition is not simply inventing traditions to fit the needs or match the experiences of the post-Easter communities but provides a rather accurate report of Jesus' deeds and

43. Jörg Frey, 'Vom Windbrausen zum Geist Christi und zur trinitarischen Person: Stationen einer Geschichte des Heiligen Geistes im Neuen Testament', *JBT* 24 (2009): 121–54 (134), rejects this understanding of a Spirit-induced authority (based only on Lk. 10.17-20, he does not discuss the Matthaean parallel). Instead Frey sees the authority of the disciples as based solely on the message of the inbreaking kingdom of God. But message and Spirit are not mutually exclusive as Mt. 8.16 demonstrates. In this summary, Jesus is said to drive out 'the spirits' of the demon-possessed 'with a word' (ἐξέβαλεν τὰ πνεύματα λόγῳ), and in 12.28 'through God's Spirit' (ἐν πνεύματι θεοῦ). In Mt. 10.7-8 exorcisms are also connected with the preaching of the kingdom message.

44. Michael Welker, *Gottes Geist: Theologie des Heiligen Geistes*, 2nd edn (Neukirchen-Vluyn: Neukirchener Verlag, 1993), 58–108; Irmtraut Fischer and Christoph Heil, 'Geistbegabung als Beauftragung für Ämter und Funktionen: Eine gesamtbiblische Perspektive', *JBT* 24 (2009): 53–92; Thiselton, *Holy Spirit*, 9–12.

45. The question of a 'biography' or 'history' ('Geschichte') of the divine persons, including elements of response and change, has been asked by Welker, *Gottes Geist*, 58–9 and elsewhere, and Frey, 'Windbrausen', 121–3, 152–3. Frey shows how the Easter events brought a decisive change in the understanding of the Spirit in such a way that it could no longer be seen apart from its relation to Christ, as God could no longer be perceived apart from his relation to the crucified Jesus. Decisive in this development were Paul, Acts and the Johannine literature. The synoptic tradition clearly represents an earlier stage (p. 134).

his teaching.[46] Even John stays mostly within the thematic range of the Synoptics and does not address the disputed topics of a later generation despite the fact that his understanding is deepened by taking subsequent experience and theological reflection more fully into account than the Synoptics.[47]

The interesting question for Matthew is, whether he leaves gaps in his narrative which are ready to be filled by his readers who probably participated in these later developments, as did, most likely, Matthew himself. Whether Matthew was written by the apostle of this name or by some unknown author as Nolland and the majority of scholars hold, and whether it was written in the 60s, the 90s or any date in between, the experiences with the Spirit referred to by Acts and the Pauline letters have clearly already taken place.[48] They were part of the believers' experience in the second half of the 1st century. Frey rightly points out that the empowerment of and fulfilment by the Spirit, which originally was the prerogative of the Messiah Jesus, became very quickly the gift to his followers after Easter.[49] Equally early is the connection between baptism and the Spirit, and also charismatic experiences of the Spirit, which originated in the earliest post-Easter communities in Judea and Jerusalem.[50]

46. E.g., M. Hengel and R. Deines, 'E. P. Sanders' "Common Judaism", Jesus, and the Pharisees: A Review Article', *JTS* 46 (1995): 1–70 (7, 11–12); Frey, 'Windbrausen', 133, points out that the Gospels do not reshape the Spirit-experience of Jesus in the light of the post-Easter experiences of the Spirit within the earliest Christian communities.

47. See Philipp F. Bartholomä, *The Johannine Discourses and the Teaching of Jesus in the Synoptics: A Contribution to the Discussion Concerning the Authenticity of Jesus' Words in the Fourth Gospel*, TANZ 57 (Tübingen: Francke, 2012).

48. Nolland, *Matthew*, 2–4, argues against the apostle as author but for a date 'before the beginnings of the buildup to the Jewish war' (17). As place of origin he suggests an 'urban environment' that 'was not too far from the heart of Judaism' (18); in support of Matthean authorship, see D. A. Hagner, *The New Testament: A Historical and Theological Introduction* (Grand Rapids: Baker Academic, 2012), 212–17; an exhaustive assessment of the recent discussion is now provided by Akiva Cohen, *Matthew and the Mishnah*, WUNT 2/418 (Tübingen: Mohr Siebeck, 2016), 32–99.

49. This is obvious from formulaic assertions like 'The Holy Spirit has been given to us', Rom. 5.5, see also Acts 8.32; 15.8; 2 Cor. 1.22; 5.5 etc.; or 'we have received the Spirit' (Rom. 8.15; 1 Cor. 2.12, etc.), and 'the Spirit of God dwells in you' (Rom. 8.9; 1 Cor. 3.16), see Frey, 'Windbrausen', 134–5.

50. Frey, 'Windbrausen', 135; also Avemarie, *Tauferzählungen*, 387–94. For the exegetical debate about baptism and Spirit, one highly charged ecclesiologically and theologically, see ibid., 129–74; William Atkinson, *Baptism in the Spirit: Luke–Acts and the Dunn Debate* (Eugene: Pickwick, 2011), and Thiselton, *Holy Spirit*, repeatedly.

But this means that the same communities, which according to Nolland and others provide the context for Matthew's Gospel, are those in which the experiences with the Holy Spirit as indwelling in the believers originated. Consequently, the reason for the silence about these things in the synoptic tradition and especially in Matthew, cannot be explained by the fact that this phenomenon was unknown to the addressees of this Gospel or its author. Nor is it likely that Matthew took an *a priori* critical position towards it. Matthew 7.22 is perhaps the clearest evidence within the first Gospel that reveals 'spiritual activities',[51] although Matthew does not name the Spirit but 'the name' of Jesus as the authority in which these miraculous feats (προφητεύειν; δαιμόνια ἐκβάλλειν; δυνάμεις ποιεῖν) have been accomplished. But this makes perfect sense as the Spirit was not yet given at this point.

Returning to the question at the beginning, what then can be said about the empty house in need of a new occupant? A cursory glance at the history of interpretation shows indeed some support both in the early church and among modern commentators for the assumption that Matthew expected his readers to see here a gap to be filled with the Holy Spirit.[52]

In conclusion, what can be said is not more than that it is *possible* that the Holy Spirit was meant to replace the seven evil spirits. For anything more Matthew does not offer enough evidence, and the same is even more true for the parable of the bridesmaids waiting for the bridegroom (Mt. 25.1-13), where the lack of oil (v. 3) has occasionally been understood as a lack of the Spirit.[53] What remains as clear positive evidence for the Spirit in the life of Jesus' disciples is therefore only the promise in 3.11, which would then point to an event beyond the temporal framework of Jesus' earthly ministry.

Jesus and Matthew

But why did Matthew not more openly address the topic of the Holy Spirit? The same question can be asked regarding other topics as well: why is forgiveness of sins – despite what is said above – not addressed

51. France, *Matthew*, 292.

52. On the early church see Manlio Simonetti, ed., *Matthew 1–13*, Ancient Christian Commentary on Scripture Ia (Downers Grove: InterVarsity Press, 2001), 259–61. Modern commentators taking this view include France, *Matthew*, 493; Wolfgang Wiefel, *Das Evangelium nach Matthäus*, THKNT 1 (Leipzig: Evangelische Verlagsanstalt, 1989), 242. Unpersuaded are Davies and Allison, *Matthew*, 2:359–61; Nolland, *Matthew*, 515; Konradt, *Matthäus*, 205.

53. See Simonetti, *Matthew 1–13*, 214–17; Davies and Allison, *Matthew*, 3:396–7.

more openly, when it plays such a dominant role in the understanding of Jesus' death and resurrection after Easter? Why is the community in Jesus' name only hinted at but its function and structure not more fully explained with words of Jesus? Is it possible that Matthew does not know about these things? Or that he rejects them and therefore does not mention them? For various reasons I take this as completely unlikely. It would place Matthew in a corner isolated from the main streams of development in the first fifty years of Christianity, and turn him into a person gloomily brooding about the 'others' who chose the wrong path and betrayed Jesus' teaching. If this were indeed the case then it becomes inexplicable how his Gospel could end up as the main Gospel for the early church. Assuming a sectarian and outsider-perspective for Matthew would rather have led to a situation similar to the fate of other Jewish Christian gospels, which disappeared with no more than some isolated quotes preserved. Alternatively, one would have to argue that those who used Matthew's Gospel alongside the other gospels and the Pauline legacy completely misunderstood him, or used him against his own intentions.

If one does not favour such a dishonest reception history of the first Gospel, a possible and quite simple solution for the above-mentioned questions is that Matthew indeed wrote a report about Jesus' life, his words and his deeds. Clearly not in a distancing, 'objective' way as something that happened in the past without meaning for the contemporary followers of this Jesus, but also not without a clear differentiation between the various epochs of God's salvation history. That he deploys salvation-historical awareness, thinking in terms of past, present and future epochs, is obvious throughout his Gospel.[54] That also means that Matthew has a clear notion of a time after Jesus' earthly presence with his disciples, and, what is more, he let his readers understand that Jesus had the same view. Matthew, perhaps more than the other Synoptics, sees Jesus as preparing his disciples for their task in leading a community in his name, comprising Jews and believers from all nations that will endure until his Parousia.[55] But despite these obvious trajectories into the future

54. For a more detailed argument see my 'The Recognition of God's Acts in History in the Gospel of Matthew: An Exercise in Salvation History', in *Acts of God in History: Studies Towards Recovering a Theological Historiography*, ed. Christoph Ochs and Peter Watts, WUNT 317 (Tübingen: Mohr Siebeck, 2013), 311–50 (334–44), and above n. 10.

55. On the ecclesial dimension of Matthew see D. A. Hagner, 'Holiness and Ecclesiology: The Church in Matthew', in Gurtner and Nolland, eds, *Built upon the Rock*, 170–86; for Hagner there can be no doubt that 'Matthew knows that disciples will be empowered with the Spirit' and that 'the Spirit will have an important role to play', p. 182); see also Konradt, *Matthäus*, 11–15 and his interpretation of

of the 'church', Matthew has not composed a manual for this future church based on the life of Jesus, but the story of its founder, and what he said about these topics, without feeling the urge to fill all the gaps.

Therefore, Matthew invites his readers to reflect about why Jesus did not talk more clearly about the Holy Spirit or the forgiveness of sins or other issues, which are so prominent in the letters of Paul and partly also in Acts. The answer to this question seems to me that Jesus could and would not talk about these issues more confidently and boldly, because they were conditioned upon his own obedience and 'success'.[56] God's plan for salvation, for which Jesus was the inaugurating agent, depended on Jesus' willingness to do the Father's will until the very end. The temptation of Jesus, not just in the beginning, but also with Peter as tempter in 16.23, and the scoffers under the cross (and the two sharing his fate on the cross) in 27.39-44, tell a story of possible failure. The outcome of Jesus' mission as Son of God on earth was not secured right from the beginning, but had to be won, as can also be seen from Jesus' inner struggle in Gethsemane (26.37-44). Accordingly, because the 'benefits' from his death could not be reaped before they were secured, they could equally not be announced or proclaimed before his final victory on the cross, where he has proven to be indeed the stronger one, who was able to bind the strong and to plunder his house (12.29). Only after the resurrection could he finally command the disciples to go out to all nations and to baptize them 'in the name of the Father and of the Son and of the Holy Spirit' (28.19), which is the fulfilment of the promise in 3.11. The trifold formula points back to the appearance of the Spirit at Jesus' baptism in 3.16-17. For the reader of Matthew's Gospel it has become clear at the latest at the baptism of Jesus, that he is intrinsically related to the realm of the Holy Spirit and the Lord God, and that his birth 'out of the Holy Spirit' (1.18, 20) sets him apart from all previous generations. Matthew allows his readers to appreciate Jesus as offspring of a divine decision brought about by the Spirit and the Lord God in fulfilment of the Scriptures which were spoken by the Lord, and, in light of 22.43, have been inspired by the Spirit. As Emmanuel he stays until the end of days with those who are 'baptised with Holy Spirit and fire'.

3.11 (p. 50), which he understands as a reference to the bestowal of the Holy Spirit on the followers of Jesus.

56. On obedience see also Konradt, *Matthäus*, 8–9, 52. For Jesus' deliberate withholding of 'explanatory allusions...until he had lived out their meaning in his everyday incarnate life', see Thiselton, *Holy Spirit*, 38, 47.

15

Jesus, the Founder of *Sabbatismos*

Craig A. Smith

Introduction

In this article, I intend to examine the meaning of rest in Heb. 4.9, where, interestingly, the author of Hebrews uses the unusual word *sabbatismos* rather than either *sabbaton*, a word used repeatedly in the Gospels, or the term *katapausis* (13 times in LXX and 8 times in Hebrews). Though different words are used, this does not mean that there is no relationship between these words and concepts. I will show there is a relationship between them, though I will make clear that by using the unique word *sabbatismos* the author of Hebrews is seeking to capture and convey an important nuance.

The second aim of this paper is to explain the argumentation which the author of Hebrews uses to show how Jesus procures the *sabbatismos* in Heb. 4.9. I will do this by showing how the author of Hebrews builds on the early church's understanding of Jesus fulfilling the promised eschatological rest as it is articulated in Mt. 11.28–12.14, connecting this with the cultic references in the Gospel of Matthew that relate to the effect of Jesus' death on the temple and priesthood.

Jesus' Relationship to the Sabbath in the Matthew 11.28–12.14

In the early 20th century, Montefiore considered the words of Jesus in Mt. 11.25-30 to be spurious because of Christ's self-disclosure and wide-reaching claims.[1] Later A. M. Hunter reflecting on the same passage

1. C. G. Montefiore, *The Synoptic Gospels*, 2 vols (London: Macmillan, 1909), 168–9.

considered Mt. 11.25-30 as 'perhaps the most important verses in the Synoptic Gospels'.[2] The importance of this text for this article is the close connection of Jesus' identity and the reference to rest within the greater context of rejection and Sabbath (Mt. 11.20–12.14). In this section I will examine the meaning of rest (ἀναπαύσω, 11.28; ἀνάπαυσις, 11.29) in Mt. 11.25-30, taking into consideration the broader context of 12.1-14. The goal is to show the probable interest and understanding the early church had in the concepts of rest and Sabbath which may provide the backdrop for the author of Hebrews' understanding of *sabbatismos* (σαββατισμός) in Heb. 4.9 and the means by which it was procured by Jesus.

In Mt. 11.28, Jesus offers those who labour and are burdened to come to him for rest. Some scholars see a strong Wisdom background in 11.25-30 because of the link created through the use of 'teaching' and 'wisdom'. Jesus is the teacher of wisdom who reveals the hidden things to the little children and offers rest to the one who draws near in the same way as that found in Sir. 51.27, 'See…that I have laboured but little and found for myself much rest (ἀνάπαυσις)'. For these scholars, rest is defined as, 'relief brought by Jesus to people from the various kinds of pressures under which they labour'.[3] The same idea is found in Mk 6.31 in which the same verb ἀναπαύσω is used. In this context, the disciples have just returned from their *tour de ministère* (Mk 6.6b-13) and Jesus suggests that they go away to a quiet place to rest and be restored. It may be that they need to learn more from Jesus and take up the yoke of his wisdom. France suggests that Jesus may be offering relief from the legalistic burdens imposed on the people (Mt. 23.4) but not release from all the obligations of the Law, as he makes clear earlier (Mt. 5.20).[4]

But some scholars[5] see the rest promised by Jesus in Mt. 11.25-30 'as the fulfillment of the Messianic rest typified by the OT Sabbath'.[6] There is much to commend this position. Matthew 11.25-30 is a *Thanksgiving*

2. A. M. Hunter, 'Crux Criticorum – Matt. 11:25-30 – A Re-Appraisal', *NTS* 8 (1962): 241.

3. John Nolland, *The Gospel of Matthew*, NIGTC (Grand Rapids: Eerdmans, 2005), 476.

4. R. T. France, *The Gospel according to Matthew: An Introduction and Commentary* (Grand Rapids: Eerdmans, 1985), 200.

5. Samuele Bacchiocchi, 'Matthew 11:28-30: Jesus' Rest and the Sabbath', *Andrews University Seminary Studies* 22, no. 3 (1984): 289–310. Andrew T. Lincoln, 'Sabbath, Rest, and Eschatology in the New Testament', in *From Sabbath to Lord's Day*, ed. D. A. Carson (Grand Rapids: Zondervan, 1982), 197–220.

6. Bacchiocchi, 'Matthew', 290.

Hymn comprised of three strophes,[7] found within the central section about the revelation of the Messiah (Mt. 11.25–12.14) which comprises the centre of the chiasm. The first strophe includes Jesus giving thanks for the revelation of 'these things' (i.e. the powerful deeds) and their significance to the 'little children' but concealed from the 'wise and learned' (11.25-26). The second strophe, a proleptic declaration of his identity as the Son, reveals his mission[8] to make the Father known (11.27). The actual declaration of Jesus as Messiah does not come until Mt. 16.16, but at this point Jesus uses the term Son as a messianic self-disclosure.[9] In the third strophe, Jesus makes the offer of his messianic rest to the weary and burdened (11.28-30). The Thanksgiving Hymn is followed by an elaboration of the messianic rest particularly in terms of its relationship to the Sabbath (12.1-14).

Because the two strophes in 11.25-27 are messianic[10] in nature it is probable, according to Bacchiocchi,[11] that the offer of rest in 11.28-30 should also have a messianic and eschatological association. Conceptually, this is not an unreasonable jump since there are many references in Jewish literature which associate the messianic age with peace and rest (Isa. 32.18; 56.4-7; 58.13-14; 65.19-23; 66.22-24; Zech. 9.9-10). The idea of rest in Mt. 11.28-30 being a messianic fulfilment of the Old Testament rest is consistent with the theme of Old Testament fulfilment found throughout the Gospel of Matthew (Mt. 1.22; 2.15, 17; 4.14). Furthermore, the juxtaposition of rest in 11.28-30 with the Sabbath in 12.1-14 also suggests that the two might be related. Carson and others[12] have observed that the use of the phrase 'at that time' connects 12.1-14 temporally and therefore theologically with 11.28-30. Similarly, the 'yoke' may provide a link between 11.28-30 and 12.1-14. Yoke is associated with willing

7. Montefiore, *Synoptic*, 169; Hunter, 'Crux', 242–9; Bacchiocchi, 'Matthew', 291.

8. Bacchiocchi, 'Matthew', 293. Joachim Jeremias, *Abba. Studien zur neutestamentlichen Theologie und Zeitgeschichte* (Göttingen: Vandenhoeck & Ruprecht, 1966), 51.

9. I. Howard Marshall, 'The Divine Sonship of Jesus', *Int* 21 (1967): 91–3; Reginald H. Fuller, *The Foundations of New Testament Christology* (New York: Charles Scribner's Sons, 1965), 31–3.

10. John Laansma, '"I Will Give You Rest": The Background and Significance of the Rest Motif in the New Testament', *TynBul* 46, no. 1 (1995): 386, and *'I Will Give You Rest': The Rest Motif in the New Testament with Special Reference to Mt. 11 and Heb. 3–4*, WUNT 2/98 (Tübingen: Mohr Siebeck, 1997).

11. Bacchiocchi, 'Matthew', 300.

12. Ibid., 301.

'submission'[13] and 'obedience' often with respect to the Law (*Pirke Aboth* 3.5), but the yoke Jesus is offering in his teaching is easy and light and will actually provide rest for one's soul. The first story in 12.1-14 provides an example of the disciples who have submitted to the yoke of Jesus and his teaching with respect to the Sabbath, thereby demonstrating that the purpose of the Sabbath is to bring relief (even from real hunger) on the basis of Christ's mercy. In the second story (12.9-14), Jesus demonstrates, through his own example, his understanding of the purpose of the Sabbath for bringing healing/restoration based on the humanitarian principle that one must do good for others regardless of the day. Matthew's argumentation in 11.28–12.14 is such that the latter text (12.1-14) appears to inform the former text (11.28-30).

Matthew is not interested in presenting a thorough treatment on the topic of the Sabbath. Instead he deals with only two aspects but looks at them through the lens of the future messianic rest; in 12.1-8 he addresses the issue of human need and in 12.9-14, the value of humanity. Matthew's high view of the Sabbath does not call for the elimination of the Sabbath day, rather he broadens its scope making mercy and Jesus' authoritative teaching the new lenses through which one interprets and lives out the Sabbath. Therefore in 12.1-14 Matthew refashions his view of the Sabbath according to Jesus' teaching, so that the Sabbath can be a day in which meeting human need surpasses the requirement and sacrifice of not working on the Sabbath. The basis for allowing David and his men to eat the showbread and for the priests to desecrate the Sabbath, is the superiority of Christ to the temple and his Lordship over the Sabbath.

Matthew does not explicitly state how Jesus fulfilled the Old Testament Sabbath and opened the way to experience this new messianic rest; rather the text simply says that Jesus is 'greater than the temple' and 'Lord of the Sabbath', the assumption being that if he is greater than the temple then he must be Lord of the Sabbath since the temple is greater than the Sabbath.[14] The cultic reference to the temple points to the death and resurrection of Jesus where he has surpassed the greatness and glory of the temple (Mt. 27.40) and became the new way into the Holy of Holies when the curtain was torn apart (27.51). I believe that the author of Hebrews builds on this background when he articulates his view of rest and presents Jesus as the high priest who procures this eschatological rest.

13. M. Maher, 'Take My Yoke upon You (Matt. 11:29)', *NTS* 22 (1976): 97–103 (98–9, 101–2).

14. Nolland, *The Gospel of Matthew*, 484.

In conclusion, it can be said, at the very least, that the argument from 11.28 to 12.14 suggests the early church was very interested in the relationship between rest, work and the Sabbath. It is difficult to be certain if the Wisdom material or the messianic rest fulfilment idea lies behind the understanding of rest in 11.28-30, though the latter interpretation is the most likely one as I have suggested. Matthew views this rest from an eschatological perspective, which means that those burdened by legalism or the onerous requirements of the Law or enduring the difficulty of living as a disciple of Jesus can experience in part this eschatological rest in the present but fully at the Parousia. Matthew, in his Gospel, connects the Sabbath with the temple and Jesus, who fulfils and even supersedes the purpose and function of the temple through his death and resurrection. As I will show, the author of Hebrews uses this temple background and early Christian understanding of the Sabbath rest and brings his unique contribution to understanding Sabbath rest as *sabbatismos* (Heb. 4.9) founded on Christ's priestly work and perfect sacrifice offered in heaven (Heb. 9.24).

It is beyond the scope of this paper to prove the issue of dating though I do take an early dating of Matthew (early 60s) and believe that Hebrews is written sometime soon after the beginning of the Neronian persecution in Rome, thus between 65 and 67 CE. Matthew's understanding of rest represents a common understanding of rest in the early church, which he puts into words for the church. The author of Hebrews' understanding is a further elaboration on this understanding. It is impossible to know whether his initial understanding comes from reading Matthew's Gospel or is simply the result of the influence of the early church's understanding of rest.

Jesus the High Priest Procures Eternal Rest

With a quick perusal of Hebrews, one can immediately note the importance of Jesus as a mediator. This theme is neatly tucked away in embryonic form in the prologue of this letter (Heb. 1.1-4) and it becomes more clearly expressed in 1.5–7.28, where Jesus is presented as the superior mediator to those who would be considered great mediators in the minds of the readers – angels (1.5–2.18), Moses (3.1–4.13), Aaron and his priesthood (4.14–7.28). Jesus' mediatory role is that of a high priest, not like those under the Aaronic priesthood (Heb. 7.11-14) but in the likeness of the priesthood of Melchizedek (7.15-28). As high priest, Jesus enjoyed a superior ministry in a superior temple and initiated a superior covenant (8.1–9.28) by offering a superior sacrifice (10.1-18).

In the previous section I showed how, according to Matthew, Jesus superseded the Sabbath law because he is greater than the temple and therefore greater than the Sabbath law. Jesus' ministry in Mt. 11.25–12.14 is significant because it marks the beginning of the new work of God in which the rituals of the temple are being surpassed by Jesus and thereby being made redundant. As Lord, Jesus has authority over the Law and the temple. Formerly the temple was considered the locus of the presence of God and an identity marker for the people of God. Matthew is pointing forward to the time when Jesus will be the centre and essence of God's presence and the one around whom the new community of God will be found (similarly Mk 11.12-25). The cumulative event when this will be realized is the death and resurrection and ascension of Jesus.[15] Matthew does not elaborate on how Christ's death, resurrection and ascension bring these about, rather he lets the reader surmise this from the rending of the curtain in the temple (Mt. 27.51) which shows two things. First, it demonstrates the judgement of God on the temple resulting in its rejection (cf. Mt. 24.32-35) and future destruction in 70 CE. Second, it shows that the entrance into God's presence has been achieved through the work of Christ. The author of Hebrews develops and builds on this truth.

Jesus the Superior High Priest

At the beginning of the section in which Christ is presented as superior to Aaron and Melchizedek (Heb. 4.14–7.28) the author of Hebrews states that the readers have a high priest, Jesus, who has passed through the heavens (4.14) and is now seated on a throne (4.16) after making purification for sins (1.3) from where he continues his ministry (8.1-2). Using the imagery of the tabernacle, the author describes, throughout Hebrews, the high priestly ministry of Jesus. In Heb. 9.1-10, the author describes the arrangement of the earthly sanctuary in such a way as to point out that 'the way into the most holy place had not yet been disclosed as long as the first tabernacle was still standing'. The reason the way into the 'holy of holies' was blocked is because the sacrifices were inadequate and inefficacious (9.7, 9-10). When Christ died and rose again he entered the 'holy of holies' by going 'through the greater and more perfect tabernacle that is not man-made, that is to say, not a part of this creation' (Heb. 9.11). In Heb. 9.24 the author clarifies his thinking, saying that Christ

15. Lane Keister, 'The Sabbath Day and Recreations on the Sabbath: An Examination of the Sabbath and the Biblical Basis for the "No Recreation" Clause in Confession of Faith 21.8 and Westminster Larger Catechism 117', *Confessional Presbyterian* 5 (2009): 232.

did not enter a 'man-made sanctuary'; rather 'he entered heaven itself' to make an offering. The difference between Christ's offering and the earthly high priests' offerings was the blood being offered. The earthly priests poured out the blood of bulls and goats whereas Jesus offered himself. To use the language of the Gospels, in light of Hebrews, when Christ died and the veil in the temple split, Jesus entered the holy of holies with the offering of himself. When he rose from the dead, the words of Jesus 'destroy this temple and I will raise it again in three days' (Jn 2.19; Mt. 26.61) were fulfilled. This in turn meant that God's judgement on the temple was complete and metaphorically the first tabernacle was no longer standing and the new way to enter the presence of God had been opened (10.19-22), to be experienced, in part now but fully later.

Jesus the Forerunner

The author of Hebrews makes another important reference to the priestly duty of Jesus in Heb. 6.18-20 found in the context of God's promise to Abraham and hope. The text says that Jesus goes behind the temple curtain, as a 'forerunner', *prodomos*. The imagery in this pericope is rich and, though the author mixes images in these verses, the meaning is quite clear. In Greek literature, a forerunner is used to refer to a soldier or group of soldiers who would go out on reconnaissance on behalf of the soldiers (*Jos. Asen.* 24.14; 26.5).[16] Here, in Heb. 6.18-20, this *hapax legomenon* carries the idea of sequence,[17] as the one who has gone ahead of his members, and of preparation (cf. Jn 14.2-3), as the one who has accomplished the work of redemption thereby preparing and opening the way to glory for his followers (Heb. 2.10). Jesus sitting on the throne of God in heaven (Heb. 1.3) is a sign that his preparatory work for them is complete and ready for them to receive. Montefiore correctly notes that, 'Jesus constitutes the advance guard who is already in heaven and who by his entry has assured the consequent entry of all who are his'.[18] Therefore, as the *prodomos*, Jesus calls out from this place as a 'herald'[19] to his brothers and sisters to flee to take hold of this hope which is secure as an anchor in heaven itself.

16. Raymond Brown, *The Message of Hebrews: Christ above All*, The Bible Speaks Today (Downers Grove: IVP, 1982), 122.

17. E. K. Simpson, 'The Vocabulary of the Epistle to the Hebrews', *EvQ* 18, no. 3 (1946): 187.

18. Montefiore as cited in R. McL. Wilson, *Hebrews*, Readings: A New Biblical Commentary, NCB Commentary (Grand Rapids: Eerdmans, 1987), 118.

19. R. P. Gordon, *Hebrews* (Sheffield: Sheffield Phoenix Press, 2008), 98.

Early Christians considered the 'anchor' to be a symbol of certain hope. The meaning of the anchor here is simply to strengthen the idea that the followers of Jesus have this hope 'moored to an immoveable object',[20] namely the throne of God upon which Jesus is seated (1.3). In other words, Christ's brothers and sisters (2.11) have a hope that an anchor metaphorically runs from their inner being to Jesus who is in heaven.[21] They are to flee from any entangling sin (12.1) and take hold of this hope set before them. The certainty of this hope is further ensured by God's oath and two unchangeable things: the promise of God and God's nature not to lie. The author's point in 6.13-17 is that in the same way God confirmed his covenant promises with Abraham (i.e. becoming a great nation, being blessed with an heir and the land of Canaan) through an oath, so the readers of Hebrews and all believers (i.e. heirs of what was promised 6.17) can be assured that the promise of this hope is secure through Jesus' death, resurrection and ascension into the heavenly throne room.

It is important at this juncture to examine a little closer the promise made to Abraham in Heb. 6.13-15. The immediate story to which the author is referring is from Genesis 22 (since the quotation is from Gen. 22.16-17) where Abraham is about to sacrifice Isaac and in essence give up all chance of receiving the promise of having an heir and becoming a great nation. God's angel stays Abraham's hand, sparing Isaac's life. From the author's perspective Abraham received Isaac back from the dead (Heb. 11.19) and in this way Abraham received the promise of an heir stated in Heb. 6.15 (ἐπέτυχεν τῆς ἐπαγγελίας). For his faith Abraham, along with others, is commended as one of those who received what was promised (cf. Heb. 11.33). It is important to note that the same verb and noun are used in both 11.19 and 11.33. Yet later in Heb. 11.39, at the end of the 'heroes of faith' chapter, the author says that, 'These were all commended for their faith, yet none of them [Abraham included] received what had been promised, *οὐκ ἐκομίσαντο τὴν ἐπαγγελίαν*. God had planned something better for us so that only together with us would they be made perfect.' There appears to be a contradiction between Heb. 6.15 and Heb. 11.39. The author's point and solution to this problem is that the author of Hebrews uses Abraham as a great example of someone who received the promise through patient endurance but 'not its final realisation and fulfillment'.[22] Abraham could not receive the final reali-

20. A. B. Davidson, *The Epistle to the Hebrews* (Edinburgh: T. & T. Clark, 1959), 199.

21. 'Heaven' is probably the best way to interpret this phrase εἰσερχομένην εἰς τὸ ἐσώτερον τοῦ καταπετάσματος (cf. Heb. 9.24).

22. McL. Wilson, *Hebrews*, 115.

zation of the promises to him because Jesus had not yet come, who is the true Son of Abraham (Mt. 1.1), the seed of Abraham through whom the promises come to those who believe (Gal. 3.16-22) and the fulfilment of the promise of land and rest. Therefore, the realization of the promise made to Abraham is for those the author calls Abraham's descendants (Heb. 2.16), who are one and the same as Jesus' brothers and sisters because they are of the same family (Heb. 2.11). Therefore, the author is saying that the hope that was offered to Abraham and his ancestors (i.e. Israel) is now available for those who have faith in Christ. To receive this hope requires the same enduring faith that Abraham demonstrated waiting for the birth of Isaac and his metaphorical resurrection (6.13-15; 11.19). But this hope, now opened up by faith, is realized in the present but fully when Christ returns.

What then is this hope that readers of Hebrews are to take hold of (Heb. 6.18)? The author uses the word for hope five times in this letter and in each case the meaning of hope is influenced directly by its context (3.6; 7.19). The reference to hope in Heb. 10.23 is more directly related to the use of hope in 6.11, 18. Here, hope is the gift for believers to enter the most holy place confidently and draw near to God because of Christ's sacrifice which opened the way to God's presence and brought cleansing of sin to allow this access.

The references to 'hope' in Heb. 6.11, 18 are found within a discussion that runs from 3.1 to 6.20. Within this section, the author gives two warnings coupled with several encouragements. The first warning is, not to ignore God's Word as Israel did and who, therefore, did not enter the rest (3.7-19). The second warning is to beware of spiritual immaturity, which will keep one from obtaining the hope (5.11–6.12). Persevering faith like Abraham's is the antidote for this immaturity. There are three encouragements within this section, which express movement with respect to God and believers.[23] The readers are *to hold onto God* by holding fast to their hope and courage (3.1-6) and holding onto their faith (4.16). They are *to move towards God* by entering his rest (4.1-11) and by entering his throne of grace to receive mercy and grace. Finally, they are *to move towards others* to help encourage one another (3.13) to enter this rest. The abundance of warnings and encouragements signals the importance of this hope on offer. Thus, the hope that the author wants his readers to experience is the rest of God he articulates in Heb. 4.1-11. This hope lies behind the curtain (6.19) and can be a present reality for them if

23. Cf. Harold W. Attridge, *Hebrews: A Commentary on the Epistle to the Hebrews*, ed. Helmut Koester, Hermeneia (Philadelphia: Fortress Press, 1989), 22.

they do not harden their hearts through unbelief (3.13, 19) or disobedience (3.18) and if they do not grow lazy (dull) in their faith through spiritual immaturity (5.11).

In this section I have shown how the author of Hebrews elaborates and expounds on the image of the torn veil in the temple found in the Gospels and the claim that Jesus is greater than the temple and Law. He does this first by showing that Jesus does not belong to the Aaronic priesthood; rather, he is a superior priest in the likeness of the priesthood of Melchizedek. Jesus as priest and his priesthood are superior because he offered a perfect sacrifice. The image of Jesus as the forerunner is significant because it shows him entering into the holy of holies before his followers and on their behalf thereby procuring for them hope (Heb. 6.11, 19). This hope is none other than the rest referred to in Heb. 4.1-11. Now it is time to examine what this rest is that the author of Hebrews believes Jesus procured for his people.

Promise of Rest for Believers

The discussion of 'rest' in Hebrews takes place within the larger section of Heb. 3.1–4.14. In Heb. 3.1-6, the author contrasts Moses and Jesus, who were both mediators of covenants, the Mosaic and new covenant (Jer. 31) respectively. Jesus has greater status and importance because he is *the Son over the house* (Heb. 3.6) whereas Moses is *a servant in the house* (3.5). For this reason, the readers of Hebrews are to consider carefully (3.1) and hold fast to Jesus (3.6) and his message which is superior to the message of the Law given through Moses. One very important part of Moses' message in the Law that the author is concerned about is 'rest/Sabbath' and he deals with this in 4.1-14. The author will show that Moses, though great and priestly[24] in his function, led Israel from bondage in Egypt to the promised land but they did not receive rest. But Jesus, who is greater and priestly, did enter the rest of God and therefore he can and will lead his people from the bondage of Satan (2.14-15) to this rest (4.3, 9).

Hebrews 4.1-11 is a unit which is held together with the phrase 'enter into the rest' which is implied or explicit eight times. Structurally, this unit is bracketed by an exhortation at the beginning and end, with an exposition on 'rest' in the middle, which is where the emphasis lies.

24. Ps. 99.6; Philo, *Her.* 182; Exod. 24.4-8; Philo, *Vit. Mos.* 1.158; 2.66-186; *Lev. Rab.* 1.14; *Sifre Zuta Numbers* 12.6-8; *Sipre Numbers* 103.

Exhortation no. 1 'Be careful no one fails to enter the rest' (4.1)

Exposition about rest (4.2-10)

Exhortation no. 2 'make effort to enter the rest' (4.11)

The first exhortation stresses the importance for the audience to pay attention (cf. Heb. 2.1-4) to God's message found in the Old Testament (i.e. Ps. 95 and Gen. 2.2), as it is understood through Jesus. His point is that there is a rest, which remains (note that it has not been 'fulfilled or withdrawn'[25]) for those who live during the period called 'Today' (i.e. the time between the first and second coming of Christ). But what is this rest that remains? Part of the difficulty identifying this rest and interpreting Heb. 4.1-11 is because there are three types of 'rest' mentioned in this text: Canaan rest, God's rest and the rest available 'Today' of which David spoke.

The Canaan rest, which Joshua brought about (4.8), had to do with taking the land (Deut. 11.8), enjoying a time of prosperity (Deut. 11.9-12) and peace with their enemies (Josh. 21.44). Clearly this is not the rest that the author is asking his audience to enter, otherwise years later David would not have spoken of another rest in Ps. 95.7. Rather, this rest predicted by David in Ps. 95.7 and fulfilled in the time of the author of Hebrews is the rest of God, which is entered through faith (4.3).

The author uses the second rule of Hillel's Seven Rules of Interpretation, a midrashic technique, called the *gezerah shawah*, whereby he takes the word 'rest' which is common to Ps. 95 and Gen. 2.2 and then proceeds to interpret the meaning of 'rest' in Ps. 95 through the lens of Gen. 2.2. Through this technique, he shows how the rest of God is the *sabbatismos* of Heb. 4.9 which is available 'Today'. So, how does the author's logic unfold?

First, when the author writes in 4.3 'they shall never enter my rest, yet my works have been done before the foundation of the world' he means that God's rest existed before Israel entered the promised land with Joshua. Israel never experienced this rest. The rest that Israel experienced was temporal and material, only a foreshadowing of God's quintessential rest.

25. David Fletcher correctly says that the readers of Hebrews find themselves in 'the same position as the wandering Israelites – faced with the choice of enduring faithfully and entering God's rest or turning away from him in rebellion and abandoning her confession of faith': 'Wandering While Resting: The Paradox of Sabbath Eschatology in Hebrews', *Pneumatika* 2, no. 1 (2014): 88–9.

Second, in 4.4 the author shows through the Gen. 2.2 text that the rest of God can be traced back to the creation account and is in some way related to the way God rested from all his works[26] on the seventh day. After each day of creation, God reflected on what he had done and said, 'It is good'. But on the seventh day after creating everything, including man and woman, he stated, 'It is very good' and he rested from his work. This process shows that 'God has given only a limited amount of himself to the task of making and upholding the heavens and the earth'[27] and therefore anything created is only a reflection of his essence. His true essence is found beyond creation in his intangible rest. It is this eternal rest that he wants to share with his people.

God consecrated the seventh day calling it the Sabbath. This day was created for Israel so that they might experience rest, which supersedes anything they could experience from what God had created in the six days. God was offering to share himself with Israel for one day each week. The purpose of the Sabbath was for Israel to separate herself from her preoccupation with the created order, leisure and work and to cleave unto God and to set her heart upon his rest. It was a day to enjoy fellowship with God with all its grace, joy and freedom. This is what Jesus had in mind when he said, 'the Sabbath was made for humankind' (Mk 11.27). The Sabbath was instated to rule out the idea that the true life could be found through one's experience of creation or through any effort or work of the individual. In fact, it is out of the Sabbath rest that the person was to labour for six days and understand the meaning of his or her labour. It is for these reasons that the penalty for breaking the Sabbath was so high (Exod. 31.14); Israel's life was at stake. The other aspect of the Old Testament Sabbath was the prophetic element because of which the Jewish believer would look forward to the messianic reign when there would be uninterrupted joy, rest and freedom.

So, the rest the author of Hebrews speaks about is not the Canaan rest or even the seventh day Sabbath rest; rather, it is the rest of God that has existed from the beginning.[28] Why could the Israelites and David not

26. Jaki sees in the Sabbath 'a divine role model for man' and an expression of God's holiness that Israel is to share when God enjoins Moses 'to tell the Israelites that the Sabbath-rest is both the expression of God's holiness and a means of making the people holy'; see Stanley L. Jaki, 'The Sabbath-Rest of the Maker of All', *Asbury Theological Journal* (Spring 1995): 38.

27. Ronald S. Wallace, *The Ten Commandments: A Study of Ethical Freedom* (Eugene: Wipf & Stock, 1998), 65.

28. W. L. Lane, *Hebrews: A Call to Commitment* (Peabody: Hendrickson, 1985), 68.

receive this rest? It is because Jesus had not come yet and made a way for the people of God to enter this rest. Jesus had to 'pass through the heavenlies' (4.15) into the heavenly sanctuary as our High Priest (6.19). By faith the believers in Hebrews and believers today can experience this rest in a limited measure not only on the Sabbath day, as the Israelites did, but every day.[29]

Further Clarification of the sabbatismos

In 4.9 the author changes the typical word for rest from *katapausis* (3.11, 18; 4.1, 3, 5, 10, 11) to *sabbatismos* (4.9). Why? The noun *katapausis* is used to refer to a 'resting place' for God (Acts 7.49; Ps. 132.14; Isa. 66.1), for God's people (i.e. Canaan; Deut. 12.9; 2 Chron. 6.41) and for the ark of the covenant (2 Chron. 6.41). In each case, rest refers to a place. This noun is also used metaphorically as the state of rest provided by God through the provision of the Sabbath rest on the seventh day (Exod. 35.2; 2 Macc. 15.1). The usage of *katapausis* in Ps. 95.11 is a mixture of the 'resting place' and 'state of rest' ideas. The author of the psalm is exhorting the people to go to this place of rest where the people can enter into God's presence and offer worship.[30] It is this understanding of *katapausis* in Psalm 95 that the author of Hebrews draws upon when he exhorts his readers to enter God's rest in Hebrews 4.[31] Just as Moses led Israel out of bondage, in the same way the readers of Hebrews are

29. The question raised among scholars is whether this rest is exclusively a future reality, entirely a present experience or something which believers can experience partially now in the present but fully later in the future; Ann Hoch Cowdery, 'Hebrews 4:1-13', *Int* (1994): 285; Richard B. Gaffin, 'Sabbath: A Creation Ordinance and Sign of the Christian Hope', *Banner of Truth* (1971): 23; Peter T. O'Brien, *The Letter to the Hebrews*, Pillar New Testament Commentary (Grand Rapids: Eerdmans, 2010), 164–6.

30. It is not clear where the people are to 'come before God'. If this is a psalm written for the Feast of Tabernacles then it could refer going out to the desert (D. Kidner, *Psalms 73–150*, TOTC (London: IVP, 1975), 375) or it may refer to meeting in the temple.

31. Some scholars do import the idea of 'resting place' in Heb. 4 which they suggest supports, I believe erroneously, their exclusively futuristic interpretation of rest in this passage. O'Brien proposes that *sabbatismos* is different from *katapausis* and the former 'explains what will take place in God's resting place, namely, an eternal, festive sabbath celebration' (O'Brien, *Hebrews*, 164–5). This is true but it is also true of what is expected to happen in the present time on earth through faith while awaiting Christ's return.

to follow in faith the path[32] set by Jesus the trailblazer (*archēgos*, Heb. 2.10), which eventually leads to the final rest (*katapausis*) of heaven itself[33] and God's full presence.[34] As these readers move towards this final rest (*katapausis*) the author of Hebrews assures them that while they are on this journey they can experience this rest presently by faith which the author calls the *sabbatismos*.

Sabbatismos is an infrequently used word. It is used in a textual variant in Plutarch, *On Superstition* 3 (*Mor*. 166A) and in four post-canonical texts (Justin, *Dial.* 23.3; Epiphanius, *Pan.* 30.2.2; *Martyrium Petri et Pauli* 1 and *Consitutiones Apostolicae* 2.36.2). The cognate verb *sabbatizein* means 'to celebrate the Sabbath or to rest' (Exod. 16.30; Lev. 26.34). Nouns ending with '*mos*' typically refer to the name of the action of the cognate verb, as in *katharismos* 'cleansing' from the verb *katharizo* 'to cleanse'. So, the meaning here probably means, 'celebrating the sabbath' or 'sabbath celebration', which is consistent with the meaning of the four other instances of this noun. It appears the author of Hebrews may have created[35] or used a rare word whose meaning of Sabbath celebration has three aspects.

Rest from Work

In 4.10 it says that the one who enters 'God's rest' is to rest from his or her work just as God rested from his work. It is not clear from what work believers are to rest. Lincoln suggests 'works' has a 'salvation connotation' in this context. This means that believers are to rest from their 'dead works' which are an attempt to earn this 'gift of eschatological salvation' instead of entering this rest through faith.[36] There is much merit in this position though more scrutiny is needed. The purpose of 4.10 is to explain how to enter this rest, namely by resting from their works just as God rested from his works, which does not suggest a works righteousness interpretation. So, if work refers to works of labour then the oddity in this

32. Philip Edgcumbe Hughes, *A Commentary on the Epistle to the Hebrews* (Grand Rapids: Eerdmans, 1977), 158.

33. James Thompson defines entering into God's rest as 'to follow Jesus into the heavenly world': *Hebrews*, Paideia (Grand Rapids: Baker Academic, 2008), 96.

34. Peter E. Enns, 'Creation and Re-Creation: Psalm 95 and Its Interpretation in Hebrews 3:1–4:13', *WTJ* 55 (1993): 277; David A. DeSilva, 'Entering God's Rest: Eschatology and the Socio-Rhetorical Strategy of Hebrews', *Trinity Journal* 21 (2000): 25–43 (32).

35. I am presuming that the author writing Hebrews (*c*. 65/67 CE) predates Plutarch (45–120 CE).

36. Lincoln, 'Sabbath', 213.

statement is that it does not look as if God has ever rested from his work. Jesus, in fact, when being confronted by the Jews about working on the Sabbath replies in his defence that 'My Father is always at his work to this very day, and I too am working' (Jn 5.17). This text clearly avers that after creation God continued to work sustaining creation and acting within human history.[37] So how are believers to rest from their works as God did?

To rest certainly, as Lincoln states, requires not trying to work to earn God's blessing of rest. But more than this, to rest is to participate in the person and essence of God. It means experiencing his glory and presence. Arnold may be correct when he says that this *sabbatismos* is 'rest for the soul' free from the incessant worries that cause believers to labour frantically (Mt. 6.28).[38] The difference for the people of God pre-Christ and post-Christ is that this experience is available 24/7 for those who have faith in Christ, and not just on the Sabbath. It is consistent with the experience of being 'in Christ' that Paul writes about. For believers of 'Today' there is no need to use work to supplement or fill an inner lacking or void which is common to all humanity because it is readily available and therefore for this reason one should make haste with a sense of urgency to enter this rest. It is from this position, from a place of rest in God's presence and glory that a believer lives. Making every effort to enter this rest is the true work of the believer (cf. Jn 6.29).

Joyful Celebration

The second aspect of the *sabbatismos* is the joyful celebration of experiencing this rest. In 2 Macc. 8.27 the soldiers celebrate the Sabbath because God sustained them and gave them victory in their battle against Nicanor's massive Gentile army. In *Jub.* 50.6-11 the author describes the Sabbath as a time for rest and celebration calling for eating and drinking, 'burning frankincense and bringing oblations and sacrifices before the Lord' (*Jub.* 50.10). The Sabbath is considered one of the sacred assemblies full of pomp and celebration (Lev. 23.3). The author of Hebrews is suggesting that this *sabbatismos*, like the Sabbath, is a sacred event though it is not relegated to just one day. Therefore, the believer today is to celebrate joyfully the *sabbatismos* 24/7 as the experience of the uninterrupted presence of God. In this sense, the *sabbatismos* resembles Paul's call to be joyful always in 1 Thess. 5.16.

37. (Philo, *Leg. All.* I, §5); Jean Hering, *The Epistle to the Hebrews* (London: Epworth Press, 1970), 32.

38. Clinton E. Arnold, 'Rest: What Does the New Testament Mean by a "Sabbath-Rest"?,' *Discipleship Journal* (2002): 316.

Eschatological Rest

As I have said earlier the purpose of the Sabbath was to take people's eyes off the world and set them on God above and to seek his presence. Yet the Sabbath day was a foretaste of what the prophets predicted would be a permanent experience during the messianic kingdom. In this sense the Old Testament Sabbath has always been typological of a future rest. This idea has biblical and extra-biblical support. There is a promise of heavenly rest in Rev. 14.13 for believers but for those who worship the beast there is no rest (Rev. 14.11). The author of *Barn.* 15.3-8 divides history into six 1,000-year days. The seventh day initiates the divine rest of God, when the Son comes in judgement for a thousand years. Then the eighth day comes which is the new world where believers experience complete and final rest.

This future eschatological rest is also associated with praise and worship (Rev. 11.17-18; 15.3-4). In *4 Ezra* 7, the author talks about seven orders of rest of which the seventh is rejoicing with boldness (*4 Ezra* 7.98). In *1 En.* 39 the elect ones are in a place of rest in which they are extolling the Lord incessantly with praise and blessing.

The Jews foresaw the new age or the messianic age coming fully in one moment but instead it partially came at the first Parousia of Jesus. The fullness and completion of God's kingdom will come at the second advent of Christ. In the meantime, believers are to experience this *sabbatismos* 24/7 by faith as mediated through Christ. It is only lack of faith, faithlessness and distractedness coupled with living in a sinful world that keeps believers from fully experiencing this *sabbatismos*. For full experience of the Sabbath rest, believers will have to wait until Christ returns.

Conclusion

Dr Nolland, during his significant career as a scholar, wrote an excellent commentary on Matthew. His work on Mt. 11.25-30 was the catalyst for this paper in which I have sought to examine this meaning of rest in relationship to the rest in Hebrews 4, in particular *sabbatismos*. I discovered that the rest in Mt. 11.28-29 is best viewed from an eschatological perspective, associated with the messianic age. Matthew does not specify how Jesus, the Messiah, fulfils the Sabbath law and becomes the Lord of the Sabbath, who opens the way for his disciples to experience this rest, though there are glimpses. Matthew proclaims Jesus is greater than the temple cult and that his death ripped apart the curtain to the holy of holies, thereby opening the way for all believers to the presence of God.

The author of Hebrews builds on this tradition, presenting a more thorough presentation of Jesus as the perfect high priest, with a perfect sacrifice, initiating a superior covenant, thereby showing how Jesus procures this eternal rest of Hebrews 4. The author of Hebrews is a creative writer and uses the image of a 'forerunner' to describe how Jesus went behind the curtain in the holy of holies to accomplish his work and prepare for his brothers and sisters to follow. This hope (i.e. rest), rooted firmly as an anchor for believers, requires them to enter this rest in the present by faith, and reject the disobedience and unbelief of the wilderness generation. The readers of Hebrews are exhorted with two commands, 'Watch out for any unbelieving heart that may turn away from God and his rest' and 'exhort one another to avoid apostasy', so that they will enter this present rest (*sabbatismos*), leading to the final rest of God in heaven.

16

Exalted Lord and Suffering Servant: The Response to Jesus in James and 1 Peter

Peter H. Davids

The Catholic Letters were bound together, either on a single scroll or in a codex, from the moment of their creation as a body,[1] but that does not mean that they are a unified composition or take a single perspective. That is even true for the letters of James and 1 Peter, the eponymous authors of which lived and worked together in the earliest stage of the Jesus movement in Jerusalem.[2] Even if one does not trust the Lukan account in Acts 1–15 in which first Peter and then James are the patriarchs of the Jerusalem Jesus community, Paul makes it clear that some type of relationship existed between the two in Gal. 1.18-19; 2.9; 2.12. Yet one would hardly guess that this relationship existed when one reads the two

1. The Catholic Epistles certainly existed as a body from the mid-3rd century and quite possibly a hundred years earlier. For instance, David Nienhuis, *Not By Paul Alone: The Formation of the Catholic Epistle Collection and the Christian Canon* (Waco: Baylor University Press, 2007), argues that James was written about 180 in order to introduce that canon and that James deliberately draws themes from the other documents in the Catholic Epistles. One does not need to accept his entire thesis (which involves arguing that the author deliberately made the document look 1st century) to accept his evidence that the Catholic Epistles existed *as a group* by 180.

2. For the purposes of this article we are bracketing the issue of whether the eponymous authors are or are not the actual authors of their respective letters or, if they are, in what sense they are the actual authors. That does not affect them theologically. For a discussion of the topic by this author, see the respective introductions to these letters in Peter H. Davids, *A Biblical Theology of James, Peter and Jude* (Grand Rapids: Zondervan, 2014).

letters and examines their respective responses to Jesus. The authors seem more situationally influenced than influenced by a common approach to Jesus, although both draw on the traditions about Jesus now enshrined in the Synoptic Gospels.

James

The problem with James is the paucity of clear direct references to Jesus, while at the same time the author makes significant use of Jesus traditions. On the one hand, Jesus is referenced by name only twice: Jas 1.1 and 2.1. In 1.1 James presents himself as the slave of two exalted individuals: θεοῦ καὶ κυρίου Ἰησοῦ Χριστοῦ δοῦλος. Notice that 'lord' is associated with 'Jesus the Anointed One'. In Jas 2.1 the 'brothers and sisters' are said to hold the faith or faithfulness τοῦ κυρίου ἡμῶν Ἰησοῦ Χριστοῦ τῆς δόξης. Again, 'lord' is a title of 'Jesus the Anointed One', but this time 'of glory' is added. While it is debated (and grammatically unclear) whether this genitive descriptor indicates the sphere the Lord belongs to, that of 'glory' ('Lord of Glory'), or whether this indicates his honorable status ('our glorious Lord'),[3] it is clear that the reference is to Jesus as exalted with reference to whom favouritism based on social status (i.e. wealth) is not appropriate.

To these two clear references one must add the repeated 'the Lord who comes' (τῆς παρουσίας τοῦ κυρίου) in Jas 5.7 and 8, for the other four times that this Parousia is combined with Lord in the New Testament (1 Thess. 3.13; 4.15; 5.2; 2 Thess. 2.1) all clearly refer to Jesus as the Lord who will come in something of a state visit. Thus it is not surprising that in the next verse one finds Jesus referred to as the one who is about to judge (ὁ κριτὴς πρὸ τῶν θυρῶν ἕστηκεν). The noun κύριος also occurs in Jas 1.7; 3.9; 4.10, 15; 5.4, 10, 11, 14, 15. Of these 1.7 probably refers to 'God', who is mentioned in 1.5, 1.9 refers to the Creator, the 'Lord and Father', 4.10 to 'God', who is repeatedly mentioned in the section, 4.15 could refer to either God or Jesus, 5.4 to God under the expression 'Lord Sabaoth', 5.10, 11 to God in the Hebrew Scriptures (although the Job is the Job of the *Testament of Job*, not of the canonical Job), but one suspects that 5.14 and 15 refer to Jesus due to the association of anointing the sick with oil with the similar action of the Twelve sent by Jesus in Mk 6.13. The point of this analysis of James is that he portrays Jesus as the exalted Lord of the community (indicated by the repeated – 17 times – address to the ἀδελφοί

3. A. K. M. Adam, *James: A Handbook on the Greek Text*, Baylor Handbook on the Greek NT (Waco: Baylor University Press, 2013), 24.

and the reference to ἐκκλησία in Jas 5.14) which meets in a συναγωγὴ, probably indicating a meal setting.[4]

If, then, Jesus is viewed primarily as the exalted ruler and coming judge of the community, it is natural that his instruction would be a significant guiding force in the community. This instruction would be both direction for the present and the standard of judgement in the future. The deeds of Jesus in the past are less remembered than his teaching, for the teaching is the present guidance of the community. When deeds of Jesus are alluded to they are his future judging and his present healing, especially through that actions of the elders.

Yet one immediately runs into the problem that there is only one verse in James that is a possible quotation of a Jesus saying also found in the Synoptics, Jas 5.12 (see Table 1):

Table 1

Mt. 5.34-37	*Jas 5.12*
μὴ ὀμόσαι ὅλως	μὴ ὀμνύετε
μήτε ἐν τῷ οὐρανῷ ...	μήτε τὸν οὐρανὸν
μήτε ἐν τῇ γῇ ...	μήτε τὴν γῆν
μήτε εἰς Ἱεροσόλυμα ...	
μήτε ἐν τῇ κεφαλῇ σου ...	
	μήτε ἄλλον τινὰ ὅρκον
ἔστω δὲ ὁ λόγος ὑμῶν	ἤτω δὲ ὑμῶν
ναὶ ναί, οὒ οὔ	τὸ ναὶ ναὶ καὶ τὸ οὒ οὔ
τὸ δὲ περισσὸν τούτων	ἵνα μὴ ὑπὸ κρίσιν πέσητε
ἐκ τοῦ πονηροῦ ἐστιν	

What one notices is that while the two sayings take the same position on the same topic and have significant overlap in terminology that appears in the same order, there is significant difference in the grammar and the Jacobean saying is shorter. The point is not that the shorter saying is definitely more original and the Matthaean saying more developed, whatever date one gives to the letters, or that they show that a given saying of Jesus existed in multiple forms in the oral tradition. The point is

4. This was first argued in an unpublished work of Daniel Streett that was presented to the Letters of James, Peter, and Jude section of the Society of Biblical Literature, but a similar argument was later published by Peter-Ben Smit, 'A Symposiastic Background to James?', *NTS* 58 (2012): 105–22.

twofold: first, that the closest one comes to a quotation of Jesus in James is paralleled only in Matthew (which closeness to the Matthaean form of the Jesus tradition will hold true throughout James) and second, that it is cited without attribution but in a way that anyone familiar with the Matthaean form of the Jesus tradition would recognize (as scholars have long since recognized). What this means is that the author of James is familiar with a form of the Jesus tradition that the scholarly world knows of as concretized in Matthew.[5] And it means that James, following the rhetorical conventions of his time, does not quote the tradition he knows, but rather weaves it into his own teaching in a way that would have been recognizable to his fellow believers who were familiar with that tradition. In other words, he uses the rhetorical technique of *aemulatio*, which was taught at the progymnastic level of education.[6]

What teaching of Jesus does James use?[7] The following (Table 2) is one listing of the 'passages' he may well use:

Table 2

James	*Matthew*	*Luke*	*Source*
1.2	5.11-12	6.23	Q
1.4	5.48		
1.5	7.7	11.9	Q
1.6	21.21		Mk 11.23-24
1.12	10.22		
1.17	7.11	11.13	Q

5. Naturally, this use of the Jesus tradition also shows the interest of the author in speech ethics, which comes out most strongly in Jas 3. See William R. Baker, *Personal Speech-Ethics in the Epistle of James*, WUNT 2/68 (Tübingen: J. C. B. Mohr, 1995).

6. See John Kloppenborg, 'The Reception of the Jesus Traditions in James', in *The Catholic Epistles and the Tradition*, ed. Jacques Schlosser, BETL 176 (Leuven: Leuven University Press/ Peeters, 2004), 93–141.

7. The following chart is taken from Peter H. Davids, *The Epistle of James*, NIGTC (Grand Rapids: Eerdmans, 1982), 48. The chart itself is developed from those in the commentaries of J. B. Mayor, *The Epistle of St. James* (London: Macmillan, 1910), lxxxv–lxxxviii and F. Mussner, *Der Jakobusbrief* (Freiberg: Herder, 1967), 48–50. A dissertation focusing on the criteria for and identification of these references to the Jesus tradition is presently being written in the Netherlands, but it cannot be cited until it is finished, accepted and defended.

1.20	5.22		
1.21		8.8	
1.22	7.24	6.46-47	Q
1.23	7.26	6.49	Q
2.5	5.3, 5; 11.5	6.20; 7.22	Q
2.6		18.3	
2.8	22.39-40		
2.10	5.19		
2.11	5.21-22		
2.13	5.7		
2.15	6.25		
3.12	7.16	6.44, 45	Q
3.18	5.9		
4.2	7.7		
4.3	7.7-8; 12.39		
4.4	6.24	16.13	Q
4.8	6.22		
4.9	5.4?	6.25	
4.10	23.12	14.11; 18.14	Q
4.11-12	7.1	6.37	Q
4.13-14	6.34		
4.17		12.47	
5.1		6.24-25	
5.2	6.19-20	6.37; 12.33	Q
5.6		6.37	
5.8	24.3, 27, 39		
5.9	5.22; 7.1; 24.33		5.9b = Mk 13.29
5.10	5.11-12	6.23	
5.12	5.34-37		Q
5.17		4.25	

Table 3. More General Parallels in Thought

James	*Matthew*	*Luke*	*Source*
1.9-10; 4.10	18.4; 23.12	9.40; 14.11; 22.26	
1.26–27; 2.14-26	7.21-23		
2.14-16	25.31-46		
3.1-12	12.36-37		
3.13-18	11.19		
4.17	12.47		
5.5		16.19	
5.7			Mk. 4.26-29
5.19	18.15	17.3	Q

What one notes is the following: (1) there are roughly 35 places where the Jesus tradition appears to influence James, which means about once every three verses. This does not count the possible presence of agrapha (e.g. Jas 3.18), which by definition were not part of the Gospels, but 'sound like' Jesus tradition. No other non-Gospel writing in the New Testament has so much influence from the teaching of Jesus.[8] (2) The overwhelming number of references point to the Sermon on the Mount tradition. There are two sections of the Matthaean Sermon that are missing, namely 6.1-18 (the teachings on pious duties) and 7.13-28 (the warnings that close the Matthaean Sermon). The main parts of the Sermon that are referenced via *aemulatio* are the reinterpretation of the Torah (including the antitheses), the teaching on wealth/possessions and the teaching on non-judgement. Where James picks up non-Matthaean Lukan concepts is mainly in the Lukan woes on the rich. This leads one to wonder whether the reference to the νόμον…βασιλικὸν in Jas 2.8 might not be to the Torah as interpreted by the King, i.e. 'our glorious Lord, Jesus Christ' (Jas 2.1). His Torah, then, is the Torah, which 'sets you free' (νόμου ἐλευθερίας), by which one will be judged. Obviously this can only be suggestive, not definitively proved. However, precisely in 2.1-13 James starts with a reference to an exalted ruling figure, 'Lord Jesus the Anointed One', moves on to refer to a 'kingdom which he has promised to those who love him' (an allusion to the first Beatitude), then mentions the summary commandment mentioned in Mt. 19.19; 22.39, but also in the end of the antitheses, and finally two of the specific commandments that Jesus reinterprets in the antitheses.

8. See also Dean B. Deppe, *The Sayings of Jesus in the Epistle of James* (Chelsea: Bookcrafters, 1989), and Patrick J. Hartin, *James and the Q Sayings of Jesus*, JSOTSup 47 (Sheffield: JSOT Press, 1991).

For James, then, the implied readers are Jesus' subjects or followers or apprentices. He is the exalted Lord before whose judgement seat they will stand at the end of the age. The expectation is that this could result in praise or condemnation, in honour or shame. Therefore, it is important to live according to his teaching, his Torah. And that is the part of the Jesus tradition that is picked up in this Diaspora letter.

1 Peter

1 Peter addresses a different situation from that of James. While in both letters the implied readers are undergoing what we might call low-grade persecution (thus Jas 1.2-4 is parallel to 1 Pet. 1.6-7), there are two critical differences in the assumptions made about the community. First, while in James it is the leaders of the surrounding community ('the rich') who lead largely economic persecution, in 1 Peter those addressed were once considered part of the larger community but are now treated as immigrants. From the description of the implied readers (they once lived as the Gentiles live, the traditions they had received from their ancestors were empty or pagan (1.18), etc.) they appear to be largely Gentile. When living as Gentiles they fit into the culture. But now they have been 'born again' of divine 'sperm' (1.23) they are no longer citizens of their native lands, but 'immigrants' or 'resident aliens' (e.g. 1.1 or 2.11). They have a new Father (1.17), a new 'milk' since they are newborn (2.2), and a new national identity, that of the people of God (2.9-10, which uses the language of Exod. 19.6, as well as that of Hosea). They are now a foreign people living among those who are still natives of their province of birth. The letter exhorts these readers to live according to the 'customs' of their new nationality or new family, despite the fact that there is a culture clash with their former compatriots, who slander them because of this.[9] They were once honorable in the eyes of their culture and are now viewed as shameful, dishonorable. They are treated as 'foreigners' are treated in such cultures (including how unassimilated Jews would have been treated). This is quite difficult for those who once belonged.

Second, because the followers of Jesus evangelized not just heads of families but also the members of the family, regardless of the wishes of

9. See Reinhard Feldmeier, *Der erste Brief des Petrus* (Leipzig: Evangelische Verlagsanstalt, 2005), particularly the discussion of the persecution of Christians in the introduction and the notes on the first chapter of 1 Peter. This does not come across as clearly in the English edition of the work, *The First Letter of Peter* (Waco: Baylor University Press, 2008).

the head of the family, this 'Jesus is the Messiah' form of Judaism was viewed as particularly pernicious. The head of the family might permit different cults to be adhered to by various family members, but only if those family members were also worshipping the familial deities. In fact, it was the right of the head of family to determine the worship of the family. The Jesus movement (viewed in the larger culture as a new variety of Judaism, which religion was despised in general) called its followers to the exclusive worship of the one God and of Jesus God's Anointed One. That meant rejecting, not just their former personal cults, but also the familial and civic cults. This was a dangerous undercutting of the foundations of the family and the city.

Within the group of those who belonged to families led by a pagan head of family were two particularly vulnerable groups. The one was that of household slaves (2.18-25), for they were in close contact with the head of household and the family cult (as opposed to slaves working on an agricultural estate). Furthermore, a master could punish or persecute them at will, for they were property and not persons, although he did have a financial interest in keeping them reasonably fit for service. For some masters, of course, what they viewed as the obstinacy of the slave (e.g. his persistence in the Jewish cult of the Messiah or Christ) could enrage them to the point that they forgot their financial interests. The second group was that of believing wives of pagan husbands (who would often also be head of family, although in some situations, instead of the husband, his father, uncle or brother might be the head of an extended family). Wives were generally responsible for the daily duties of the domestic cult (e.g. making the daily ritual offerings to the domestic deities, whether it be incense, food, or fire) and helping out in the larger familial and civic celebrations (such as cooking the festal meal). Women also could be abused and mistreated within the family and they could be pressured to engage in behaviour which followers of Jesus believed to be improper. If this mistreatment escalated enough, some cultures in Asia Minor might allow them to divorce their husbands (although probably at the cost of leaving their children) and some not.[10] If they were able to leave, they might have limited opportunities of where to go if their family of origin was pagan and would not want such a 'shameful woman' to return to their home.

10. Roman law did allow women to divorce their husbands, while at least in Achaia women could not divorce, much as in Jewish law women could not divorce. Rome may well be the culture of origin for 1 Peter, but many towns near the western and northern coasts of Asia Minor were Ionian Greek in origin and probably followed some form of Greek customary law.

These two conditions, then, shaped what aspects of the traditions about Jesus were relevant to 1 Peter. He talks about judgement, but basically about the judgement of pagans who will be forced to confess that the behaviour of the believers in Jesus was honourable. Unlike James, he is especially focused on the rejected Jesus and the traditions that relate to the passion.

Gerhard Maier is one of many who have outlined the contact between 1 Peter and the Jesus tradition. See Table 4 for his list.[11]

Table 4

1 Peter	*Matthew*	*Mark*	*Luke*	*John*
1.3, 23				3.3-6
1.8				15.11-15; 20.29
1.9	16.24-26			
1.10-12	13.17		24.25-27	8.56
1.15	5.48			
1.22				13.34-35; 15.12
1.23	13.18-20		8.11-15	
2.4-8		12.10-12 (Ps. 118.22)		
2.9	5.14-16			8.12
2.13-17	17.25-27	12.17	20.25; 22.15-17	
2.19-21	5.10-11; 16.24			
4.7-8	3.2; 4.1; 10.7; 13.49-51 26.41; 28.20		21.31-33	
4.8				13.34-35; 15.12
4.10			12.42-44	
4.12-16	5.11-12; 26.41		6.22-23	
5.3-5	20.20-22			13.4-6; 21.15-17
5.7	6.25-27		12.22-24	
5.8-9	24.42-44			

11. Peter H. Davids, *The First Epistle of Peter*, NICNT (Grand Rapids: Eerdmans, 1990), 27, citing Gerhard Maier, 'Jesustraditionen im 1. Petrusbrief?', in *Gospel Perspectives*. Vol. 5, *The Jesus Tradition Outside the Gospels*, ed. D. Wenham (Sheffield: Sheffield University Press, 1984), 85–128. Many commentaries have their own lists, but this one is sufficient to show the contours of the use of Jesus traditions.

What one notes first of all is that there is basically no Gospel narrative that is cited directly or via *aemulatio*. This, of course, contrasts with 2 Peter, which has its famous reference to the transfiguration (2 Pet. 1.16-18). The traditions used are basically of three types: (1) teaching material (note the multiple parallels with the Sermon tradition), (2) *testimonia* (e.g. the rejected stone saying in 2.4-8, which is in fact combined with – and probably circulated with – two passages from the prophets) and (3) references to the passion. One should comment briefly on each of these.

First, the *testimonia* are interesting in two ways. On the one hand, they illustrate 1 Peter's relatively heavy use of the Hebrew Scriptures, which contrasts with the practice of both James and 2 Peter. James may allude to the Hebrew Scriptures (as in Jas 2.19, which may well allude to the *Shema'*) or mention narratives (always in the form that they were known in Second Temple literature), but he does not quote (except in Jas 4.5, where an unknown text is cited as 'scripture'). 1 Peter does indeed quote (e.g. 1 Pet. 1.24-25; 2.6-9; 3.10-12; 4.18; 5.5), but some of these passages are also referred to by Jesus in the Gospels, so it is likely that 1 Peter thinks of them as selected by or interpreted by Jesus. That is, for him they were embedded in Jesus traditions.

Second, the teaching of Jesus is that which calls his followers to live holy lives (1 Pet. 1.15//Mt. 5.48) or that which promises reward in the coming age. When it comes to speech-ethics, 1 Peter is not concerned with those within the community as much as he is concerned with behaviour towards those outside the community. Nor does one find the same concern with wealth/the rich in 1 Peter, for while there may be deprivation, it is not by members of the community. They are, so to speak, all in the same boat.

Third, and most importantly, when it comes to the passion (1 Pet. 1.2, 19; 2.21-24; 3.18; 4.1, 13; 5.1) and by implications the resurrection (1.3, 21; 3.21), there is a focus on *imitatio Christi*. It is true that Jesus' death in 1 Peter is sacrificial (which is more Johannine than Synoptic) and redemptive, a theme found in the Synoptic Gospels on the lips of Jesus (e.g. Mk 10.45//Mt. 20.28), even if rarely, but these are almost passive – a lamb is slain and its blood is applied by a priest, not by the lamb,[12] so Jesus appears to supply the blood, but the sprinkling is done by someone else. The Passion Narrative is applied, then, in two ways. Jesus is the sacrificial victim the blood of which redeems one from one's former way of life, from one's former nationality (being redeemed from one's former way of life seems to pair with being born again into the nationality of the

12. It is true that in Heb. 10 the Anointed One is priest as well as victim, actively offering his own blood, but in 1 Peter the priestly interpretation of Jesus' actions is absent.

people of God). Jesus' passion and resurrection are also the model for the believer. This comes out very clearly in 1 Pet. 2.21-24 in which the slave is to behave in his suffering as Jesus did in the Passion Narrative. In this case it is not what is narrated in the Gospels that is critical, but what is *not* narrated, i.e. Jesus' silence in the face of abuse, apparently read in the light of his teaching in Matthew 5 and Luke 6 (indeed, in Luke 6 it is highlighted by the lack of some of what is in Matthew 5). But, as one can see in three of the passages that start this paragraph, the present experience of the passion and its results is connected to a future experience of the resurrection. While not a Synoptic Gospel theme *per se* (although it does occur in John), the resurrected and ascended Jesus draws his followers after him.

This creates another contrast with James. While both 1 Peter and James have an exalted, glorified Jesus the Anointed One, which surely draws, at least indirectly, on the exalted Son of Man sayings in the Synoptics,[13] they differ in its application. In 1 Peter this rule, which is presently cosmic (1 Pet. 3.22), is eventually revealed to those on earth (1 Pet. 1.7). However, while in James, as pointed out above, Jesus is the coming judge, in 1 Peter God appears to be the judge (1.17; 2.12;[14] 3.17). Those judged have slandered his people as lawbreakers, have rejected his designated Anointed One, but some of them are also his people now, who are being purified. One would hardly want to say that 1 Peter could not conceive of Jesus as eschatological judge, but the emphasis of his portrait is that of Jesus as exalted Son of Man,[15] with God the Father judging those who reject his designated one.[16]

Where we see 1 Peter drawing from the Synoptic tradition, then, appears to be first from the *testimonia*, the selection of which were attributed to Jesus in Synoptic narrative. These showed that far from being

13. One can hardly imagine someone familiar with the Synoptic tradition not knowing and being influenced by Mk 14.62//Mt. 26.64//Lk. 22.69 since this saying of Jesus appears in all three versions of the tradition.

14. While in Lk. 19.44 visitation from God (ἐπισκοπή) is the advent of Jesus, which should have been positive for the Jews, in other uses of the expression in biblical literature (e.g. Wis. 3.7, 13; Sir. 18.20; Isa. 23.17 LXX) the expression is used for either God's providential care or his judgement.

15. One thinks of such texts as Mk 14.62, where one has the exalted Son of Man and the coming Son of Man combined. The hidden is being revealed.

16. Of course, there are Synoptic traditions attributed to Jesus in which the Son of Man judges, with Mt. 25.31-46 being the most famous. Since 1 Peter shows affinities with Matthaean tradition, it may well be that our author knew this tradition as well. But he does not refer to it explicitly.

an isolated act of evil and vindication, the passion and resurrection of Jesus were anticipated in Hebrew prophetic literature (which included the Psalms)[17] and so were part of an ancient plan. Then he drew, second, from the ethical teaching of Jesus, chiefly from the general call to holiness and being like 'the Father'. This appears to be more a call to perseverance than a correction of problems. Third, he drew from the suffering and exaltation of the Son of Man, never citing the Son of Man sayings themselves, but drawing on the content to which they pointed. Thus the suffering of the Son of Man/Jesus has meaning as a sacrificial lamb or as a ransom.[18] It is only in this context that he dips into narrative, pointing out that Jesus lived the verbal non-violence that he taught[19] and calling on his followers, in particular slaves, to imitate his demeanour. But there are also the sayings about the exalted and coming Son of Man (as well as the narrated experience of the resurrection). These give hope, giving meaning to the ethics and reframing the suffering of the believer. As they have identified with the suffering of Jesus in being 'sprinkled' with his blood or in their being 'ransomed' from their old behaviour and even now are invited to identify with it by imitating his demeanour in their own sufferings, so they will share identification with the exalted and coming Son of Man, in particular when he will be 'revealed' by God the Father. This fits the situation of those whom 1 Peter addresses, for these implied readers, while in reality the renewed people of God, the heirs of the promises to Israel in Exod. 19.6, are being treated by the societies in which they grew up as immigrants, foreigners, even lawbreakers. To them 1 Peter

17. Technically the Psalms are part of the Writings, not the Prophets, but (1) the boundaries of the Writings was fluid in the 1st century and (2) one of the fluid boundaries was between the Writings and the Prophets. Thus Daniel is presented as one of the wise, a sage, but also as a prophet. Jesus refers to David as prophesying (speaking 'in the Spirit') in the Psalms (Mk 12.36//Mt. 22.43) as do the Twelve (Acts 1.16; 2.30; 4.25). And, of course, Jude cites *1 En.* 1.9 as a prophecy, not to mention that 'The Book of the Watchers' of *1 Enoch* lies behind not only Jude, but also 1 and 2 Peter.

18. This re-frames what could be viewed as gratuitous suffering as meaningful suffering, doing so without defining the meaning of sacrificial lamb or ransom – they remain in the world of metaphor drawn from the cult of Israel (probably the Passover, although this is not certain) and the practice of ransoming prisoners.

19. 1 Peter assumes that his readers knew enough about the Passion Narrative, at least about Jesus' silence and the lack of invective in his words from the cross, perhaps also the 'Father, forgive them…' saying (although its textual basis in Luke has issues) so as to nod when he writes about Jesus' behaviour. This would make most sense if he is also assuming that they knew about Jesus' teaching on the treatment of enemies or oppressors, e.g. in the Sermon tradition.

presents a glorified Anointed One with whom they can identify and who gives meaning to their situation, while the God whom they call Father (perhaps an allusion to Jesus' reference to God as Father and his teaching his followers to pray to God as Father), while not to be trifled with, will in the coming judgement shame those who presently shame them.

Conclusion

It is difficult to conceive of any group of followers of Jesus, even in the 1st century, among whom the narratives about and teaching of Jesus did not circulate.[20] There is, first of all, the evidence of the Letters, but there is also, second, the evidence of the Gospels themselves: if they were indeed written as Gospels, i.e. as the good news, then the narrative and teaching that they contain served as the foundation narrative for the Jesus community, just as the narrative and teaching of at least parts of the Pentateuch served as the foundation narrative for ancient Israel. It is also clear that James and 1 Peter in particular are heavily influenced by the narratives about and teaching of Jesus. Whether they knew any written Gospel or are instead influenced by oral (or partly written) traditions that would form the Gospels is, of course, a matter for debate. One can say that the closest one comes to an actual citation is Jas 5.12.

However, that being said, it is also clear that they receive and apply the Jesus tradition in a different manner, one determined by the perceived needs of their respective addressees. James perceives his addressees as, under the pressure of low-grade persecution (largely economic disadvantaging and verbal dishonouring), giving way to the pressure of human desires and sinning. His purpose statement is clear in Jas 5.19-20: he is trying to return sinners from the error of their ways. That also fits Jas 4.1-10. The trials come from the outside, but the effects are seen inside the community in economic discrimination, stinginess and verbal arguments. That shapes how he uses the Jesus tradition.

20. This includes the Pauline churches, for it is difficult to read 1 Corinthians, for instance, without assuming that Paul expects his intended readers to know both the Passion-Resurrection Narrative and significant parts of the teaching of Jesus (e.g. 1 Cor. 6–7, for starters, often pick up on teachings of Jesus). Furthermore, there are the words of institution in 1 Cor. 11, which are referred to as a tradition Paul received (and which the Corinthians should recognize), as is the Passion-Resurrection Narrative that starts 1 Cor. 15.

In James there is no reference to the passion of Jesus.[21] He is interested in the exalted Son of Man[22] who sits at the right hand of the Father. This Son of Man, the Lord, is the one who reinterpreted the Torah, and this interpretation of the Torah is binding on those who claim to be his followers. It is possible, therefore, that this Torah that gives freedom (Jas 1.25), i.e. the Royal Torah (Jas 2.8), is the Torah as interpreted by Jesus, especially since this expression is followed by a reference to a Torah passage, which passage was used by Jesus, according to the Jesus tradition (Mk 14.28-34 and parallels). He is also the coming Son of Man who will judge on the basis of ethics, as in Matthew 25. In fact, he seems to be the primary judge for James, one who 'is at the door'. All of this means that it is Jesus' ethical teaching that James finds most useful, whether in his speech-ethics of James 3 and 5.12, his economic ethics of James 2 or his ethics of trials and suffering in James 1. Thus the bulk of the echoes of Jesus that one hears are those of the Sermon tradition, although there also seem to be echoes of the testing tradition (e.g. Matthew 4). James is closer to the Matthaean tradition than any other except when it comes to pronouncing woes on the rich.

1 Peter is aimed at an audience that is perceived differently. They were once at home in their culture of birth, but due to their rebirth into the people of God they now find themselves immigrants in the lands of their physical birth. They are experiencing rejection, calumny and the like at the hands of the majority culture. For those who are particularly vulnerable, i.e. the slaves of pagan masters and the wives of pagan husbands, there is the added reality of physical abuse (although in the case of the wives it may be threatened, resulting in fear). While there are ethical exhortations aimed at the faithful, the major burden of the letter sees the threats to the community from the outside and the need of the community to re-frame their experience in terms of the Jesus narrative and their expectation of the coming Son of Man.

It is no surprise, therefore, that 1 Peter speaks about the passion, using images also found in the Jesus tradition that portray that passion as being for the advantage of Jesus' followers. He also uses the passion in an *imitatio Christi* sense so that suffering slaves can re-frame their

21. Some read Jas 5.6 as a reference to Jesus as the Righteous One killed by the rich, in which case this would be the sole fairly cryptic reference to the passion. However, Davids, *James*, 179–80, argues that this is quite likely not the meaning of this passage.

22. James, of course, does not use the term 'Son of Man', just as 1 Peter also does not. The picture of Jesus that James uses is found in the Jesus tradition in the Son of Man sayings.

experience in terms of identification with Jesus. This identification also tells them how to behave in the situation. 1 Peter is very much aware of the exalted Son of Man, but that exaltation is after his human rejection. His coming is actually the revelation of that present exaltation, not something 'new' in that sense that he did not rule before. In language that seems to echo the Johannine Jesus; Jesus is pictured as 'shepherd'. There is, then, a shepherd protecting the presently harassed flock. And, just as Jesus appointed Twelve to be with him and exercise his authority for him in the Gospels, so there are those he has appointed and gifted to exercise his authority over his community during his apparent absence. Finally, as Jesus was at pains to show the continuity of the people of God in the Hebrew Scriptures with the community he was gathering, noting that those very Scriptures indicated both his rejection and exaltation, along with his community, so 1 Peter draws on the *testimonia* attributed to Jesus in the tradition and uses them to re-frame the experience of his largely Gentile communities in terms of their identity as the regathered Israel, the people of God.

These are two letters, one a Diaspora Letter from the Patriarch in Jerusalem and one an encyclical from the Patriarch in Rome.[23] Both draw heavily on traditions about or stemming from Jesus, as well as on how those traditions developed in the ensuring years. But given the different situations of the two sets of implied readers, while they overlap in their use of the Sermon tradition and the exalted Son of Man, they select differently from the rest of the tradition according to their different needs.

23. Again, we are talking about attributed and perceived authorship, not necessarily actual authorship, which would require a much more significant discussion.

17

Jesus, the Theological Educator: Lessons in Transformational Teaching from the Gospel of Luke

Eeva John

I. *Introduction*

In a climate of stretched resources and declining church attendance, theological educators of mainstream churches – at least in the UK – are wrestling with searching questions about the nature of Christian education for ministry, and how these relate to the day-to-day teaching and learning within theological education institutions, and to the flourishing of the church they seek to serve. Yoked to the infrastructures and ideologies of higher education, there is considerable chafing: educators and church leaders rush to underscore the importance of spiritual formation and the development of dispositions in addition to the acquisition of theological understanding and ministerial skills. Educators reach for first-century words such as *paideia*, *phronesis* and *habitus* to describe the distinctiveness of an education that is about much more than the earning of academic awards or even the attainment of professional competences.[1]

1. See, e.g., Edward Farley, *Theologia: The Fragmentation and Unity of Theological Education* (Augsburg: Fortress Press, 1994); Robert Banks, *Reenvisioning Theological Education* (Grand Rapids: Eerdmans, 1999); Bonnie J. Miller-McLemore, 'Practical Theology and Pedagogy: Embodying Theological Know-How', in *For Life Abundant: Practical Theology, Theological Education and Christian Ministry*, ed. Dorothy C. Bass and Craig Dykstra (Grand Rapids: Eerdmans, 2008), 170–90.

While this pertains largely to the theological education of individuals called to ordained or other forms of authorised ministry, there is a growing recognition that not all is well when it comes to the Christian education of the laity either. Theological educators bemoan the declining levels of literacy in relation to the Bible and an often superficial embodiment of Christian discipleship among aspiring ordinands. At the same time church leaders are waking up to the effects of decades of clericalism on the whole people of God, the *laos*, especially as the church's inability to produce and maintain enough clergy to feed the one minister–one church model becomes a self-evident reality.

There are many signs of hope, however, as theological educators, church leaders and even ordinary Christians are beginning to re-imagine Christian education in response to the changing environment in which Christian educators are called to serve the church. The calling to a vocation is beginning to be seen as much more of a continuum from the vocation of the laity as the coal-face missionaries of the church to the range of ecclesially regulated forms of authorized and ordained ministries.[2] The silos of the Berlin school of theological education are beginning to be allowed to merge into one another as the importance of interdisciplinary approaches is recognized. And the emergence of practical theology with its emphasis on theological reflection, reflective practice, contextual and experiential dimensions of learning are beginning to seep into the curriculum as a whole, rather than being tacked on as a separate entity to the predominantly academic programme of studies.[3]

Beneath these hopeful undercurrents are a number of questions that theological educators – and church leaders – are asking. How are our practices of theological education for discipleship and ministry theologically informed? To what extent are they shaped and possibly even encumbered by the prevailing tenets of higher education? Does learning 'stick' and is it life changing? How well are we fusing academic content with Christian character? Do we pay sufficient attention to the bodily and affective nature of learning? Does experiential and contextual learning really permeate theology in the classroom as well as it could? How effective is the church's education for discipleship? Who should be involved in this? How are we forming educators who can facilitate learning that is transformative, life changing?

2. The General Synod of the Church of England, *GS1977 Developing Discipleship* (Archbishops' Council, 2015).

3. David Heywood, 'Educating Ministers of Character: Building Character into the Learning Process in Ministerial Formation', *Journal of Adult Theological Education* 10 (2013): 4–24.

The purpose of this essay is to bring some of these concerns to Luke's account of Jesus the teacher. It is not a systematic study of the relationship between Jesus the teacher and his disciples in the context of 1st-century Jewish practice, nor does it scrutinise or systematize Jesus' methods of teaching: others have done this.[4] Nor does it offer a hermeneutical rationale for making connections between Jesus' approach to teaching and learning and that of the 21st-century church. Rather its purpose is to draw some inspiration from the Gospel of Luke that will bring fresh insights, prompt new questions and suggest energizing challenges for the vital task of educating 21st-century Christians for discipleship and ministry within the mission of God.

But why Luke? After all, Mark is the one to describe Jesus as teacher most frequently. Luke, however, frames his Gospel as an educational endeavour: it is written so that 'Theophilus' might 'know the truth concerning the things about which you have been instructed' (Lk. 1.4). After recounting Jesus' baptism, Luke asserts that 'Jesus began his work'. Luke is almost emphatic in describing this work as that of teaching: after his testing in the wilderness 'he began to teach in their synagogues and was praised by everyone'. Furthermore, Luke begins his sequel, the book of Acts, by reminding Theophilus that the first book was 'about all that Jesus did and taught'. Indeed, the very last verse of Acts has Paul 'proclaiming the kingdom of God and teaching about the Lord Jesus Christ with all boldness and without hindrance'. The purpose of the Gospel was to educate, it tells of Jesus the educator, and its sequel finishes with an educational mandate as exemplified by Paul.

II. *Integrity: Life-infused Teaching*

Luke describes Jesus' first teaching session as being in the synagogue in Nazareth (Lk. 4.16), and then carrying out what sounds like a teaching tour in the 'synagogues of Judea' (Lk. 4.44). Apart from two further occurrences (Lk. 6.6 and 13.10), Luke makes it clear that although Jesus saw the synagogue as a regular teaching venue, he did not confine his teaching ministry to the synagogue. He taught the crowds from a boat on Lake Gennesaret (Lk. 5.3) and in a house (Lk. 5.17-19). He taught

4. See, e.g., Herman Horne, *Jesus the Teacher: Examining His Expertise in Education*, rev. and updated Angus M. Gunn (Grand Rapids: Kregel Publications, 1998); Samuel Byrskog, *Jesus the Only Teacher: Didactic Authority and Transmission in Ancient Israel, Ancient Judaism and the Matthean Community* (Stockholm: Almqvist & Wiksell International, 1994).

outdoors 'in a level place' (Lk. 6.17), in the home of Martha, Mary and Lazarus (Lk. 10.39), while dining in the homes of Pharisees (Lk. 11.37-52; 14.1) and in towns and villages 'on his way to Jerusalem' (Lk. 13.22). He taught the crowds that followed him while he was travelling (Lk. 14.25) and, for many consecutive days, it seems, in the temple in Jerusalem (Lk. 19.47; 20.1; 21.37). He taught his disciples in the intimacy of the upper room before facing the events leading to his crucifixion (Luke 22) and, risen and incognito, on the Emmaus road and in the inn.

While Jesus seemed to see the synagogue as the natural 'classroom' for teaching, Luke depicts Jesus as teaching wherever there is a demand or an opportunity. His vocation as an educator was, it seems, a 24/7 occupation. Most forms of formal theological education in Britain involve at least some element of teaching and learning in a residential context and therefore seem to wish to model such a holistic approach. Indeed, as the church ponders how best to disburse its limited resources for formal theological education, residential colleges make much of the benefit of theological training and formation in such a residential setting. Sharing meals, daily worship, leisure time – as well as teaching and learning – are assumed to be deeply formational and a means of effecting the dispositional transformation that is the ultimate goal of ministerial training.[5] In the pressurized and highly regulated environment of having to 'deliver' higher education that is packaged in the shape of modules or courses, however, I wonder if the aspiration to offer 'whole life' teaching and learning is not as realized as it might be in residential learning communities. Theological educators are consumed by the demands that higher education 'quality assurance' systems make on teaching, learning and assessment – not to mention the committees and examination boards that make large claims on time and energy. Add to all this an underlying *zeitgeist* of individualism and professionalism, and it is no wonder that theological educators struggle to give of themselves as teachers in the way that Jesus appeared to do. In fact, it may well be that such self-giving is more possible in part-residential programmes, where students and teachers gather for weekends or weeks at a time away from 'the institution', and therefore during which teachers are more able to immerse themselves in the life of the learning community.[6]

5. See this argued, e.g., in Paul R. House, *Bonhoeffer's Seminary Vision: A Case for Costly Discipleship and Life Together* (Wheaton: Crossway, 2015).

6. Ian McIntosh, 'Formation in the Margins: The Holy Spirit and Living with Transitions in Part-Residential Theological Education', *Journal of Adult Theological Education* 11 (2014): 139–49.

Jesus' approach to teaching suggests that the calling of a theological educator for ministry and discipleship is a calling to a shared life with learners beyond the classroom. It suggests that the teacher has the physical availability and the mental, emotional and spiritual capacity to be alert to learning opportunities in the everyday places of living: around a meal table, in intimate conversations, among crowds and when on the move.

III. *Authority: Performative Teaching*

Practical theologians make much of the need for reflective practice in ministerial training.[7] Typically, students undertake placements where they both observe and engage in ministerial tasks and experiences. They record these in learning journals and, back in the classroom, reflect on their own practice or that of those they have been observing. The missions of the twelve and of the seventy, and the feeding of the five thousand, seem to approximate such an approach to teaching and learning. The students practise and then reflect and learn. But more frequently, Jesus appears to operate back to front and inside out: he teaches and then he practises. Luke repeatedly recounts how Jesus' teaching is often interrupted by or concludes with an act of healing, rebuking demons or absolving an individual of his sins, usually in response to needs presented to him while he was teaching. In the synagogue at Capernaum, for example, Jesus is accosted by, and liberates, a man with an unclean spirit (Lk. 4.33-34). The friends who lowered the paralysed man through the roof of a house did so while Jesus was teaching. Jesus appears to incorporate this interruption into his teaching as he performs both healing and absolution.

Early in the Gospel, Luke recounts that such a pattern of expectation had been set up that the crowds came 'to hear him and to be healed of their diseases; and those who were troubled with unclean spirits were cured'. There is no indication that Jesus' performative acts were in any way an attempt to validate his teaching, since Luke emphasizes how the hearers were astounded by the authority of Jesus' teaching (Lk. 4.32) and were 'spellbound by what they heard' (Lk. 19.48). It is impossible to know whether the content of Jesus' teaching on those occasions related in any way to his actions. What is clear, is that it is not only the disciples who are sent to 'practise', as in the sending of the twelve and of the seventy, but also the teacher who supplements his teaching by practising in the

7. Laurie Green, *Let's Do Theology: Resources for Contextual Theology* (repr., London: Bloomsbury, 2012).

disciples' presence. The authoritative nature of Jesus' teaching flows into authoritative action with a spontaneous inevitability rather than a rehearsed intentionality.

The classrooms of today's theological educators and their students seem to be a far cry from the varied situations and contexts in which Jesus both taught and healed. Nevertheless Jesus performed his healing actions even in the 'classroom' situation of his day, namely the synagogue. So at the very least it would suggest that authoritative teaching – namely teaching that evokes a transformative response – is accompanied by performative acts on the part of the teacher. Perhaps such an approach is more easily translated into an apprenticeship model of learning, as in a curacy or a lay internship, where the student has many opportunities to observe her supervisor at work, and where teaching and learning take place more publicly than in a classroom, the doors of which are not generally open to bystanders wanting to be ministered to.[8] Perhaps the challenge is for 'classroom teachers' to spend time with their students outside the classroom in active ministry, breaking down the artificial division that is often operative between educators and practitioners. Even in situations and contexts where the teacher is also a practitioner as part of their 'day job', the practices of teaching and ministry are separate. In some – but not all – models of context-based training, both the 'educator' from the theological institution and the context 'supervisor' (usually the minister or vicar of the placement church) are actively engaged in the life of the context church together with the students, as well as in the classroom: a hopeful move towards more transformative learning as student and teacher alike 'perform' in each other's presence.[9]

IV. *Discernment: Inquisitive Teaching*

A prevailing tension among theological educators is the concern to impart sufficient subject content at an appropriate depth while teaching in a way that encourages critical thought, inquisitiveness and a desire to learn more. Educators ply students with armloads of resources to read before and after a class, while students are often more intent on acquiring handouts and

8. The practice of supervision is key to this form of education and is described in Michael Paterson and Jessica Rose, eds, *Enriching Ministry: Pastoral Supervision in Practice* (London: SCM Press, 2014), and in Jane Leach and Michael Patterson, *Pastoral Supervision: A Handbook* (London: SCM Press, 2010).

9. E. John, R. Barden and M. Volland, *Context Based Learning for Discipleship and Ministry: The PC^3 Approach* (Cambridge: Grove Books, 2017).

PowerPoints than engaging with the questions raised by the subject matter there and then in the classroom. Higher education ideology insists that teachers teach to pre-determined 'learning outcomes' and students duly demonstrate they have achieved them by completing carefully designed assessment tasks. Little is left to chance and spontaneous detours are to be discouraged.

Luke is the only one of the Gospel writers to tell us about his boyhood educational experience in the temple. The anxiety-ridden Mary and Joseph find him 'sitting among the teachers, listening to them and asking them questions' (Lk. 2.46). When Jesus begins his adult work of teaching, questions continue to play an important and varied part. He uses questions to arouse interest and to clarify the purpose of his teachings. By punctuating his teaching discourses with questions, Jesus elicits active and memorable engagement with his listeners.

Jesus often frames his parables within an opening question that indicates what he wants his hearers to understand: 'What is the kingdom of God like?' is the question Jesus asks and answers with the parables of the Mustard Seed and the Yeast (Lk. 13.18-21). Still other parables – such as the parables of the Lost Sheep and the Lost Coin – pose a question that immediately arouses the interest of the listeners as they pertain to an experience with which they readily identify.

Luke's account of Jesus' teaching is often a series of miniature parables in the form of a question. The discourses on not worrying (Lk. 12.22-34) and on the cost of discipleship (Lk. 14.25-33) are good examples of this approach. The concluding assertions, almost proverbial in quality, are all the more powerful as a result of this shower of questions and answers.

On a number of occasions Jesus responds to questions from 'the audience' by recounting a parable which itself often begins and concludes with a question. The parable of the Rich Fool (Lk. 12.13-21), for example, is Jesus' response to a family quarrel about inheritance, whereas the parable of the Narrow Door (Lk. 13.22-30) answers a listener's question about whether only a few will be saved.

Luke also records Jesus as perceiving the unspoken questions on people's minds and responding to these, often with a question. Jesus reads the Pharisees' minds, for example, and catches them off guard as he responds to their *sotto voce* grumbling. After forgiving the paralytic, Luke recounts: 'When Jesus perceived their questionings, he answered them, "Why do you raise such questions in your hearts?"' (Lk. 5.22). The parables of the Lost Sheep and the Lost Coin are prompted by the Pharisees' grumbling about the company Jesus kept (Lk. 15.2). Jesus' response often takes the form of a question that reveals their motives, thereby startling the Pharisees into silence and amazing the other onlookers. The disciples, too, are sometimes subjected to Jesus' disarming ability to discern their inner thoughts, as in the question about which one of them was the greatest (Lk. 9.46-48).

When Jesus' teaching touches the central truth about his identity Jesus leaves the questions for his hearers to answer for themselves. Thus, the disciples are asked, 'Who do you say that I am?' (Lk. 9.20) and the Sadducees are given a riddle-like question about David's son (Lk. 20.41-44). Some questions, it seems, are best left for learners to work out for themselves.

Contemporary teaching and learning is often framed in propositional statements, such as the learning outcomes in higher education frameworks mentioned at the beginning of this section.[10] Luke's account of Jesus' inquisitive approach to teaching that begins, ends and is shot through with questions is a salutary reminder that teaching and learning is about creating curiosity and addressing the real – perhaps even unspoken – questions that students have about a subject. What would it look like if aims and learning outcomes were conveyed as a series of questions that related to students' lives and God's mission in today's church? How could we create a classroom culture that not only allows but encourages interruptions and questions that go beyond checking understanding? What if teaching preparation involved spending time discerning the real questions that students have about a subject? Might a more inquisitive approach to teaching and learning have a longer 'shelf-life' in the memory of the students? Might tackling students' 'real' questions about a subject be transformative as well as intellectually illuminating?

V. *Attentiveness: Relevant Teaching*

We have seen how Jesus allows requests for healing or questions to shape his approach to teaching. On several occasions, it is Jesus himself who makes an observation and uses it as a prompt to embark on a particular discourse. 'When he noticed how the guests chose the places of honour, he told them a parable' (Lk. 14.7). He was unafraid to challenge self-righteous behaviour (Lk. 18.9) with a parable and the action of blessing children; he noticed how the rich and the poor gave gifts into the temple

10. For a theological defence of learning outcomes, see Clive Marsh, ' "Learning Outcome" as a Theological Concept: Skills, Competences, and Personal Development in Theological Education', *Journal of Adult Theological Education* 11 (2014): 110–22.

treasury (Lk. 21.1-4). In today's pedagogical language we would describe Jesus' teaching as being contextual and theologically reflective. Jesus designs his curriculum not only according to the questions he perceives are on the minds of his hearers, as we saw in the previous section, but according to observed behaviours among his hearers or in their immediate surroundings and culture. He notices and dares to comment, running the risk of offending his hearers.

This aspect of Jesus' teaching points to the challenge of teaching both contextually and critically, daring to ask questions about the culture around us, including the students in front of us, and being prepared to reflect theologically even when there may be obvious implications for learners' life choices and behaviours. This is learning that 'sticks' and has consequences. It goes against the individualistic and objectified grain of contemporary higher education ideology.

VI. *Imagination: Memorable Teaching*

Theological education today takes place in an ocean of accessible resources unimaginable in previous decades. Furthermore, ministerial and discipleship teaching and learning programmes take place over months and years of sustained teaching and learning. Although the disciples were with Jesus for three years, they had neither the capacity nor the resources to 'store' Jesus' teaching in the way that today's ministerial students can – by lining their bookshelves and filling their electronic filing systems, or even keeping recordings of the teaching sessions. Furthermore, Jesus' vocation as a peripatetic teacher meant that he had just one opportunity to teach a crowd in a particular place before moving on.

Could it be that today's students can lull themselves into a false sense of learning, by relying on being able to turn to their resources when they didn't 'get' a particular teaching point or when, only a matter of weeks later, they have forgotten the content of a teaching session? According to Meyers and Jones, 'Research has shown that learners retain in six weeks perhaps 5 per cent of what is learned through traditional teaching strategies (lecture, question and answer), and in two years the recall is inconsequential'.[11]

11. Perry Shaw, *Transforming Theological Education: A Practical Handbook for Integrative Learning* (Carlisle: Langham Global Library, 2014), 182, quoting C. Meyers and T. Jones, *Promoting Active Learning: Strategies for the College Classroom* (San Francisco: Jossey Bass, 1993).

Clearly Jesus' teaching was memorable, as evidenced by the Gospels themselves, and it was transformative, as testified by the existence of the worldwide Christian church today. All this without the aid of books, PowerPoints or virtual learning platforms. I am not suggesting that we dispense with the rich resources that two thousand years of scholarship and reflection offer, or ignore the role of the Holy Spirit in memory and transformation, but that we take note of some of Jesus' pedagogical strategies to help make teaching and learning more memorable and transformative.

Undoubtedly influenced by the teaching methods of contemporary Judaism, Jesus' imaginative and prolific use of story as a key teaching tool is perhaps the first strategy that comes to mind. Drawing on familiar everyday experiences and employing humour and hyperbole, Jesus' teaching must have been entertaining as well as instructive. Some parables were lengthy narratives with all the components of a good storyline. Others were one-line metaphors. All conjured up images rather than words and aroused emotion as well as reason.

However, the parables often had a riddle-like quality which meant that even the disciples struggled to get the point (Lk. 8.9-10) at times. The parables were not designed to spoon-feed the audience with propositional truth statements, but left the hearers with a puzzle to work on, with unanswered questions and searching for meaning. It is harder to let go of an unsolved mystery and the effort of solving it deepens the experience of learning. Leaving students with unanswered questions, at least for a time, may be a means of enabling deeper, more transformative learning to take place.

Jesus also used imaginative actions to reify his teaching. When calling the disciples, Luke alone tells the story of Jesus asking Simon Peter to put his nets down on the other side of the boat, making the call to become 'fishers of people' an unforgettable one. Jesus taught about the nature of greatness by drawing a child to himself (Lk. 9.46-48), and revealed his identity in the breaking of bread (Lk. 24.30). Jesus understood the power of physical acts – as opposed to mere words or even images – to make a point that was life-changing, not just mind-changing.

It would appear that Jesus was not only able to think on his feet, but to imagine on his feet. When teaching engages learners' imaginations, learning takes on emotional, spiritual as well as intellectual dimensions. New connections are made and new possibilities are opened up. However, preparing imaginative approaches to teaching is time-consuming and creative delivery involves taking risks as students' preconceptions about what constitutes teaching and learning is challenged, and their response is not guaranteed. Furthermore, classrooms are often not configured in a way that makes creative approaches to teaching easy. Nevertheless, the reward of facilitating learning that is memorable and even transformative is well worth the effort and seems, in some small way, to mimic Jesus, whose teaching had his hearers 'spellbound' (Lk. 19.47).

VII. *Patience: Prayerful Teaching*

A central tenet of higher education systems is the need to assess whether learning has taken place. At the end of a course, students complete specific assessment tasks that are designed to test whether and to what extent the requisite knowledge and skills of a particular subject have been acquired. Theological education that is framed within university awards must comply with such an approach, while recognizing that acquiring knowledge and skills is only a part of the goal of discipleship or ministerial training: developing Christ-like dispositions, virtues, character and habits forms the backdrop of the whole learning experience, without which, it is of limited value. However, attempts to capture whether this 'deeper' level of transformation is taking place are far from straightforward, even though this kind of transformation is by far the more significant. As a result, the effort and energy of students and teachers alike are focused on the more formal and quantifiable assessment of knowledge and skills.

Jesus' itinerant teaching of the crowds that tenaciously surrounded him did not give him the opportunity to 'assess' whether his teaching had been effective, nor did he seem to be concerned to find out. As in his own parable of the Sower, Jesus seemed more preoccupied with exposing as many people and places as possible to his teaching than ensuring that the crowds had understood his message: 'And the crowds were looking for him; and when they reached him, they wanted to prevent him from leaving them. But he said to them, "I must proclaim the good news of the kingdom of God to other cities also; for I was sent for this purpose"' (Lk. 4.42b-44). It could be argued that Jesus considered himself to be preaching rather than teaching – although Luke describes Jesus as teaching, telling, proclaiming and saying seemingly interchangeably.

Jesus' attitude to the disciples is somewhat different. He explains the parable of the Sower to them, asserting that to them 'has been given to know the secrets of the kingdom' (Lk. 8.10). He rejoices over the successful mission of the seventy and declares the disciples to be blessed 'to see what you see […] and to hear what you hear' (Lk. 10.23-24). On two occasions Jesus draws the disciples to one side and seems to want to find out what they have understood. In the first instance, after spending time in prayer, Jesus asks the disciples, ‘Who do you say that I am?’, eliciting Peter’s declaration of him as the Messiah (Lk. 9.18-20). In the second incident, Jesus impresses upon the disciples the need for him to suffer, be killed and to rise again (Lk. 18.31-34), but Luke reports that the disciples neither understood nor grasped what Jesus meant – which must have been painful for Jesus. It is not until the two disciples are taught by the risen Christ on the road to Emmaus that true, life-changing learning took place.

The learning journey of these first disciples was, of course, unique and not directly transferable to the training of disciples and ministers of today. However, even with these first disciples, Jesus seemed to exercise a patient trust in his Father that as events unfurled, the disciples would indeed learn what they needed to ‘know’ in order to become missionaries of the gospel. In the same way, perhaps theological educators for ministry and mission are called to tread a narrow pedagogical path that balances patient trust in God with periodic ‘touchstone’ questions prayerfully timed and articulated in a way that ensures students focus their efforts – not on assessments and academic achievements – but on the deeper learning of ‘the Way’ that embraces following Jesus to the cross in the power of his resurrection.

VIII. *Concluding Thoughts*

A theological educator who seeks to imitate Jesus as teacher embarks on a high calling. Luke’s account of Jesus the teacher suggests that it is a call on the whole of a teacher’s life. It calls for a vulnerability that is authoritative as the teacher not only teaches but ministers alongside her students. It invites the teacher to model inquisitiveness: to ask questions, to discern unspoken questions and to stimulate a deep curiosity about God. It seeks to be deeply attentive to the student and to the realities of the culture and context in which learning is taking place. It urges teachers to take risks and use their imagination to inspire deep, transformative learning. And it is a call to prayerful, trusting patience in the God who alone brings about transformation in the lives of his disciples, in the life of the church and, through them, in his world.

18

Lives that Speak: ἡ λογικὴ λατρεία in Romans 12.1

Eckhard J. Schnabel

Context

Paul begins the fourth and final section of his description of the justification of sinners through God's salvific revelation in Jesus Christ with a statement of the fundamental reality that is to characterize the everyday being and behaviour of the believers in Jesus, focused on the metaphor of self-sacrifice. As Jewish and Gentile believers in Jesus have experienced the mercies of God, accorded to them in Jesus' atoning death and resurrection when they were sinners, they will, they shall and they can worship God in the context of everyday life in a manner that reflects the fact that they are not controlled by the values and standards of society but by the will of God which they fulfil as people who are being renewed in their thinking in the midst of the realities of everyday living (Rom. 12.1-2). These two verses have been described as formulating the main theme of 2.1–15.13,[1] as introduction,[2] summary,[3] heading,[4]

1. Ernst Käsemann, *Commentary on Romans* (Grand Rapids: Eerdmans, 1980), 326; Romano Penna, *Lettera ai Romani*, Scritti delle origini cristiane 6 (Bologna: Dehoniane, 2010), 807.

2. C. E. B. Cranfield, *The Epistle to the Romans*, ICC (Edinburgh: T. & T. Clark, 1975–79), 2:595.

3. James D. G. Dunn, *Romans*, 2 vols, WBC 38 (Dallas: Word Books, 1988), 707; Anton Grabner-Haider, *Paraklese und Eschatologie bei Paulus. Mensch und Welt im Anspruch der Zukunft Gottes*, NTA 4 (Münster: Aschendorff, 1968), 116–17.

4. Otto Michel, *Der Brief an die Römer*, 5th edn, KEK IV (Göttingen: Vandenhoeck & Ruprecht, 1978), 365; Ulrich Wilckens, *Der Brief an die Römer*, EKK 6/1–3 (Neukirchen-Vluyn: Neukirchener Verlag; Einsiedeln: Benzinger Verlag, 1978–82), 3:1.

or a combination of 'basic rule' and 'heading'.[5] The connections between 12.1-2 and Paul's exposition of the gospel in chs 1–11 are significant: Paul describes in 12.1–15.13 the ethos of the believers in Jesus in the historical, theological and christological context of the gospel.[6]

Paul exhorts (παρακαλῶ) the believers in Jesus, who are brothers (ἀδελφοί) as adopted children in God's family (cf. 8.14-17), to offer their bodies to God as sacrifice (παραστῆσαι τὰ σώματα ὑμῶν θυσίαν). The metaphor of 'sacrifice' means, among other connotations, that their bodies do not belong to themselves – they belong to God, which means that the actions that they carry out with their bodies are determined by the new life which consists in the newness of God's Spirit who shapes their daily lives (θυσίαν ζῶσαν, 6.4; 7.6), by the holiness of the righteousness that God has granted them (θυσίαν ἁγίαν; cf. 6.19, 22) and by personal and communal correspondence to God's expectations as they have become obedient from the heart and as they have set their mind not on the flesh but on God's Spirit (θυσίαν εὐάρεστον; cf. 6.17; 8.7-9).

The use of the term 'sacrifice' as a metaphor that describes not what happens in the temple in Jerusalem but in the everyday lives of Jewish and Gentile believers in the city of Rome underscores the significance of 3.25: the 'holy of holies' where God revealed his atoning presence has been replaced by God's atoning revelation in Jesus' death who, as the Crucified and Risen One, mediates the salvation of sinners, access to God and the life of God's people who embody in their daily existence the life, the holiness and the will of God (3.20–8.39).

The appositional phrase ἡ λογικὴ λατρεία ὑμῶν comments on the believers' presentation of their bodies as sacrifice. The term λατρεία, generally translated in English versions as 'worship' (AV, KJV, NET Bible translate 'service', NASB 'service of worship'), is used in literary and documentary texts in the sense of 'service (for wages), work' by order of a superior, then 'labour, effort', as well as cultic 'service' in the sense of the 'veneration' or 'worship' of the gods.[7] Paul uses the term λατρεία here to describe the behaviour of the believers in Jesus in their

5. Wolfgang Schrage, *Die konkreten Einzelgebote in der paulinischen Paränese. Ein Beitrag zur neutestamentlichen Ethik* (Gütersloh: Mohn, 1961), 124.

6. Cf. Jürg Buchegger, *Erneuerung des Menschen. Exegetische Studien zu Paulus*, TANZ 40 (Tübingen: Francke, 2003), 144–8.

7. Cf. H. Strathmann, 'λατρεύω, λατρεία', *TDNT* 4:58–65; H. Balz, 'λατρεύω, λατρεία', *EDNT* 2:cols 344–5. Paul uses the noun λατρεία in Rom. 9.4; 12.1, the verb λατρεύω in Rom. 1.9 (service for the gospel); 1.25 (pagan veneration of deities); Phil. 3.3; 2 Tim. 1.3; cf. Acts 24.14; 26.7; 27.23.

everyday lives which they are to surrender to God. Believers in Jesus serve and worship God not only in their regular assemblies in which they pray to God and read and study God's word, but also, and foundationally, in their everyday actions.

Translations of λογικός

The interpretation of the adjective λογικός in Rom. 12.1 is not without difficulties, as a survey of the standard translations shows. We find 'intelligent' (Phillips), 'by mind and heart' (NEB), 'proper' (TNIV), 'reasonable' (AV, KJV, NET), 'spiritual' (ESV, Moffat, NASB, NCV, NIV 1984, NRSV, RSV), 'true' (GNB; cf. NLT), 'true and proper' (NIV 2011) and 'worthy' (JB). Essentially the same range of glosses is found in the commentaries: 'logical',[8] 'rational' or 'reasonable',[9] 'spiritual',[10]

8. Paul J. Achtemeier, *Romans*, Interpretation: A Bible Commentary for Teaching and Preaching (Louisville: Westminster John Knox Press, 2010), 195; Stanley E. Porter, *The Letter to the Romans: A Linguistic and Literary Commentary*, New Testament Monographs 37 (Sheffield: Sheffield Phoenix Press, 2015), 231 ('logical and reasonable', 'logical or reasonable').

9. Joseph A. Fitzmyer, *Romans*, AB 33 (New York: Doubleday, 1993), 637, 640; Brendan Byrne, *Romans*, SP 6 (Collegeville: Liturgical Press, 1996), 362; Thomas R. Schreiner, *Romans*, BECNT 6 (Grand Rapids: Baker, 1998), 642, 645; Charles H. Talbert, *Romans*, Smyth and Helwys Bible Commentary (Macon: Smyth & Helwys, 2002), 283 (285: 'true worship'); Robert Jewett, *Romans*, Hermeneia (Minneapolis: Fortress, 2007), 724; Richard N. Longenecker, *The Epistle to the Romans*, NIGTC (Grand Rapids: Eerdmans, 2016), 921. Cf. Hans Wenschkewitz, *Die Spiritualisierung der Kultusbegriffe Tempel, Priester und Opfer im Neuen Testament*, Angelos Beiheft 4 (Leipzig: E. Pfeiffer, 1932), 127; Georg Klinzing, *Die Umdeutung des Kultus in der Qumrangemeinde und im Neuen Testament*, SUNT 7 (Göttingen: Vandenhoeck & Ruprecht, 1971), 216–17; Franz-Josef Ortkemper, *Leben aus dem Glauben. Christliche Grundhaltungen nach Römer 12–13*, NTAbh 14 (Münster: Aschendorff, 1980), 27; George H. van Kooten, *Paul's Anthropology in Context: The Image of God, Assimilation to God, and Tripartite Man in Ancient Judaism, Ancient Philosophy and Early Christianity*, WUNT 232 (Tübingen: Mohr Siebeck, 2008), 389–90; idem, 'Man as God's Spiritual or Physical Image? Theomorphic Ethics versus Numinous Ethics and Anthropomorphic Aesthetics in Early Judaism, Ancient Philosophy, and the New Testament', in *Anthropologie und Ethik im Frühjudentum und im Neuen Testament. Wechselseitige Wahrnehmungen*, ed. M. Konradt and E. Schläpfer; WUNT 322 (Tübingen: Mohr Siebeck, 2014), 99–138 (129–31).

10. John Murray, *The Epistle to the Romans* (1959/1965; repr., NICNT; Grand Rapids: Eerdmans, 1977), 2:112 ('spiritual…Reasonable or rational is a more literal rendering'); Matthew Black, *Romans*, 2nd edn (1973; repr., NCB Commentary;

'thoughtful',[11] 'true',[12] or 'understanding'.[13] The suggested translations often morph into each other, for example from 'rational' to 'reasonable' or from 'spiritual' to 'true', generally without explanation.[14] W. Schmithals goes so far as to assert that Paul uses the phrase λογικὴ λατρεία without assuming a particular meaning.[15]

The Stoic Polemic against Religious Cult Practice and 'Reasonable' Worship

Most scholars think that Paul took over the concept of 'rational', 'reasonable' or 'true' worship from the polemic of Stoic popular philosophy

Grand Rapids: Eerdmans; London: Marshall, Morgan & Scott, 1989), 167; C. K. Barrett, *The Epistle to the Romans* (1957/1962; repr., BNTC; London: Black, 1971), 231; F. F. Bruce, *Romans*, rev. edn, TNTC (1963; repr., Leicester: InterVarsity Press, 1985), 226; Dunn, *Romans*, 707, 711–12; Leon Morris, *The Epistle to the Romans* (Grand Rapids: Eerdmans; Leicester: InterVarsity Press, 1988), 434; James R. Edwards, *Romans*, New International Biblical Commentary 6 (Peabody, MA: Hendrickson, 1992), 283–4; Frank J. Matera, *Romans*, Paideia (Grand Rapids: Baker Academic, 2010), 286–7. Cf. Wolfram Strack, *Kultische Terminologie in ekklesiologischen Kontexten in den Briefen des Paulus*, BBB 92 (Weinheim: Beltz Athenäum, 1994), 297–8: λογικὴ λατρεία has the sense of πνευματικός; Hanna Stettler, *Heiligung bei Paulus. Ein Beitrag aus biblisch-theologischer Sicht*, WUNT 2/368 (Tübingen: Mohr Siebeck, 2014), 465 ('geistgewirkte[r] Gottesdienst').

11. Colin G. Kruse, *Paul's Letter to the Romans*, PNTC (Grand Rapids: Eerdmans, 2012), 463 ('true and proper').

12. Douglas J. Moo, *The Epistle to the Romans*, NICNT (Grand Rapids: Eerdmans, 1996), 753 combines the meanings 'spiritual' in the sense of 'inner' and 'spiritual' in the sense of 'rational' (752).

13. Cranfield, *Romans*, 595, 603–4 ('intelligent understanding').

14. William Sanday and Arthur Cayley Headlam, *A Critical and Exegetical Commentary on the Epistle to the Romans*, 5th edn, ICC (1902; repr., Edinburgh: T. & T. Clark, 1964), 353: 'a service to God such as befits the reason (λόγος), i.e., a spiritual sacrifice and not the offering of an irrational animal'; N. T. Wright, 'The Letter to the Romans', in *The New Interpreter's Bible*, Vol. 10 (Nashville: Abingdon Press, 2002), 393–770 (705, 'the thing that *thinking* creatures ought to recognize as appropriate', emphasis Wright); Grant R. Osborne, *Romans*, IVP New Testament Commentary 6 (Downers Grove: InterVarsity Press, 2004), 320–1 (who combines 'logical or reasonable', 'rational', 'spiritual' and 'understanding'); Ben Witherington and Darlene Hyatt, *Paul's Letter to the Romans: A Socio-Rhetorical Commentary* (Grand Rapids: Eerdmans, 2004), 285 ('reasonable' or 'logical').

15. Walter Schmithals, *Der Römerbrief. Ein Kommentar* (Gütersloh: Mohn, 1988), 429 ('ohne mit ihr eine bestimmte Deutung zu verbinden').

against the superstition of the sacrificial cults which were 'unreasonable' since the deity was worshipped with material gifts rather than, as befits the deity's nature, with the mind (or reason).[16] Epictetus's statement in *Diatr.* 1.16.20-21 is often quoted in support of this interpretation: 'If, indeed, I were a nightingale, I should be singing as a nightingale; if a swan, as a swan. But as it is, I am a rational (λογικός εἰμι) being, therefore I must be singing hymns of praise to God. This is my task; I do it, and will not desert this post, as long as it may be given me to fill it; and I exhort you to join me in this same song' (trans. W. A. Oldfather, LCL). In Stoic popular philosophy, nature was described as λόγος which was also the nature of the divine. Diogenes Laertius writes:

> And this is why the end may be defined as life in accordance with nature, or, in other words, in accordance with our own human nature as well as that of the universe, a life in which we refrain from every action forbidden by the law common to all things, that is to say, the right reason (ὁ ὀρθὸς λόγος) which pervades all things, and is identical with this Zeus, lord and ruler of all that is. And this very thing constitutes the virtue of the happy man and the smooth current of life, when all actions promote the harmony of the spirit dwelling in the individual man with the will of him who orders the universe (7.88; trans. R. D. Hicks, LCL).

The λόγος is the power of reason which characterizes human beings as 'rational beings', as Epictetus (2.9.2-3) writes:

16. G. Kittel, 'λογικός', *TDNT* 4:141–3; H.-W. Bartsch, 'λογικός', *EDNT*, 2:col. 355; Wenschkewitz, *Die Spiritualisierung der Kultusbegriffe Tempel, Priester und Opfer im Neuen Testament*, 49–66; Hans Lietzmann, *An die Römer*, 5th edn, HNT 8 (Tübingen: Mohr Siebeck, 1971 [orig. 1906]), 108–9; Käsemann, *Romans*, 328–9; Cranfield, *Romans*, 602–3; Michel, *Römer*, 370; Wilckens, *Römer*, 3:4–6; Eduard Lohse, *Der Brief an die Römer*, KEK IV (Göttingen: Vandenhoeck & Ruprecht, 2003), 336; Lohse, *Römer*, 336; Christopher Evans, 'Romans 12.1–2: The True Worship', in *Dimensions de la vie chrétienne (Rm 12–13)*, ed. L. De Lorenzi, Sezione biblico-ecumenica 4 (Rome: St Paul's Abbey, 1979), 7–33 (17–21); Folker Siegert, 'Die Synagoge und das Postulat eines unblutigen Opfers', in *Gemeinde ohne Tempel. Zur Substituierung und Transformation des Jerusalemer Tempels und seines Kults im Alten Testament, antiken Judentum und frühen Christentum*, ed. B. Ego, A. Lange and P. Pilhofer, WUNT 118 (Tübingen: Mohr Siebeck, 1999), 335–56 (351–2); cf. Georg Strecker and Udo Schnelle, eds, *Neuer Wettstein. Texte zum Neuen Testament aus Griechentum und Hellenismus. Band II: Texte zur Neutestamentlichen Briefliteratur und zur Johannesapokalypse* (Berlin: W. de Gruyter, 1996), 177–80.

> For what is a man? A rational, mortal animal (ζῷον λογικὸν θνητόν), someone says. To begin with, from what are we distinguished by the rational element? From the wild beasts. And from what else? From sheep and the like. See to it, then, that you never act like a wild beast; if you do, you will have destroyed the man in you, you have not fulfilled your profession.

Since human beings have λόγος, 'they are also, it is declared, godlike (ἔχειν γὰρ ἐν ἑαυτοῖς οἱονεὶ θεόν); for they have something divine within them; whereas the bad man is godless' (Diogenes Laertius 7.119). For this reason, the true veneration of the gods is not the offering of animal sacrifices to anthropomorphically imagined deities but veneration of the divine with pure reason:

> Will you think of God as great and placid, and a friend to be reverenced with gentle majesty, and always at hand (*semper in proximo*)? Not to be worshipped with the immolation of victims and with much blood – for what pleasure arises from the slaughter of innocent animals – but with a pure mind (*mente pura*) and with a good and honourable purpose (Seneca, *Frag.* 123, in Lactantius, *Inst.* 6.25.3; trans. W. Fletcher).

In the philosophical mysticism of the *Corpus Hermeticum*, this notion is transposed into the transcendent. Commentators on the phrase λογικὴ λατρεία ὑμῶν in Rom. 12.1 often quote the final prayer in Poimandres: 'Holy is god, the father of all… Holy are you, mightier than praises. You whom we address in silence, the unspeakable, the unsayable, accept pure speech offerings (δέξαι λογικὰς θυσίας ἁγνάς) from a heart and soul that reach up to you' (*Corp. Herm.* 1.31; trans. B. P. Copenhaver).[17] The phrase λογικὴ θυσία is used several times (13.18, 19, 21). The same phrase occurs in Nag Hammadi: 'Receive from us these spiritual sacrifices (*logeikē thusia*)' (*The Discourse on the Eighth and Ninth*, Codex VI, 57.18-19; trans. P. A. Dirkse, D. M. Parrott).[18] Porphyry uses a similar expression:

17. Brian P. Copenhaver, *Hermetica: The Greek Corpus Hermeticum and the Latin Asclepius in a New English Translation, with Notes and Introduction* (1992; repr., Cambridge: CUP, 1995). Cf. Jens Holzhausen, *Das Corpus Hermeticum Deutsch. Übersetzung, Darstellung und Kommentierung in drei Teilen*, 2 vols, Clavis Pansophiae 7 (Stuttgart–Bad Cannstatt: Frommann-Holzboog, 1997), 1:22, who translates the phrase λογικὰς θυσίας ἁγνάς 'in heiligen Worten dargebrachte Opfer'. Note G. Strecker on the difficulty of translating λογικός in this text; cf. Strecker and Schnelle, *Neuer Wettstein II*, 179 n. 3.

18. James M. Robinson, ed., *The Nag Hammadi Library in English*, 3rd edn (1977; repr., San Francisco: Harper, 1988). Siegert, 'Synagoge', 351, suggests 'Wortopfer' (sacrifice consisting in words) as translation of λογικὴ θυσία.

> Both inward, therefore, and external purity pertain to a divine man, who earnestly endeavours to be liberated from the passions of the soul, and who abstains from such food as excites the passions, and is fed with divine wisdom; and by right conceptions of, is assimilated to divinity himself. For such a man being consecrated by an intellectual sacrifice (τῇ νοερᾷ θυσίᾳ), approaches to God in a white garment, and with a truly pure impassivity of soul, and levity of body, and is not burdened with foreign and external juices, and the passions of the soul (*Abst.* 2.45; trans. T. Taylor).

Similar motifs are found in contemporary Jewish texts. *Testamentum Levi* 3.6 describes the heavenly worship of the archangels as presenting 'to the Lord a pleasing odor, a rational and bloodless oblation (λογικὴ καὶ ἀναίμακτος θυσία)' (trans. H. C. Kee).[19] Philo writes in his explanation of the incense offering which precedes the bloody animal sacrifice, 'This symbolical meaning is just this and nothing else: that what is precious in the sight of God is not the number of victims immolated but the true purity of a rational spirit (πνεῦμα λογικόν) in him who makes the sacrifice' (*Spec. Leg.* 1.277; trans. F. H. Colson, LCL). Since God is more interested in the 'rational spirit' than in the animal sacrifice, he is less interested in the perfection of the sacrificial animal than in the question whether the person's 'own mind (διάνοια) stands free from defect and imperfection (ὁλόκληρος καὶ παντελής)' (*Spec. Leg.* 1.283). Philo concludes, 'And thus we have the clearest proof that he holds the sacrifice to consist not in the victims but in the offerer's intention and his zeal (τὴν διάνοιαν προθυμίαν) which derives its constancy and permanence from virtue' (*Spec. Leg.* 1.290). Philo's interpretation shows that Stoic notions of 'rational' sacrifice had been taken up by Jewish authors who agreed with the contrast between true sacrifices and true worship on the one hand and material animal sacrifices on the other.

Interpretations of ἡ λογικὴ λατρεία in the Context of Stoic Motifs

The specific relevance of the Stoic critique of anthropomorphic cults and animal sacrifices for the phrase ἡ λογικὴ λατρεία in Rom. 12.1 has been variously assessed. A few examples shall suffice. H. D. Betz translates the phrase λογικὴ λατρεία as 'rational religion', which he understands to be 'enlightened religion, not an irrational, diffuse superstition'.[20]

19. J. H. Charlesworth, ed., *The Old Testament Pseudepigrapha*, 2 vols (Garden City: Doubleday, 1983–85).

20. Hans Dieter Betz, 'Das Problem der Grundlagen der paulinischen Ethik (Röm 12,1–2) [1988]', in *Paulinische Studien. Gesammelte Aufsätze III* (Tübingen:

O. Michel detects an implicit antithesis to animal sacrifices which are stipulated in Old Testament and Jewish tradition, as well as an emphasis on the 'reasonable understanding' of worship that corresponds to the eschatological situation of the Christian believers.[21] C. E. B. Cranfield also highlights both the Stoic as well as the Old Testament and Jewish parallels and argues against C. K. Barrett who thinks that the distinction between inward sacrifice and material sacrifice in the Old Testament (Ps. 51.17) influenced Paul's thinking more than the Stoic parallels,[22] and that the reference to τὰ σώματα ὑμῶν in v. 1 makes it difficult to interpret λογικὴ λατρεία in terms of the 'inwardness' of true Christian worship; Paul does not contrast internal and external or immaterial and material worship but rational and irrational worship; he asserts that 'rational' (λογικός) does not refer to the natural rationality of human beings but to 'being consistent with a proper understanding of the truth of God revealed in Jesus Christ'.[23] J. D. G. Dunn thinks that Cranfield's explanation is contextually correct but asserts that it reads too much into the wording of 12.1; the implied contrast with ritual worship should not be overplayed but not disregarded either, as for Paul the worship of the new community of Christians is distinct from the cultic hallmarks of traditional Judaism; Paul does not simply speak of a worship offered by the mind but, in contrast to the Hermetic literature, of a worship expressed in the bodily reality of everyday living; the worship he calls for is λογική in the sense of 'being proper for man the creature – the logical expression of his creatureliness properly understood, and lived out'.[24]

E. Käsemann asserts that Paul picks up motifs and terminology of the Diaspora synagogues when he adapts the Stoic polemic against sacrificial cults in his description of the Christians' spiritual worship; Paul emphasizes neither noetic reasonableness nor mystical detachment – he incorporates all life and he stresses corporeality 'as the characteristic sphere of this worship' – but he asserts, in an 'anti-cultic thrust', that 'Christian worship does not consist of what is practiced at sacred sites, at sacred times, and with sacred acts (Schlatter). It is the offering of bodily

Mohr Siebeck, 1994), 184–205 (198) (author's translation). He specifically rejects an interpretation in terms of 'spirituality' or 'spiritualization' which, according to Betz, say little (ibid.).

21. Michel, *Römer*, 370 ('Einsichtigwerden'); he comments: 'Nicht nur das rechtliche, sondern auch das kultische Denken kommt in unserem Brief unter dem eschatologischen Gesichtspunkts zur Entfaltung'.

22. Barrett, *Romans*, 231.

23. Cranfield, *Romans*, 604–5.

24. Dunn, *Romans*, 711–12, quotation 712.

existence in the otherwise profane sphere 'which is constantly demanded and which takes place in daily life'.[25] U. Wilckens asserts similarly that while Paul uses the term λογικός for its hermeneutical function in Stoic and mystical usage where it distinguishes between the true cult and the plurality of existing 'improper' cults, Paul departs both from Stoicism and mysticism by focusing the believers' total commitment to God not on an internal *logos* but, rather, on the salvific reality of God's grace and by highlighting the bodily existence of the believers as the realm in which their 'spiritual worship' takes place.[26]

R. Jewett grants that the phrase 'reasonable worship' may have been mediated from Stoic tradition by the Hellenistic synagogue, but argues that it more clearly 'signals the desire to set claim to a broad tradition of Graeco-Roman as well as Jewish philosophy of religion'; in contrast to 'the enlightened individual, touted by Graeco-Roman philosophers', Paul emphasizes 'the rationality of a redeemed community committed to world mission'.[27] J. A. Fitzmyer interprets the phrase as 'a cult suited to your rational nature' which is a 'spiritual cult' governed 'by the *logos*, as befits a human being'; it is 'worship governed by the *logos*, as befits a human being with *nous* and *pneuma*, and not merely one making use of irrational animals. This cult is a way of expressing Christian noetic dedication. Faith living itself out through love enables Christians to live according to the highest aspects of their beings.'[28]

F. Siegert concedes that the phrase λογικὴ θυσία in *Corp. herm.* 1.31; 13.18, 19, 21; Nag Hammadi Codex VI, 57.18-19 and Porphyry (*Abst.* 2.45), all later texts, could represent the after-effects of Rom. 12.1; he believes, however, that the fixed expression more likely derives from the philosophical critique of religion of the Pythagoreans and Stoics; he highlights the parallels between the synagogue services which consisted

25. Käsemann, *Romans*, 329; the reference is to Adolf Schlatter, *Gottes Gerechtigkeit. Ein Kommentar zum Römerbrief* (1975; repr., Stuttgart: Calwer, 1935), 333; cf. Adolf Schlatter, *Romans: The Righteousness of God* (German edn 1935; Peabody: Hendrickson, 1995), on Rom. 12.1.

26. Wilckens, *Römer*, 3:6, with reference to Philipp Seidensticker, *Lebendiges Opfer (Röm 12,1). Ein Beitrag zur Theologie des Apostels Paulus*, NTA 20 (Münster: Aschendorff, 1954), 256–63; Heinrich Schlier, *Der Römerbrief*, 3rd edn, HTKNT VI (1987; repr., Freiburg: Herder, 1977), 358. Wilckens uses the phrase 'geistiger Gottesdienst' which can be translated 'spiritual worship' or 'mental, intellectual worship'; 'geistig' can be, but is not necessarily identical with, 'geistlich'.

27. Jewett, *Romans*, 730, 731.

28. Fitzmyer, *Romans*, 640.

in listening to the words of Moses, oral instruction and prayers, and the 'pure' and 'bloodless' worship of the gods in Pythagorean and Stoic tradition.[29] A philosopher attending a synagogue service would have been surprised about the modernity of synagogal worship in which no animals were slaughtered, in which purely verbal prayers were offered and in which instruction took place in terms of the reading of and reflection upon the words of a master.

Lives That Speak: ἡ λογικὴ λατρεία *as Communication*

Since Paul speaks of the sacrifice of the believers' bodies (σώματα), and since λογικός is not limited to the meaning 'rational, reasonable, intellectual', an interpretation of λογικὴ λατρεία becomes possible in which the primary semantic field is determined by the meaning 'speech, speaking, word' (communication). Some scholars have alluded to the possibility of understanding λογικός in the sense of 'word'.[30] Michel renders λογική as 'dem Wort gemäß', without explanation and without evaluating the consequences for Paul's statement which he interprets in terms of an implicit contrast between animal sacrifices and the understanding of worship that results from the truth of the gospel, identifying at one point λογικὴ λατρεία with 'the will of God'.[31] He seems to think of a connection between λογικός and the 'word' (λόγος) of the gospel that is being proclaimed, highlighting the revelatory dimension of Christian worship. Cranfield mentions Michel's translation which he calls 'not quite satisfactory' and then apodictically asserts the 'fact' (with the qualifier 'as it surely is') that the word λογική 'is here used with reference to λόγος in its sense of

29. Siegert, 'Synagoge', 336–45; the following point ibid., 343. Siegert is followed by Volker Gäckle, *Allgemeines Priestertum. Zur Metaphorisierung des Priestertitels im Frühjudentum und Neuen Testament*, WUNT 331 (Tübingen: Mohr Siebeck, 2014), 343–5. Unconvinced by Siegert's evaluation of the importance of *T. Lev.* 3.6, Gäckle asserts that λογική has the same metaphorical meaning as ζῶσαν and expresses resignation regarding the possibility of defining λογική more precisely ('was auch immer λογική bedeuten mag'); cf. 343, 344–5.

30. Michel, *Römer*, 367; Ernst Käsemann, 'Gottesdienst im Alltag der Welt. Zu Römer 12 [1960]', in *Exegetische Versuche und Besinnungen* (1960/1964; repr.; Göttingen: Vandenhoeck & Ruprecht, 1970), 2:198–204, 201; Ulrich Kellermann, *Das Achtzehn-Bitten-Gebet. Jüdischer Glaube in neutestamentlicher Zeit. Ein Kommentar* (Neukirchen-Vluyn: Neukirchener Verlag, 2007), 92; Martin Vahrenhorst, *Kultische Sprache in den Paulusbriefen*, WUNT 230 (Tübingen: Mohr Siebeck, 2008), 303.

31. Michel, *Römer*, 370.

“reason” rather to λόγος in its sense of “word”’.[32] Siegert considers the meaning ‘worship in the word’, without elaboration.[33]

The derivation of the phrase λογικὴ λατρεία from Hellenistic motifs and traditions is not as certain as scholars think. First, the expression λογικὴ λατρεία is not attested before Paul, and the post-Pauline evidence in Christian literature is scant. In the first and second centuries CE, the expression occurs, outside of Rom. 12.1, only six times: Irenaeus, *Fragmenta deperditorum operum* 36; Athenagoras, *Leg.* 13.4; Origen, *Comm. Rom.* 12.2; *Comm. Jo.* 13.25.148; *Sel. Ezech.* 13.785.44; *Fr. Luc.* 123.4. Both Irenaeus and Origen’s commentary on Romans quote Rom. 12.1.[34]

Second, only six of the nearly 750 uses of λογικός in Greek literature before 100 CE are used in contexts that explicitly refer to sacrifice, distinguishing proper or real sacrifices from material sacrifices: *T. Lev.* 3.6; Philo, *Spec. Leg.* 1.277; *Corp. herm.* 1.31; 13.18, 19, 21 (see the quotations above). The *Corpus Hermeticum* is post-Pauline, originating between the late 1st and 3rd centuries CE, compiled in the 10th or 11th century by Byzantine scholars;[35] the four references are thus not relevant for interpreting Rom. 12.1. Since *Testamentum Levi* was originally written in Hebrew, with the *Urfassung* being lost, and since the *Testaments of the Twelve Patriarchs* underwent a Christian revision, the significance of the reference in *T. Lev.* 3.6 remains restricted.[36] This leaves one single reference – Philo’s *Spec. Leg.* 1.277 – which uses the phrase πνεῦμα λογικόν (‘rational spirit’). In sum, the expression λογικὴ λατρεία is neither a fixed formula nor attested before Paul.

32. Cranfield, *Romans*, 605 n. 1.

33. Siegert, ‘Synagoge’, 351 (‘Gottesdienst im Wort’). Cf. Peter Wick, *Die urchristlichen Gottesdienste. Entstehung und Entwicklung im Rahmen der frühjüdischen Tempel-, Synagogen-, und Hausfrömmigkeit*, BWANT 150 (Stuttgart: Kohlhammer, 2002), 182.

34. Angelika Reichert, ‘Gottes universaler Heilswille und der kommunikative Gottesdienst. Exegetische Anmerkungen zu Röm 12,1-2’, in *Paulus, Apostel Jesu Christi*, Festschrift G. Klein, ed. M. Trowitzsch (Tübingen: Mohr Siebeck, 1998), 79–95 (88–9 n. 41).

35. Cf. J. Holzhausen, ‘Corpus Hermeticum’, in *Brill’s New Pauly: Encyclopedia of the Ancient World*, ed. Hubert Cancik, Helmuth Schneider and Manfred Landfester, 22 vols (Leiden: Brill, 2002–2012), 3:cols. 846–50; Holzhausen, *Corpus Hermeticum Deutsch*.

36. Cf. Harm W. Hollander and Marinus de Jonge, *The Testaments of the Twelve Patriarchs: A Commentary*, SVTP 8 (Leiden: Brill, 1985), 138, who point to related formulations in *Christian* texts regarding *T. Lev.* 3.6 to related formulations in *Christian* texts.

Third, the word λογικός has different meanings in different contexts. *LSJ* distinguishes two main meanings, the first of which denotes 'speech':[37] I.1. *of* or *for speaking* or *speech*,[38] 2. *of* or *in eloquence*,[39] 3. *suited for prose*;[40] II.1. *possessed of reason, intellectual*,[41] 2a. *dialectical, argumentative*,[42] 2b. substantive, ἡ λογική *logic*;[43] 3. of the 'dogmatic' school of physicians.[44] The evidence for λογικός I comes from documentary and literary texts contemporary to Paul. One should note that in some texts, 'rationality' and 'verbal articulation' are closely linked; see Philo, *Op. Mund.* 119.5 ('words issue from it [the head], words which are deathless laws of a deathless soul, by means of which the λογικός life is steered'); *Leg. All.* 1.10.1 ('They say a man becomes λογικός in his first seven years, by which time he is already capable of expressing ordinary nouns and verbs through having acquired the λογικός faculty').[45]

BDAG prejudices the evaluation of the sense of λογικός. The meaning λογικός I (*LSJ*) is ignored, while we read that the term is 'a favorite expr[ession] of philosophers since Aristot[le]'; λογικός is defined as 'pert[aining] to being carefully thought through', and 'thoughtful' is suggested as a gloss; the phrase λογικὴ λατρεία in Rom. 12.1 is translated

37. LSJ, 1056, s.v. λογικός.

38. μέρη λ. 'organs of speech'; Plutarch, *Cor.* 38: ἡ λογική, 'speech', opposed to μουσική, Dionysius of Halicarnassus, *Comp.* 11; *Stoicorum Veterum Fragmenta* 2.61: λ. φαντασία 'expressed in speech'. Cf. Theon, *Prog.* 97.11-13, 16; 98.21; 99.4; 101.24, 30; 102.8 for the technical use of λογικός designating one of the subgenres of the *chreia* which focuses on a *word* (rather than on an action or a mixture of word and action).

39. Philostratus, *Vit. Soph.* 1.22.1: ἀγῶνες; *SEG* II 184, 6 (Tanagra, 2nd cent. BCE): ἀκροάσεις λ. καὶ ὀργανικαί.

40. Demetrius Phalereus, *De Elocutione* 42: ὁ ἡρῷος σεμνὸς καὶ οὐ λ.; Diogenes Laertius, *Vitae Philosophorum* 5.85: λογικοί of persons, 'writing in prose'; *IG* IX,2 531, 43 (Larisa, late 1st cent. BCE/early 1st cent. CE): ἐγκώμιῳ λ. 'in prose'.

41. Timaeus Locrus 99e: μέρος; Chrysippus, *Stoic.* 3.95: τὸ λ. ζῷον; Aristotle, *Eth. Nic.* 1108b9: ἀρεταὶ λ. – διανοητικαί, opposed to ἠθικαί.

42. οἱ λ. διάλογοι of Plato, such as the *Theaetetus* and *Cratylus* (Diogenes Laertius, *Vitae Philosophorum* 3.58); in Aristotle usually like διαλεκτοκός, λ. συλλογισμός (*Pol.* 93a15; cf. *Top.* 162b27; *Meta.* 1080a10: διὰ λογικωτέρων καὶ ἀκριβεστέρων λόγων 'more abstract'); but also, 'logical': *Rhet.* 1355a13: λ. συλλογισμοί, opposed to ῥητορικοί.

43. Cicero, *Fin.* 1.7.22; also τὰ λογικά, *Tusc.* 4.14.33.

44. ἡ λ. αἵρεσις, Galen, *De Sectis Ingredientibus* 1.

45. Dan G. McCartney, 'λογικός in 1 Peter 2,2', *ZNW* 82 (1991): 128–32 (131–2). See also Dionysius of Halicarnassus, *Comp.* 11.119; 14.86, 108 (Epitome); Plutarch, *Alc.* 2.5.

as '*a thoughtful* service', with the explanatory comment 'in a dedicated spiritual sense'.[46]

There is no *a priori* reason why the meaning of λογικός in the expression ἡ λογικὴ λατρεία should denote 'reason' or 'intellect' rather than 'speaking' or 'speech'. Since λογικός occurs in different contexts with different meanings related to either 'speaking' (λογικός I, *LSJ*) or 'reason' (λογικός II, *LSJ*), and since the expression λογικὴ λατρεία is not attested before Paul, it is possible that the phrase λογικὴ λατρεία was coined by Paul himself.[47] Since Paul uses the word λόγος nearly always in a context related to speech, speaking and word(s),[48] it is plausible to ask whether λογικός in Rom. 12.1 can be understood in the sense of λογικός I.

The only New Testament passage apart from Rom. 12.1 that uses the word λογικός is 1 Pet. 2.2. In the context, Peter speaks of the new birth caused by the 'living and enduring word of God' (διὰ λόγου ζῶντος θεοῦ καὶ μένοντος, 1.23), the imperishable seed that is 'the word of the Lord' (ῥῆμα κυρίου) that 'endures forever' (1.25a) – 'that word is the good news that was announced to you' (τοῦτο δέ ἐστιν τὸ ῥῆμα τὸ εὐαγγελισθὲν εἰς ὑμᾶς, 1.25b). The description of the Christian believers as 'newborn babies' in 2.2 picks up the reference to their new birth mentioned in 1.23. This means that the expression τὸ λογικὸν γάλα, which most English versions translate as 'spiritual milk' (ESV, GNB, NIV, NLT, NRSV, RSV), refers to the λόγος that effected the believers' new birth, the 'word' of the proclamation of the gospel. This means that the expression τὸ λογικὸν γάλα means 'the milk of the word' (KJV, NASB),[49] 'having to do with the Word [of God]',[50] 'the milk of God's word'.[51]

46. BDAG, 598 s.v. λογικός.

47. Reichert, 'Gottesdienst', 90; cf. Evans, 'Worship', 23.

48. Paul uses λόγος 84 times; for Rom. cf. 3.4; 9.6, 9, 28; 13.9; 14.12; 15.18; for 1 Cor. cf. 1.5, 17, 18; 2.1, 4 (2×), 13; 4.19, 20; 12.8 (2×); 14.9, 19 (2×), 36; 15.2, 54. For meanings not connected with 'speaking', 'speech' or 'word' cf. Rom. 14.12; Phil. 4.15, 17; cf. BDAG, 600 s.v. λόγος 2 'computation, reckoning'.

49. John H. Elliott, *1 Peter*, AB 37B (New York: Doubleday, 2000), 394, 400–401. Cf. Reinhard Feldmeier, *Der erste Brief des Petrus*, THKNT 15/I (Leipzig: Evangelische Verlagsanstalt, 2005), 83 ('Milch des Wortes [Gottes]'), 84 ('Wortmilch').

50. McCartney, 'λογικός', 132.

51. Paul J. Achtemeier, *1 Peter*, Hermeneia (Minneapolis: Fortress Press, 1996), 143; in the context of 1.23, 25, 'some relationship between the divine word and the adjective λογικός seems most likely' (ibid., 146). Cf. Norbert Brox, *Der erste Petrusbrief*, EKK 21 (Zurich: Benziger; Neukirchen-Vluyn: Neukirchener Verlag, 1979), 92: 'das Wort Gottes und dessen reine, unverfälsche Wahrheit'. Also Leonhard Goppelt, *Der erste Petrusbrief*, KEK 12/1 (Göttingen: Vandenhoeck & Ruprecht,

The meaning of λογικός in the sense of 'having to do with speech' is not only attested in non-Jewish Hellenistic texts but also in Jewish texts (cf. Philo, *Vit. Mos.* 1.84; *Somn.* 1.106; *Praem. Poen.* 2). This renders it plausible that Paul uses the word λογικός with reference to 'speech' or 'word'. The objection that this meaning would be unique[52] is unconvincing: the expression λογικὴ λατρεία itself is unique. Paul does not take up a fixed formula.

The expression ἡ λογικὴ λατρεία in Rom. 12.1 is most plausibly understood in terms of 'speech' that is communicated by the λατρεία ('worship') of Christian believers. Paul, after using the term θυσία ('sacrifice') in a metaphorical sense, indicated by the adjective ζῶσα ('living') and the reference to τὰ σώματα ('the bodies') of the believers, uses a second metaphor: the believers' λατρεία 'speaks', their worship 'communicates'.[53]

First, the interpretation of λογικός in the sense of 'speaking' and of λογικὴ λατρεία in the sense of 'worship that speaks' takes up the exhortation in v. 1 that believers in Jesus shall present their bodies (τὰ σώματα ὑμῶν) as a 'living sacrifice' (θυσίαν ζῶσαν). The word σῶμα ('body')[54] describes here the personal bodily existence of the individual Christian,[55] a corporeality which, as E. Käsemann emphasizes, 'is the nature of man in his need to participate in creatureliness and in his capacity for communication in the widest sense, that is to say, in his relationship to a world with which he is confronted on each several occasion [*sic*]'.[56] The verb παραστῆσαι ('present') describes, as U. Wilckens explains, 'the realization of this

1978), 136: he translates 'spiritual milk' but interprets λογικός as 'von der Art des Wortes und Geistes Gottes', 'eine dem Logos der Christen, d.h. dem Evangelium (1,25), entsprechende geistliche Nahrung' (n. 47).

52. Gäckle, *Priestertum*, 343 ('ein völlig singulärer Wortgebrauch').

53. The following arguments are adapted and expanded from Reichert, 'Gottesdienst', 88–94; Angelika Reichert, *Der Römerbrief als Gratwanderung. Eine Untersuchung zur Abfassungsproblematik*, FRLANT 194 (Göttingen: Vandenhoeck & Ruprecht, 2001), 240–47. Reichert's research has been overlooked by most scholars. Reichert differentiates her results from Michel in the sense that the latter implied the revelatory nature of the church's λατρεία whereas she emphasizes its communicating power.

54. Cf. Rom. 1.24; 4.19; 6.6, 12; 7.4, 24; 8.10, 11, 13, 23; 12.1, 4, 5.

55. Cf. Rudolf Bultmann, *Theologie des Neuen Testaments*, 9th edn, ed. Otto Merk (1948–1953; repr., UTB 630; Tübingen: Mohr-Siebeck, 1984), 196–7; Karl-Adolf Bauer, *Leiblichkeit, das Ende aller Werke Gottes. Die Bedeutung der Leiblichkeit des Menschen bei Paulus*, SUNT 4 (Gütersloh: Mohn, 1971), 179–80.

56. Ernst Käsemann, 'On Paul's Anthropology', in *Perspectives on Paul* (Philadelphia: Fortress Press, 1971), 1–31 (21); cf. Ernst Käsemann, 'Zur paulinischen Anthropologie', in *Paulinische Perspektiven*, 3rd edn (1969; repr., Tübingen: Mohr

communication which takes places first and foundationally with God in specific obedience (vv. 1[-2]) and then in living together in the Christian community in brotherly love (vv. 9[-21])'.[57] Since the body of the believer is the place where the powers of the present world and God's salvific will encounter each other, and since the body of the believer is no longer at the disposition of the believer but, as the dwelling place of the Holy Spirit, is called to faithful obedience by which he glorifies God (8.1-17; cf. 1 Cor. 6.19-20), the body of the believer is not only 'one's self-understanding in the present world' but also expresses the fact of 'being incorporated into God's creative saving act'.[58] Since the latter happened not only in Jesus' death on the cross and in the believer's past conversion to faith in Jesus, but also in the life of the believer in the context of the community of believers, the communication of God's saving revelation in and through Jesus continues to take place in the everyday life of the believer. When Christians commit their body, i.e. their way of life in all aspects of everyday living, to holy behaviour that pleases God, this will not remain a hidden reality. The life of the individual believer and the life of the local community is λογικός – their lives 'speak', communicating to believers and unbelievers alike their commitment to God whom they serve.

Second, the interpretation of ἡ λογικὴ λατρεία in the sense of 'the worship that speaks' takes up the phrase οἱ οἰκτιρμοὶ τοῦ θεοῦ ('the mercies of God') in v. 1, which marks the authority of and the reason for the exhortation of the believers to present their bodies as a living sacrifice. As the body of a human being communicates with the world, the bodies of the believers communicate to the world the reality of God's mercies which redeemed them from the power of sin (1.18–3.20; 5.12-21; 7.7-25) as a result of Jesus' saving death and resurrection (3.21–5.11), and which transforms their life as persons who experience the freedom of the 'law of the Spirit of life in Christ Jesus' as they walk according to the Spirit, thus pleasing God (8.1-8). The λατρεία of the believer which takes place in everyday living is worship that communicates the gospel as 'the power of God for salvation to everyone who has faith, to the Jew first and also to the Greek' (1.16). Since the believers experienced the gracious mercies of God in their own lives, the continual and consistent presentation of their bodies to God in everyday living is 'worship that speaks' in that they exemplify the reality and the consequences of God's mercies in the

Siebeck, 1993), 9–60 (43): 'in seiner Fähigkeit zur Kommunikation im weitesten Sinne, nämlich seiner Bezogenheit auf eine ihm jeweils vorgegebene Welt'.

57. Wilckens, *Römer*, 3:3 (author's translation).

58. Udo Schnelle, *Apostle Paul: His Life and Theology* (Grand Rapids: Baker Academic, 2005), 498.

world. The life of the believers in Jesus is 'worship that speaks' in the everyday realities of life in the world – the visible, observable exterior of the community which is stamped by God's mercies and which is made to participate in the mission of God who is merciful to all, both Jews and Gentiles (11.32).[59]

Third, the interpretation of ἡ λογικὴ λατρεία in the sense of 'the worship that speaks' connects Paul's statement with the negative and positive exhortation in v. 2. The refusal to live according to the values and patterns of behaviour of the present world living in rebellion against God (μὴ συσχηματίζεσθε τῷ αἰῶνι τούτῳ) and the continual transformation that happens as a result of the renewal of their minds (μεταμορφοῦσθε τῇ ἀνακαινώσει τοῦ νοός) constitute the two foundational dimensions of the believers' worship that speaks to the world. The mercies of God removed the believers from the sinful powers that control the present world. As they actively refuse the temptations of a mindset shaped by the reality of sin that seeks to occupy the self (7.7-25), willing to risk persecution for the sake of the cross (Gal. 6.12), their non-aligned behaviour participates in the revelation of God's wrath against all godlessness and wickedness (1.18) and exemplifies and communicates to the world God's judgement on the sinful desires of people's hearts (cf. 1.24). If and when believers present their bodies as 'living sacrifice' that 'speaks' to the world, they prove God to be true as his words (λόγοι) of judgement will prevail (3.4) – the promises of sin are unmasked as deception (7.7-11), God's law is shown to be holy and his commandments to be holy, just and good (7.12). And as the mercies of God cause the believers' transformation to renewed reasoning, thinking and desires, their lives, controlled by God's Holy Spirit (8.1-8), communicate to the world that it is possible to fulfil 'the just requirement of the law' since they are people 'who walk not according to the flesh but according to the Spirit' (8.4), and that it is possible to 'discern what is the will of God' and to do 'what is good and acceptable and perfect' (12.2).

Fourth, the interpretation of λογικὴ λατρεία as 'worship that speaks' connects with Paul's description of his proclamation of the gospel with the verb λατρεύω in 1.9. As Paul 'serves' God (ὁ θεός ᾧ λατρεύω) by announcing the gospel of his Son (ἐν τῷ εὐαγγελίῳ τοῦ υἱοῦ αὐτοῦ), believers individually and communally are engaged in the 'service'

59. Reichert, 'Gottesdienst', 94: the 'worship that speaks' is 'die wahrnehmbare Außenseite der Gemeinde, die von Gottes Erbarmen überwunden und geprägt ist und die für dessen Tendenz auf "weiteren Raumgewinn in der Welt" in Anspruch genommen wird', quoting Günter Klein, 'Der Friede Gottes und der Friede der Welt', *ZTK* 83 (1986): 325–55 (340).

(λατρεία) of God which 'speaks' as they live out the reality of God's grace revealed in Jesus Christ in 'word and deed' (λόγῳ καὶ ἔργῳ, 15.18).[60]

Conclusions

The interpretation of ἡ λογικὴ λατρεία in Rom. 12.1 in the sense of 'reasonable' or 'true' worship, in the context of a perceived contrast between external, material worship (with animal sacrifices) and internal, immaterial worship (involving the heart and mind),[61] or in the context of a perceived contrast between worship that is, or is not, consistent with a proper understanding of the gospel,[62] is plausible. The main reasons for the plausibility of this interpretation are the context in 12.2 where Paul speaks of the renewal of the Christians' νοῦς, Paul's exposition of Jesus as the 'place' of God's atoning presence (3.25) in the context of Romans 1–8 and Paul's exposition of Israel's quest for righteousness which can be attained only through the Messiah Jesus (Romans 9–11).

The interpretation in terms of a 'worship that speaks' is at least as plausible, if not more so, given the equally standard meaning of λογικός as 'speaking', the meaning of λογικός in 1 Pet. 2.2 and the context in Rom. 12.1-2 in which Paul exhorts the believers to present their 'bodies' with which they 'communicate' with the world as a 'living sacrifice'. Paul reminds the believers of the missional power of the 'mercies of God', and he exhorts the believers to refuse the sinful values of the present world and to submit to God's renewal of their minds, transforming them into people who discern the will of God and do what is good, acceptable and perfect. This happens in and through they 'body' as they 'serve' God in the manifold realities of everyday living. The life of a believer in Jesus and the life of each local congregation of believers 'speaks' of the transforming power of God's mercies and thus of God's reality and power, 'for the glory of God' (15.7) and for the salvation of Jews and Gentiles (1.16).

60. Cf. Vahrenhorst, *Sprache*, 299–303, who accepts Reichert's interpretation but connects λογικός more closely with λόγος in the sense of 'word of God'; he renders λογικὴ λατρεία as 'botschaftsgemäßer', 'wortgemäßer Gottesdienst' (p. 303). However, in 12.1 Paul does not refer to God speaking through his word but to the life of the believers which 'speaks' as they present their bodies to God as living sacrifice.

61. Karl Barth, *Der Römerbrief*, 15th edn (1922/1989; repr.; Zurich: Theologischer Verlag, 1919), 416–17; Schlatter, *Römerbrief*, 333; Barrett, *Romans*, 231; Käsemann, *Romans*, 317; Wilckens, *Römer*, 3:4–6, 8; cf. Strack, *Terminologie*, 297–301; Stettler, *Heiligung*, 462–5.

62. Cranfield, *Romans*, 605. Cf. Schreiner, *Romans*, 645: 'Since God has been so merciful, failure to dedicate one's life to him is the height of folly and irrationality'.

Index of References

Index of Authors

Lightning Source UK Ltd.
Milton Keynes UK
UKHW020050220819
348363UK00006B/432/P

9 780567 69006